CONFEDERATE
SHARPSHOOTER
MAJOR
WILLIAM E. SIMMONS

MERCER
UNIVERSITY PRESS

Endowed by
TOM WATSON BROWN
and
THE WATSON-BROWN FOUNDATION, INC.

CONFEDERATE SHARPSHOOTER

MAJOR

WILLIAM E. SIMMONS

Through the War with the 16th Georgia Infantry
and the 3rd Battalion Georgia Sharpshooters

JOSEPH P. BYRD IV

Mercer University Press | Macon, Georgia | 2016

MUP/ H914

© 2016 by Mercer University Press
Published by Mercer University Press
1501 Mercer University Drive
Macon, Georgia 31207

9 8 7 6 5 4 3 2 1

Books published by Mercer University Press are printed on acid-free
paper that meets the requirements of the American National
Standard for Information Sciences—Permanence of Paper for
Printed Library Materials.

ISBN   978-0-88146-568-6
Cataloging-in-Publication Data is available from the Library of
Congress

Contents

Preface vii

Acknowledgments xi

1. A Family of Distinction 1

2. Will Simmons's Early Years 6

3. The War Begins 12

4. Straddling the Peninsula 23

5. The Seven Days Battles 31

6. A Narrow Escape 36

7. The Bloody Lane 44

8. The Sunken Road 50

9. Victory at Chancellorsville 65

10. Wofford's Georgia Sharpshooters 75

11. Raid on the Ironworks 83

12. The Peach Orchard and Wheat Field 89

13. Retreat from Gettysburg 98

14. Deployment to Chattanooga 103

15. Assault on Fort Sanders 110

16. Another Bitter Winter 121

17. Back to the Wilderness 129

18. Slaughter at the Bloody Angle 136

19. A Well-deserved Promotion 143

20. The Major's Last Battle 150

21. Captured and Imprisoned 158

22. The Prisoners' Oath 169

23. Home at Last 174

24. The Young Legislator 181

25. Family and School Ties 186

Afterword 195

Exhibit 1. Acceptance Letter of Commissions by
        Officers of the Gwinnett Volunteers 199

Exhibit 2. Letter from D. M. Byrd Jr. to J. P. Byrd III 200

Exhibit 3. The Simmons Journal at Fort Delaware Prison 203

Exhibit 4. Resolution to Continue Service to the CSA 205

Exhibit 5. William E. Simmons Obituary 206

Statistical Summary   209
Third Battalion Georgia Sharpshooters Roster   211
Bibliography   275
Index   285

Preface

For as long as I can remember, I have been fascinated with the American South and its colorful people, culture, and traditions. As a boy I grew up listening to stories about my Georgia kinfolks. Although I was born in Savannah, I spent most of my formative years in Oklahoma and Colorado, far away from the place of my birth. Perhaps the great distance made the stories and the people more interesting than they would have been had I grown up in the home of my ancestors.

This book grew out of the love of my family, coupled with a longtime interest in American history. I have always been fascinated by the War Between the States, or in the words of my grandfathers, the "War for Southern Independence." More than anyone or anything, my late father helped to cultivate this abiding interest. Until he reached his nineties, he was blessed with an extraordinary memory and a wonderful talent for storytelling. He left behind a veritable storehouse of information on our family history. One relative my father greatly admired was his great uncle, William E. Simmons, a Confederate war hero, whom he vividly remembered from frequent childhood visits to his father's home town of Lawrenceville, Georgia.

Our family ties to Uncle William are by marriage. In 1869, he wed Mary Ambrose, the sister of my great-grandmother, Georgia Ambrose Byrd.[1] My father fondly remembered joining Uncle William and Aunt Mary and other members of the family for dinner at the Simmons's Victorian home on the Courthouse Square in Lawrenceville. At every meal he observed the distinguished, white-haired gentleman with a neatly trimmed moustache seated at the head of the table. William Simmons was well into his eighties by that time, always immaculately groomed and attired in a coat, vest, and tie. To a youth from Tulsa, the old man seemed to be a figure of nobility, complete with regal bearing and manners. Regardless of his formality, my father always remembered him to be "jovial and friendly." In later years he wrote about these childhood visits:

> One of the highlights of our Georgia vacations was a visit to see my Uncle William Simmons and his wife Mary—a great uncle and aunt of mine. Uncle William had been a major in the Confederate army, and although he was an elderly man when I was a youngster, I always enjoyed visiting in his home in Lawrenceville. I have many fond memories of those early visits—

---

[1] The Ambrose family Bible shows six children born to George Washington Ambrose and Mary Ann Wood Ambrose: Charles (b. 1847), Mary (b. 1849), Charlton (b. 1853), Sallie (b. 1855), Georgia (b. 1860), and Eudora (b. 1865). A photocopy of the page from the Ambrose family Bible is in the author's possession.

the boxwood hedges and their fragrance, the old gingerbread house exterior, the beaten biscuit machine that was in the dining room, a beautiful music box, and other rare and fascinating items that I had never seen before. Upon entering Georgia Tech in the fall of 1934, I had occasion to visit in the President's office sometime during the first semester of my freshman year. As I shook hands with…Dr. Marion Luther Brittain, I happened to look over his shoulder. On the wall above his desk was a picture of the Board of Regents of the Georgia University System with Uncle William on the front row attired in full academic regalia. I asked the President if he knew William Simmons, and it turned out that my great uncle was one of his closest friends. He had been a mentor of Dr. Brittain in days gone by, both of them having graduated from Emory College.[2]

After returning to the state of my birth several years ago, I began to research my family roots after attending a family reunion. I prevailed on my father to share what information he had on William Simmons and the Ambrose branch of our family. He responded with information that was taken from memoranda furnished to Clark Howell, who was editor of the *Atlanta Constitution* for many years and a close friend of Uncle William. My father also provided me with several newspaper articles and excerpts from a journal that Uncle William had kept while he was in the Confederate army during the War between the States. Later, he sent me a manuscript of a book about Uncle William with the working title *Them Brave Georgians*. The manuscript was prepared (but never published) by my late second cousin, Daniel Madison Byrd Jr. (whom my father always called "Madison") sometime in the early 1960s.[3] Like my father, Madison was a great admirer of his great uncle William and cultivated a special relationship with him as he grew up next door to the Simmons's home in Lawrenceville. As Madison recalled, "Uncle William was ninety-one when he died in 1931. I was sixteen. My memories are as vivid as the green kudzu which shaded us as we rocked on the wide veranda which half circled the house. There we rocked while I pulled from him some of his tales about the exploits of the 16th Georgia Regiment."[4]

Madison Byrd's project was inspired by a journal of Uncle William's war experiences, meticulously kept while he served as an infantry officer in the Confederate army. To supplement the journal information, Madison thoroughly

---

[2] J. P. Byrd III, "From Civil War Battlefields to the Moon," *Tech Topics* 28/1 (Fall 1991): 4B.

[3] Daniel M. Byrd Jr., *Them Brave Georgians*, manuscript, pg. iv–v, Gwinnett Historical Society Archives, Lawrenceville, GA (Fort Delaware Society Library, Delaware City, DE, also has a copy.).

[4] Daniel M. Byrd Jr. to Bill Baughman, president, Gwinnett Historical Society, 29 December 1992, Simmons file, Gwinnett Historical Society Archives, Lawrenceville, GA.

researched the records of Simmons's military company, regiment, and battalion to provide a more detailed account of his war experiences. Most of the documentation came from sources at the Georgia Department of Archives and History in Atlanta, the University of Georgia library in Athens, the National Archives and Library of Congress in Washington, DC, and his personal library, which included a complete set of the *Official Record of the War of the Rebellion*, commonly referred to as the *OR*. His manuscript contains a trove of fascinating information and family legends and reflects Madison Byrd's extensive knowledge of genealogy, military history and Southern culture.[5]

The working title of my late cousin's manuscript was taken from a passage contained in a favorite book of his on the War between the States that was given to him by a friend. The book, titled *Recollections of War Times: How I Got In, and How I Got Out,* was written by William A. McClendon, a native of Alabama, who served in the 15th Alabama Infantry Regiment in the Army of Northern Virginia. In his book, McClendon, a man of limited education, provides a moving account of the courage exhibited by Major Simmons's 16th Georgia Infantry Regiment and others in their attempt to storm Fort Sanders at the Siege of Knoxville on a frigid November morning in 1863.

> We stood…and watched them brave Georgians as they moved out to the assault. I knew…that it would be a desperate undertaking and many a brave Georgian would bite the dust. I imagined the carnage to be in the ranks of them brave fellows. The Georgians moved on, without wavering. Each man picked his own way to advance, but they moved on, shot, shell, grape, and canister dealing death at every step. They gave the "Rebel Yell," and…made a dash for the fort. They were repulsed with heavy loss, but the charge upon Fort Sanders by them Georgians will ever live in the memory of the living and adorn a page in history testifying to the devotion of them Georgians to the "Lost Cause."[6]

The qualities embodied by the men of the 16th Georgia and other regiments in that ill-fated assault and the battalion of sharpshooters who laid down covering fire for them, courage, dedication, resourcefulness and obedience, were all strong characteristics of William Simmons, not just as an infantry officer in a terrible war, but throughout his life.

William Simmons was the son of a respected Georgia lawyer and political leader. He was a devoted husband and a man of unassailable character. Throughout his life he was successful in a number of endeavors. He graduated at the top of his class at Emory College at the age of eighteen. Before he turned

---

[5]For more information on D. M. Byrd Jr.'s research, see Exhibit 2.
[6]W. A. McClendon, *Recollections of War Times by an Old Veteran while under Stonewall Jackson and Lieutenant General James Longstreet* (1909; reprint, Tuscaloosa: University of Alabama Press, 2010) 220–21.

twenty, he became the editor and publisher of a thriving newspaper. At the age of twenty-four he was a major in the Confederate army and acting commander of an elite battalion of North Georgia sharpshooters the following year. By the time he was thirty, he was serving as a representative in the Georgia legislature. Beginning in 1894, he served on the Georgia University Board of Regents over a period of thirty-two years as a trustee of the state's two great institutions of higher learning. In many respects he followed in the footsteps of his father and became one of the most influential and prominent men in Georgia. Despite his fame and fortune, he tended to avoid the limelight. He was always modest about his achievements and the recognition they brought. He died in 1931, a few months shy of his ninety-second birthday, having lived a full and rewarding life. In his obituary in the *Atlanta Constitution*, he was acclaimed as "one of Georgia's most distinguished pioneers." By all accounts, he was truly an exceptional man who lived an extraordinary life.

It is my sincere desire in writing this book to provide a more complete portrait of William E. Simmons and shed light on the exploits of his regiment and sharpshooter battalion during the War Between the States. This book is not an attempt to document a comprehensive regimental or battalion history. Rather, it focuses on a truly remarkable man, his many accomplishments, and the people, places, and events that touched his life. It follows his footsteps through nearly a century along with his family, fellow Georgians, and comrades-in-arms. Given the scarcity of primary resources on Confederate sharpshooters, however, I have added additional detail, as appropriate, about Major Simmons's 3rd Georgia Sharpshooter Battalion, and to a lesser extent, the 16th Georgia Infantry Regiment.

Acknowledgments

During the time I was researching and writing this book, I ran across a quote by Grant Foreman, who served on the legal staff of the Dawes Commission in Indian Territory prior to Oklahoma statehood. Foreman, a native of Chicago, fell in love with the land and left his job in 1903. He later became a noted historian, along with his wife Carolyn, and devoted the rest of his life to an arduous career of uncovering and recording the history of Oklahoma and its Indians. As noted by fellow historian, Angie Debo, he once said,

> To me there is no avocation, no occupation so interesting and so fascinating...as historical research. To follow a clue to the lair of an elusive historical event; to capture the fact and make it my own brings a glow of satisfaction I would not yield to any big game hunter (or gold seeker). The treasure I extract in the mother lode of rich old historical records not only dims the big game trophy or glitter of the metal for pure joy of discovery and possession, but it has the greater value of being mine...to share with others, without fear of theft or loss.[7]

Grant Foreman's words resonated with me as I was in the process of discovering my true calling late in life. Along the way, I discovered a few "hidden treasures" of my own to share with others, but much more was freely given to me by others who share my passion.

I am indebted to a number of people for their support and assistance in researching and writing this book. In particular I am deeply grateful to the dedicated volunteer staff of the Gwinnett Historical Society in Lawrenceville, Georgia, especially Elaine Roberts, Harriet Nichols, Phyllis Davis, Bill Baughman, and Alice Smythe McCabe.

There are a number of my compatriots in the Major William E. Simmons Camp 96, Sons of Confederate Veterans, who have been very supportive of my research, including Commander Joe Bath, David Floyd, Bob Collins, Bill Grimes, Bill Winn, Rick Clarke, Cecil Pinner, Greg Beavers, and many others.

The staff and volunteers of the Hiram Parks Bell Family Research Center in Cumming, Georgia, are always generous with their time and expertise, especially Frank Clark, Clark Rye, and Leighton Young.

David Vaughan, past president of the Atlanta Civil War Roundtable, provided useful and timely information on images of soldiers who fought in the Civil War and access to his world-class collection of original images of Georgia

---

[7]Grant Foreman, *Indian Removal: The Emigration of the Five Civilized Tribes of Indians*, vol. 2 in The Civilization of the American Indian Series (1932; reprint, Norman: University of Oklahoma Press, 1989) 3.

Confederate soldiers in uniform. My association with David led me to the Richard Russell Special Collection Building and the Hargrett Rare Book and Manuscript Library on the campus of his alma mater, the University of Georgia.

Dr. Keith Bohannon of West Georgia University shared valuable information and advice and allowed me to peruse his files on the three regiments and two legion infantry battalions of the Wofford/DuBose Brigade, Army of Northern Virginia. Thanks also to Wayne Dobson and his comrades of the Jackson Rifles (Company G, 16th Georgia) Re-enactor Group for their interest and support. I am also indebted to Dan Bennett, Ted Brooke, Mike McAlpin, Cliff Roberts, Mike and Jenny Fleming, Kurt Graham, Tom Despard, Gerald Sanders, Hugh McMillian, Guy Condra, and my brother, Bill Byrd, for their encouragement, information and advice.

I also want to acknowledge the advice and encouragement given to me by Dr. Brian Steel Wills, director of the Civil War Center at Kennesaw State University and a prolific author of books on the Civil War.

A special note of appreciation goes to Marc Jolley and the staff at Mercer University Press, including Marsha Luttrell and Mary Beth Kosowski. They always provided valuable advice and assistance in keeping me on course to complete this project.

Finally, I want to thank my wife, Sandi, for her support, patience, and perspective over the years I have pursued the dream of publishing this book.

This book is dedicated to the memory of my late father, Joseph P. Byrd III, and to my late cousin, Daniel Madison Byrd Jr., who lies at rest beside the graves of William and Mary Simmons at Shadowlawn Cemetery in Lawrenceville, Georgia.

Joseph P. Byrd IV

Emory College, Oxford, Georgia. Class of 1858. Will Simmons is on the left end of the top row. *Gwinnett Historical Society Archives; D. M. Byrd Jr. family collection.*

Howell Cobb, prominent political leader and the first commander of William Simmons' 16th Georgia Infantry Regiment. Cobb was later promoted to brigade command and Major General.

ABOVE: Confederate dead beside the post and rail fence along the Hagerstown Road. The 16th Georgia was accidentally positioned at this point during the Battle of Sharpsburg. *Photograph by Matthew Brady. Library of Congress.* BELOW: The Infamous Sunken Road was the site of the fiercest fighting at Fredericksburg. It was at this position that Cobb's Brigade and other regiments held off numerous major assaults. *Drawing from* Battles and Leaders of the Civil War, Volume 3.

Brigadier General Thomas R. R. Cobb led the 16th Georgia and other brigade regiments at the Battle of Fredericksburg where he was killed in action. *Courtesy the Museum of the Confederacy, Richmond, Virginia.*

ABOVE: General William Tatum Wofford, a fellow Georgian, took over command of Simmons' brigade after General T. R. R. Cobb was killed at the Battle of Fredericksburg. *Library of Congress.* BELOW: Regiments of Confederates relieve the tedium of their winter bivouac near Fredericksburg with a huge snowball fight. *Drawing from* Battles and Leaders of the Civil War, Vol. III.

Mary Ambrose, daughter of George W. and Mary Ann Wood Ambrose, Lawrenceville, Georgia. *Byrd family collection.*

Charles Ambrose (1847–1888). Older brother of Mary Ambrose, Lawrenceville, Georgia, ca. 1866. *Byrd family collection.*

Clinton family, ca. 1894. (left to right), Louise Atkins Clinton, Fred Severs Clinton, Paul Clinton, Lee Clinton, and Mary Vera Clinton. *Byrd family collection.*

Clinton home (constructed, ca. 1884) in Red Fork, Creek Nation, Indian Territory.
Byrd family collection.

Joseph Pitts Byrd family, Lawrenceville, Georgia. First row (left to right) Lucille (m. Sam Martin), J. P. Byrd Sr., Georgia Ambrose Byrd, Georgia (m. Scott Candler); Second row (left to right), Hallie (m. Wilbur Blake, Mary (m. Lovick Martin), Cora, and Dan (the Major's "son"); Back row (left to right) George Harold, Fred, and J. P. Byrd Jr. Picture taken at the Methodist Campground near Lawrenceville, Georgia, ca. 1914. *Byrd family collection;* Vanishing Gwinnett, Volume II.

William E. Simmons with his "Tulsa" family, ca. 1920. The picture was most likely taken in Hot Springs, Arkansas, a favorite vacation spot of the Major's. (Left to right), Susan Merrill Clinton, the Major, Vera Clinton McBirney, Ruth Clinton, James Hugh McBirney, and Lee Clinton. *Byrd family collection.*

William E. Simmons, ca. 1910. The Major served as an at-large member on the University of Georgia Board of Trustees under thirteen different governors. His tenure spanned more than thirty-two years. *Byrd family collection.*

Vera Clinton, the Major's "Dear Little Girl." *Byrd family collection.*

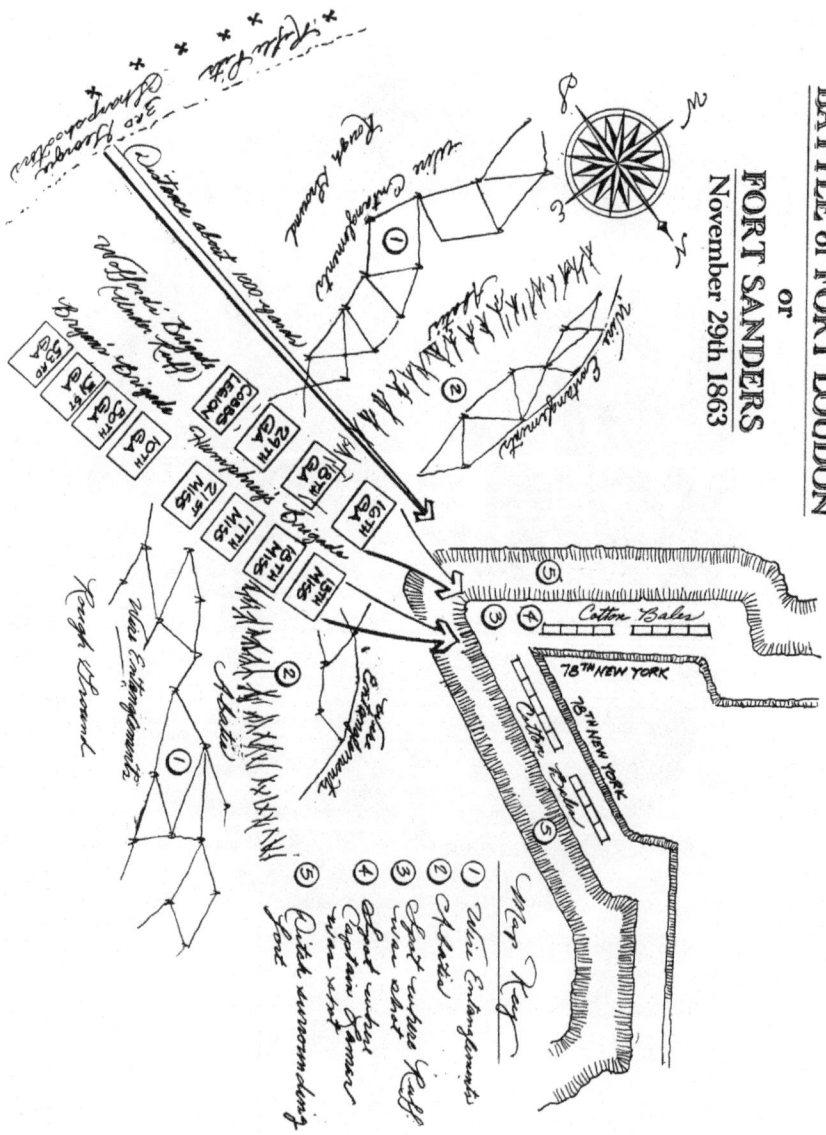

Map sketch by Mike Fleming.

Map sketch by Mike Fleming.

Federal
2nd Position

To Winchester

Crawford Run

4th Virginia

Wofford

3rd Virginia

Shenandoah River

Guard Hill

Federal 1st Position

North Fork

Manassas Gap Railroad

2nd Dismounted
Virginia

To Strasburg

Wickham's Brigade

1st Virginia

2nd Virginia

To Manassas

South Fork

4th Virginia

3rd Virginia

Richardson's Hill

North

To Front Royal

ACTION
AT
GUARD HILL, VIRGINIA
August 16th 1861

Map sketch by Mike Fleming.

1

A Family of Distinction

People will never look forward to prosperity who never look backward
to their ancestors.

—Edmund Burke

William Eleazer[1] Simmons came into the world on 26 August 1839. He was the
second child and eldest son of eight children born to James Pinckney Simmons
and Eliza Terrell Simmons of Gwinnett County, Georgia. Will, as he was called
in his younger days, was born fourteen years after his family had come to
Georgia from North Carolina by way of Tennessee. He was a direct descendant
of James Simmons of Montgomery County, North Carolina, who was born in
1752. In 1777, James served in the Continental Army in the Revolutionary War.
He later married Sara Quimby, and in 1786, a son, Adam Quimby Simmons,
was born.[2]

Adam Q. Simmons grew up in North Carolina, and at the age of nineteen
he married Anna West (b. 1785). After ten years of marriage, Adam and Anna
decided to leave their home and move further west. Early in 1815 they packed
their worldly possessions and with their three young children traveled by horse
and wagon to Rutherford County, Tennessee. They were accompanied by
Anna's brother and his family. Several weeks after beginning their long and
difficult journey, the two families reached the Cumberland Plateau in Middle
Tennessee and stopped in Warren County. There they found shelter in a small
log cabin, originally erected for a hatter's shop—but more recently was used as a
stable. That humble abode was the birthplace of James P. Simmons.

Not long after the family arrived in Tennessee, Adam Simmons purchased
land near the present-day city of Murfreesboro where he farmed and raised
livestock. In 1825 he moved his family, now consisting of his wife and eight

---

[1]William Simmons's middle name was taken from the Bible and likely chosen by
his father, a devout Christian. It was a variation in the spelling of Eleazar, the son of
Aaron and nephew of Moses and Miriam. Eleazar succeeded his father as High Priest,
one of the most important positions in Israel. Eleazar is mentioned in five different books
of the Old Testament: Exodus, Leviticus, Numbers, Deuteronomy, and Joshua.

[2]A more detailed account of the Simmons family appears in James C. Flanigan,
History of Gwinnett County, Georgia, 1818–1960, vol. 2 (1959; reprint, Lawrenceville:
Gwinnett Historical Society, 1999) 588–92.

children, to the northwest corner of Georgia. They settled in the little town of Ringgold, several miles southeast of Chattanooga, Tennessee.[3]

About this time, Adam Simmons began the practice of medicine and created a medical formula widely known as *Dr. A. Q. Simmons' Vegetable Liver Medicine* and *Simmons' Liver Regulator*. It was said to contain mandrake, senna, snakeroot and cloves. It was a very popular medical product and was still in use 100 years after its beginning. In a relatively short time Dr. Simmons built a successful practice and business in the small northwest Georgia community. A strong believer in education, he sent four of his five sons to the University of Tennessee. Of the four, two became doctors and another, Caswell W. Simmons, became a minister in Lawrenceville, Georgia.[4]

After the death of his wife, Anna, in January 1829, Adam Simmons retired from the medicine business. By that time he had accumulated a considerable fortune. His sons, grandsons and great-grandsons carried on the business for many years and became very wealthy selling the *Liver Regulator*.

In 1831, at the age of forty-five, Adam Simmons moved to the western portion of Gwinnett County, Georgia, where he had acquired 2,000 acres of land in a small rural community known as Level Creek. Today the land he purchased is filled mostly with single family homes in suburban Atlanta, situated in the adjacent cities of Buford and Suwanee. It was his home for twenty-five years.

Gwinnett County had been in existence for only thirteen years when Adam Simmons and his family settled in the area. The county was established in 1818 by the Georgia legislature, one of three adjacent counties in the state bearing the names of the Georgia delegates who signed the Declaration of Independence: Button Gwinnett, Lyman Hall and George Walton.[5]

Until Gwinnett County was formed, two great Southeastern Indian tribes, the Creeks and the Cherokees, inhabited the land. The Creeks occupied the land in the southern section and the Cherokees lived along the Chattahoochee River in the northwestern portion of the county. The creation of the county and its settlement came about directly as a result of hostilities between the Creek Indians and the U.S. government. One faction of the Creeks, the "Red Sticks," sided with the British in the War of 1812 while another faction, the more assimilated "White Sticks," aligned with the United States. In March 1814 the Red Sticks were defeated at the Battle of Horseshoe Bend. Andrew Jackson commanded the U.S. forces, which consisted of 2,700 Tennessee militiamen,

---

[3]"The Simmons of Gwinnett" by T. E. Simmons in Flanigan, *History of Gwinnett County*, 2:589.

[4]Ibid.

[5]Joyce Rovetta, "Gwinnett County: The First 150 Years," in Alice Smythe McCabe, ed., *Gwinnett County Families, 1818–1968*, Gwinnett Historical Society (Atlanta: Cherokee Publishing Company, 1980) 1–2.

and a Native American contingent of 600 Cherokees, Choctaws, and Creek White Stick warriors.

After the defeat at Horseshoe Bend, the Creeks ceded 1.5 million acres of land to the United States, including a large portion of the state of Georgia. Gwinnett County was created partly from the former Creek lands and partly from a portion of Jackson County, Georgia, which had been established in 1796. The population of the new county grew rapidly after a land lottery in 1820, the establishment of Lawrenceville as the county seat the following year, and the relocation and removal of the Native American population over the next two decades.[6] The town was named for Captain James Lawrence, the American naval hero who fought in the War of 1812.[7]

Soon after Adam Simmons and his children settled in the Level Creek Community, four veins of gold were found on his land. As assayed in 1831 by the United States Mint at Charlotte, North Carolina, the veins contained gold powder or "pulverized sulfides of gold" valued at $392.73 per ton and gold ore valued at $604.54 per ton. In 1852, twenty-one years after gold was discovered on his land, Adam Simmons sold his property. By that time he and his family had added greatly to their wealth.[8]

The Simmons mine was on the southern edge of the gold fields in North Georgia, site of the nation's first major gold rush. The discovery was on land inhabited by Cherokee Indians, and first reported in August 1829. Before long, thousands of fortune hunters descended on the Georgia frontier. The center of activity was around the boom towns of Auraria and Dahlonega, about fifty miles northwest of Level Creek. Soon Congress authorized the establishment of a Federal Branch Mint at Dahlonega.[9] From its opening in 1838 until 1861, the Dahlonega mint produced 1.5 million coins with a face value of more than six million dollars.

----

[6]According to Census records, the population of Gwinnett County was 4,589 in 1820, 13,289 in 1830 and 10,804 in 1840, reflecting the rapid influx of white settlers and the departure of native Cherokees and Creeks.

[7]James C. Flanigan, *History of Gwinnett County, Georgia*, vol. 1 (1943, reprint; Lawrenceville: Gwinnett Historical Society, 1995) 29.

[8]J. Tracy Power, "Simmons Finds Gwinnett Gold," *Gwinnett Daily News* (Lawrenceville, GA), 13 July 1975. The Simmons gold strike came three years after gold was discovered in Lumpkin County near Dahlonega in the north Georgia Mountains. As a high school student, Tracy Power became a regular contributor to the *Gwinnett Daily News*, writing a weekly column on local history. He later earned his PhD in History at the University of South Carolina, and headed up the South Carolina Department of Archives and History. Dr. Power is the author of *Lee's Miserables: Life in the Army of Northern Virginia from the Wilderness to Appomattox* (Chapel Hill: University of North Carolina Press, 1998).

[9]The name "Dahlonega" comes from the Cherokee word for "gold."

Adam Q. Simmons was married three times. In 1850, at the age of sixty-four and after more than twenty years as a widower, he wed a Mrs. Trimble of Newton County, Georgia. The couple had two children. Following the death of his second wife, Simmons married Ida Lamar, who bore three more children. Adam Simmons sold his holdings in 1852 and later moved to Parker County, Texas, west of Fort Worth. He died in the county seat of Weatherford in 1863 at the age of seventy-seven.[10]

Adam Simmons's precocious son, James, attended Lawrenceville Academy from January 1834 to September 1835. After completing his schooling, the younger Simmons began studying law in the office of Nathan Louis Hutchins, and he was admitted to the Lawrenceville bar on 4 April 1836, his twenty-first birthday. James had a prosperous career as a lawyer as evidenced by the fact that for many years he was one of the Gwinnett County's largest taxpayers. He was also one of the largest landowners in the area. Prior to the War Between the States, he owned 1,300 acres of land, as recorded in the 1860 Census, with cotton the principal crop.[11]

In 1849, James Simmons was one of four lawyers in Lawrenceville who were deeded corner lots on the public square that surrounded the Gwinnett County Courthouse.[12] The action was taken by the County Commission to keep out wandering farm animals that had been trampling and fouling the courthouse grounds. Livestock often disrupted court proceedings by entering the courthouse building. Before the new ruling could be implemented, the Georgia State legislature had to pass a special act. The only stipulation made in the offer was that each property owner erect a commercial building and maintain "a substantial fence around the square" to keep out the intrusive animals. The first fence under the agreement was built of chestnut rails. It stood eight feet high with a stile on each side. In those days, placing a fence around the courthouse was important as there were free range laws in Georgia that allowed livestock to roam at will.[13]

---

[10]Flanigan, History of Gwinnett County, 1:589–90.

[11]Bob Wynn, "Simmons Fills Local History Books," *Gwinnett Daily News*, 18 February 1984, 2A.

[12]Marvin Nash Worthy, *A Land, Its People, Their Heritage*, vol. 3 of *History of Gwinnett County, Georgia, 1818–1993* ([Lawrenceville]: Gwinnett Board of Commissioners, 1994) 152. In addition to James P. Simmons, the other recipients included Charles H. Smith, Nathan L. Hutchins Sr., and T. W. Alexander. In later years, Smith gained widespread fame as a humorist and newspaper columnist under the pseudonym of "Bill Arp."

[13]Mary Frazier Long, *About Lawrenceville* (Madison, GA: Southern Lion Books, 2008) 173–74. Mrs. Long's research revealed that "The chestnut rail fences served well for several years and they began to disappear. It was found that certain individuals decided that they made excellent firewood."

Throughout most of his adult years, James Simmons was a dedicated member of the Lawrenceville Baptist Church, serving as clerk and deacon. He contributed regularly and liberally to the support of his church and to numerous charitable and civic needs. He was licensed by his denomination to preach and often filled the pulpits of area churches when requested to do so. A skilled writer, he published his first article, "Angels, Devils, and Men," in a Georgia religious newspaper in 1852 with the anonymous signature, "Layman."[14] During the 1870s, Simmons authored three books on theological subjects: *War in Heaven, Peace on Earth,* and *Origin of Man.*[15]

Although he was an accomplished writer and speaker from the pulpit, James Simmons's primary interest was the law. He was actively involved in political life, serving in the Georgia House of Representatives in 1841 and as a state senator for two terms, in 1847–1848 and 1851–1852. He was said by some to have been the most active member of the Georgia Secession Convention of 1850. There he fought hard against the movement to secede from the Union and was successful. In May 1858, he attended the Southern Commercial Convention in Montgomery, Alabama, having been appointed as a delegate to represent the state's Sixth Congressional District by Georgia governor Joseph Emerson Brown.

In addition to his law practice and agricultural interests, James Simmons was the principal owner and president of the Gwinnett Manufacturing Company, a Lawrenceville cotton mill that employed more than 100 workers. The business enterprise was very successful until it was destroyed by fire during the War between the States. In later years, Simmons moved to Norcross, in the western portion of Gwinnett County, where he was instrumental in the early formation of that city and the establishment of a weekly newspaper.[16]

During his lifetime, he became known as one of the "leading men of the state" according to F. W. Avery in his book, *The History of Georgia.*[17]

---

[14]James P. Simmons, *War in Heaven* (1872; reprint, Lavergne, TN, publisher unknown, 2014) 10.

[15]J. Tracy Power, "Why Lawyers Know Bible Better," *Gwinnett Daily News,* 4 December 1977. All three of James P. Simmons's theological books are available as reprints.

[16]Bob Wynn, "Gwinnett's Best Ever? It Could Be James Simmons?" *Gwinnett Daily News,* 23 November 1986, 3D. In addition to his many other accomplishments, James P. Simmons is credited as the founder of the First Baptist Church of Lawrenceville, where he was the first clerk and served as Sunday school superintendent for many years.

[17]F. W. Avery, *History of Georgia* (New York: Brown and Derby, 1881) 72.

Will Simmons's Early Years

The love of learning, the sequestered nooks,
and all the sweet serenity of books.

—Henry Wadsworth Longfellow

James P. Simmons was an exemplary role model to his eldest son, Will. Madison Byrd recalled hearing that, as a youngster, Will excelled in his studies at the Lawrenceville Academy[1] where his father had once been an outstanding student.

> From a very early age, the boy began to develop ideas and convictions of his own, and often engaged in spirited discussions with his father about the issues of the day. James Simmons took great pleasure in these discussions with Will. They demonstrated that the young man could think for himself and that he was showing great aptitude for the law. If they agreed on nothing else, they did agree, that upon graduation, Will would study law in his father's office, a small brick building located on the family property not more than a hundred feet from the front door of their home.[2]

In 1854, a few days after his fifteenth birthday, Will enrolled at Emory College in Oxford, Georgia. By that time, he had developed strong convictions and a very stubborn nature. A relative recorded a family story he remembered hearing about how young Simmons was sometimes the victim of his own hard-headedness:

> When Will arrived at Emory he found himself somewhat bewildered in the presence of so many new acquaintances. At supper, when a steaming dish of grits was passed to him interrupting a conversation, he was momentarily taken aback, and said, "No thank you, I never touch them." This caused much comment at the table. Throughout the rest of his days at college, he always declined grits, although it was a favorite dish of his and frequently

---

[1]James C. Flanigan, *History of Gwinnett County, Georgia*, vol. 1 (1943; reprint, Lawrenceville: Gwinnett Historical Society, 1995) 69. The Lawrenceville Academy was one of the first schools established in Gwinnett County. Rev. Dr. John S. Wilson was rector and superintendent from 1826–1838. Because the school charged tuition, his students came from the most prosperous families in the area.

[2]Daniel M. Byrd Jr., *Them Brave Georgians*, manuscript, Gwinnett Historical Society archives, Lawrenceville, GA, pg. 5 (Fort Delaware Society Library, Delaware City, DE, also has a copy.).

served at college meals. He ate his fill at home, but his particular sense of dignity and plain stubbornness would not allow him to lose face at college by indulging in that staple of Southern cooking.[3]

There was another family legend about Will Simmons's impulsiveness and quick temper recorded by Madison Byrd:

On the eve of graduation from Emory in 1858, Will learned that the college planned to deny him his rightfully earned top honors. The coveted award was to be given to the scion of one of the college's more generous benefactors. Upon learning of this action, Will became indignant, and left the college immediately. In his words, his diploma and commencement could "go to blazes."[4]

He did not return to campus until his fiftieth class reunion in 1908. In his memoirs, he simply wrote, "Graduated [from] Emory College with degree of A. B. in 1858."[5]

After graduating from Emory College, Will Simmons returned to his home town to pursue a law career and help his father manage the family's farm property. However, circumstances soon prevailed to route him in the direction of journalism as a field of endeavor. His father had advanced a considerable sum of money to some parties to establish a newspaper, *The Lawrenceville News*. The investors failed to purchase the plant, and the elder Simmons made his son a present of it.[6] The paper was now his, either to publish or to sell to another owner. To help get the new publication off the ground, Isaac Pilgrim was named as the first editor. The younger Simmons soon found that it was very difficult to find a qualified buyer for a small town Georgia newspaper. Thus, he became an editor and publisher at the tender age of nineteen to keep it going.[7] His dream of becoming a lawyer would have to wait.

---

[3]Byrd, *Them Brave Georgians*, 6. D. M. Byrd refers to this as a "family legend," and he likely heard it from his father.

[4]Ibid. Records of Emory College were destroyed when Sherman's army occupied the building in Oxford, GA, on its "March to the Sea" in November 1864.

[5]"Reunion of the Class of 1858 a Feature of Emory Commencement," *Atlanta Constitution*, 10 June 1908. William E. Simmons was one of eight members of his graduating class to attend their Emory College fiftieth reunion in Oxford, GA. Other class members, all from Georgia, who attended the commencement included Dr. H. L. Wilson of Atlanta, W. Simmons of St. Marys, S. P. Orr of Athens, J. F. Senife of Camilla, Julius A. Peek of Polk County, William Allen Turner of Newnan, and Frank L. Little of Sparta.

[6]Byrd, *Them Brave Georgians*, 7. Simmons also collected autographs of fellow prisoners, visitors, a few poems and notes. Some of the names appear in Flanigan, *History of Gwinnett County*, 1:244–45.

[7]Byrd, *Them Brave Georgians*, 7.

The first issue of the *News* appeared on 16 November 1858. Despite Will Simmons's youth and lack of experience, he quickly made it a lively and aggressive publication. Subscriptions poured into the offices of the *News* from all over the Sixth Congressional District in North Georgia. The venture was successful, and by the end of the first year the *News* had the legal advertising of the six counties in his district, and a good circulation in all of them.

From the very start, Simmons's newspaper took a firm stand on the hot issue of the day—the extension of slavery to the western territories from which new states were to be created.[8] Will's father, though profiting from the use of his slaves, was not completely sympathetic with the institution of slavery. He was regarded as a "Unionist" by his fellow planters. In fact, some of his peers referred to him as an "abolitionist," a name occasionally applied in the 1850s in the Deep South to anyone who was opposed to the extension of slavery and its protection by the laws of the United States. Despite the unkind words his neighbors had for his position, James Simmons remained steadfast in his support of the Union and continued his opposition to any measure that would place Georgia in a hostile attitude towards the federal government. His son took a different position, however. On the pages of the *Lawrenceville News*, young Simmons strongly advocated the secession of Georgia and the Southern states from the Union.[9]

In June 1859, three months before his twentieth birthday, Will Simmons was selected as a delegate from Gwinnett County to attend the Democrat Party Gubernatorial Convention in the state capital of Milledgeville. On that occasion, he was joined by Thomas H. Jones, D. W. Spence, H. Allan, Hugh Duncan, A. Pool, and Nathan L. Hutchins Jr., the son of his father's mentor.

In April of the following year, the Democrat Party National Convention was held in Charleston, South Carolina. Most Northern Democrats, determined to reject the demand of the party's Southern wing for a pro-slavery plank, arrived for the opening gavel. A large segment of Northern delegates backed Stephen Douglas, a candidate clearly not acceptable to the majority of voters in the South. The Southern faction strongly favored John Cabell Breckinridge of Kentucky. When the Northerners refused to accept the Southerners' demands, fifty Southern delegates walked out of the convention. This action made it extremely difficult for any candidate to gain the necessary votes of two-thirds of the remaining convention delegates. After fifty-seven ballots, the delegates decided to adjourn until 18 June and resume their proceedings in Baltimore, a somewhat less partisan location. During that time the party was without a presidential nominee.[10]

---

[8]L. T. Griffith and J. E. Talmadge, *Georgia Journalism 1763–1950* (Athens: University of Georgia Press, 1951) 381.

[9]Byrd, *Them Brave Georgians*, 7–9.

[10]Avery, *History of Georgia*, 115.

When the convention resumed in Baltimore, the northern faction adopted a plank supporting the position of Stephen Douglas. Once again, a large number of Southern delegates walked out, with the Georgia delegation hopelessly split. Without agreement to support one candidate, the presidential election was destined to be won by the more unified Republican Party, which nominated Abraham Lincoln at their convention in Chicago.

Back in Georgia, three different state conventions were hastily convened, one for each of the two Democrat Party platforms, and one for the newly-formed Constitutional Union Party and its standard-bearer, John Bell of Tennessee. Faithful to his more moderate convictions, James P. Simmons attended the "National" Democrat State Convention as a delegate from the Sixth Congressional District where he and sixty-three delegates from twenty-four Georgia counties supported the Douglas platform.[11] At the same time, Will Simmons served as a delegate from the Sixth District at the state convention that backed John C. Breckinridge. There he and 340 delegates from 112 counties adopted the majority Charleston platform that called for protection of slaves in U.S. territories.[12] Two other Gwinnett County delegates, Nate Hutchins Jr. and James Polk, accompanied young Simmons to the convention.

After father and son returned home from their respective conventions, father Simmons prevailed upon Will to allow the *News* to offer differing viewpoints of the day's major issues in its columns. Will stubbornly refused his father's plea and affirmed his stand as editor that the newspaper would only support Breckinridge for president and Joseph Lane of Oregon for vice president. The paper had been advocating their views on slavery in the territories from the start of his editorship and would continue to do so. Despite his sharp difference of opinion with his son, the senior Simmons acknowledged Will's convictions and allowed him to continue running the newspaper.[13]

Later, when it became evident that Abraham Lincoln would be elected president, the *News* advocated secession as "the only safe and honorable course left to the South." According to Madison Byrd,

> Father Simmons was appalled. Will might be twenty-one years of age and a successful editor, but destruction of the Union was a doctrine that he felt no Simmons should advocate. Sharp words ensued before wiser reflection permitted a compromise, perhaps the only successful one in the nation during that fateful year of 1860. Will relinquished his editorship of the *News* and a cousin from Atlanta was brought to Lawrenceville to take control.[14]

---

[11]Ibid., 121.
[12]Ibid., 120.
[13]Byrd, *Them Brave Georgians*, 7–8.
[14]Ibid., 10. See also Griffith and Talmadge, *Georgia Journalism*, 381.

Despite the differences with his son and the growing sentiment in the Lower South, James P. Simmons continued to oppose the advocates of disunion. He traveled to many places throughout Georgia and the Southeast to speak against secession. In January 1861, he represented Gwinnett County as a member of the Georgia Secession Convention held in the state capital of Milledgeville. Along with two other Gwinnett County delegates, Richard D. Winn and Thomas J. P. Hudson, he cast his vote against Georgia seceding from the Union. In a fiery speech before the delegates Simmons bluntly exclaimed in conclusion, "Gentlemen, secession means war; and in such an unevenly matched war, we are practically licked even now before we start! Are we crazy?"[15]

Contrary to the growing support for secession in the Lower South, James Simmons's position was not unique among delegates from the North Georgia counties where there were relatively few large plantations and slave owners. According to the 1860 Census, there were only twenty-three Gwinnett County farms of more than 1,000 acres. There were 330 Gwinnett residents out of a total population of over 10,000 who claimed to own slaves, and most had no more than one or two in servitude (James P. Simmons owned seven slaves in 1860).[16] Despite the efforts of all three Gwinnett County delegates, however, the resolution to secede passed by a vote of 208 to 89, dissolving Georgia's ties with the United States of America.

After the result of the secession vote was announced, James P. Simmons offered the following resolution, which was recorded in the journal of the proceedings of the convention and printed on the Georgia Ordinance of Secession.

> We, the undersigned delegates to the convention of the State of Georgia now in session, while we most solemnly protest against the action of the majority in adopting an ordinance for the immediate and separate secession of this state, and would have preferred the policy of cooperation with our southern sister states, yet as good citizens we yield to the will of a majority of her people as expressed by their representatives; and we hereby pledge "our lives, our fortunes, and our sacred honor" to the defense of Georgia, if necessary, against hostile invasion from any source whatever.[17]

Six delegates signed the protest resolution, including James P. Simmons of Gwinnett County, Thomas M. McRae and F. H. Latimer of Montgomery County, Davis Whelchel and Phillip May Byrd of Hall County, and James Simmons (no relation) of Pickens County. Georgia's fate was sealed, and the

---

[15]James C. Flanigan, *History of Gwinnett County, Georgia, 1818–1960*, vol. 2 (1959; reprint, Lawrenceville, GA: Gwinnett Historical Society, 1999) 591.

[16]Flanigan, *History of Gwinnett County*, 1:182.

[17]Allen D. Candler, *The Confederate Records of the State of Georgia* (Atlanta: C. P. Byrd State Printer, 1909–1911) 17.

state officially seceded from the Union at 2:00 P.M. on 10 January 1861. She was the fifth state to do so. The next month, delegates from the seceding states, with the exception of Texas, convened in Montgomery, Alabama, and formed a provisional government. By 11 March, with the support of Texas, they had adopted a constitution. The Confederate States of America was now a reality.

The War Begins

Go forth to meet the shadowy future without fear and with
a manly heart.

— Henry Wadsworth Longfellow

After Georgia seceded from the United States and war became inevitable,
several influential Lawrenceville citizens issued a call to arms to form a volunteer
company to defend their newly created government. Will Simmons and eighty-
three other men attended the very first meeting at the county courthouse on
Tuesday, 7 May 1861.[1] That evening each man present signed an oath of loyalty
to Georgia and elected officers to lead the new company, called the "Gwinnett
Volunteers." Henry Phillip Thomas was elected captain by acclamation. Thomas
was a respected local lawyer, former state senator and representative, and a large
land owner.[2] Will Simmons was one of three lieutenants elected, along with
Nathan Louis Hutchins Jr. and John A. Mitchell.[3]

---

[1]Nathan Louis Hutchins Jr. to Howell Cobb, 9 June 1861, Howell Cobb Papers,
box 51, Folder 26 ms. 1376 Hargrett Rare Book and Manuscript Library, UGA, Athens.

[2]James C. Flanigan, *History of Gwinnett County, Georgia*, vol. 1 (1943; reprint,
Lawrenceville: Gwinnett Historical Society, 1995) 351–53. Henry P. Thomas was born
10 May 1810 in Franklin County, GA. He was a classmate of Howell Cobb, Alexander
Hamilton Stephens, and William H. Crawford Jr. at Franklin College (University of
Georgia), class of 1832. A man of great intellect, Thomas received second honors at
graduation, surpassed only by Alexander H. Stephens. Thomas was admitted to the bar
in 1835 and came to Lawrenceville the following year. Later, he distinguished himself as
an officer in the Mexican War, serving on the staff of General Winfield Scott. Thomas
had four sons who served in the Confederate army. His brother, Edward L. Thomas,
would become commanding officer of the 35th Georgia Infantry. A nephew, Lovick P.
Thomas, would lead the 42nd Georgia Infantry. For additional information see "Henry
P. Thomas—In Memoriam," *Georgia Historical Quarterly* 19/3 (September 1935): 264–
65.

[3]During the war, the Gwinnett Volunteers were commonly referred to as the
"Hutchins Guards" in honor of their captain, Nathan L. Hutchins Jr., and his father,
Judge N. L. Hutchins, who released several men charged for minor offenses on condition
that they would enlist in the company for service in the Confederate army. Some of the
Lawrenceville area residents who attended the 7 May 1861 meeting included William M.
Adair, Julian Bowran, James H. Braziel, John T. Clark, G. W. Davis, Samuel Z. Dyer,
Andrew J. Farill, Asa McMillan, George N. Morgan, Thomas P. Nelms, Charlton H.
Strickland, and Ed Thomas. In spring 1863, six of this group (Adair, Clark, Farill,

To help swell the ranks of the volunteer company, Judge Nathan L. Hutchins Sr. discharged some eighteen or twenty Gwinnett County men indicted for minor offences, on condition that they would enlist in the Army.[4] Soon after the company was formed, the five Judges of the Gwinnett Superior Court were directed to make provision for the families of those "who are called off to defend their country." The judges, W. R. Bracewell, Daniel Madison Byrd, W. F. Kennedy, John Mills and Adam Robinson, arranged to borrow enough money to equip the volunteers and care for their dependent families.[5] To provide a means to pay back the money borrowed, the Gwinnett Superior Court judges levied a tax and exempted all volunteers from it.[6]

During the following month the Superior Court made provisions to secure uniforms and arms for the Gwinnett Volunteers. The court arranged for the purchase of cloth and engaged William A. Harvey, a local tailor, to measure each soldier and cut his uniform. Relatives and friends then sewed "day and night" to make apparel for the hometown boys.[7] Lieutenant Simmons, a blue-eyed, fair-haired young man of twenty-one, must have cut a fine figure in his new gray uniform, standing erect to make the most of his five feet ten inches.[8] He was always meticulous about his appearance and bearing, a trait that was characteristic throughout his life.[9]

About two weeks after the company was organized, Captain Thomas notified the Governor of the formation of the company and selection of officers. A response was received from General Henry C. Wayne in a letter dated 20 May 1861, acknowledging the company's formation and enclosing commissions for each of the officers. On 4 June, the Gwinnett Volunteers responded in a

---

McMillan, Nelms, and Strickland) would be selected to serve in the elite 3rd Georgia Sharpshooter Battalion under the leadership of Nathan L. Hutchins Jr.

[4]Faye Stone Poss, abstractor, *The Southern Watchman Athens, Georgia: Civil War home front coverage, 1861–1865* (Snellville, GA: Faye Stone Poss, 2008) 14.

[5]Daniel Madison Byrd (1826–1880) was the grandfather of Daniel Madison Byrd Sr. (1885–1934) and nephew of Phillip May Byrd, who signed James Simmons's resolution that appears on the Georgia Ordinance of Secession.

[6]Flanigan, *History of Gwinnett County*, 1:190.

[7]Ibid., 1:191.

[8]William E. Simmons's height, eye and hair color were noted and recorded on his release from Fort Delaware Prison on 24 July 1865 at the signing of the amended Oath of Allegiance to the United States.

[9]Daniel M. Byrd Jr., *Them Brave Georgians*, manuscript, Gwinnett Historical Society archives, Lawrenceville, GA, p. 16. (Fort Delaware Society Library, Delaware City, DE, also has a copy.).

letter signed by all four company officers. The original letter is held in the Georgia Department of Archives and History (see Exhibit 1).[10]

While waiting for completion of their uniforms and assignment to a regiment, the newly formed company remained encamped on the courthouse lawn in Lawrenceville and drilled each evening after supper during the remaining hours of daylight. It was at that time that they were contacted by Howell Cobb, a prominent Georgian, who issued an invitation to the volunteers to join in the formation of a regiment he was organizing. The members of the company were delighted that they had been approached by such a distinguished leader and responded that they were ready and willing to follow his command. On 9 June Lieutenant Nate Hutchins was chosen to reply on behalf of the Gwinnett Volunteers given his father's close friendship with Howell Cobb. In his letter Hutchins emphasized that all the members of the company "readily and cheerfully agree to go into your regiment." He also asked Cobb to keep the company informed on the plans for the regiment.[11]

Howell Cobb (1815–1868) was a native of nearby Jefferson County, Georgia, and an 1834 graduate of Franklin College.[12] For much of his life Cobb was prominent in the political world. After four years in the Georgia legislature, he served in the U.S. Congress from 1843 until 1851 and was Speaker of the House from 1849 to 1851. In 1851, he was elected governor of Georgia for one term until 1853. The following year he was again elected to Congress. Soon after taking the Oath of Office in 1857, President James Buchanan appointed Cobb to be Secretary of the Treasury, a position the Georgian held until his resignation on 10 December 1860.[13]

In his new role, Cobb was ably assisted by his adjutant, Lieutenant James Barrow, who was appointed on 19 July 1861. Barrow's distinguished service record and reputation as a good officer preceded him in the North Georgia countryside and helped to make him a very effective recruiter. In March 1862 Barrow was promoted to captain and assistant adjutant general to Howell Cobb. The following year he received a promotion to lieutenant colonel and was given command of the 64th Georgia Infantry. In February 1864 Barrow was killed at

---

[10]Ibid., 17. The officers of the Gwinnett Volunteers were a serious band of men. These soldiers were known as "war troops," men who had enlisted for the duration of the war rather than for a specific chronological term of service.

[11]N. L. Hutchins Jr. to Howell Cobb, 9 June 1861, Howell Cobb papers, box 51, folder 26, ms. 1376, Hargrett Rare Book and Manuscript Library, University of Georgia, Athens.

[12]Franklin College later became the University of Georgia (though Franklin College was retained as the name of the College of Arts and Sciences).

[13]Horace Montgomery, "Howell Cobb's Confederate Career," in *Confederate Centennial Studies* no. 10, ed. William S. Hoole (Montgomery, AL: Confederate Publishing Company, 1959) 17, 20.

Olustee (Ocean Pond), the only major land battle fought in Florida during the War Between the States.[14]

While Simmons and his comrades in the Gwinnett Volunteers were awaiting orders, a number of impatient young men from the Gholston and Reader communities in the western part of the county were organizing a volunteer company of their own. A meeting was called at the Byrd Martin store, and officers were elected. Ben Gholston was chosen captain; Ed Reader, 1st lieutenant; James M. Liddell, 2nd lieutenant; and W. T. Smith, 3rd lieutenant. Because of its good shelters and access to fresh water, the group decided to go into training at the campground near Flint Hill.

As recounted by William M. Hunnicutt, a private in the outfit, some serious differences arose over "payments for uniforms between the Gholston and Reader factions, which were about evenly divided and threatened to break up the company." To settle the controversy the company met on a specified date and representatives of each faction made fiery speeches. Fortunately older and wiser heads were present and a compromise was reached. Gholston and Reader were persuaded to resign their offices and become privates. This move seemed to bring harmony, and new officers were elected. Moses Richardson was chosen captain, E. F. Gober of Marietta became the 1st lieutenant, and Liddell and Smith were re-elected as 2nd lieutenants. Peace prevailed and company was named the "Flint Hill Grays."[15]

In late July, after the appropriate arrangements were made, Lieutenant Simmons and the rest of the Gwinnett Volunteers marched to Stone Mountain, Georgia, sixteen miles from Lawrenceville, and boarded a train for the 660-mile ride via Chattanooga and Knoxville to Richmond, where Howell Cobb was to assemble his regiment. In all the journey took a week, and the men were worn out by the time they arrived safely at their destination around the first of August.[16]

Several days later, on 11 August, the Flint Hill Grays traveled by rail to Richmond, following a different route from the one taken earlier by the Gwinnett Volunteers. One member of the Grays wrote that their first stop was Augusta, where they received a warm welcome from the local citizens. From Augusta the volunteers journeyed to Charleston, South Carolina, and then on to

---

[14]E. Merton Coulter, *Lost Generation: The Life and Death of James Barrow, C. S. A.*, no. 1 in Confederate Centennial Studies, ed. William S. Hoole (Montgomery, AL: Confederate Publishing Company, 1956) 56–59.

[15]"Remembrances of William M. Hunnicutt" in "Flint Hill Grays from Gwinnett County, Georgia" in *Bible Records, Military Rosters and Reminiscences of Confederate Soldiers*, vol. 9 of United Daughters of the Confederacy Bound Transcripts, pp. 19–104, Georgia Department of Archives and History, Morrow, GA. The original is in the Washington Library and Archives in Macon, GA.

[16]Byrd, *Them Brave Georgians*, 21.

Wilmington, North Carolina, where they crossed the Cape Fear River by steamboat. They then boarded another train for their destination by way of Kinston, North Carolina, and Petersburg, Virginia.[17]

Earlier, the Cobb Infantry from nearby Habersham County had traveled from Atlanta to Richmond. According to Captain B. Edward Stiles, commanding officer of the company, their route was through Dalton, Georgia; Chattanooga, and Knoxville. He described the journey in a letter to his mother dated 1 August 1861. Later that month his unit would be assigned to the 16th Georgia along with the two Gwinnett County companies.[18]

When they arrived in Richmond in early August, Lieutenant Simmons and his companions may have been disappointed at the appearance of the Confederate capitol building. In addition to describing the State House as "a dilapidated old rookery," the *Charleston Mercury* continued, "As a public building it would not have been a credit even to a decadent country and its dismal appearance was made more pronounced by the contrasting beauty of its grounds. Well-tended flower beds, hedges and graceful trees made the State House stand out as a thorn among so many roses."[19]

A very different perspective of the Confederate capitol was expressed by Private Eli Pinson Landers of the Flint Hill Grays. Soon after arriving at camp in mid-August, he wrote that he was granted a pass to leave camp and visit the city.

> I got permission from my Captain and went up in town today. There I saw the greatest place I ever did see! Atlanta is nothing more than a kitchen to the Big House! I will tell you folks that there is no use in trying to compare nothing to what I have saw since I left home! I saw Washington's Monument. It is away up on a stack of fine rock and he is on the largest horse that I ever saw. Washington is on his horse with his sword in his hand. The horse and man look as natural as nature itself.[20]

---

[17]Eli P. Landers to Susan Landers, 11 August 1861 [in?] Elizabeth Whitley Roberson, *Weep Not for Me Dear Mother* (Gretna, LA: Pelican Publishing Company, 1998) 23. The complete letters of Private Landers are contained in Elizabeth Whitley Roberson, *In Care of Yellow River* (Fort Lauderdale: Venture Press, 1994).

[18]B. Edward Stiles Jr. to his mother, 1 August 1861, McKay-Stiles papers, Southern Historical Collection, University of North Carolina, Chapel Hill. Stiles served in Company E (Cobb Infantry from Habersham County) of the 16th Georgia Infantry Regiment. Samuel C. Elam also describes a trip from Atlanta to Richmond in the 7 November 1861 issue of *Southern Confederacy*, a newspaper published in Atlanta.

[19]Charleston (SC) Mercury, 26 April 1861.

[20]Eli P. Landers to Susan Landers, 18 August 1861, in Roberson, *Yellow River*, 21. See also Henry Woodhead, ed., *Soldier Life: Voices of the Civil War* (Alexandria, VA: Time Life Books) 62–63.

The hustle and bustle of the city was something else. War fever was in the air. Teams of mules and horses rumbled over the bridges and clogged the streets. Thousands of troops were everywhere, barely avoiding each other as they paraded about the city. Since most of the streets were not surfaced, great clouds of dust trailed each regiment as the men marched off to training camps and more distant destinations.[21] A *Charleston Mercury* reporter observed that "All business seems to be suspended, except the sale of arms, military clothes and equipment. The hotels are crowded to their utmost capacity, and the corridors glitter with arms, epaulettes, and gold lace."[22]

Amidst the confusion, Lieutenant Simmons and his comrades in the Gwinnett Volunteers were assigned a site to make camp. They were met by Howell Cobb, who had arrived in Richmond on 13 June following a trip to Norfolk to see his three sons already in uniform.[23]

Upon his return, Cobb eagerly appealed to the Confederate government to grant him the authority to form a regiment. Although he lacked military experience, his powers of leadership were needed by Confederate army and his request was quickly granted by the Confederate Congress. Over the next two months, assisted by Staff Adjutant James Barrow, he completed the task of recruiting enough men to be organized into ten companies.[24]

In Richmond, the Gwinnett Volunteers joined up with the Flint Hill Grays, the Cobb Infantry from Habersham County and seven other North Georgia companies recruited by Howell Cobb to form a regiment. There were about 900 men present, including two companies from Madison County, the Madison County Greys and the Danielsville Guards; the Jackson Rifles, also known as the Jackson County Volunteers; the Centre Hill Guards (also from Jackson County); the Hartwell Infantry from Hart County; the Ramsey Volunteers from Columbia County; and a company from Walton County.[25]

On 15 August 1861, the men of Howell Cobb's new regiment assembled to elect officers. A cry immediately went up for Cobb to take command, and he was made regimental colonel by acclamation. The next officer in the chain of command was Lieutenant Colonel Goode Bryan, a West Point graduate (class of 1834) and Mexican War veteran. Bryan brought a wealth of military experience to the regiment, having served for more than twelve years as an

[21] Fitzgerald Ross, *Cities and Camps of the Confederate States* (Urbana: University of Illinois Press, 1958) 23; "Address of Colonel Edward McCrady Jr. before the Virginia Division of the Army of Northern Virginia at Their Reunion on the Evening of October 21, 1886," *Southern Historical Society Papers* (hereafter *SHSP*) 14 (January–December 1886): 192.

[22] *Charleston (SC) Mercury*, 26 April 1861; "Address of Colonel Edward McCrady Jr.," 192.

[23] *Richmond (VA) Dispatch*, 28 May 1861 and 15 June 1861.

[24] Coulter, *Lost Generation*, 56–59.

[25] *Southern Banner* (Athens GA), 6 November 1861.

officer with the Alabama and Georgia militias. During the Mexican War, he held the rank of major in command of the First Alabama Volunteers. After the regiment was disbanded in 1847, he continued his service on the staff of General Worth until the following year.[26]

Rounding out the top leadership of the regiment was Gwinnett County's own Henry P. Thomas, who was elected major. The regiment was designated the 16th Georgia, and the Gwinnett Volunteers became Company I. The elevation of Thomas to the regimental staff left a vacancy among the officers of the 16th Georgia. Nathan L. Hutchins Jr. was promoted to captain in the elections. William Simmons was selected as 1st lieutenant and E. B. Thomas replaced Simmons as 2nd lieutenant. The title of 3rd lieutenant was dropped, and John Mitchell became the company's other 2nd lieutenant.[27]

Lieutenant William Simmons was undoubtedly pleased with his promotion and that of his friend Nathan L. Hutchins Jr. (b. 1835), who was selected to fill the position of company commander (previously held by Captain Henry P. Thomas). As Emory College graduates, natives of Lawrenceville, and sons of prominent lawyers, Simmons and Hutchins had a great deal in common.[28] In the days to come, the Gwinnett Volunteers would be more commonly referred to as the "Hutchins Guards."

After the regiment was formed, Hutchins and Simmons became acquainted with the captains who commanded the other nine companies of the 16th Georgia: James S. Gholston, Company A (Madison County Grays); Abner M. Reynolds, Company B (Center Hill Guards); John H. Skelton, Company C (Hartwell Infantry); John N. Montgomery, Company D (Danielsville Guards); Benjamin Edward Stiles Jr., Company E (Cobb Infantry); John H. D. McRae, Company F (Walton Volunteers); Augustus C. Thompson, Company G

---

[26]Goode Bryan was born in Hancock County, GA, on 31 August 1811. His record at West Point was less than stellar, and he was required to repeat his second year. He graduated in 1834. After service in the Mexican War he settled in Jefferson County, GA, and later resided in Richmond and Lee counties in Georgia. In January 1861 he attended the Georgia Secession Convention in Milledgeville. See Stewart Sifakis, *Who Was Who in the Civil War* (New York: Facts on File Publications, 1988) 83.

[27]Simmons service records, in Byrd, *Them Brave Georgians* 26.

[28]Nathan Louis Hutchins Sr. was born in the Pendleton District of South Carolina on 11 April 1799. After settling in Georgia, he became a widely respected lawyer and served as judge of the Western Circuit from 1857 to 1868. His daughter Harriet Harris Hutchins (b. 1837) married Alfred Iverson Jr. in 1856. Judge Hutchins was likely very proud of his son-in-law, who served as a cavalry officer in the Confederate army. After honorable service in the Battle of Sharpsburg, Iverson was promoted to brigadier general. His brigade suffered heavy casualties at Gettysburg, and he was later transferred to Georgia. In July 1864, outnumbered two-to-one, he was victorious over Major-General Stoneman's cavalry in Jones County near Macon, capturing Stoneman and 600 of his men. See Sifakis, *Who Was Who in the Civil War*, 332–33.

(Jackson Rifles); Nathaniel Reader, Company H (Flint Hill Grays); and Robert J. Boyd, Company K (Ramsey Volunteers). Once the officers were chosen to lead the regiment, Cobb selected the men to serve on his staff, including James Barrow, adjutant; Lewis S. McGuire, commissary; Robert Thomas, quartermaster; William Flinn, chaplain; and R. M. Smith, surgeon.[29]

As soon as organizational matters were completed, the 16th Georgia moved to Camp Lee on the Richmond Fairgrounds. It was there that Cobb, with the assistance of some cadets from the Virginia Military College (VMI), began the task of training himself and his regiment in the duties and disciplines of soldiers. After drill was concluded each day, he assembled the regimental officers for more intense study and a discussion of military tactics. The few military books available were passed from officer to officer. Lieutenant Simmons and his fellow officers agreed that they learned more from the *United States Ordinance Manual* than from any other military book.[30]

Soon after their arrival in Richmond, many of the soldiers in the 16th Georgia and their neighbors in camp became afflicted with sickness and disease. During the ten weeks the regiment was in Richmond, hundreds of men became sick and were not able to carry out their duties. By the end of August, the situation was critical. A young private from the Yellow River Community[31] in Gwinnett County wrote that there were at least 100 men in the 16th Georgia who were sick, including all the commissioned officers except one. One week later, in a letter to his mother, he described how the situation had deteriorated to the point that more than twice as many men were seriously ill:

> Times is bad here and getting worse. There is so much sickness here that there is about 250 sick in this regiment. They are dying dayly. There has been about fifteen died since last Sunday morning. Last Thursday, there was six died. Though I have not been sick but one day since I left home, the sick [soldiers] is just lying thick through the camps on a little straw with their knapsacks under their heads. It's like Brutus to see a man die in such places but they can't help theirself for Col. Cobb won't allow them to be moved out of camp if he can help it but the most of them gets their friends to go out and get a house for them and then we steal them off to the house. We have forty-two sick in our company [Flint Hill Grays]. We are badly wearied waiting on them.[32]

---

[29]Clement A. Evans, *Georgia*, vol. 6 of *Confederate Military History* (Atlanta: Confederate Publishing Company, 1899) 37.

[30]J. L. Brent, *Memoirs of the War between the States* (New Orleans, n.p., 1940) 128.

[31]Eli P. Landers to Susan Landers, 29 August 1861, in Roberson, *Yellow River*, 22–23.

[32]Eli P. Landers to Susan Landers, 5 September 1861, in Roberson, *Yellow River*, 24–25.

Sickness and suffering among the soldiers of the 16th Georgia in camp remained widespread through the remaining weeks of summer. As was the case with the men in Private Landers's company, most of the soldiers came from isolated homes in rural areas of Northeast Georgia. They were suddenly packed into crowded camps with poor sanitation and inadequate nursing care. As early as 27 August, measles broke out, followed by mumps.[33] By 7 September, seven men had died from these diseases. From then until the epidemic subsided in October, about thirty were lost.[34] In letters to his mother and sister, Private Landers wrote about how the measles outbreak took the lives of three of his comrades.

> There has been two of the Lawrenceville County died since we come here. Their names was Cadell and Underwood. Underwood died yesterday with the measels. I have not bin sick, only with diarrhea, but I am cooking every day when I am able....[35] We have had a very serious time since yesterday morning for we have witnessed the death of one of our fellow solgers to wit Thomas Sanders. He died with a relapse of the measles. He got most well of them and exposed hisself in the rain. His relapse was very hasty to death. He died last night about 1 o'clock. It was a very solemn occasion. He was out of his senses all of the time. I was detailed to wait on him twenty-four hours. It almost wearied me down for he was trying to skip off all the time. He said he was going home but the poor fellow will return home with his eyes closed.[36]

Despite the problems with sickness and disease, spirits were high at Camp Lee that summer. Recruits were pouring into Richmond at the rate of 500 to 1,000 a day, and the South was building a great Army. The Confederates had already won a convincing victory at Manassas on 21 July under the leadership of generals Pierre G. T. Beauregard and Joseph E. Johnston, and the men of the 16th Georgia were anxious to see action in battle.

Regardless of the desire expressed by the men of Simmons's regiment to join the fighting, deployment to the battlefield would take several months.

---

[33]B. Edward Stiles to his mother, 27 August 1861, McKay-Stiles papers.

[34]Howell Cobb to Mary Ann Cobb (nee Lamar), 4 October 1861, Howell Cobb papers, box 51, folder 26, ms. 1376, Hargrett Rare Book and Manuscript Library, University of Georgia, Athens. See also James O. Bredeen, "Joseph Jones and Confederate Medical History," *Georgia Historical Quarterly* 54/3 (Fall 1970): 372.

[35]Eli P. Landers to Susan Landers, 15 September 1861, in Roberson, *Yellow River*, 30. According to his service records, Private John H. Underwood of Company I died on 14 September 1861. He was buried in Hollywood Cemetery, Richmond. No record was found of a soldier named "Cadell" in either of the Gwinnett Companies of the 16th Georgia.

[36]Eli P. Landers to Susan Landers and Hildy Carolina Landers, 6 October 1861, in Roberson, *Weep Not For Me*, 41.

Howell Cobb was a leading member of the Confederate Congress, and his regiment remained at their camp in Richmond while he served in the dual capacity as legislator and military commander. During this time, the 16th Georgia was placed under Brigadier General John Bankhead Magruder, who commanded all Confederate forces around Richmond and the Lower Peninsula, the strategic stretch of land southeast of Richmond between the York and James rivers.[37]

There was another reason that the 16th Georgia was not deployed in the early months of the war. Relatively few of the men were adequately equipped with firearms. In the first week of September, Cobb received news that the blockade runner *Bermuda* had slipped through the Union lines with a large shipment of rifles from England and Germany. He immediately sent a requisition to Savannah for enough rifles to equip his regiment. Unfortunately Georgia governor Joseph Emerson Brown denied the request and had the rifles impounded. When Cobb learned what had happened, he lost his self-control, excoriated Confederate authorities, and demanded such interference cease.[38] He then registered an official complaint protesting Governor Brown's action.[39]

After several weeks' delay, Brown relented and 1,000 British Enfield rifles[40] were shipped by rail from Savannah, finally arriving in Richmond around the middle of October. To Cobb's dismay, the rifles were so rusty that they could not be used. It took another week to have the defective weapons cleaned and repaired before the regiment could be properly equipped.

Despite the condition of the rifles upon arrival, when restored they provided the regiment with some of the best infantry weapons in the Confederate army.[41] The 1853 Enfield rifle was about fifty-five inches in length; the same as the Enfield rifle musket, which was the standard weapon of the British Army. A shorter, less-common model, the 1858 Enfield, was about forty-nine inches long and referred to as the "Sergeant's Enfield." During the war more than 400,000 Enfield rifles were smuggled past Federal blockades to help arm the Confederate army.

After rumors arose regarding the provision of weapons for the brigade, Private Samuel A. Burney of Cobb's Georgia Legion Infantry Battalion at nearby Camp Washington wrote his wife in Georgia about finally leaving camp for a combat assignment: "I think we have had about half dozen days appointed

---

[37]Douglas Southall Freeman, *Lee's Lieutenants: A Study in Command*, vol. 1 (New York: Charles Scribner's Sons, 1942) 16, 40.

[38]Richard N. Current, ed., *Encyclopedia of the Confederacy*, vol. 1 (New York: Simon & Schuster, 1993) 360.

[39]Roberson, *Weep Not For Me*, 37–38.

[40]Current, *Encyclopedia of the Confederacy*, 1:360.

[41]Briscoe G. Baldwin to Howell Cobb, 14 October 1861, Howell Cobb papers; *Southern Banner* (Athens GA), 23 October 1861.

upon which we would leave this place. I can say that we are here and no more. Cobb knows no more when we will leave than I do. I will write to you and let it be known after we have moved. This much is true—we expect to leave every day."[42]

The 16th Georgia remained in Camp Lee during the days of late summer and early fall. As they watched regiment after regiment leave for the theater of war, the tedium of camp life set in for the men left behind. One very homesick fellow, William Sisk, said that he would give his horse, which he thought to be worth eighty dollars, to be home.[43] To Lieutenant Simmons, camp life was exceedingly dull. He and his companions in the 16th Georgia were not fond of the tiresome routine. For most men in the regiment there was only one certain relief, a letter from home. Some were so bored that even an encounter with the Yankees would have been a welcome relief.[44]

In mid-October, Simmons and the men of his regiment learned that they would soon be leaving the confines of their camp in Richmond. On 17 October, in preparation for their departure, the soldiers gathered in a nearby field for a special ceremony. Colonel Joseph Davis, brother of President Jefferson Davis, presented a stand of colors and a sword to their commanding officer, Colonel Howell Cobb. Confederate secretary of state R. M. T. Turner and other high officials of the Davis administration participated in the ceremonies and a military band added to the festivities.[45] It was a fitting sendoff for the 16th Georgia Infantry Regiment.

---

[42]Samuel A. Burney to Julia Ann Burney (nee Shields), 8 October 1861, in Nat Turner, ed., *A Southern Soldier's Letters Home: The Civil War Letters of Samuel Burney, ANV* (Macon: Mercer University Press, 2002) 246. See also *Soldier Life: Voices of the Civil War* (Alexandria, VA: Time Life Books) 158.

[43]B. Edward Stiles to his mother, 27 August 1861, McKay-Stiles papers. The soldier mentioned in Stiles's letter was William S. Sisk of Company E, Cobb Infantry, 16th Georgia, from Habersham County. Sisk enlisted as a private at the age of 26 on 24 July 1861 and later in the war was promoted to captain. He was captured leading his company at Front Royal, VA, on 16 August 1864. Sisk was sent to Fort Delaware Prison and was released in June 1865 to return to his family in Homer (Banks County), GA.

[44]Byrd, *Them Brave Georgians*, 29; see also Carlton McCarthy, "Detailed Minutiae of Soldier Life in the Army of Northern Virginia," *SHSP* 2/3 (September 1876): 129.

[45]*Southern Banner* (Athens GA), 23 October 1861; Coulter, *Lost Generation*, 60–61.

4

Straddling the Peninsula

Be ever soft and pliable like a reed, not hard and unbending
like a cedar.
                                                    —The Talmud

On the morning of 19 October, the 16th Georgia finally left camp under orders
to report to General Magruder at Yorktown, Virginia.[1] After breaking camp,
Lieutenant Simmons and his comrades traveled on the Richmond & York
Railroad to West Point and then embarked on the *CSS Logan* for Yorktown.
The trip down the York River was a welcome relief to the men who had been
confined so long at camp in Richmond. Bands played and several of the men
amused themselves by shooting birds from the main deck. Relaxation was the
"order of the day."[2]
     The 16th Georgia soon arrived at Yorktown and marched three miles
down the Newport News Road to take up positions near Crafton Church.[3]
Their new home was named Camp Bryan in honor of Lieutenant Colonel
Goode Bryan, who was acting commander of the regiment while Howell Cobb
was home on leave. The regiment remained at that location from 22 October
until 12 December.[4] Later, winter quarters were constructed at a better site
along the Yorktown-Williamsburg Road.[5] The men named their new home
Camp Lamar in honor of John B. Lamar, the brother of Howell Cobb's wife.
Construction of the new site was supervised by Goode Bryan, who remained in
charge of the regiment while Howell Cobb presided over the Confederate

---

[1] *The War of the Rebellion: A Compilation of the Official Records of the Union and
Confederate Armies* (70 vols. in 128; Washington, DC, 1880–1901), ser. I, vol. 51, pt. 2,
288 (hereafter cited as *OR*). The original orders were dated 11 September 1861.
    [2] *Southern Banner* (Athens GA), 6 November 1861.
    [3] B. Edward Stiles to his mother, 22 October 1861, McKay-Stiles papers, Southern
Historical Collection, University of North Carolina, Chapel Hill.
    [4] *Southern Banner* (Athens GA), 6 November 1861. See also William S. Smedlund,
Camp Fires of Georgia's Troops, 1861–1865 (Kennesaw, GA: Kennesaw Mountain Press,
1994) 77–79.
    [5] Smedlund, *Camp Fires*, 181; Horace Montgomery, "Howell Cobb's Confederate
Career," in *Confederate Centennial Studies* no. 10, ed. William S. Hoole (Montgomery,
AL: Confederate Publishing Company, 1959) 31.

Congress in Richmond.[6] The regimental camp was located at the site where General Washington's army had camped before the British army under Cornwallis surrendered in the Revolutionary War. At Camp Lamar, housing for the soldiers consisted of log cabins, some as large as sixteen feet by eighteen feet, with rough planks along the walls for beds. There was also a hospital presided over by Dr. James Mercer Green.[7]

William Simmons and most of the men in the 16th Georgia appreciated the comforts and diversions of Camp Lamar that first winter, especially as they reflected on their experiences in later years. Joseph White Woods, a private in Company D (Danielsville Guards) of the 16th Georgia, fondly remembered his days in camp during winter 1861–1862:

> We built winter quarters, good comfortable cabins with stick and dirt chimneys. There we remained until spring, drilling and doing guard duty. We had a good time there, comfortable and warm quarters, plenty to eat and time to write letters, time to enjoy ourselves in various ways with no fighting.[8]

Another private from the 16th Georgia also had favorable words about the conditions at Camp Lamar. In January 1862, after returning from two months of sick leave, he wrote to his family in Georgia about the regiment's accommodations: "All the boys is well and hearty and are as fat as pigs. They have eat so much beef 'til they favor a cow. They threwed away enough beef the other day to make a good milk cow! Today we drawed flour and pork and molasses. We will live well 'til it is gone. I tell you the truth, we are well fixed."[9]

The regiment remained at Camp Lamar throughout the winter while preparing for the inevitable assignment to the battlefront in the spring. Colonel Cobb noted that the regiment was subjected to nightly alarms of impending Yankee attacks. There were frequent marches to defensive positions and long waits in inclement weather for an enemy that never appeared. The men may

---

[6]Howell Cobb to Mary Ann Cobb (nee Lamar), 9 December 1861, Howell Cobb papers, box 51, folder 26, ms. 1376, Hargrett Rare Book and Manuscript Library, University of Georgia, Athens.

[7]Dr. James Mercer Green to John B. Lamar, 16 December 1861, Howell Cobb papers.

[8]"History of Service of Joseph White Woods, Soldier in the War between the States: Written by Himself after the War," in *Bible Records, Military Rosters and Reminiscences of Confederate Soldiers*, vol. 9 of *United Daughters of the Confederacy Bound Transcripts*, pp. 134–51, Georgia Department of Archives and History, Morrow, GA. Woods was one of a handful of men from the 16th Georgia who surrendered at Appomattox on 9 April 1965.

[9]Eli P. Landers to Susan Landers, 27 January 1862 in Elizabeth Whitley Roberson, *In Care of Yellow River* (Fort Lauderdale: Venture Press, 1994) 61–62.

have resented the discomforts of the alarms, but they provided a spark to life in the camp and served as a reminder that they were soldiers on active duty.[10]

In February 1862 the pace of camp life quickened. On the thirteenth of the month, Howell Cobb was promoted to brigadier general and assigned to command the 2nd Brigade of General Magruder's forces, which included the 16th Georgia. Goode Bryan succeeded Cobb to fill the vacancy as regimental commander. In addition to his former regiment, Cobb's Brigade included the 24th Georgia, the 2nd Louisiana, the 15th North Carolina, and Cobb's Legion Infantry Battalion, which was established and commanded by Cobb's younger brother, Colonel Thomas R. R. Cobb. The brigade also included Page's Virginia Artillery Battery. From Cobb's Brigade, the military chain of command extended up through Major General Lafayette McLaws's 2nd Division and Magruder's Army of the Peninsula.

With the promotions of Howell Cobb and Goode Bryan, Henry P. Thomas was elevated to second in command of the regiment with the rank of lieutenant colonel. In turn, Thomas's vacancy was filled by Captain James S. Gholston of the Madison County Greys, Company A of the 16th Georgia.[11]

Early in March, Cobb's Brigade was transferred from Magruder's command for a brief period of time to reinforce troops under Major General William Wing Loring, who was busily engaged at Suffolk, Virginia, in checking Federal attempts to separate Richmond from the Deep South. This campaign had begun on New Year's Day 1862 when Union forces commanded by General Ambrose E. Burnside slipped out of Hampton Roads, Virginia, by boat and occupied several towns along the North Carolina coast. Burnside's primary objective was to sever two important railroads extending from Suffolk to Petersburg, Virginia, and Weldon, North Carolina.

Leaving their comfortable quarters at Camp Bryan, the 16th Georgia and the rest of the Howell Cobb's 2nd Brigade joined up with forces from Randolph's Brigade and headed south for Suffolk, Virginia, arriving by train on 7 March. After two weeks in Suffolk, the two brigades were ordered to Goldsboro, North Carolina, about 120 miles to the southwest. Here they served briefly as part of a defense force of about 20,000 men under Major General Theophilus H. Holmes. This move was implemented to protect the two railroads and contain the Union forces that had recently captured the town of New Bern, North Carolina.

After arriving on 22 March, Cobb's Brigade marched about three miles outside Goldsboro to a pine grove and made camp. Their new home was named in honor of George W. Randolph, the newly appointed Confederate secretary of

---

[10]Cobb to his daughter Mary Ann, 13 January 1862, Howell Cobb papers.
[11]Clement A. Evans, *Georgia*, vol. 6 of *Confederate Military History* (Atlanta: Confederate Publishing Company, 1899) 39.

war.[12] The days at Camp Randolph were difficult ones for Lieutenant Simmons and his comrades in the brigade. In their move from the Peninsula, they had outdistanced their wagon trains, supplies, and equipment.[13] To add to the misery, the location of Camp Randolph proved to be unhealthy and inadequate. Soon, there was an outbreak of pneumonia among the soldiers. The 16th and 24th Georgia regiments were particularly hard hit, with men dying every day.[14]

While in Goldsboro, the four regiments and one infantry battalion of Cobb's Brigade participated in a review in honor of General Holmes. The review was held on 12 April and Holmes was favorably impressed with the 16th Georgia, pronouncing it the "best in the brigade." The general was not so complimentary of the performance of the 24th Georgia, composed largely of companies from the highlands of North Georgia, and he did not spare its commanding officer, Colonel McMillan, in his comments.[15]

Later in April, after successfully driving off the Federals from Goldsboro, Cobb's Brigade was ordered back to the Peninsula. The men were soon pressed into service to head off a large force of Federal troops, commanded by Major General George B. McClellan, that had landed at Fort Monroe on Hampton Roads and initiated an advance toward Yorktown, Virginia, about twenty miles away. It was at this time that Cobb's Brigade was transferred from the Army of the Peninsula to the Army of Northern Virginia.

After a hard three-day march, Cobb's men took up positions near the Warwick River, a body of water that begins about a mile and a half south of Yorktown and flows southwest across the Peninsula into the James. Along the river, the Confederates constructed a series of dams to back up the water and

---

[12]T. R. R. Cobb to Marion Cobb (nee Lumpkin), 24 March 1862, Thomas Reade Roots (T. R. R.) Cobb papers, box 1, file 12, ms. 448, Hargrett Rare Book and Manuscript Library, University of Georgia, Athens; *Southern Banner*, 9 April 1862.

[13]Howell Cobb to Mary Ann Cobb (nee Lamar), 29 March 1862; John H. Cobb to his mother, 1 April 1862, Howell Cobb papers.

[14]According to regimental service records, there were at least twenty-four deaths recorded from sickness or disease in the 16th Georgia between 18 March and 21 April 1862, most from pneumonia. The death toll was likely higher as some of the records do not contain a specific date or location of death. Included were four men from Gwinnett County: Private Asa H. Pitman of Company I; and privates J. W. White, W. H. Dickerson and Moses L. Herrington of Company H. In a letter dated 25 March 1862 and completed two days later, Private Eli P. Landers, of the 16th Georgia Flint Hill Grays, wrote to his mother that there were about 150 men in the regiment who were left behind in Suffolk. He expressed great sorrow at the death of his friend Private William H. Dickerson of Company H: "This is what I hate to tell. We had to witness the death of one of our worthiest solgers last night to wit, William Dickison. He died at four o'clock. We all mourn the loss of him very much...he died in Triumph of Honor" (Roberson, *Yellow River*, 70–72).

[15]B. Edward Stiles to his mother, 4 April 1862, McKay-Stiles papers.

make the Warwick impassable for attacking infantry or artillery. Confederate forces guarded each of the dams. Cobb's Brigade was assigned to Dam Number 1, near Lee's Mill, which was considered to be the most vulnerable place in the line of defense. On arrival, the brigade was put to work clearing trees from their front and constructing entrenchments. It was here on 16 April that Simmons and his regiment participated in their first "real" battle. The attacking Union forces were under the command of Brigadier General William F. "Baldy" Smith, who was dispatched by General McClellan to stop the Confederates from strengthening their defenses at Dam Number 1.[16]

For most of the day, Federal artillery pounded the Confederate earthworks across the Warwick River. The men of Cobb's Brigade prudently took shelter away from the barrage and were mostly hidden from view and suffered few casualties. Later in the afternoon, General Smith sent the Vermont Brigade forward to the banks of the Warwick. Four companies from his old regiment, the 3rd Vermont, forded the river and quickly drove the Confederates from their rifle pits along the opposite shore. Once the 3rd Vermont was dug in, three companies of the 4th Vermont were sent on a charge over the dam while additional troops from the 6th Vermont crossed the river at the ford. At this time it appeared that the Confederate line had been broken, but confusion reigned in the Union ranks and no decisive action was taken to widen the breach. After clinging to their foothold for about forty minutes, the Vermonters were counterattacked by Confederate forces under Howell Cobb, including Lieutenant Simmons's 16th Georgia. Of the 192 Union soldiers engaged in the reconnaissance, eighty-three were killed, wounded, or captured. By the end of the day, there were 165 Union casualties. The carnage inflicted on the Vermonters continued throughout the next three years as the brigade earned the dubious distinction of losing more men than any other brigade on either side during the war.[17] Simmons's report of the action was very brief, simply stating that his regiment was "...attacked by [Union General] Smith's Corps." He

---

[16]Stephen W. Sears, *To the Gates of Richmond: The Peninsula Campaign* (Wilmington, MA: Mariner Books, 1992) 55. See also Ronald H. Bailey, *Forward to Richmond: McClellan's Peninsular Campaign* (Alexandria, VA: Time Life Books, 1983) 102.

[17]"The Vermont Brigade had the dubious honor of losing more men than any other brigade in the Civil War," *America's Civil War* 6/6 (January 1994): 77–84. Of the nearly 10,600 men who served in the brigade during the War Between the States, more than 50 percent—some 5,440—became casualties. Of that number, more than 2,500 men lost their lives, nearly 24 percent of all who fought in that brigade. The battle at Lee's Mill was the Vermonters' first major encounter. They also fought valiantly at Savage Station, Banks's Ford, Funkstown, the Wilderness, Spotsylvania, Cold Harbor, Opequon, Cedar Creek, and Petersburg.

added that "The attack was repulsed." There were relatively few Confederate losses on that day.[18]

The 16th Georgia was in the thick of the fighting on 16 April. At 3:00 P.M. the regiment was in a position about a half a mile behind the Confederate breastworks north of the Warwick River when the firing commenced. Private Eli P. Landers of the Flint Hill Grays provided a more detailed description in a letter to his mother:

> We all went in double quick to the rescue of our brothers and when we got there the enemy was nearly to our breastworks, in fact they had part of them in possession and we run in an[d] opened fire on them. We did not have time to organize our regiment. We just run in and shot when we had the chance and never formed no line. If a man could get behind a tree it was alright. Some of the boys never fired a gun. Some lay behind logs as close to the ground as young rabbits till the battle was over…. The fight lasted until about dark when the enemy retreated. Old Mr. Gassaway was killed dead and one of Captain [John Hampton] Skelton's men was killed.[19] I was standing in three feet of him [Gassaway] when he was shot.[20]

After the battle had ended, Cobb's Brigade moved its camp closer to Dam Number 2 and named it in honor of Miss Sally Twiggs. The young lady was betrothed to Colonel Bryan, who was a widower. For a while the 16th Georgia was known as the "Sally Twiggs" regiment.[21] The camp became the brigade's muddy home until the first week of May when the Confederate forces began to withdraw from the fortifications along the river.

On the evening of 3 May, a furious cannonade was begun by the Confederates as a signal to begin the retreat.[22] The following day, the 16th Georgia left their camp on the Warwick River, and slogged toward Richmond through a sea of churned mud. Before noon, the men had passed through Williamsburg, stopping about two miles to the west, past a place where Longstreet's men had rested. After a brief pause, they resumed the march in the

---

[18]Daniel M. Byrd, Simmons biographical sketch, drawer 19, box 80, Georgia Department of Archives and History, Morrow, GA; *Them Brave Georgians*, 44.

[19]According to service records, "Old Mr. Gassaway" who was killed alongside Landers was Private S. F. Gassaway of Company H. There were two soldiers killed from Captain John Hampton Skelton's Company C (Hartwell Infantry) of the 16th Georgia, 1st Sergeant Angus N. Masters and Private Willis Newton Barron.

[20]Eli P. Landers to Susan Landers, 23 April 1862, in Roberson, *Yellow River*, 73. Landers wrote that "the 7th, 8th, 11th, and 16th Georgia Infantry Regiments were engaged in the fight along with the 5th North Carolina and a Louisiana Regiment [the 2nd Louisiana]." Cobb's Legion Infantry Battalion also took part in the battle.

[21]Colonel Goode Bryan's report of the Battle of Dam Number 1 (or Lee's Mill) is headed "Bivouac Sally Twiggs" (*OR*, ser. I, vol. 11, pt. 1, 419).

[22]*OR*, ser. I, vol. 11, pt. 1, 602.

early evening.[23] On 7 May, Magruder's Division stopped to form a line of defense at the Paumunkey River. The 16th Georgia took up positions to defend the York River Railroad on the extreme left of the Army.[24] They camped for five days near the Baltimore Crossroads[25] before resuming their withdrawal. After an agonizingly slow journey that took two weeks, they arrived at their camp on 17 May near the Fairfield Racetrack just outside Richmond.

The grueling march was described by a young officer in Cobb's Legion Infantry Battalion of Cobb's Brigade:

> We left Dam no. 2 on Saturday night…just a little after dark. It took us until broad day to get to Williamsburg, 12 or 14 miles. The roads were very muddy and much cut up. A mud hole or a narrow passage will delay the rear of a large army from one-half to one and two hours. The men became overcome with fatigue and want of sleep and were to be seen on each side of the road at every ten or twenty steps, lying wrapped in their blankets. [On one occasion] we got entirely out of provisions. I went out with my men and, after visiting several poor families, could get nothing but six eggs for which I paid 35 cents. Others went out four or five miles, pressed in meal but no bread could be found.[26]

Not long after the exhausted men of the 16th Georgia returned to the relative safety and comfort of the Racetrack Camp, Lieutenant Simmons became ill. He was granted a thirty-day sick furlough, and on 29 May he departed for Lawrenceville.[27] While resting at home Simmons enjoyed the company of his beloved family, including his four-year-old brother, James; his older sister, Sarah Elizabeth (b. 1837); and three younger sisters, Anna Eliza (b. 1844), Eillene (b. 1851), and Ida (b. 1853). He made a swift recovery before returning to his regiment on 27 June.[28]

While Simmons was on leave, his comrades were very busy. On 31 May and 1 June, the battle of Seven Pines, called Fair Oaks by the North, claimed over 6,000 casualties and resulted in the wounding of Confederate General

---

[23]Ibid., 275–76.

[24]William Allan, *The Army of Northern Virginia in 1862* (Cambridge: Houghton Mifflin and Company, 1892) 27; Joseph L. Brent, *Memoirs of the War between the States* (reprint; New Orleans: n.p., 1940) 120.

[25]General Joseph E. Johnston had his headquarters in a fire house here, probably the home of Robert Stubbs (Brent, *Memoirs*, 120); Douglas Southall Freeman, *Lee's Lieutenants: A Study in Command*, vol. 1 (New York: Charles Scribner's Sons, 1942) 232.

[26]Joel C. Barnett to his wife, 13 May 1862, in Mills Lane, ed., *"Dear Mother: Don't Grieve About Me. If I get Killed, I'll Only be Dead": Letters from Georgia Soldiers in the Civil War* (Savannah, GA: Beehive Press) 119. Barnett led Company G, called the Panola Guards, from Morgan County, GA.

[27]Simmons service records, in Byrd, *Them Brave Georgians*, 54.

[28]Ibid.

Joseph E. Johnston on the first day of battle. The commander was taken off the battlefield with a musket ball in his right shoulder and his chest torn by a heavy shell fragment.[29] Neither the 16th Georgia nor any of Magruder's command were directly engaged. Since 1 June, General Robert E. Lee had been in command of the Confederate forces.

---

[29]Drury L. Armistad, "The Battle in Which General Johnston Was Wounded," *Southern Historical Society Papers* 18 (1890): 186–87. See also "General Johnston's Report of the Battle of Seven Pines," *SHSP* 18 (1890): 182–85.

5

The Seven Days Battles

Perseverance is not a long race; it is many short races one after
another.

—Walter Elliott

While Lieutenant Simmons was on sick leave, the massive Army of the Potomac
advanced to the outskirts of Richmond and was threatening the capital of the
Confederacy. The soldiers of 16th Georgia Infantry Regiment witnessed, but
did not engage in, combat during the first three days of the Seven Days Battles,
which began on 25 June at Oak Grove. Fighting continued on the following day
at Mechanicsville and on 27 June at Gaines Mill. During this time, the 16th
Georgia had been kept under arms day and night in reserve to advance at a
moment's notice to the field of battle.[1]

On 29 June, two days after William Simmons returned to duty from his
furlough, the 16th Georgia, expecting to find the enemy still occupying the
strong line of fortification immediately in front of their position, moved from its
trenches at the Burnt Chimney on the Nine Mile Road.[2] Slowly their pickets
moved out and forced some small Union detachments to retreat behind their
fortifications. Charging faster, the pickets mounted the fortifications only to
find them deserted. Along with its companion regiments, the 16th Georgia set
off in hot pursuit along the Richmond & York River Railroad towards Savage's
Station to the east.

Upon arriving at Fair Oaks they again discovered that the Union lines had
been evacuated.[3] The regiment continued its advance on the north side of the
railroad tracks to Savage's Station where they joined Kershaw's Brigade of South
Carolinians and Griffith's Mississippi Brigade to engage the Union forces. A
few well-directed shots from accompanying artillery effectively silenced the
enemy's fire.[4] Cobb's Brigade advanced another 400 yards and occupied a
position on the outskirts of some woods with an open field to their front. Here
they slept briefly with rifles ready. Although they had been under fire all day,
most of the fighting took place south of the railroad tracks. The Battle of

---

[1]*The War of the Rebellion: A Compilation of the Official Records of the Union and
Confederate Armies* (70 vols. in 128; Washington, 1880–1901), ser. I, vol. 11, pt. 2, 748;
hereafter cited as OR.

[2]Ibid., 668

[3]Ibid., 748

[4]Ibid., 749

Savage's Station was memorable to the men of the 16th Georgia because they witnessed the first firing of a cannon mounted on a steam-driven flatcar.[5]

Early on the morning of 30 June, Magruder's entire command, including the 16th Georgia, received orders to march back toward Richmond on the Williamsburg Stage Road and then proceed to Timberlake's Store on the Darbytown Road.[6] After arriving in the early afternoon, the column rested for two hours before resuming their march. Later in the day they were directed to relieve General James Longstreet's forces at positions north of Malvern Hill, a large plateau about 150 feet above the James River. Their arrival was delayed for several hours because they were ordered to take a needless detour on a country lane that passed through intervening farms until it reached New Market Road.[7] About 11:00 P.M. the brigade finally occupied the trenches vacated by the troops under Longstreet.[8] The men were worn out after a long day of marching without rest or food, and the detour and delay had caused them to miss the Battle of Frayser's Farm. That night, Simmons and his comrades experienced the shallow sleep caused by hunger and fatigue.

After waking at dawn, Magruder's command continued marching throughout the day. Once again the men were led astray, due primarily to the lack of good maps. Precious time was spent marching away from the battlefield, which cost more than three hours and upset General Lee's plan for deployment.[9] Magruder finally arrived at 4:00 P.M. in close proximity to the Federal forces at Malvern Hill.[10] At that location, a furious battle had been raging since 11:30 that morning.[11] As they approached the conflict, the men were afforded a full view of the entire battle scene. In the distance, on a ridge behind a farmhouse, were 100 Yankee artillery batteries and an estimated 25,000 to 30,000 soldiers in blue.[12]

Upon their arrival, Lieutenant Simmons and the men of the 16th Georgia learned that Confederate forces under Brigadier Generals Lewis Armistead and Ambrose R. Wright had been under heavy enemy fire since 1:00 P.M. and had taken shelter in a heavily wooded ravine.[13] Cobb's Brigade continued their advance to the summit of a hill where withering Yankee fire forced them to fall

[5]Ibid., 664; Brent, *Memoirs*, 188.
[6]Ibid., 666; Brent, *Memoirs*, 191–93.
[7]*OR*, ser. I, vol. 11, pt. 2, 666.
[8]Ibid., 667.
[9]Stephen W. Sears, *To the Gates of Richmond: The Peninsula Campaign* (Wilmington, MA: First Mariner Books, 1992) 314–15.
[10]*OR*, ser. I, vol. 11, pt. 2, 814.
[11]Ibid., 813.
[12]Ibid., 812.
[13]Ibid., 818.

back to the ravine. They remained there while Union artillery continued to fire from their commanding position.[14]

At 5:30 P.M. Armistead ordered a Confederate charge and rushed forward with two of his regiments and one battalion.[15] Howell Cobb followed immediately with three of his regiments while the 16th Georgia remained in reserve, sheltered in the relative safety of the ravine. Cobb skillfully placed his men in front of Armistead's three remaining regiments, which had never been under fire in a major battle.[16] Soon the 16th Georgia joined the advance on the Union positions along with additional reinforcements from Anderson's and Semmes's Brigades. Throughout the late afternoon and evening, the advancing Confederate troops fired volley after volley with deadly precision into the Federal ranks but never broke through the battle line.

The assault at Malvern Hill was witnessed by General Daniel Harvey Hill, who later wrote that [he] "never saw anything more grandly heroic than the advance after sunset of the nine brigades under Magruder's orders." Hill added, "Unfortunately they did not move together, and were beaten in detail. Not only did the brigades that were engaged suffer, but also the inactive troops and those brought up as reserves too late to be of any use. The Confederate forces sustained many casualties from the fearful artillery fire which reached all parts of the woods."[17]

This horrible conflagration was described by noted historian, Stephen W. Sears:

> General Lee was at the very center of the battlefield, trying to sort out and salvage a fight that had burst out of his control. He was with Lafayette McLaws's Division...when a call for help from Magruder reached him. He advanced McLaws personally and sent word to Magruder to redirect his assault more toward the right, against the enemy's flank....
>
> Magruder's own division, [made up of] the brigades of Howell Cobb and William Barksdale, was the first to arrive and the first to go in. Barksdale's Mississippians charged into what their commander called a "terrible fire" of every type of artillery missile imaginable, and they lost one-third of their numbers. Cobb's Brigade...passed through the wreckage of Armistead's Virginians and met the same terrible fire....
>
> Virtually every Confederate who stormed Malvern Hill and left a record of his experience spoke in awe of the Federal guns. ...D. H. Hill,

---

[14]Ibid., 823.

[15]Ibid.

[16]Ibid., 670, 673.

[17]Daniel Harvey Hill, Lieutenant General, CSA, "McClelland's Change of Base and Malvern Hill" in *North to Antietam*, vol. 2 of *Battles and Leaders of the Civil War* (1887; reprint, New York: Thomas Yoseloff, 1956) 394.

looking back on Malvern Hill after four years of war, believed more than half the Confederate casualties that day were a result of artillery fire, a circumstance that he called "unprecedented."[18]

Called up from their relatively secure position in the ravine, Lieutenant Simmons and the 16th Georgia joined in the final assault of the day against the well-defended Federal positions. Sears continues, "A final desperate charge was made by Lafayette McLaws's two thinned brigades, along with remnants of brigades from earlier attacks. For its full length the crest of Malvern Hill was wreathed in battle smoke, with only angry red flashes to mark the positions of the guns and waving flags to mark the battle lines"[19]

Private Eli P. Landers of the Flint Hill Grays was among the men of the 16th Georgia who made that final desperate charge. He described his experiences in vivid terms in a letter to his mother in Gwinnett County, Georgia. Although he did not mention the name of the battle, his description and the date of his correspondence leave no doubt as to his eyewitness account of the Battle of Malvern Hill.

> In the evening we came up with the Yankees in line of battle in a noble position with a heavy battery in good range of us. We made an immediate attack and with large forces on both sides. But they having all the advantages of high ground and our men not expecting them so close by, our men was not properly organized for the engagement but we had run on them and we was obliged to fight or retreat. The first command given was to fix bayonets and charge the battery which the gallant men in great heroism did but we had to charge through an open field for about a half mile under the open and well directed fire of a heavy battery well supported with infantry. The grapeshot and bombs cut our lines down so rapidly our officers found it could not be taken. We was ordered back to reform and tried it again but did not succeed and retired the second time. It is amazing strange how any of us got through to tell the fate of the others for all this time we were under the fire of their cannons with the grapeshot and bombshells flying round us as thick as a hailstorm.[20]

The battle raged until nearly 9:00 P.M. at which time the exhausted soldiers collapsed. Soon the enemy was seen with lanterns busily engaged in gathering the wounded and burying the dead. That night, a nervous McClellan

---

[18]Sears, *To the Gates*, 332–33.

[19]Sears, *To the Gates*, 334.

[20]Eli P. Landers to Susan Landers, 6 July 1862, in Elizabeth Whitley Roberson, *In Care of Yellow River* (Fort Lauderdale: Venture Press, 1994) 86. Private Landers indicated that the letter was written at the "Crews farm near Richmond, Virginia." The camp was at the site where the deadly Union artillery batteries were positioned in the Battle of Malvern Hill. Numerous references are made to "Crew Hill" as the epicenter of the battle.

pulled back his army to Harrison's Landing where it remained for six weeks before withdrawing from the Peninsula. The Seven Days Battles had cost the Federals nearly 16,000 men and ended a chance for a quick capture of the Confederate capital. Southern losses were even greater, with more than 20,000 casualties.

Cobb's Brigade suffered severe losses at Malvern Hill. On Saturday, 29 June, when they left for battle, there had been 2,700 men. Fatigue and exhaustion gradually reduced the ranks to 1,500, and the fighting had taken another 415 casualties. The toll on the 16th Georgia was sixty-three men killed, wounded, or missing.[21] Of the men who served in the two Gwinnett companies of the 16th Georgia, only two soldiers from the Flint Hill Grays were injured. Private David Wayne Haney was wounded in the knee, and 1st Sergeant Thomas L. D. Medlock suffered an eye injury from a bomb blast. No fatalities were recorded.[22]

The 16th Georgia had been tried and tested in the vortex of the battle. For forty-eight hours prior to the engagement at Malvern Hill, they had neither rest nor food. Cobb praised the men of his command, in particular the 16th Georgia, who was "found foremost in the fight."[23] After the guns were silenced, Lieutenant William E. Simmons counted his blessings. He and his company mates had come through some of the fiercest fighting of the War unscathed.

---

[21] *OR*, ser. I, vol. 11, pt. 2, 979.

[22] Letter from Eli P. Landers to Susan Landers, 6 July 1862, in Roberson, *Yellow River*, 85, 86. Landers wrote that "There was several of our regiment killed and a good many wounded but none of our company was killed." His company was short-handed for the battle. According to Landers, "not more than 20 went in to it. [Of those who did not participate], Some was sick, some tired down and left behind, some lost, and I expect some just slipped out. We did not have narry a Commissioned Officer with us." According to 16th Georgia service records, there were at least seven men killed in action and one fatally wounded: Private Robert J. Boyd and Private James T. Wood of Company B, Private A. Y. Evans and Private J. Earl Gaines of Company C, Private Bailey Smith of Company E, Private William Palmer of Company F, and Private Joseph S. Bell of Company G. 1st Corporal John Daniel Johnson of Company F died of wounds on 15 July 1862.

[23] *OR*, ser. I, vol. 11, pt. 2, 749.

6

A Narrow Escape

Keep your fears to yourself, but share your courage with others.
—Robert Louis Stevenson

After remaining for about one week in the vicinity of Malvern Hill, McLaws's Division was directed to relocate to positions closer to Richmond. On 9 July they began an "easy march" to new positions prescribed by General Lee for all commands.[1] Their new home proved to be an ill-chosen site for camp. The soldiers were cramped for space and lacked a good supply of clean water and fresh air. Many of the men became ill and suffered greatly. On 27 July, after recognizing the hazards, General Lee informed McLaws that he could select a new position "best conducive to health" of the command.[2]

The new camp was appreciated by the men of the 16th Georgia, in particular, Private Eli P. Landers. In a letter to his mother in early August, he referred to the location as "Camp Lee."

> We are still at the same place, one of the beautifulest camps and a plenty of the best kind of water, but I am afraid that we will not stay here long for they have commenced their fighting again with the Yankee fleet on the James River. We have all enjoyed ourselfs finely since we have bin permitted to rest. We all appreciate this kind of living as hi as we used to at our own homes.[3]

During the respite following the Seven Days Battles, there were several changes to the organization of brigades in the Army of Northern Virginia. For some time President Jefferson Davis had advocated that troops from the same state be brigaded together, particularly his fellow Mississippians. On 26 July General McLaws was ordered to form a new brigade of five Louisiana regiments, including the 2nd Louisiana and Coppen's Zouave Chasseurs. These

---

[1] *The War of the Rebellion: A Compilation of the Official Records of the Union and Confederate Armies* (70 vols. in 128; Washington, 1880–1901), ser. I, vol. 11, pt. 3, 636, 637. Hereafter cited as OR.

[2] Ibid., 656. According to service records, there were at least ten soldiers in the 16th Georgia who of typhoid fever or "disease" between mid-July and early August 1862, most likely due to the poor conditions at their camp near Richmond. Among the victims were privates John Ethridge and E. Daniel of Lieutenant Simmons's Company I.

[3] Eli P. Landers to Susan Landers, 4 August 1862, in Elizabeth Whitley Roberson, *In Care of Yellow River* (Fort Lauderdale: Venture Press, 1994) 93–94.

regiments later made up Starke's Brigade of Jackson's Division.[4] As a part of the reorganization, Cobb's Brigade would soon become an all-Georgia unit and placed in General Lafayette McLaws's Division under Longstreet's Command. They were joined by the men with whom they had previously served under Magruder.[5] Cobb's Brigade was now made up of the 16th Georgia, the 24th Georgia, Cobb's Georgia Legion Infantry Battalion and the 15th North Carolina.

The soldiers in the 16th Georgia did not remain in their new camp very long. On 5 August Confederate cavalry reported that the enemy was returning to Malvern Hill in a "considerable force."[6] Lieutenant Simmons and his comrades must have dredged up dreadful memories of the earlier assault on Malvern Hill as they advanced once more with their regiment.[7] On 7 August they approached the heights, but only encountered a small number of Union cavalry pickets. This time the Union rain of artillery fire from the hill was missing. The enemy force was soon driven back and a small number of Yankees were killed or captured.[8] Cobb's and Evans' brigades advanced and cleared the field of battle by nightfall. Confederate casualties were light.[9] After gathering equipment and arms from the battlefield, the brigades withdrew to camp for the night.[10] The next day, the enemy left the area, and by 17 August there were no Union forces on either side of the James River. The stage was set for the Army of Northern Virginia to take the initiative as Lieutenant Simmons and the 16th Georgia joined the march northward in late August.

During the first week of September, Cobb's Brigade forded the Potomac near Leesburg and marched into Maryland. Crossing the Potomac brought great joy, particularly to the Maryland troops. Bands played "Maryland, My Maryland," and rebel cheers filled the air. The festive mood helped the soldiers forget about their wretched uniforms, battered shoes, and a steady diet of green corn.[11]

---

[4]*OR*, ser. I, vol. 11, pt. 3, 656.

[5]Ibid., 671.

[6]*OR*, ser. I, vol. 11, pt. 2, 956.

[7]Daniel M. Byrd Jr., *Them Brave Georgians*, manuscript, Gwinnett Historical Society archives, Lawrenceville, GA, p. 75 (Fort Delaware Society Library, Delaware City, DE, also has a copy.).

[8]*OR*, ser. I, vol. 11, pt. 2, 962–63.

[9]According to service records, Private Berry Broadhill of Simmons's Company I was killed in action soon after the return to Malvern Hill.

[10]*OR*, ser. I, vol. 11, pt. 2, 956, 963.

[11]William Miller Owen, *In Camp and Battle with the Washington Artillery of New Orleans* (1885; reprint, Baton Rouge: Louisiana State University Press, 1999) 130; Ezra Carman, *South Mountain*, vol. 1 of *The Maryland Campaign of September 1862*, ed. Thomas G. Clemens (New York: Savas Beatie, 2010) 90–91. Clemens cites several

After spending four days at an encampment near Frederick, Maryland, General Lee ordered McLaws's command to resume its march to Middletown and join with General Richard H. Anderson's division.[12] A brief halt in Middletown produced an unexpected diversion. Several of the local ladies of easy virtue could not resist the opportunity to solicit customers from the invading army. From their porches, they let the men know by familiar gestures that they were interested in conversing with them. Several men broke ranks to discover that for the sum of $2.50 they could have their pick of the ladies for an entire night.[13] The soldiers refused the invitations and resumed their march to positions at Brownsville near the base of South Mountain.[14] There they camped on the night of 11–12 September.[15]

The next morning General McLaws made assignments to the brigades under his command and the men resumed marching.[16] Cobb's Brigade was directed to cross Pleasant Valley, march along the base of Elk Ridge (to the west of South Mountain) and maintain contact with General Joseph Kershaw's forces moving south along the top of the ridge. If Kershaw met with any disaster, Cobb's men were to come to his aid.[17]

Cobb's Brigade marched to Sandy Hook on 13 September where they spent the night. Sandy Hook was a key point on the route along the Potomac from Harper's Ferry east to Frederick. About noon the following day, Cobb received orders from General McLaws to return his brigade to Brownsville and then proceed to Crampton's Gap to relieve the troops under Brigadier General Paul J. Semmes."[18]

During the march Cobb encountered General James Ewell Brown ("Jeb") Stuart, the cavalry commander of the army, and some of Stuart's staff returning from a reconnaissance of the passes in South Mountain. The two generals held a brief conference where Stuart assured Cobb that the Union forces at the base of

---

sources that documented the singing of "Maryland, My Maryland" by the Southern army as they crossed the Potomac.

[12]*OR*, ser. I, vol. 19, pt. 2, 603.

[13]N. Coker to his wife, 5 October 1862, Florence Hodgson Heidler Collection of Letters, Hargrett Rare Book and Manuscript Library, University of Georgia, Athens.

[14]Horace Montgomery, "Howell Cobb's Confederate Career," in *Confederate Centennial Studies* no. 10, ed. William S. Hoole (Montgomery, AL: Confederate Publishing Company, 1959) 70; D. Augustus Dickert, *History of Kershaw's Brigade* (1899; reprint, Wilmington, NC: Broadfoot Publishing Company, 1990) 147; Douglas Southall Freeman, *Lee's Lieutenants: A Study in Command*, vol. 2 (New York: Charles Scribner's Sons, 1943) 186.

[15]*OR*, ser. I, vol. 19, pt. 1, 870; Dickert, *Kershaw's Brigade*, 147.

[16]*OR*, ser. I, vol. 19, pt. 2, 603.

[17]*OR*, ser. I, vol. 19, pt. 1, 853.

[18]John G. Oeffinger, ed., *A Soldier's General: The Civil War Letters of Major-General Lafayette McLaws* (Chapel Hill: University of North Carolina Press, 2002) 31.

Crampton's Gap consisted of cavalry and three regiments, the equivalent of a brigade.[19] Earlier that day, Stuart dispatched his Laurel Brigade, led by Colonel Thomas Munford, to support William Mahone's Infantry Brigade under the temporary command of William A. Parham, positioned at the base of the mountain.[20] They were soon joined by the 10th Georgia Infantry Regiment of Semmes's Brigade.

Cobb arrived at Brownsville around 4:00 P.M. but made no attempt to size up the situation. An hour later he received an urgent plea from Munford, whose cavalry was guarding the flanks at Crampton's Gap to hold back a large attacking Union force. Cobb then sent the 24th Georgia and Cobb's Legion Infantry Battalion to the field of battle. Minutes later he received a second request, this time from Parham's courier, and immediately ordered his remaining two regiments, the 16th Georgia and the 15th North Carolina (368 and 402 officers and men respectively), forward to engage the enemy.[21] As Cobb hurried forward, he was overtaken by Major McIntosh, McLaws's assistant adjutant general, with orders to "hold the gap if it cost the life of every man in his command."[22]

About this time reconnaissance disclosed that large numbers of Union infantry and artillery were advancing from Burkittsville toward the base of South Mountain. Cobb later determined that two divisions of Franklin's VI Corps took part in the battle, led by major generals Henry Slocum and William F. "Baldy" Smith. The size of the Federal force was estimated to be 12,000 men, which was more than five times the number of Confederate soldiers who were positioned to guard the pass.[23] The gross mismatch was the result of Stuart's underestimation the Union forces, coupled with faulty Union intelligence that indicated a much larger Confederate force at Crampton's Gap. This placed Cobb's Brigade and the defenders under Parham and Munford in a vulnerable position.

Meanwhile, Howell Cobb led his remaining forces to join the other two regiments in an attempt to hold the Confederate position at Crampton's Gap. Riding ahead, he soon overtook the 16th Georgia and 15th North Carolina regiments. After arriving at Crampton's Gap, he went to Colonel Munford, who explained the position of the defenders and offered to turn over command.

---

[19]Stuart's estimate of a brigade-size Union force was consistent with his report to General McLaws, who stated that "[Stuart] told me he did not believe there was more than a brigade of the enemy" (*OR*, ser. I, vol. 19, pt. 1, 854). See also Stuart's report in *OR*, ser. I, vol. 19, pt. 1, 817, 873.

[20]Carman, *South Mountain*, 300.

[21]John Michael Priest, *Before Antietam: The Battle for South Mountain* (Shippensburg, PA: White Mane Publishing Company, Inc., 1992) 292.

[22]*OR*, ser. I, vol. 19, pt. 1, 870. See also Stephen W. Sears, *Landscape Turned Red: The Battle of Antietam* (New Haven: Ticknor & Fields, 1983) 144–45.

[23]Bill Welsh, "Firing the Gap," *America's Civil War* 6/6 (January 1994): 41.

Although Cobb was the ranking officer present, he declined since he was relatively inexperienced and unfamiliar with the terrain and the deployment of troops.[24] Moreover, Cobb was ill-suited for hard campaigning. Nearing fifty years of age and overweight, he suffered from the rigors of the field.

By the time they arrived at the battle line, Lieutenant Simmons and his comrades were completely exhausted. For several hours prior to their arrival, the 16th Georgia had participated in a forced march for the purpose of cutting off Union supplies to Harper's Ferry. More than half of the men in the regiment involved in this action were too worn out to continue fighting and remained behind. This left Simmons with only a fraction of his company fit for battle.

After their arrival, the 16th Georgia and 15th North Carolina had only a few moments to survey the battlefield where they were to meet the Yankees' advance. Directly in front lay a descent to the bottom of the mountain through a narrow defile, wooded on both sides. At the base of the mountain was a low stone wall, now separating Confederate and Union forces by less than a quarter of a mile.[25]

According to Simmons's account, Cobb's Brigade was initially placed behind a stone wall to provide a strong defensive position, but was ordered by a ranking cavalry officer (most likely Colonel Munford) to proceed further down the mountain. The ground was very steep and rough below the stone wall, but Cobb's men firmly held their position.[26] About 5:30 P.M. the brigade advanced toward the Union forces down the mountainside. To guard against a flanking attack, the 16th Georgia and 15th North Carolina turned to the left of the road through the gap while the 24th Georgia and Cobb's Legion Infantry Battalion formed on the right side.[27]

In the midst of the smoke and confusion, the battle-weary Confederate troops under Munford and Parham incorrectly assumed that the approach of Cobb's Brigade signaled their long overdue relief, and they began to fall back.[28] At that moment, a renewed Federal attack began along the entire battle line. Initially the Confederate forces fought well and maintained their ground against vastly superior forces, but when the enemy was within twenty paces of the stone wall, the center of the Confederate line gave way. In sudden panic many veteran Confederate soldiers reacted like a "flock of frightened sheep" according to one first-hand account.[29] As evening approached, Yankee and Confederate units became intermingled in the fierce fighting and the color bearer, Corporal

---

[24]*OR*, ser. I, vol. 19, pt. 1, 826.

[25]Ibid., 375, 394, 870, 826.

[26]Daniel M. Byrd, Simmons biographical sketch, drawer 19, box 80, Georgia Department of Archives and History, Morrow, GA; Byrd, *Them Brave Georgians*, 90.

[27]*OR*, ser. I, vol. 19, pt. 1, 870.

[28]Ibid., 827.

[29]Ibid.

William McMullin of Company B, 16th Georgia, was killed.[30] General Cobb grabbed a regimental flag and attempted to rally his men. A federal bullet shattered the flagstaff, and Cobb gave it up and followed his troops in their retreat over the pass and to the western base of the mountain.

In his journal, Lieutenant Simmons, who was commanding Company I of the 16th Georgia, described his predicament during the melee. Looking back over his shoulder, he "saw the United States flag floating over the stone wall and General Cobb vainly trying to rally his panic stricken troops to the right of the 16th Georgia." When the center of the line gave way, Simmons was cut off from the main body of his regiment. He was left to fight his way out as best he could.

By this time, Simmons could count only five men from his company and ten from other regimental units. Just as the last daylight faded into evening shadows, he took charge of this group and immediately began to lead his men in a desperate attempt to escape the enemy who now controlled the battlefield. With Simmons in front, the little band began the dangerous climb up the mountainside surrounded by enemy soldiers. Using his sidearm, he fought stubbornly against Union skirmishers during the long ordeal up the steep incline until darkness intervened, most likely saving his men and himself from capture.[31]

After three hours of hard fighting, the Yankees had seized Crampton's Gap, taking 531 casualties against an estimated 800–900 or more for the Confederates.[32] Of the Confederate casualties, most were from Cobb's Brigade, which accounted for roughly three-fourths of the total. There were four fatalities among the officers in Cobb's Brigade, including Colonel John B. Lamar, Cobb's volunteer aide and his wife's only brother. While rallying the troops, Lamar received a mortal wound from which he died the next day.[33] The 16th Georgia suffered greatly. A total of 368 officers and men from the regiment had marched

---

[30]*Hallowed Banners: Historic Flags in the Historic Georgia Capitol Collection* (Atlanta: Georgia Secretary of State, 2005) 14. McMullin was shot by Sergeant Anderson of Company K, 96th Pennsylvania Infantry. The captured flag was later returned to Georgia where it is displayed in the capitol in Atlanta.

[31]Byrd, Simmons biographical sketch.

[32]Stephen W. Sears, "Fire on the Mountain: The Battle of South Mountain September 14, 1862," *Blue & Gray* 4 (December–January 1986–1987): 21. Sears wrote that nearly all of the Union casualties at Crampton's Gap were from Slocum's Division. Specific Confederate casualty returns are not on record, but it appears that there were about 400 killed or wounded, and another 400 taken captive. Ezra Carman's estimates were higher. Based on references from the *OR* and estimates given by survivors, there were 962 Confederate casualties, including 70 killed, 289 wounded, and 442 missing or captured (Carman, *South Mountain*, 312).

[33]*OR*, ser. I, vol. 19, pt. 1, 871.

to Crampton's Gap. After the smoke of battle had cleared, 24 were killed, 56 wounded, and 107 were missing or taken prisoner.[34]

As darkness approached, General Franklin decided that his men had had enough and ordered them to bed down on the mountain. During the night, the remnant of Cobb's Brigade fell back to a hastily formed line across Pleasant Valley south of Brownsville where they were joined by reinforcements from McLaws's Division. While the new line was being formed, Lieutenant Simmons and his fifteen comrades were groping their way over the mountain in the darkness and cautiously advancing in a southerly direction toward Harper's Ferry.

The next morning, Simmons led his men down the mountain and into Pleasant Valley in an attempt to locate the confederate lines. Around 10:00 A.M. they came within sight of a line of Federal troops across the valley facing a line of Confederates, with each side poised for battle. Suddenly, a nearby signal station relayed welcome news. The Union forces had surrendered at Harper's Ferry. After a brief silence, a soul-stirring rebel yell swept up the valley, and the little band knew that the Confederates had prevailed. A path was opened for McLaws's command to rejoin the rest of the Army. It took the remainder of the day for Simmons and his handful of men to follow the windings of the rugged terrain back to Harper's Ferry, and they arrived about dark.[35]

Earlier, after the Confederates fell back from Crampton's Gap, General McLaws, Jeb Stuart, and several staff members arrived to find Howell Cobb seemingly helpless amid the chaos as his disorganized brigade retreated down Pleasant Valley.[36] Heros von Borcke, Stuart's dashing Prussian aide, later reconstructed Cobb's frantic greeting: "Dismount, gentlemen...your lives are dear to you. The enemy is within fifty yards of us. Oh, my dear Stuart, that I should live to experience such a disaster. What can be done? What can save us?"[37]

Throughout 15 September, Cobb continued bitterly grieving over the loss of a large portion of his brigade and was certainly saddened by the death of his beloved brother-in-law, John B. Lamar, known affectionately as "White John"

---

[34]Ibid., 861. According to service records, there were at least eight men killed or wounded in Simmons's Company I of the 16th Georgia on 14 September 1862: Private William H. Bowring was killed; Private James Light died from wounds on 7 October 1862; and privates Nathan B. Clark, Buckner J. Harris, William J. McCune, S. Jasper Mitchell, John Porter, and Nathan Russell were wounded.

[35]Byrd, Simmons biographical sketch, 96, 97. Byrd, *Them Brave Georgians*, 90.

[36]Burke Davis, *Jeb Stuart: The Last Cavalier* (New York: Fairfax Press, 1988) 201.

[37]Ibid. Davis writes that Cobb said that the Yankees were 200 yards behind. After hearing Cobb's assessment, Stuart sent men out to determine if the enemy was close at hand. After an hour they returned to report that there were no Union soldiers within a mile (Heros von Borcke, *Memoirs of the Confederate War for Independence* [1866; reprint, Dayton, OH: Morningside Press, 1985] 217–18).

to the Lamar family. That evening Cobb was seated on a stoop above a sidewalk in Harpers Ferry when he heard the voice of William Simmons, who was one of his favorites. Cobb rose up and hugged the weary lieutenant, saying, "You were reported dead by a soldier who said he saw you fall and shot while running up the mountain between the lines. I am overjoyed to see you alive!" It was true that Simmons fell as described and that a Yankee soldier fired on him at close range while he was down, but the bullet that hit him did not break the skin. Upon examining his uniform, Simmons found one bullet hole through his hat brim and fourteen through his clothes and haversack, including five through his pants! Miraculously, he suffered no wounds.[38]

Thanks to Lieutenant Simmons's courage and leadership, he and fifteen Confederate soldiers were able to overcome nearly impossible odds and escape almost certain capture or death at the hands of Union forces. As he rested his exhausted body that night little did he realize that this was only the first of what would be many close calls during his years of service in the Confederate army.[39]

---

[38]Byrd, Simmons biographical sketch; Byrd, *Them Brave Georgians*, 90.
[39]*Hallowed Banners*, 15. In the three and a half years they were in the field during the war, the 16th Georgia participated in no fewer than 55 battles and skirmishes.

7

The Bloody Lane

Duty is the sublimest word in our language. Do your duty in all
things. You cannot do more. You should never wish to do less.
—Robert E. Lee

After the fall of Harper's Ferry, the Union army became more determined than
ever to stop the Confederate advance into Maryland. The siege on that strategic
river town had been successful largely due to the ability of General Thomas J.
"Stonewall" Jackson's forces in Maryland to divert attention from the
Confederate forces under the command of General Lee. This maneuver allowed
Jackson to take Harpers Ferry, capture 14,000 Federal soldiers, and possess vast
quantities of supplies, food, and weapons.[1] The victory was short-lived, however,
due to the superior number of Union forces in the area. Jackson needed help to
get back to Virginia, so reinforcements were sent to support his withdrawal.

On 16 September, the 16th Georgia, as part of McLaws's Division, was
ordered to resume marching. Lieutenant Simmons and a small number of his
battle-weary comrades left Harper's Ferry at 3:00 P.M. and proceeded to
Shepherdtown where the troops rested until midnight. They resumed their
march and crossed the Potomac at Botelers Ford.[2] Around sunrise on 17
September, the head of the column reached General Lee's headquarters near the
town of Sharpsburg. Soon they were joined by the 16th Georgia and the rest of
McLaws's Division. In the distance the soldiers could hear the Union artillery
being answered by Confederate guns closer by and the noise of rifles
accompanied by the shouts of soldiers.

At 9:00 A.M. McLaws received orders to reinforce the left of the
Confederate line in the west near the Dunker Church, about one mile north of
Sharpsburg.[3] The left flank of the Southern line, defended by Stonewall
Jackson's forces, was in danger of being broken. Since the early dawn the
Yankees had attacked the position in overwhelming numbers, and Jackson's
brigades had suffered a large number of casualties.[4] During a lull in the fighting,

---

[1] *The War of the Rebellion: A Compilation of the Official Records of the Union and
Confederate Armies* (70 vols. in 128; Washington, 1880–1901), ser. I, vol. 19, pt. 1, 629.
Hereafter cited as OR.

[2] *OR*, ser. I, vol. 19, pt. 1, 857.

[3] Ibid., 149, 857; James Longstreet, *From Manassas to Appomattox: Memoirs of the
Civil War in America* (1896; reprint, New York: Barnes & Noble, 2006) 199–201.

[4] *OR*, ser. I, vol. 19, pt. 1, 956.

McLaws began to form his line of battle with Cobb's Brigade, now under the command of Lieutenant Colonel C. C. (Christopher Columbus) Sanders, positioned to the right of Jackson and to the left of General Daniel Harvey Hill. Casualties and sheer exhaustion had taken their toll on Cobb's Brigade, including on General Cobb himself. Just 357 officers and men went into battle, down from over 2,900 who made up the brigade during the Peninsula Campaign.[5] Lieutenant Simmons had only five men under his command.[6]

About thirty minutes after leaving General Lee's headquarters, McLaws ordered Sanders to march Cobb's Brigade by the left flank. In the noise and confusion, Sanders either did not hear or misunderstood the command and marched straight ahead to take a position along the Hagerstown Road at the junction of a sunken road leading to the east.[7] This placed the 16th Georgia and the rest of Cobb's Brigade in the center of the Confederate line, fighting beside troops under General Robert E. Rodes of General D. H. Hill's command. Cobb's Brigade was now completely separated from the rest of McLaws's Division.

Colonel Sanders placed his soldiers behind a post and rail fence along the east side of the Hagerstown Road.[8] Directly in front and to the east ran a narrow road, sunken below the levels of the adjacent fields by years of erosion, which connected the Hagerstown Road with the Boonsborough Road. General Rodes's troops and all of Hill's Division were stretched along this natural rifle pit. The dusty road soon would become a bloody lane and go down in history with that distinction. Although the fence provided some protection from enemy fire, the men were constantly raked by heavy shelling from Union artillery from a hill across Antietam Creek.[9]

For an hour Sanders and his men remained inactive while awaiting orders. At midday, after a Union attack on the center failed, General Hill took the initiative and ordered a countercharge. All the troops in the sunken road and those behind the fence along the Hagerstown Road responded. Cobb's depleted brigade joined the others and advanced straight ahead to the top of a small hill in front of their position. The soldiers were subjected to withering fire, but held their position until Sanders ordered the men to fall back behind the protection of the fence and the road bank.[10]

---

[5]Ibid., 861–62, 871.

[6]Daniel M. Byrd Jr., *Them Brave Georgians*, manuscript, Gwinnett Historical Society archives, Lawrenceville, GA, 102–103 (Fort Delaware Society Library, Delaware City, DE, also has a copy.).

[7]William Allan, *The Army of Northern Virginia in 1862* (Cambridge: Houghton Mifflin and Company, 1892) 415.

[8]*OR*, ser. I, vol. 19, pt. 1, 871.

[9]Ibid., 872

[10]Ibid.

Not long after returning to their former position, confusion developed in the ranks on the sunken road and General Rodes's troops began to retreat. It became imperative for Colonel Sanders and his small force to join the withdrawal so that they would not be flanked. Cobb's Brigade pulled back to a safer position behind a stone fence near the Hagerstown Road next to the 4th South Carolina Infantry Battalion.[11]

From their new vantage point, Lieutenant Simmons saw the Yankees pouring across the sunken road and advancing toward the reformed Confederate battle line. To bolster the defenses, General Hill directed new-arrived artillery batteries to fire upon Yankee guns on the other side of Antietam Creek. Soon grape and canister had a telling effect on the attacking bluecoats. In turn the Federal soldiers concentrated their fire on the batteries. So desperate was the situation that General Longstreet held the horses of his staff officers while they took the places of the fallen gunners.[12]

As the men of Cobb's Brigade remained in their position behind the stone wall, General D. H. Hill rode up to Colonel Sanders and discussed the possibility of another countercharge. Soon, other regimental officers also came forward to confer. All agreed to participate if General Hill would lead.[13] When the order to advance was given, Colonel Sanders was too exhausted to lead his men. All day he had suffered from an illness. He then turned over command of Cobb's Brigade to Lieutenant Colonel William McRae of the 15th North Carolina.[14]

Throughout the afternoon the fighting heated up in the vicinity of the sunken road. Confederate dead numbered in the hundreds. Simmons' regiment carried on valiantly while incurring a large number of casualties.

After several hours of intense fighting, Cobb's men had spent almost all of their ammunition. Colonel McRae gave the order to fall back and join the remnants of two other regiments. For the remainder of the day, they took up positions on the Confederate left between Jeb Stuart's Cavalry and Kershaw's Brigade. By 5:30 P.M. most of the fighting had ended. From that day on, the battle would be called Antietam by the North, named for the meandering stream that ran through the area. In the South, it was known as the Battle of Sharpsburg, named after the nearby town. By either name, it was the bloodiest single day of the Civil War. A tabulation of Cobb's men showed that 17 had been killed, 129 wounded and 10 missing or captured. Almost half of the 357

---

[11]Ibid.; Longstreet, *From Manassas to Appomattox*, 249.

[12]G. Moxley Sorrel, *Recollections of a Confederate Staff Officer*, ed. Bell Irvin Wiley (Wilmington, NC: Broadfoot Publishing Company, 1995) 105.

[13]*OR*, ser. I, vol. 19, pt. 1, 872, 1024.

[14]Ibid., 872.

officers and men going into battle were lost forever or until serious wounds were healed.[15]

Although the Army of Northern Virginia remained in position on the battlefield at the end of the day, it was a costly outcome from which the only major accomplishment was the opportunity it gave for the Confederate forces to withdraw across the Potomac. After the debacle on South Mountain, the men of Cobb's Brigade had acquitted themselves with honor. Lieutenant Colonel McRae praised the "gallant little band" when reporting to General Cobb, who arrived in Sharpsburg early the next morning to resume command of his battered but proud brigade.[16]

On 18 September the two exhausted armies lay facing each other. Not a shot was fired to the considerable relief of the Confederates. That afternoon, General Lee ordered his army to return to Virginia. The supply trains started back, and soon after dark the troops followed. By sunrise the next morning, the entire army had left Maryland, crossing the Potomac at Botelers Ford.[17]

The following day, 20 September, Cobb's thin and exhausted brigade arrived at Camp Lizzie, which was situated about two miles from Martinsburg, Virginia.[18] After a brief stay, the brigade moved to Camp Tom in the Shenandoah Valley, seven miles west of Winchester.[19] Throughout the following week, a steady stream of soldiers thought to be dead or deserters rejoined their comrades. As a rule, soldiers who had been taken prisoner by the enemy were released on parole and returned to their regiments. Such was the case of 2nd Lieutenant W. G. Brannon of Company D (Danielsville Guards), 16th Georgia. According to Brannon's service records, he was captured at Crampton's Gap on 14 September 1862. He was sent to Fort Delaware and released for exchange on 2 October. He returned to the regiment on 21 October 1862, two weeks after being exchanged at Aiken's Landing on 6 October.

---

[15]Ibid., 862.

[16]Ibid., 871.

[17]E. Porter Alexander, *Military Memoirs of a Confederate: A Critical Narrative* (1907; reprint, Dayton, OH: Press of Morningside Bookshop, 1977) 269; John G. Walker, Major-General, CSA, "Sharpsburg," in *North to Antietam*, vol. 2 of *Battles and Leaders of the Civil War* (1887; reprint, New York: Thomas Yoseloff, 1956) 682; *OR*, ser. I, vol. 19, pt. 1, 872.

[18]Howell Cobb to Mary Ann Cobb (nee Lamar), 24 September 1862, Howell Cobb papers, box 51, folder 26, ms. 1376, Hargrett Rare Book and Manuscript Library, University of Georgia, Athens. While he was a brigade commander, Howell Cobb usually named each camp after a family member. Camp Lizzie camp was named for one of his eleven children, Elizabeth Craig Cobb, a practice he continued during the Maryland Campaign.

[19]Camp Tom was named for Howell Cobb's youngest child, Thomas Reade Rootes Cobb (b. 1861), who did not survive early childhood.

Throughout the fall the brigade's ranks were further bolstered by an influx of new recruits. Within a few weeks the brigade grew in size to 1,600 men, over four times the number who fought at the Battle of Sharpsburg, but still significantly smaller than its original complement.

After Lee's Army returned to the safer confines of Virginia, Howell Cobb came under severe criticism by his superior for his conduct during the Maryland Campaign. McLaws felt that Cobb failed to understand his responsibilities and had been a great bother. On 24 September Cobb requested a transfer for himself and his brigade to another division. McLaws promptly and politely turned down the request.[20]

Cobb's troubles continued after the brigade located to Camp Tom. He developed a nasty infection in his foot that became so painful and swollen that he was unable to put a boot on to greet General Longstreet when he arrived to review McLaws's Division. With Howell Cobb not able to perform his duties, temporary command of the brigade was turned over to his younger brother, Colonel Thomas R. R. Cobb.[21] Like his older sibling, Tom Cobb was a graduate of the University of Georgia (class of 1841). The following year he was admitted to the bar and began to build a solid reputation as a constitutional lawyer. He became actively involved in political life and served as a delegate to the Confederate Convention in Montgomery, Alabama. Early in the war, he recruited Cobb's Georgia Legion, of which he was commissioned colonel in August 1861 and became commanding officer of the legion's infantry battalion. On 27 October 1862 General Lee recommended Tom Cobb for the grade of brigadier general, and the commission was made official on 6 November.[22]

Several days before his brother's promotion and still sidelined from his infected foot, Howell Cobb decided to take a furlough and return home to Georgia. He was in his home state on 5 November when he learned that he was being transferred to the District of Middle Florida.

Back in Virginia, the ranks of Cobb's Brigade continued to steadily grow, along with the other brigades of McLaws's Division. By 10 November, the division numbered more than 9,000 officers and men present. However, this good news was tempered by the fact that many of the men were woefully short

---

[20]George Montgomery Jr., *Georgia Sharpshooter: The Civil War Diary and Letters of William Rhadamanthus Montgomery* (Macon: Mercer University Press, 1997) 75–76; T. R. R. Cobb to Marion Cobb (nee Lumpkin), 20 October 1862, Thomas Reade Roots (T. R. R.) Cobb papers, box 1, file 12, ms. 448, Hargrett Rare Book and Manuscript Library, University of Georgia, Athens; Thomas R. R. Cobb, "Extracts from Letters to His Wife February 3, 1861–December 10, 1862," *Southern Historical Society Papers* (hereafter *SHSP*) 28 (1900): 296.

[21]Howell Cobb to Mary Ann Cobb (nee Lamar), 4, 6, 10 October 1862, Howell Cobb papers.

[22]William B. McCash, *Thomas R. R. Cobb: The Making of a Southern Nationalist* (Macon: Mercer University Press, 2004) 313; *OR*, ser. I, vol. 19, pt. 2, 683, 699.

of arms, clothing, and equipment. With winter on the horizon, General McLaws and his subordinates were concerned that one in seven soldiers had no shoes and an even greater proportion were without blankets.[23] Unfortunately the situation would get much worse in the days to come.

---

[23] *OR* 19 part 2, 713, 721. The reported number of men in the division without shoes was 1,475. See *OR*, ser. I, vol. 19, pt. 2, 674, 702–703.

8

The Sunken Road

Charity looks at the need and not at the cause.

—German Proverb

On 18 November camp was broken. That day, McLaws's and Ransom's divisions of Longstreet's Corps began a march to Fredericksburg, a prominent Virginia town on the southern/western bank of the Rappahannock River.[1] To reach their destination the men once again plodded down muddy roads in cold, rainy weather. The journey was especially difficult for the large number of rebel soldiers without shoes who marched barefooted or with their feet wrapped in rags or straw. After they arrived, the 16th Georgia and Cobb's other regiments went into camp west of Fredericksburg behind a local landmark called "Federal Hill." From Federal Hill one could view the home where the mother of generals Howell and Tom Cobb was born and married.[2]

The topography in the vicinity of Fredericksburg clearly revealed where the best defensive line should be established for General Lee's army. West of the town, separated by an open plain several hundred yards wide, ran a range of hills nearly parallel with the Rappahannock where it flowed past Fredericksburg. This higher ground near Fredericksburg is known as Marye's Heights or Marye's Hill. As soon as they arrived, the Confederate soldiers went to work in the heights constructing breastworks on the crest of each hill at the most favorable positions. Where the hills leveled off, the line was extended by rifle pits and abatis. All along the foot of the hills more rifle pits were dug out of the cold, hard soil. The high ground provided the Confederates with an excellent defensive position and allowed a clear view of an open plain leading to Fredericksburg and the Rappahannock River beyond. When completed, the

---

[1]*The War of the Rebellion: A Compilation of the Official Records of the Union and Confederate Armies* (70 vols. in 128; Washington, 1880–1901), ser. 1, vol. 21, 1017. Hereafter cited as OR.

[2]T. R. R. Cobb to Marion Cobb (nee Lumpkin), 22 November 1862, Thomas Reade Roots (T. R. R.) Cobb papers, box 1, folder 21, ms. 448, Hargrett Rare Book and Manuscript Library, University of Georgia, Athens; Thomas R. R. Cobb, "Extracts from Letters to His Wife February 3, 1861–December 10, 1862," *Southern Historical Society Papers* (hereafter *SHSP*) 28 (1900): 296.

Confederate fortifications stretched six miles from a point about a mile and a half north of the town to four or five miles south of it.[3]

Across the Rappahannock loomed the mighty Army of the Potomac, now under the command of Major General Ambrose Everett Burnside. The Federal forces were massing in great numbers on Stafford Heights to the east of Fredericksburg. Burnside was anxious for his army to cross the river and advance on the entrenched Confederates, but he had to wait for several days for the delivery of pontoons necessary to bridge the deep river. To further delay the Federal advance, Barksdale's Mississippi Brigade was deployed to defend the town and river crossings. They were also responsible for holding up the assembly of Burnside's pontoon bridges at Fredericksburg until the Confederates could be alerted and take positions in their fortifications.[4]

While preparing for the inevitable battle, General Lee made several organizational changes to his Army of Northern Virginia. The 15th North Carolina Infantry Regiment of Cobb's Brigade was transferred to Cooke's Brigade in Ransom's Division. The same order replaced the 15th North Carolina with Phillips Georgia Legion Infantry Battalion from Drayton's Brigade and added the famed 18th Georgia Infantry Regiment from Robertson's Brigade of Hood's Division. From this point in time until the end of the war, Cobb's Brigade would be an all-Georgia outfit.[5]

In the beginning the men of the 18th Georgia did not relish the idea of leaving their old companions in arms, but General Tom Cobb soon won them over.[6] The transition for the 18th Georgia went smoothly. There was a mutual respect among the men involved in the re-organization. According to one officer of the 18th Georgia,

> Their outfits [regiments of Wofford's Brigade] were well known as being hard fighters, yet all of them knew of the [Hood's] Texas Brigade's reputation and seemed to hold us in particular regard. It wasn't long before we all fell in together, for being Georgians, there were many common friends and even family among us. Upon our reformation, we were called together and General Tom Cobb was introduced. He gave us a fiery speech noteworthy for his eloquence and spirit, yet he looked to me at least, more

[3]*OR*, ser. 1, vol. 21, 552, 585; E. Porter Alexander, *Military Memoirs of a Confederate: A Critical Narrative* (1907; reprint, Dayton, OH: Press of Morningside Bookshop, 1977) 289.

[4]*OR*, ser. 1, vol. 21, 573.

[5]Ibid., 1033.

[6]James Madison Folsom, *Heroes and Martyrs of Georgia: Georgia's Record in the Revolution of 1861* (Macon: Burke & Boykin, 1864) 16.

like a politician than a soldier. Still he seemed a good sort and brave fellow.[7]

Although Tom Cobb was pleased with the changes, there were some concerns. The newly assigned 18th Georgia, commanded by Lieutenant Colonel S. Z. (Solon Zacharias) Ruff, lacked sufficient arms and equipment: 100 men had no weapons, and 150 had no shoes. The weather was getting colder in late November and early December, and the thinly clad Southerners suffered greatly, especially those on picket duty where fires were not allowed.[8] On 24–25 November, the overnight temperatures dropped several degrees below freezing, and there was a heavy frost.[9] The lack of adequate clothing and footwear was not confined to the 18th Georgia, however. In a letter to his mother in late November, Eli P. Landers, a private in the 16th Georgia wrote,

> I have got no shoes yet nor no prospect of getting any. The weather is getting very cold. I tell you we suffer for the want of blankets to sleep under. Some nights we don't sleep hardly a bit on account of being so cold. We have just one blanket to lie on and one to cover with. I want you to send me my overcoat and wool shirt by the first passing for I don't expect we will ever get them things at Richmond.

Three days later, Landers completed the letter he had started on 26 November:

> We stayed on picket for 48 hours down in Fredericksburg. I am not so very well today. My cold seems to get worse. I have got a very bad cough and I am so bad stopped up till I sometimes almost smother. I am fearful that I will be sick. We have a very fair prospect for snow now soon. I dread it very bad without we was better prepared for it. I don't know what we will all do if we don't get shoes.[10]

Private Landers was correct about the "fair prospect of snow." On the night of 5 December, Cobb's men stood picket duty in a driving snowstorm.[11]

During the next week there was a period of relative inactivity. The two armies faced each other across the river with only an occasional shot fired. It was

---

[7]James Lile Lemon, *Feed them the Steel! Being the Wartime Recollections of Captain James Lile Lemon Company A, 18th Georgia Infantry C.S.A.* (Acworth, GA: printed by Mark H. Lemon, 2008) 36.

[8]Alexander, *Military Memoirs*, 292.

[9]Robert K. Krick, *Civil War Weather in Virginia* (Tuscaloosa: University of Alabama Press, 2007) 77. The temperature readings for the two days were taken at 7:00 A.M. in nearby Washington, DC, where it was 28 degrees both mornings.

[10]Eli P. Landers to Susan Landers, 29 November 1862, in Elizabeth Whitley Roberson, *In Care of Yellow River* (Fort Lauderdale: Venture Press, 1994) 104–105.

[11]T. R. R. Cobb to Marion Cobb (nee Lumpkin), 6 December 1862, T. R. R. Cobb papers; T. R. R. Cobb, "Extracts from Letters to His Wife," 300.

the calm before the storm, and soldiers on each side grew eager for battle.[12] On the evening of 10 December, after three weeks of delays caused by inclement weather and lack of materials for the pontoon bridges, the Army of the Potomac finally made its move. Confederate signal guns were fired as the enemy began to erect pontoon bridges to enable a river crossing. The signal alerted the troops to leave their camps and march to their positions along the line.[13] By 5:00 A.M. Cobb's Brigade was armed and in place along its entrenchments.

At midmorning, General McLaws ordered Cobb to send reinforcements to the troops on the river just to the north of Deep Run, one of the locations where the Yankees were attempting to cross the Rappahannock.[14] Cobb dispatched the 16th Georgia to support the 18th Mississippi of Barksdale's Brigade, which had been trying to hold off the construction of a pontoon bridge at that site since daylight. Despite a hail of fire from the Confederates, boats were thrown out and planking was laid for the first bridge.[15]

The 16th Georgia arrived at the river about noon and took up positions to the left of the 18th Mississippi. The two regiments were soon joined by the 15th South Carolina of Kershaw's Brigade, led by Colonel W. D. DeSaussure.[16] All three Confederate regiments endured constant enemy artillery and rifle fire from the opposite river bank as they held their position on the river. After an hour, the first bridge was completed and the bluecoats poured over the structure, firing as they crossed. The Confederate regiments fell back slowly to a better defensive position at Bowling Green Road. There the 16th Georgia and the two other regiments remained on picket duty during the frigid night of 11 December.[17]

The next morning at daybreak the 16th Georgia returned from picket duty to their position on the Confederate line. When they arrived, they discovered that the rest of their brigade had been relocated to a position along Telegraph Road at the foot of Marye's Heights, where they directly faced the town of Fredericksburg. Rather than rejoining their fellow Georgians, the 16th Georgia was ordered to proceed to Howison's Mill and remain there until further notice.[18] Their new position was located on the south side of Hazel Run, a creek

---

[12]*OR*, ser. 1, vol. 21, 552.

[13]Ibid., 569; Edward J. Stackpole, *The Fredericksburg Campaign: Drama on the Rappahannock* (New York: Bonanza Books, 1957) 133.

[14]At the point where the Union pontoon bridge was constructed, the Rappahannock is about 400 feet wide. After the Confederates were driven off, five more pontoon bridges were quickly put in place (David S. Heidler and Jeanne T. Heidler, eds., *Encyclopedia of the American Civil War*, vol. 2 [Santa Barbara, CA: ABC-CLIO, 2000] 777).

[15]*OR*, ser. 1, vol. 21, 604.

[16]Ibid., 599.

[17]Ibid., 588.

[18]Ibid., 608.

that runs perpendicular to the heights and empties into the Rappahannock just below Fredericksburg.

The Federal assault began early on the morning of 13 December in the midst of a thick fog. After three days of intense skirmishing, the Union forces now occupied Fredericksburg. William Simmons and the 16th Georgia began the day defending their position at Howison's Mill while T. R. R. Cobb's other regiments and the 24th North Carolina remained at their forward position on Telegraph Road, which was from three to five feet below ground level. Known as the "Sunken Road," the lane was protected by a four-foot-high, 400-yard-long stone wall on the Fredericksburg side of the byway. To shore up their defenses, the Confederates dug a ditch behind the wall and packed the scooped-out earth against the stones of the exposed side for added protection. There were approximately 2,000 men stationed at this location with an additional 7,000 troops held in reserve behind the ridge. The defenders were backed up by the famed Washington Artillery of New Orleans, which manned nine pieces positioned on higher ground behind the stone wall.[19] The Sunken Road and stone wall would soon become the site of the most deadly fighting during the battle of Fredericksburg.[20]

The fog lifted about 10 A.M., and one hour later General William H. French's Division of bluecoats moved out from the town in a dense formation led by General Nathan Kimball's Brigade. From behind the wall, the poorly-clad Confederates marveled at the immaculate uniforms and bright accouterments of the enemy glistening in the sun and flags crowning each regiment in the breeze.[21] As the first wave of Union soldiers approached the stone wall, General Cobb pulled off his hat, waved it over his head and said, "Get ready boys, here they come."[22] Once the bullets began to fly, Cobb moved from point to point along the Confederate line and shouted to his soldiers, "Aim low boys, aim low, that's the style."[23] The bluecoats got within forty yards of the Georgians behind the stone wall before retreating in a hail of Confederate gunfire. After Kimball's Brigade came French's 3rd Brigade under the command of Colonel John W. Andrews. In a little more than fifteen minutes, nearly half of Andrews's Brigade had been killed or wounded.

About 1:00 P.M. a courier arrived at Howison's Mill with orders from General McLaws. Colonel Goode Bryan, commanding officer of the 16th Georgia, was directed to lead his regiment to Telegraph Road where Cobb's

---

[19]Ibid., 573.

[20]Ibid., 554, 589; Alexander, *Military Memoirs*, 289.

[21]Lemon, *Feed them the Steel*, 37.

[22]William R. Montgomery to Aunt Frank in Marietta, GA, 17 December 1862 (George Montgomery Jr., *Georgia Sharpshooter: The Civil War Diary and Letters of William Rhadamanthus Montgomery* [Macon: Mercer University Press, 1997] 77).

[23]Lemon, *Feed them the Steel*, 37.

Brigade was positioned behind the stone wall.[24] To reach their destination, the regiment proceeded double-quick down the line of earthworks, continued on the Telegraph Road behind the lines, turned left and climbed a new military road to the crest of Marye's Heights.[25] From this height they had an appalling view of the carnage inflicted on the advancing Yankees from above and below.

Not long after the 16th Georgia reached the heights, a courier brought bad news. The report indicated that General Tom Cobb had fallen, suffering a wound to his thigh from a sharpshooter's bullet after the first Union attack. At that time, no one yet knew the seriousness of the wound.[26] Colonel Robert McMillan of the 24th Georgia was now in command of the brigade. The men of the 16th Georgia immediately raced down the heights back to the Telegraph Road to join their brigade positioned behind the stone wall.

When the 16th Georgia arrived, Colonel McMillan placed the regiment on the right of his line, doubling with the 18th Georgia. By mid-afternoon there would be eleven regiments packed in behind the stone wall.[27] During the

---

[24]*OR*, ser. 1, vol. 21, 580, 608.

[25]Ibid., 588, 608, 626.

[26]Ibid., 608. Among the accounts of General Cobb's death behind the Stone Wall, there are several contradictions. Captain Stephen Dent recalled that Cobb was killed by shrapnel from artillery fire rather than a bullet. See Stephen Dent, "With Cobb's Brigade at Fredericksburg," *Confederate Veteran* 22/11 (November 1914): 501. Others report that the wound was in the calf rather than the thigh. In his account of the battle, Lafayette McLaws wrote that Cobb was "wounded by a musket-ball in the calf of the leg." McLaws based the statement on the authority of Surgeon Todd of Cobb's Brigade, who says he saw the wound. See Lafayette McLaws, Major-General, C. S. A., "The Confederate Left at Fredericksburg," in *Retreat from Gettysburg*, vol. 3 of *Battles and Leaders of the Civil War* (1887; reprint, New York: Castle Books, 1956) 94. In the same volume, Longstreet writes that Cobb "fell from a wound to the thigh and died in a few minutes from loss of blood." See James Longstreet, Lieutenant General, C. S. A., "The Battle of Fredericksburg" (81). Surgeon Eldridge examined Cobb after he was carried to the Widow Stevens house, and determined that a shattered thigh bone had ruptured main arteries. To further complicate matters, there was some speculation that Cobb was killed by a disgruntled Confederate private who he had recently chastised for a minor infraction.

[27]The regiments behind the stone wall included the 16th, 18th, and 24th Georgia regiments and Phillips Legion Infantry Battalion from T. R. R. Cobb's Brigade; Ransom's 24th and 25th North Carolina regiments; Cooke's 27th and 46th North Carolina regiments, and three regiments of Kershaw's Brigade: the 2nd, 8th, and 15th South Carolina (William Allan, *The Army of Northern Virginia in 1862* [Cambridge: Houghton Mifflin and Company, 1892] 503). D. Augustus Dickert noted that these and additional Confederate units "held the stone wall *and* Marye's Hill," including a third regiment from Cooke's Brigade, Cobb's Infantry Legion, the 3rd Battalion of Kershaw's Brigade and two Artillery Batteries: the Washington Battery of New Orleans and Alexander's Battery from Virginia (D. Augustus Dickert, *History of Kershaw's Brigade*

remainder of the day, the formation along the line was four deep. The new arrivals were instructed to follow General Cobb's tactics by calmly holding their fire until Yankee coat buttons could be counted.[28] The 16th Georgia had not been in position for very long before they helped to drive off a third Federal attack, led by Colonel Oliver H. Palmer's Brigade. Within a few minutes, a struggle equally as fierce and bloody as its predecessors raged along the entire base of Marye's Heights. Lieutenant Simmons witnessed a barrage of fire that enveloped the head and flanks of the Union battle line.[29]

Generals Robert E. Lee and James Longstreet observed the inferno from the summit of Lee's Hill, located to the south of Marye's Heights. Longstreet noted that by the time the third attack was repulsed, the open ground between the stone wall and Fredericksburg was so covered with bodies that it impeded the approach of the attacking Federals. Lee became uneasy when he saw the attacks so promptly renewed and feared that the line might be broken. Longstreet assured Lee that his defenders, if provided with enough ammunition, could hold their position even if every man north of the Potomac were put on the field of battle.[30]

Despite the continued slaughter of his men in blue, Burnside ordered a fourth attack on the Confederates, led by Zook's Brigade of Hancock's Division. This charge came closest to reaching the Confederate line along the Sunken Road, but only one Union soldier came within 100 feet of the wall before he fell to the ground.[31] After the fourth attack was repulsed, Thomas Francis Meagher's Irish Brigade of 1,300 was called on to advance from Fredericksburg. The Irish were tough, experienced soldiers who had fought valiantly at Frayser's Farm and Malvern Hill during the Seven Days Battles and at the Bloody Lane at Antietam, but they fared no better than their predecessors. The brigade paid a heavy price that afternoon with 545 killed, wounded, or missing/presumed dead, a 42 percent casualty rate.

[1899; reprint, Wilmington, NC: Broadfoot Publishing Company, 1990] 192–93). See also A. A. Timmons, "Sixteenth Georgia at Fredericksburg," *Confederate Veteran*, 7/12 (December 1899): 546.

[28]*OR*, ser. 1, vol. 21, , 608; *Confederate Veteran* 7/7 (July 1899): 309.

[29]Daniel M. Byrd Jr., *Them Brave Georgians*, manuscript, Gwinnett Historical Society archives, Lawrenceville, GA pg. 132 (Fort Delaware Society Library, Delaware City, DE, also has a copy.).

[30]James Longstreet, Lieutenant-General, C. S. A., "The Battle of Fredericksburg," in *Retreat from Gettysburg*, vol. 3 of *Battles and Leaders of the Civil War* (1887; reprint, New York: Castle Books, 1956) 81.

[31]Ibid. In his official report, General McLaws wrote that (from the fourth attack), "The body of one [Union] man, believed to be an officer, was found within about thirty yards of the stone wall, and other single bodies were scattered at increased distances until the main mass of the dead lay thickly strewn over the ground at something over one hundred yards (and beyond)...."

By mid-afternoon the Washington Artillery on Marye's Heights had run out of ammunition, but the batteries were quickly relieved by Colonel E. Porter Alexander's Artillery Battalion. The replacements were in position when Burnside launched a sixth attack around 5:30 P.M. At dusk, the final charge was made by Caldwell's Brigade, which met with disastrous results. The Union death toll mounted through the day until there were more than 7,000 dead and wounded covering the 300 yards in front of the stone wall.

When the battle had ended, Chaplain R. K. Porter[32] told the men of the 16th Georgia that their esteemed brigade leader had died. His wounding had taken place after the first Union assault had been beaten back and a second attack was being formed on the plain below the stone wall. During the lull in the fighting, Cobb was conferring with General John R. Cooke and a group of officers behind a building when a random artillery shell hit the side of the building. Cooke and several others were wounded, including Tom Cobb, who was knocked to the ground with a wound to the leg.[33] Cobb was then carried to a nearby house that had been pressed into service as a hospital.[34] The surgeon arrived quickly, and his examination revealed a shattered thighbone and a ruptured artery. The general soon sank into a coma and bled to death. He was thirty-nine years old. Simmons and his comrades wept at the sad news.

The details of Cobb's tragic death were chronicled by Stephen Dent, one of Cobb's staff, several years after the War ended:

> [From the top of Marye's Heights] I sent the rowels into the flanks of my horse, making a dash for the foot of the hill and friendly shelter of the stone wall. Feeling, though not seeing, the flash of the fatal shrapnel, the explosion of which gave General Cobb his death wound, I found myself

---

[32] Byrd, *Them Brave Georgians*, 134. In the Byrd manuscript, the chaplain is referred to as Reverend R. K. *Ponder*. All eleven cards of his service record identify him as R. K. *Porter*, chaplain of T. R. R. Cobb's Georgia Legion Infantry Battalion, with the rank of captain. The reverend described T. R. R. Cobb's final minutes to General Howell Cobb in a letter dated 9 January 1863, which is printed in the *Confederate Veteran* 7/7 (July 1899): 309. In Stephen Dent's account of Cobb's death published in the *Confederate Veteran* 22/11 (November 1914): 50, the chaplain is incorrectly referred to as P. K. Ponder. Reverend Porter was a Presbyterian minister from Waynesboro, GA, and was a personal friend of Tom Cobb (William B. McCash, *Thomas R. R. Cobb: The Making of a Southern Nationalist* [Macon: Mercer University Press, 2004] 88).

[33] "With Cobb's Brigade at Fredericksburg," *Confederate Veteran* 22/10 (October 1914): 500–501.

[34] W. Roy Mason, Major, C. S. A., "Notes of a Confederate Staff Officer," in *Retreat from Gettysburg*, vol. 3 of *Battles and Leaders of the Civil War* (1887; reprint, New York: Castle Books, 1956) 100. The home belonged to Mrs. Martha Stevens, a widow. According to Major W. Roy Mason, the lady "attended the wounded and dying fearless of consequences, and refused to leave her house...[which stood] just between the line of the advancing enemy and the stone wall."

bundled up in the middle of the road with the firm belief that my horse's head had been shot off and myself fatally hurt. I was aroused by Captain Rutherford asking, "Are you hurt, Dent?" Shaking myself, I found that I was not hurt and so replied. "Then get Dr. Eldridge[35] at once! General Cobb is dangerously wounded." Captain Rutherford was flat in the road, holding General Cobb's head in his lap, and had applied a tourniquet in his endeavor to stop the flow of blood that was pouring from the femoral artery. Recovering my horse, I started for the doctor and met him with Mr. Ponder [Porter], our chaplain, together with four men bearing stretchers. General Cobb was borne to the old Telegraph Road, placed in our ambulance and carried to his headquarters, attended by Dr. Eldridge, Mr. Ponder, Captain Rutherford and myself. The last order from his lips was addressed to me. Rising on his elbow, he said, "Steve, report to Colonel McMillan. He has no one with him. You are the only one I can send; the others are dead."[36]

Another eyewitness to the event was Sergeant William R. Montgomery of Company L, Phillips Legion Infantry Battalion, who was in close proximity to General Cobb when disaster struck:

The whole time of the engagement [first Union assault] our brave and gallant General Cobb was encouraging on his men until a shot from the enemy's cannon gave him his mortal wound. He was on the right of our company, only a few feet from me when wounded. Payson Ardis being one of our litter bearers ran to him & I shall never forget his last look as they laid him on the litter to bear him from the field. His last words to his men were, "I am only wounded boys, hold your ground like brave men."[37]

With the coming of night a stiff wind picked up and the temperature dropped. Many critically wounded Union soldiers quickly perished and froze solid. Others wounded less seriously suffered through the long night in the bitter cold before dying. Still others who were ordered to hold the advance position lay prone on the blood soaked field and spent the dark hours in agony from the cold and thirst, surrounded by the dead and dying.

Meanwhile, Lieutenant Simmons and his exhausted, hungry comrades remained behind the stone wall along the Sunken Road. The night was filled with the eerie moans and desperate pleas of the wounded and suffering on the battlefield. The next morning as the fog cleared, large numbers of Union

---

[35]According to service records, Dr. Erwin J. Eldridge was the chief surgeon of Cobb's Brigade. He began his service in July 1861 and was assigned to the 16th Georgia as assistant surgeon before being promoted to brigade staff.

[36]Stephen Dent, "With Cobb's Brigade at Fredericksburg," *Confederate Veteran* 22/11 (November 1914): 500.

[37]William R. Montgomery to Aunt Frank in Marietta, GA, 17 December 1862, in Montgomery, *Georgia Sharpshooter*, 77.

soldiers were sighted along the riverbank, but there was no attempt to resume the battle or remove the dead and wounded from the battlefield. From the Sunken Road, the cries of the wounded Union soldiers could still be heard above the sporadic gunfire. This was too much for one Confederate soldier to bear as documented in several accounts of the battle:

> Suddenly from behind the wall rose a youthful Confederate sergeant; laden with canteens. He walked to the nearest wounded foe. Tenderly he raised the fallen soldier's head and gave him a comforting drink. Not a Federal rifle interfered with his efforts to aid their fallen and deserted comrades, who identified themselves from the dead men by cries of "Water, water; for God's sake, water."[38]

This kind deed was witnessed and recorded by General Joseph Kershaw and very likely had a touching effect on all who still huddled behind the stone wall along the Sunken Road. The principal player in this drama was Richard Rowland Kirkland, a young sergeant from the 2nd South Carolina Regiment of Kershaw's Brigade. Throughout the morning the nineteen-year-old soldier went about his errands of mercy while Yankee sharpshooters held their fire. As his canteens were emptied, the compassionate young man returned for refills until his task was completed. From that day on, he would forever be immortalized as the "Angel of Marye's Heights." Several months later, Kirkland would be mortally wounded at the Battle of Chickamauga.[39]

The Confederate army held their positions for two more days until the Union forces withdrew across the Rappahannock. The celebration of a great victory was dampened by the wholesale destruction of what was once a beautiful town. After the citizens fled and the Confederate defenders were driven back to the safety of Marye's Heights, the Union soldiers broke open and occupied every house, smashed up furniture, and threw personal items into the streets. Pews in the town churches were torn out, and the floors of many of the homes were covered in blood and dead Union soldiers.

Captain B. Edward Stiles of the 16th Georgia was enraged at what he saw:

> The poor people have suffered terribly. [We] are now taking up a subscription for them. It was a pitiable sight to see the women and children those dreadfully cold nights streaming along the road streaming from the city stopping at every fire to keep from freezing with nothing in the world

---

[38]Gregg S. Clemmer, "The Angel of Marye's Heights" in *Valor in Gray: The Recipients of the Confederate Medal of Honor* (Staunton, VA: Hearthside Publishing Company, 1998) 16–23.

[39]General J. B. Kershaw, "Richard Kirkland, the Humane Hero of Fredericksburg," *SHSP* 8 (January–December 1880): 187–88; William D. Thrantham, "Wonderful Story of Richard R. Kirkland," *Confederate Veteran* 16/3 (March 1908): 106; Clemmer, "The Angel of Marye's Heights," 16–23.

but what they had on their backs. I do believe after seeing all I have I could murder the devils [Union soldiers] in cold blood, but I suppose Providence will punish them in His good time. This morning [21 December] just after sunrise I was patrolling the city with a detail and heard a woman's voice. I went in and found two women and one old man, the latter frozen to death. The Yankees had actually taken his mattress from under him. One of the women said she would have taken him to her house but she had none. It had been burnt by the Yankees.[40]

As soon as Burnside's forces had withdrawn across the Rappahannock, Lee's soldiers immediately went to work felling trees for firewood and constructing winter quarters on Marye's Heights. From experience gained the previous winter, many men built log huts with chimneys to keep out the cold. Others dug holes and covered themselves with remnants of tents. Still others built shelters, open to the south, covered them with pine brushes and warded off the chill by huge log fires in the front.[41]

For William Simmons and the men of his brigade, the warm glow of a great Confederate victory was tempered by the frigid weather and the loss of their leader, General Tom Cobb. Simmons also grieved for the loss of four men in his regiment, including one of the original members of the Gwinnett Volunteers, 2nd Lieutenant Julius S. Bowran, who was acting adjutant of the 16th Georgia. Bowran's brother, William, was killed three months earlier at Crampton's Gap.[42] Another sixty-two men in the 16th Georgia were wounded and four were captured.[43]

On 20 December the leaderless brigade went into winter quarters on the eastern slope of Marye's Heights,[44] but a final decision to remain in the encampment near Fredericksburg was not made until the next month when inclement weather made the roads impassable. Soon the conditions made it impractical for either side to undertake an active campaign. It was during this time that a renewed attack by Burnside became hopelessly stalled and was

---

[40]B. Edward Stiles to his aunt in Georgia, 21 December 1862, McKay-Stiles papers, Southern History Collection, University of North Carolina, Chapel Hill.

[41]Douglas Southall Freeman, *Lee's Lieutenants: A Study in Command*, vol. 2 (New York: Charles Scribner's Sons, 1943) 430.

[42]According to service records, the name is also spelled "Bowring" and "Bowran." Other fatalities from the 16th Georgia included Private A. J. Ambrose of Company I, 4th Sergeant James Kilgore of Company F, and 3rd Corporal John R. Lay of Company G. A(ndrew) J(ackson) Ambrose was a first cousin of Mary Ambrose, who would marry William Simmons in 1869.

[43]*OR*, ser. 1, vol. 21, 583; Byrd, *Them Brave Georgians*, 135. Of the wounded men, six were from Lieutenant Simmons's Company I of the 16th Georgia: privates T. F. M. Benningfield, J. N. Cates, James Glosson, Lewis A. Glosson, Edward D. Sammon, and W. B. Wright.

[44]Freeman, *Lee's Lieutenants*, 2:381.

thereafter known as the "Mud March."[45] There would be no more major conflicts until spring 1863.

The 16th Georgia and the rest of Cobb's Brigade carried on without a commanding officer for more than a month following the battle of Fredericksburg.[46] On 19 January 1863, General Robert E. Lee announced the selection of Colonel William Tatum Wofford of the 18th Georgia as the new brigade commander. Wofford was well known to Simmons and many of his fellow North Georgians, having been born in nearby Habersham County in 1823. At the age of thirteen, after the untimely death of his father, he enrolled in the Gwinnett Manual Labor Institute near Lawrenceville. In 1839 he entered the University of Georgia (Franklin College) in Athens. He later studied law under Judge Nathan L. Hutchins Sr. in Lawrenceville and began a law practice in Cassville, Georgia, in 1845.[47]

Like many of the high-ranking officers on both sides of the conflict, Wofford fought in the Mexican War. He received an appointment from Georgia governor George Towns in 1847 and raised a company of mounted volunteers. Wofford and his men saw action near Vera Cruz and at the village of Matesordera.[48] After the war, Wofford returned to his home in Cassville and resumed his law practice. He soon rose to prominence in politics, serving as a member of the Georgia legislature from 1849 through 1853. Wofford's political views were similar to those of James P. Simmons. He initially opposed the war, but he changed his position and cast his lot with the Confederacy when Georgia seceded from the Union. He was among the overwhelming majority of convention delegates who signed the Ordinance of Secession on 21 January 1861.[49]

In May 1861 Wofford was elected colonel of the 1st Regiment, 4th Brigade, Georgia State Volunteers. Two months later the 4th Brigade was disbanded and Wofford's regiment was sent to Richmond. On 9 August, the

---

[45] *OR*, ser. 1, vol. 21, 753–54.

[46] The following year there was a moving ceremony in Athens for the fallen general with four distinguished speakers selected by Nathan L. Hutchins Sr., judge of the Superior Courts of the Western Circuit of Georgia (*Southern Watchman* [Athens GA], 2 September 1863). See also "Confederate Necrology: Tribute of Respect Tuesday Morning 11th Day of August, 1863," *Georgia Historical Quarterly* 19/2 (June 1935): 63–64.

[47] Gerald J. Smith, *One of the Most Daring of Men: The Life of Confederate General William Tatum Wofford*, vol. 16 of Journal of Confederate History Series, ed. John McGlone (Murfreesboro, TN: Southern Heritage Press, 1997) 1–3; Bradley M. Gottfried, *Brigades of Gettysburg: Union and Confederate Brigades at the Battle of Gettysburg* (Cambridge, MA: Da Capo Press, 2002) 419.

[48] Smith, *One of the Most Daring of Men*, 4–5.

[49] For more in-depth information on Wofford's political life, see Smith, *One of the Most Daring of Men*, 9–23.

regiment was re-named the 18th Georgia and assigned to the brigade commanded by Brigadier General Louis T. Wigfall, a South Carolinian. In March 1862, following Wigfall's resignation, Colonel John Bell Hood was promoted to brigadier general and assumed command of the brigade. From that time on the unit would be known as "Hood's Texas Brigade."

After Hood was elevated to division commander in July 1862, Wofford, as senior colonel, assumed command of the Texas Brigade and led his men in the thick of the fighting for the rest of the year. When Wofford reported to his new assignment, he saw many familiar faces, including Nathan L. Hutchins Jr., the son of his mentor, whom he remembered from the time he studied law in Lawrenceville. Wofford's command was now an all-Georgia brigade that included his old regiment, the 18th Georgia, which had been re-assigned after the battle of Sharpsburg. This action was taken by President Jefferson Davis to place regiments from the same state together.

On the day after Wofford's promotion was announced, the bad weather worsened. A heavy rain fell continuously for two days. Another storm followed on 27 January and did not let up until more than six inches of snow fell on the shivering, ill-fed men.[50] Hundreds of Confederate soldiers had no covering of any kind for their feet. Many others lacked blankets and warm clothing. As the winter progressed, symptoms of scurvy began to appear as food supplies dwindled. Each regiment was directed to send out daily details to gather sassafras buds, wild onion, garlic, lamb's quarter, and poke sprouts to substitute for vegetables.[51]

The construction of shelters and large fires to deal with the frigid weather took its toll on the area forests, making it difficult to obtain fuel. By late February, the area was barren, as described by a young soldier in a letter to his family in Gwinnett County, Georgia:

> We have had some awful bad weather here of late. Last Sunday was the coldest day I ever saw. I think the snow is now one to two feet deep. We have had nothing but snow here lately. I have saw more snow this winter than I ever saw in my life. I am willing to leave this place for we have burned up all the wood around here. We have to burn old field pine bushes or tote our oak wood over a half a mile. This part of the country is ruined for all of the timber is cut down.[52]

---

[50]Krick, *Civil War Weather*, 83. There was a report of a six-inch snowfall at nearby Washington, DC, the night of 28–29 January 1863.

[51]*OR*, ser. 1, vol. 25, pt. 2, 687; Alexander, *Military Memoirs*, 318.

[52]Eli P. Landers to Susan Landers, 25 February 1863, in Roberson, *Yellow River*, 116. With regard to the snowfall and frigid temperatures, Landers was referring to the weekend of 22 February when nine inches of snow fell on Washington, DC. A week earlier there was a ten-inch accumulation in the capital (Krick, *Civil War Weather*, 88).

Despite the inclement weather and short rations, the soldiers engaged in a number of activities to relieve the tedium of camp life. There were numerous minstrel shows for entertainment, along with games of cat, town ball, and bull pen. Religious meetings also helped to fill the lonely hours. In the 16th Georgia Regiment, soldiers from a number of denominations formed the Christian Soldiers' Association. Each evening after roll call, the group gathered for prayers, hymns, and inspirational messages.[53]

During the winter camp, there was a snowball fight that began with a handful of soldiers and ultimately involved 9,000 officers and men. The good-humored "battle" was touched off after a late January snowfall by spirited Texas and Georgia troops, many of whom had never seen snow before joining the Confederate army. Regiments formed in line of battle and went at each other, firing volleys of packed snow while employing battlefield maneuvers. The regiments of Wofford's Brigade were in the thick of the action as described by an officer in the 18th Georgia:

> After our lines were formed we observed the 16th Georgia advancing on us. We met them head-on, officers joining the men and the balls flew fast and furious. We sent a flanking company of skirmishers who pelted the "enemy" from flank and rear and they gave way, with us following and firing our ice-bombs. After their defeat, we joined with them and went after the 24th [Georgia], which was late getting into line, as they had been building breastworks of snow. We assaulted their works in fine style, mounted and took the works, and then met them hand to hand. Boys were laughing as they fought one another, rolling about head over heels in the snow. After this last assault we were all about played out, and returned to our quarters exhausted but in good spirits.[54]

This monstrous but good-humored battle in the deep snow was also recounted by a soldier in Cobb's Legion Infantry Battalion in a letter to his brother in early February:

> I am well at present, except a bad cold which I caught playing in the snow. Yesterday, Cobb's [now Wofford's] Brigade formed in line of battle and marched about two miles in the snow to Kershaw's Brigade. All our officers was out, too. The field officers was on their horses.... Benjamin, great God, I never saw snow balls fly so in my life. I tell you it got so tight that some got to throwing rocks and then some to fighting sure enough, and

---

[53]"History of Service of Joseph White Woods, Soldier in the War between the States: Written by Himself after the War," in *Bible Records, Military Rosters and Reminiscences of Confederate Soldiers*, vol. 9 of *United Daughters of the Confederacy Bound Transcripts*, pp. 134–51, Georgia Department of Archives and History, Morrow, GA.

[54]Lemon, *Feed them the Steel*, 39.

then the snow balls and rocks flew, so that I got out of it as quick as possible.[55]

Throughout the cold winter months, Lieutenant Simmons and the 16th Georgia remained in their camp on Marye's Heights. Much of their time was spent shoring up the defenses by constructing field works and rifle pits. This was done to deter the Union army from crossing the Rappahannock by fords that would be passable by spring. Soon they would be on the march once again.

[55]James C. Mobley to Benjamin Mobley, 1 February 1863, Emory University Library Archives, Atlanta, GA. See also Mills Lane, ed., "*Dear Mother: Don't Grieve About Me. If I get Killed, I'll Only be Dead*": *Letters from Georgia Soldiers in the Civil War* (Savannah, GA: The Beehive Press) 220–21. Mobley served in Company E (Poythras Volunteers) from Burke County, GA, just south of Augusta. He said that the snow was "twelve inches thick" [at the campground] on the day he wrote and "nine [inches] deep where we fought the battle" the previous day.

9

Victory at Chancellorsville

We should always be booted and spurred, and ready to go.
—Montaigne

Shortly after assuming his new command, General Wofford began to draw up detailed plans to form an elite battalion of sharpshooters that would be selected from the three regiments and two battalions of his brigade.[1] In May of 1862 the Confederate Congress formally authorized the formation of sharpshooter battalions for each brigade to be made up of men who had demonstrated bravery under fire.[2] The captains of each company making up these battalions were to be appointed by the brigadier general, approved by the commanding general and commissioned by the secretary of war. Each sharpshooter captain was granted the authority to select such men as he desired and organize them into a permanent military component. Under the provisions of the statute, all promotions to officer were to be made for gallantry on the field and not by rank or seniority, as in the balance of the army, where the death of a regimental or line officer automatically enabled the promotion of the person in the next grade below. The men to be selected by company and regimental officers were to be excellent marksmen and possess the qualities of a good scout, especially the capacity for independent thought.[3] Confederate soldiers of all ranks now had a chance to be considered for a commission.

General Wofford carefully weighed the qualifications of all his young officers by considering their records, temperament, health, and physical abilities. After a careful review he selected Captain A. H. Patton to command the battalion. Wofford was well acquainted with Patton as one of his top officers in

---

[1] Gerald J. Smith, *One of the Most Daring of Men: The Life of Confederate General William Tatum Wofford*, vol. 16 of Journal of Confederate History Series, ed. John McGlone (Murfreesboro, TN: Southern Heritage Press, 1997) 65–66.

[2] The details are found in the Confederate War Department General Orders No. 34, dated 3 May 1862, and signed by Samuel Cooper, adjutant and inspector general. Subsequently, the War Department sent additional orders pertaining to sharpshooter training (target practice, judging distance, drill arms inspection, etc.), and organizational matters (Fred L. Ray, *Shock Troops of the Confederacy: The Sharpshooter Battalions of the Army of Northern Virginia* [Asheville, NC: CFS Press, 2006] 339–45).

[3] James Lile Lemon, *Feed them the Steel! Being the Wartime Recollections of Captain James Lile Lemon Company A, 18th Georgia Infantry* C.S.A. (Acworth, GA: printed by Mark H. Lemon, 2008) 39.

the 18th Georgia Infantry Regiment who served as his assistant adjutant general.[4] Also high on his list was Captain Nathan L. Hutchins Jr. and Lieutenant William E. Simmons of the 16th Georgia, Lieutenant Frederick E. Ross of Cobb's Legion, and several others who were considered worthy of promotion.

Although Wofford put a great deal of time and effort into the organization of his new sharpshooter battalion, there was strong opposition from a large segment of his brigade. Many soldiers had no desire to leave their friends and were determined to remain in their respective regiments. One officer from Cobb's Legion Infantry Battalion expressed is feelings in a letter to his wife several days before the Battle of Chancellorsville.

> I have been mad all week. General Wofford is trying to organize a battalion of sharpshooters from the Brigade. He has appointed an officer [Ross] from the Legion to raise a company from the Legion. The boys of our Company [G, the Panola Guards] to a man are opposed to leaving their old company.... It is mean to take men from the company of their choice against their wishes and put them in a company whose officers they do not like. The feeling against it in the Brigade is bitter, and if Wofford organizes the battalion, he will do it in the face of universal opposition.[5]

There were other reasons why many in Wofford's Brigade were opposed to his plan. Some felt that Wofford was only interested in providing promotions for his friends.[6] Many officers were concerned that the formation of such a unit would strip their regiment or company of its best men. Commanders of ordinary units were never happy about losing their most reliable men who could be counted on to hold the unit together in adverse situations.[7] One young

---

[4]Smith, *One of the Most Daring of Men*, 66. Patton was captain and brigade adjutant when he was considered and selected for promotion to lieutenant colonel by General Wofford. He previously commanded Company E (the Stephens Infantry from Gordon County) of the 18th Georgia Infantry Regiment.

[5]Samuel Burney to Sarah Elizabeth ("Sallie") Burney (nee Shepherd), 24 April 1863, in Nat Turner, ed., *A Southern Soldier's Letters Home: The Civil War Letters of Samuel Burney, ANV* (Macon: Mercer University Press, 2002) 246. The "officer from the Legion" was Captain Frederick E. Ross of Carroll County, Georgia, who was selected to become the officer in charge of Company D in the 3rd Battalion Sharpshooters. Despite what Burney described as "universal opposition," according to service records (Burney stated "the boys of our company to a man are opposed to leaving their old company"), at least 48 men from Cobb's Legion Infantry Battalion served in the sharpshooter battalion. Of this group, all but two were assigned to Company D.

[6]Ibid.

[7]Russell K. Brown, *Our Connection With Savannah: A History of the 1st Battalion Georgia Sharpshooters* (Macon: Mercer University Press, 2004) 2.

lieutenant complained that "eleven men will be forced to leave our company and join [the sharpshooters]. We will hate to lose eleven men, but they must go."[8]

Wofford was anxious to secure official approval and complete the training of his new sharpshooter battalion, but more urgent matters faced the Confederate high command. With improving weather, the Union army initiated another aggressive campaign to take Richmond. On 28 April Yankee forces slowly crossed the Rappahannock River on the upper fords. The Army of the Potomac was now under the command of Major General Joseph Hooker, who was appointed by President Lincoln shortly after Burnside's disastrous "Mud March" ended in January. Hooker was transferred from the Western Theater of war where he had once boasted that "while in command of the army of the west he had only been able to see the backs of the Confederate soldiers." When he took command of the Army of the Potomac, he dated his general orders "Headquarters in the saddle."[9] Hooker had a reputation as a hard drinker who was often arrogant and impulsive, but the North was desperate for a decisive victory. This was the fifth attempt in less than two years for the Union army to advance on the Confederate capital.

Hooker elected to pick up where Burnside had left off, and crossed the Rappahannock in a feint three miles below Fredericksburg. While this movement progressed half of his forces made river crossings above the Confederate fortifications.[10] Early in the morning of 29 April artillery and small arms fire along the river indicated that the Federals were massing for an attack on Confederate positions.[11] Within a few minutes Wofford's command moved to the front to block the advance of the northern troops. The men held their position for two days until Barksdale's Brigade relieved them just after midnight on 1 May. They then made a night march up the Plank Road with the brigades of Kershaw and Semmes to intercept Union forces advancing from United States Ford and from the nearby crossroads of Chancellorsville. By 6:00 A.M. the three brigades were in position at Smith's Hill and joined up with General Anderson's command.[12]

---

[8]Samuel Burney to Sarah Elizabeth ("Sallie") Burney, 26 April 1863, in Turner, ed., *A Southern Soldier's Letters Home*, 248. According to service records, thirteen men from Burney's company served in the 3rd Sharpshooter Battalion. Among this number were 2nd Lieutenant James M. Almond, Sergeant William J. Hogan, and Privates Rufus D. Brown, William H. Minton, Wesley Short, Lucious L. ("Luke") Wittich, Elijah D. Young and James H. Young.

[9]Christopher Columbus Sanders, "Reminiscences of the Battle of Chancellorsville," *Atlanta Journal*, 23 November 1902.

[10]*The War of the Rebellion: A Compilation of the Official Records of the Union and Confederate Armies* (70 vols. in 128; Washington, 1880–1901), ser. I, vol. 25, pt. 1, 796–97. Hereafter cited as OR.

[11]Ibid., 829, 833.

[12]Ibid., 797, 824.

Later that morning Stonewall Jackson and his forces reached the front and immediately launched an attack.[13] McLaws quickly collected his brigades to join the battle. They were then joined by Mahone's and Perry's brigades of Anderson's Division. After proceeding about a mile, skirmishers in advance of the troops began to fire on the Federal forces. Under a scattering fire from enemy infantry and artillery some 400–500 yards in the distance, a line of battle was formed across the turnpike with Mahone's and Wofford's brigades making up the center.[14]

A short advance brought the gray line to the edge of a wooded area overlooking open fields where the enemy was deploying. Soon the Union infantry pushed forward. When they were within easy range, the order was given to commence firing. The Federals recoiled, took cover, and returned the fire. A bluecoat charge ensued but was promptly repulsed. As the gray line began to advance, Wofford's and Perry's brigades encountered no resistance. The enemy had fallen back without firing. Together the two Confederate brigades captured several prisoners and found some abandoned munitions and commissary stores.[15]

By 4:00 P.M. the Union forces were finally driven from the battlefield, leaving knapsacks, blankets, overcoats, and other valuable articles behind them. Confederates pursued the enemy for more than two miles until darkness found them directly facing the Federals' strongly entrenched position at Chancellorsville. Here they bivouacked for the night.[16]

The next day General Wofford received orders to distract the enemy while Stonewall Jackson's forces executed a flanking movement.[17] Careful reconnaissance had revealed that the right of the Yankee battle line in front of Chancellorsville was unprotected. If it could be reached, the entire line might be driven back to the river. Slowly, the entire gray line moved to the left, bringing Wofford's men to a position straddling the turnpike. Near the close of the day Simmons and his comrades heard the sound of firing, which signaled the onset of Jackson's flanking attack. Although faint at first, it grew steadily louder, suggesting that the enemy was being driven back. General McLaws then gave orders for his division to advance along the whole line and engage the Federal skirmishers. They were directed to threaten and harass the enemy, but not to launch a full-scale attack. This was done to deter reinforcement of the Yankee battle line.[18]

Although Wofford's sharpshooters were not formally designated, the battalion was actively engaged in the fighting in the Battle of Chancellorsville.

---

[13]Ibid., 825, 833.
[14]Ibid., 833–34, 874.
[15]Ibid., 825, 830, 834.
[16]Ibid., 834.
[17]Ibid., 798.
[18]Ibid., 826.

One participant was Lieutenant A. J. Reese of Phillips's Legion, who was put in charge of a company of fifty-three sharpshooters.[19] Around 10:00 P.M. on 2 May, Reese's company and the rest of the sharpshooters pushed ahead in front of the brigade to confront the enemy. Wofford personally led the charge of his newly formed battalion on horseback. This was something seldom done by a brigadier, but Wofford wanted to inspire his men. His brigade followed, and according to McLaws, "[Wofford] became so seriously engaged that I directed him to withdraw…his men in good spirits after driving the enemy to their entrenchments."[20] This bold move was witnessed by an officer in the 18th Georgia who watched the sharpshooters follow Wofford into battle:

> General Wofford gallantly rode at the head of the…sharp-shooters and advanced so impetuously that they became separated from the rest of us. We followed quickly behind and soon emerged into a clearing on the edge of which we spied a Yankee battery. Wofford and the sharp-shooters were heavily engaged with them and had nearly overrun and captured the guns. We moved up quickly to their support and began a hot exchange of fire with the infantry supports. We began to slowly drive them from their positions and had nearly broken their lines, when we were ordered back, much to our fury and astonishment.[21]

Darkness prevented further attacks and the men slept that night along the battle line they then held.

The Saturday evening charge was described by William R. Montgomery, who had recently been selected from the ranks to become an officer in the sharpshooter battalion. In a letter to his mother and sister written after the battle, he wrote how well the men had performed in their new role: "I tell you we done it [performed well in our first engagement]…to perfection. You ought to hear General Wofford praise us. Saturday evening our little battalion charged the Yankies breast work, one whole brigade behind it, charged three times but the fire was hot from the enemy. We had to fall back."[22]

---

[19]A. J. Reese to his uncle, 8 May 1863, in "Collection of Confederate Letters," drawer 186, box 31, Georgia Department of Archives & History, Morrow, GA. Reese was from Company E (Blue Ridge Rangers) in Phillips Legion Infantry Battalion. According to service records, he returned to lead his company in Phillips Legion soon after the Battle of Chancellorsville (Mills Lane, ed., *"Dear Mother: Don't Grieve About Me. If I get Killed, I'll Only be Dead": Letters from Georgia Soldiers in the Civil War* [Savannah, GA: Beehive Press] 231).
[20]Smith, *One of the Most Daring of Men*, 68; *OR*, ser. I, vol. 25, pt. 1, 826.
[21]Lemon, *Feed them the Steel*, 40.
[22]William R. Montgomery to Elizabeth Ann Montgomery (nee Young) and sisters, 7 May 1863 (George Montgomery Jr., *Georgia Sharpshooter: The Civil War Diary and Letters of William Rhadamanthus Montgomery* [Macon: Mercer University Press, 1997]

Just before sunrise on Sunday 3 May, the battle resumed in earnest. The Confederates launched a fierce attack that lasted for about a half an hour. A second charge carried the Southerners within a few yards of the Federal breastworks. After an hour of intense fighting, the Confederate forces withdrew, reformed, and charged for a third time. By this time, the Union ranks were seriously depleted.[23]

The third hour-long attack was followed in a few minutes by a fourth. In the midst of combat, the newly-formed sharpshooters and the rest of Wofford's Brigade showed the tempered qualities that had been forged in some of the hardest fought engagements of the war. The Federals in their breastworks directly in front of the 16th Georgia had left an opening for their retreating skirmishers to get to cover. This opening had been filled with logs, but no earth had been thrown against them, nor had ditches been dug in front. The abatis of felled trees with sharpened branches pointing toward the assaulting force was also fairly sparse and no soldiers were positioned behind it. Led by the sharpshooters, the men of the 16th Georgia immediately advanced and probed this weak point in the Yankee line. They planted their battle flag within 100 feet of the breastworks and held their position despite heavy fire on both sides.[24]

Once again, General Wofford boldly led his men into battle. Nearby, Lieutenant James L. Lemon of Wofford's old regiment (the 18th Georgia) noted that after emerging from thick woods into a clearing, they faced "galling fire" from the Yankee infantry well-posted behind their works:

> General Wofford gallantly led us towards the works, hat in hand as was his style, and calling in a loud voice, "Press them my boys, that's the way." In the face of enfilading fire, Wofford was forced to withdraw his troops back to the protection of the woods at the far edge of the clearing. From that vantage point, the general and his staff carefully observed the enemy's activity, and after a very short time called his men to assemble for yet another charge. The order was given to fix bayonets, and move out of the timber. Wofford was again waving his hat as he rode and yelling, "Charge them boys, charge them with a will!" and "Give them some steel!" This time the brigade surged through the breastworks, and after a sharp fight, the Yankees fled from their defensive position.[25]

About 9:00 A.M., after the Federal forces began to fall back, General Wofford ordered a portion of his command to take up positions behind the retreating bluecoats in a wide encircling movement to prevent the escape of a considerable body of the enemy. Once surrounded, the entrapped Federals sent

---

77). At the time he wrote the letter, Montgomery was waiting for confirmation of his officer's commission and promotion to lieutenant.
[23]*OR*, ser. I, vol. 25, pt. 1, 343.
[24]Ibid., 344.
[25]Lemon, *Feed them the Steel*, 40–41.

out a flag of truce. Wofford's decisive action resulted in the capture of 340 Union officers and men, including a large portion of the 27th Connecticut and 145th Pennsylvania. Although the two Union regiments surrendered to General Paul Semmes, General McLaws concluded that Wofford deserved a great deal of the credit.[26]

Later that day, Wofford's Brigade was ordered to new positions at the junction of the Plank and Mine Roads to cut off the Union movement down either of these routes that threatened the Confederate rear. When it became apparent that an advance was unlikely, the brigade joined up with the remainder of McLaws's Division on the Plank Road at Salem Church, only three miles from Fredericksburg.[27] The combined force literally swept the enemy from the field. In their haste the retreating Federals left behind a treasure trove of weapons and accouterments.[28] Over the course of three days the 16th Georgia and other regiments under McLaws had marched from Fredericksburg, fought and defeated greatly superior forces, reversed their steps, and were now prepared to meet new masses of the enemy. As the day came to an end, Wofford's men held their position at Salem Church and spent the night. The new sharpshooter battalion was actively engaged until after midnight, according to a young sergeant who had been selected from Phillips Legion Infantry Battalion:

> We still moved forward, pressing them at every point until 1 o'clock at night, capturing many prisoners. Sharp Shooters made a charge in a pine thicket, not knowing anybody was in it, dark as Egypt, fired a volley and you ought to have heard the Yanks beg for quarter. [We] took a Lieutenant Colonel and about a half a regiment. We pushed forward as far as we thought prudent in the night. Layed down on the road side to sleep.[29]

The following morning, Monday 4 May, Wofford's Georgians were thrown forward along with Kershaw's Brigade of South Carolinians against a much larger Union force. Being badly outnumbered, the two brigades soon withdrew to their original positions, where they spent the rest of the day awaiting orders.[30]

Finally at 6:00 P.M. three guns fired in rapid succession, signaling the attack on the enemy. Through a dense thicket of tangled brushwood and fences

---

[26]*OR*, ser. I, vol. 25, pt. 1, 336, 344, 826, 83; Ray, *Shock Troops*, 56–57; Montgomery, *Georgia Sharpshooter*, 84. Montgomery claimed that "800 or 900 men [Union soldiers] had surrendered to a small band of sharpshooters," but a more accurate number was somewhere around 350. The Union soldiers who were surrounded actually surrendered to Brigadier General Paul J. Semmes of McLaws's Division.

[27]*OR*, ser. I, vol. 25, pt. 1, 827, 835.

[28]Lemon, *Feed them the Steel*, 41.

[29]William R. Montgomery to Elizabeth Ann Montgomery (nee Young) and sisters, 7 May 1863, in Montgomery, *Georgia Sharpshooter*, 85.

[30]*OR*, ser. I, vol. 25, pt. 1, 827.

Wofford's Brigade progressed slowly and with great difficulty, harassed by a constant fire of shell and canister. However, when they emerged from the woods into open ground they discovered that the enemy had fled. It was now beginning to get dark and visibility was limited, but noise of great confusion came from the direction of Banks Ford where the Yankees were in full retreat. The 16th Georgia and Wofford's other regiments rushed toward the River Road, engaging the Union forces and driving them toward the river.[31]

In their pursuit of the Union troops, Wofford's Brigade came upon a house where a small detachment of Union infantry was making a stand. After a well-aimed volley, the force of about forty soldiers and a lieutenant colonel surrendered. Wofford spoke to the owner of the house, who volunteered his services to guide them to the river through the woods in the growing darkness. The brigade came within three-quarters of a mile of the enemy's pontoon bridges at Banks Ford. Since his brigade was "perilously" in advance of the Confederate forces and given the darkness, Wofford realized that he and his men were in danger of taking friendly fire and ordered the troops to halt. Signal flares were fired to mark the location and a courier was sent to General McLaws. The order quickly came back to not advance any further. Wofford became "white-hot with rage" upon receiving the order. He was convinced that the bridge at Banks Ford could have been taken with little difficulty and a large number of the Union army could be cut off and captured. That night, the exhausted soldiers "laid on their arms" and slept beside the road.[32]

By the next morning, the Union army had retreated across the Rappahannock. A heavy fog clung to the river, limiting visibility to twenty yards. Skirmishers were thrown out, but nothing of the enemy was found except its dead and wounded and some discarded munitions. The wounded soldiers left behind alternately called for help and heaped curses on friends who had abandoned them in their distress.[33] Southern soldiers now buried the dead, attended to the wounded, and collected Federal arms and accouterments discarded the night before. Errands of mercy were abruptly curtailed at 2:30 that afternoon by a severe wind and rainstorm that continued into the next day.

After the fighting had ceased, Eli P. Landers wrote down his recollections of the battle in a letter to his mother:

> We have had some awful times here for the last ten days. We have been in line of battle all of the time marching through the woods, mud, and swamps and some part of the army was fighting all the time. The 3rd of May our Brigade got into it heels overhead and our regiment lost more men than we ever have in arry fight yet.... We fought desperately to gain

---

[31]Ibid., 828, 831.

[32]Lemon, *Feed them the Steel*, 42.

[33]D. Augustus Dickert, *History of Kershaw's Brigade* (1899; reprint, Wilmington, NC: Broadfoot Publishing Company, 1990) 219.

the day but after all our destruction we captured the whole passel of the line that was fighting us. They raised from their trench with a white flag and surrendered to us like lambs. Three cheers for the Army of the Potomac! I must brag although our brigade suffered worse than any other, but my heart is full of thanks for the great skill that has been manifested among us. During the fight we have defeated the enemy…. We have drove old Hooker and his bluecoats back over the Dare Mark [Rappahannock], but thousands of them will never get back.[34]

Although the soldiers of Wofford's Brigade were exhausted after days of intense marching and fighting, they were thankful for a great victory. One young lieutenant from Phillips Legion shared his thoughts in a letter to his uncle in Georgia: "I am well worn out going through what we have had to go through with for the last week or more. But I feel thankful that I am still spared and now with the living. This has been one of the great battles of the war. There was fighting for upwards of 30 miles up and down the river."[35]

Chancellorsville was one of the hardest-fought battles in the War Between the States. The Army of Northern Virginia had won a great victory against an enemy more than twice their size, but the men were shocked and saddened by the news that Stonewall Jackson had been seriously wounded by a Southern sentry who mistook him for an enemy soldier. Their concern turned to grief several days later when they learned that Jackson had died from his wounds.

The battle had taken its toll on Wofford's Brigade, which suffered 562 casualties, including 70 men killed, and 448 wounded or missing.[36] Of the brigade's dead and wounded, 133 were from the 16th Georgia with 18 killed and 115 wounded. There were also casualties among the men who made up the newly formed sharpshooter battalion. The greatest loss was the commanding officer, Captain A. H. Patton, who had been recommended for promotion to lieutenant colonel. Two other sharpshooters who had served in Phillips Legion were killed: 2nd Lieutenant Peyton W. Fuller and 4th Corporal William E. Ruede. Seventeen others were wounded, including three men from the 16th Georgia: 2nd Sergeant Oscar Benson, and privates G. W. Davis and James R. Wood.[37] Once again, William Simmons came through the battle unscathed.

---

[34]Eli P. Landers to Susan Landers, 8 May 1863, in Elizabeth Whitley Roberson, *In Care of Yellow River* (Fort Lauderdale: Venture Press, 1994) 122–23.

[35]A. J. Reese to his uncle, 8 May 1863, "Collection of Confederate Letters," drawer 186, box 31, Georgia Department of Archives & History, Morrow, GA; Lane, *Dear Mother*, 231–32.

[36]Lemon, *Feed them the Steel*, 42.

[37]According to service records, most of the sharpshooter casualties came from men who had served in Phillips Legion Infantry Battalion and the 18th Georgia Infantry Regiment. Among the wounded were 2nd Lieutenant Joseph W. Barrett, and privates Henry J. Fincher, Thomas W. Griffin, Jonathan King, Newton J. Rich, Thomas J.

Shoemaker and A. J. Shular from Phillips Legion; 1st Corporal L. M. Mann, and privates C. H. Humphries, Eli Jenkins and S. J. Richardson from the 18th Georgia; and 2nd Lieutenant Joseph G. Nichols, and privates Elias W. Boss and Littleton M. Wall from the 24th Georgia.

10

Wofford's Georgia Sharpshooters

> Neither talent without instruction, nor instruction without talent can
> produce the perfect craftsman.
>
> —Vitruvius

After the great victory at Chancellorsville, the Army of Northern Virginia was given a well-deserved rest. For the next month, the officers and men remained at their camp near Fredericksburg and prepared for further campaigns. There was a light schedule of drilling and refitting. The ranks of the Army swelled in number with the addition of conscripts and the return of wounded soldiers to duty.[1]

During the lull in the action, General Wofford again turned his attention to administrative matters. On 25 April 1863, just before the Battle of Chancellorsville, he had requested formal approval of his plan to form a sharpshooter battalion.[2] He realized that in the early months of the war, little thought had been given to building fortifications and taking positions behind earthworks. At that time, most Confederate soldiers had a great disdain for digging trenches, which they considered to be work for slaves. Besides, they felt that they were too brave and daring to hide behind a pile of dirt.[3]

Once they had been in combat, however, these soldiers quickly began to realize the importance of fortifications on the battlefield. In spring 1862, they had taken their places behind earthworks at Yorktown where they successfully held off the Yankees who had tried to wade through the chilly waters of the Warwick River in front of Magruder's trenches. At Williamsburg, large numbers

---

[1]D. Augustus Dickert, *History of Kershaw's Brigade* (1899; reprint, Wilmington, NC: Broadfoot Publishing Company, 1990) 221–23; G. Moxley Sorrel, *Recollections of a Confederate Staff Officer*, ed. Bell Irvin Wiley (Wilmington, NC: Broadfoot Publishing Company, 1995) 150–51.

[2]General W. T. Wofford to Major J. M. Goggin, Assistant Adjutant General, McLaws's Division, 25 April 1863. Filed with the personal papers of Nathan L. Hutchins Jr., 16th Georgia Regiment, in the National Archives, Washington, DC, are the originals of letters dated 23, 25, 27 April 1863 and 11 May 1863 (in *Compiled Service Records of Confederate Soldiers Who Served in Organizations from the State of Georgia*, microcopy 266, RG 109, National Archives and Records Administration, Washington, DC). This correspondence was captured by Federal forces following the fall of Richmond. Correspondence from this collection is hereafter cited as Hutchins letters.

[3]Joseph L. Brent, *Memoirs of the War between the States* (New Orleans: 1940) 128.

of minie balls were absorbed and deflected by the earthworks that protected them. At Malvern Hill, when the 16th Georgia attacked Hiram Berdan's Sharpshooters arrayed in front of the Union battle line, the Georgians were sheltered by deep ravines at the foot of a high plateau that formed a natural trenching. At Fredericksburg the Southerners decimated wave after wave of Union soldiers from behind the bolstered stone wall along the sunken Telegraph Road. Based on these experiences disdain for fortification began to disappear. Self-preservation caused a demand for entrenching tools as well as firearms. The spade and mattock became an important part of an infantry soldier's equipment, along with his rifle and ammunition.[4]

Trenches were also dictated by other considerations. Given the smaller population of the Confederate States, public policy required the husbanding of every life. Disease, wounds, and death were decimating the Confederate army faster than volunteers or conscripts could fill the dwindling ranks. The preservation and effective utilization of limited forces led to the use of trenches whenever a battle line was formed. Often pickets on duty scooped up protective piles of dirt and rocks for protection.

As the war progressed, advance troops became more responsible for the outcome of a battle. In the early months of the war they were often chosen at random. Men and officers selected as necessity dictated for a specific situation might come from several brigades, unknown to each other. Such conditions made coordination and concerted action difficult. The pickets and skirmishers were so important, however, that it was imperative to improve their training and organizational structure.[5]

Following the guidelines set forth by the Confederate Congress, General Wofford carefully considered candidates for the new sharpshooter battalion, which he believed would improve the efficiency of his brigade in combat. He decided to establish six companies of fifty men from among his three infantry regiments and two legion battalions, and select a sharpshooter battalion commander and subordinate officers. In a letter to Major J. M. Goggin, assistant adjutant general of McLaws's Division, Wofford wrote, "It is imperative that good marksmen of tried courage and steadiness be chosen."

After appointing a commanding officer for the battalion, Wofford selected six sharpshooter captains from among the lieutenants in his brigade, including two from the 16th Georgia. He felt that the men he selected "were most distinguished for good conduct in battle and general qualifications as officers."

---

[4]John D. Young, "A Campaign with Sharpshooters," in *The Annals of the War: Written by Leading Participants, North and South* (1879; reprint, Gettsyburg, PA: Civil War Times, 1974) 267.

[5]Daniel M. Byrd Jr., *Them Brave Georgians*, manuscript, Gwinnett Historical Society archives, Lawrenceville, GA p. 156 (Fort Delaware Society Library, Delaware City, DE, also has a copy.).

Each of the newly appointed officers was then directed to recruit fifty-three men from volunteers in their regiment. From each of these newly formed companies, Wofford then selected the three most distinguished in battle and good conduct as lieutenants.[6]

By 25 April the selection process was completed, and Wofford sent a detailed report to Major Goggin.[7] "I have labored," he wrote, "and taken great pains to select those who are best qualified and who are entitled to promotion for their gallantry upon the field of battle and general good conduct since entering the service." He continued, "All these officers without exception are young, healthy, and athletic, and from the best evidence that I could procure, are moral intelligent gentlemen. In point of courage, intelligence, and morality, I feel justified in saying that they are equal if not superior to the officers of any regiment or battalion in this brigade." By the name of each officer he wrote a concise statement of their qualifications and how they distinguished themselves in battle. Next to Lieutenant Simmons's name Wofford wrote, "He is a young officer of fine education and attainments; distinguished in battle for coolness and courage."[8]

After learning that he had been selected to lead one of the six companies in the newly formed sharpshooter battalion, Lieutenant Simmons was delighted about the prospect of his promotion and new assignment. His excitement was shared by a sergeant in Phillips Legion Infantry Battalion, William R. Montgomery, one of three enlisted men in his company who were selected for an officer's commission. In a letter sent to his mother and sister several days after the Battle of Chancellorsville, Montgomery wrote,

> I forgot to tell you about the Sharp Shooters. Gen. Wofford had 50 men detailed from each Regt in the brigade to form a battalion of Sharp Shooters. Bill Anderson[9] is recommended to the President for Capt., [and] myself for first lieutenant.... Perhaps you don't know what our duty is. We are always in front of the Brigade, about 300 to 400 yds. to clear out the way.[10]

The formation of the new sharpshooter battalion, with its attendant

---

[6]General W. T. Wofford to Major J. M. Groggin, 28 April 1863, Hutchins letters.
[7]Ibid., 25 April 1863.
[8]Byrd, *Them Brave Georgians*, 159; General W. T. Wofford to Major J. M. Groggin, 25 April 1863, Hutchins letters.
[9]Lieutenant William D. Anderson, formerly of Company M in Phillips Legion Infantry Battalion. The company was initially established in Cobb County during the early months of the war as the Denmead Volunteers.
[10]William R. Montgomery to Elizabeth Ann Montgomery (nee Young) and sisters, 7 May 1863, in George Montgomery Jr., *Georgia Sharpshooter: The Civil War Diary and Letters of William Rhadamanthus Montgomery* (Macon: Mercer University Press, 1997) 83–84.

promotions and assignments, was also noted by Eli P. Landers of 16th Georgia, now a sergeant, in an undated letter to his mother:

> Tell A. W. [Archibald "Arch" Washington McDaniel, a cousin] that our sharpshooters is all fixed up now. Lieutenant Martin[11] and Simmons is now company captains, and Captain Hutchins is now Colonel of the Battalion, and John W. King from Cobb's Legion is company captain.[12] We will have another lieutenant to elect to fill the vacancy of Lieutenant Martin. The Captain and 1st lieutenant and sergeants from the "Hutchins Guards" [the more commonly used nickname for the Gwinnett Volunteers] joined the sharpshooters. They will have to elect two Lieutenants.[13]

On 28 April Major General Lafayette McLaws endorsed his approval of Wofford's recommendations and directed that the proposals be immediately submitted to higher authorities. However, the Union crossings of the Rappahannock and the subsequent Battle of Chancellorsville delayed the normal process and the papers remained at McLaws's division headquarters. By 21 May the misplaced papers were located and McLaws endorsed a second approval, with which Longstreet concurred. Four days later General Robert E. Lee gave his personal approval, adding in his own handwriting, "For companies of the size proposed, I think a captain and three lieutenants would be sufficient, if the law permits it."[14] On 5 June, the secretary of war gave his final approval and Wofford's recommended promotions became official.[15]

News of the secretary's approval reached General Wofford three days later when his brigade was camped at Culpeper Court House. That day Wofford formally announced the formation of the 3rd Georgia Sharpshooter Battalion, along with the promotions and the commissions of the new officers. In addition to Simmons, Martin, Anderson, and King, the other new sharpshooter captains included M. F. Crumley and Garnett McMillan.[16]

---

[11]2nd Lieutenant John F. Martin served in Private Landers's Company H of the 16th Georgia. He was selected by General Wofford to lead Company E of the Sharpshooter battalion.

[12]John W. King was a private in the Bowdon Volunteers (Company B of Cobb's Legion Infantry Battalion) before taking over leadership of Company D of the Sharpshooter Battalion.

[13]Eli P. Landers to Susan Landers, undated, in Elizabeth Whitley Roberson, *In Care of Yellow River* (Fort Lauderdale: Venture Press, 1994) 41.

[14]Byrd, *Them Brave Georgians*, 160–61; General W. T. Wofford to Major J. M. Goggin, 11 May 1863, Hutchins letters. The reverse of the letter from this date contains all approvals as well as General McLaws's explanation of the delay in forwarding the recommendations.

[15]General W. T. Wofford to Major J. M. Goggin, 11 May 1863, Hutchins letters.

[16]The six sharpshooter captains were assigned to companies designated as follows: Company A, M. F. Crumley; Company B, Garnett McMillan; Company C, William E.

The commanding officer selected to replace R. H. Patton and lead the new battalion was Simmons's close friend and fellow townsman, Captain Nathan L. Hutchins Jr. of Company I, 16th Georgia, who was promoted to lieutenant colonel. Wofford greatly admired the new sharpshooter commander and had known him since childhood. He praised Hutchins as "a young man of fine natural ability and attainments, great gallantry, and in every way qualified to fill the position for which he is recommended."[17]

Upon hearing the official news of his promotion and new position, Captain Simmons wrote that he was delighted with his promotion. He felt a sense of pride to be included among a group of new officers to lead a battalion of "picked men who had displayed such valor on the battlefield." It was, in itself, a singular honor to be recommended by General Wofford, approved by generals McLaws, Longstreet, and Lee, and commissioned by the secretary of war.[18] Simmons described the important role of the sharpshooters in battle in his journal:

> In the future, when the brigade meets the enemy, the men of the sharpshooter battalion march in advance and, after locating the enemy's lines, fire the opening shots of the engagement. Once the opposing lines are engaged, the sharpshooters rejoin the ranks and act as file closers, in order to prevent any soldier or officer from skulking. They would be the first advance and the last to retreat.[19]

Soon after its formation, the new sharpshooter battalion was sent to a separate camp for training and placed on an independent footing, reporting directly to brigade headquarters. The new commander started at once to improve the proficiency of the sharpshooters in specialized skills and tactics. Skirmish drill, target practice, bayonet exercise and practice in estimating distance were prerequisites to achieving successful operations.[20]

Although he had no experience in training sharpshooters, Wofford had the opportunity to observe the training regimen of General Robert Rodes's sharpshooter battalion during the winter lull that followed the Confederate victory at Fredericksburg.[21] The training was led by a young Confederate officer

---

Simmons; Company D, John W. King (replaced Frederick E. Ross, who declined); Company E, John F. Martin; and Company F, William D. Anderson.

[17]The other sharpshooter captains received similar praise from Wofford. One of the group, William D. Anderson, had been promoted from the ranks as a private. Wofford recognized his courage and leadership and noted that "He is qualified to fill any regimental or company office" (General W. T. Wofford to Major J. M. Goggin, 25 April 1863, Hutchins letters).

[18]Byrd, *Them Brave Georgians*, 162–63.

[19]Ibid., 161–62.

[20]Ibid.

[21]Fred L. Ray, *Shock Troops of the Confederacy: The Sharpshooter Battalions of the Army of Northern Virginia* (Asheville, NC: CFS Press, 2006) 50. The author wrote that "a

and native Virginian, Eugene Blackford. In the early months of the war Captain Blackford raised an infantry company in Alabama and attached it to Rodes's 5th Alabama Regiment, which was assigned to the Army of Northern Virginia. Blackford and Rodes became good friends and worked closely together to share what they had learned from their battlefield experience.

Rodes felt strongly about the need of trained skirmishers instead of the haphazard way of calling for details from each company when approaching the enemy. He knew from experience that when confronted with this situation, company officers would often select less qualified men so that they could keep their best soldiers in the main body of the regiment. He wanted to remedy this problem by making the corps of sharpshooters into an elite unit of volunteers.[22]

Under Rodes's system, each regiment detailed a sharpshooter company, commanded by a lieutenant, with a sergeant "to act as a guide orderly" and a second non-commissioned officer. As an incentive these chosen men were exempt from routine camp duties. Only the best soldiers were selected, men who met the standards of soldiering, marksmanship and "fidelity to the Southern Cause." The soldiers selected were also rewarded by being provided with the best line weapons available. It is likely that Enfield rifles were employed, given their relative availability and proven accuracy at longer ranges.[23]

In training Rodes's sharpshooters, Blackford introduced a number of innovations to the troops. Rather than shouting or relying on one bugler to send out commands to the skirmish line, he used three or four buglers to be heard above the din of battle at great distances. Blackford added new bugle calls, and even worked out a system of indicating ranges with them. To emphasize their new role, he trained his men to estimate distances before they began target practice. To improve accuracy in range estimation, Blackford hid men in front of the battalion at various ranges known only to him. He then had his buglers call up each man with a series of notes. As soon as each man appeared, the rifleman would estimate the range. The estimate would then be compared to the actual distance and recorded to determine accuracy and the progress of each shooter.

To speed up target practice, Blackford had four-foot deep pits dug in front of the targets and placed a man in each pit with a long-handled paddle, black on one side and white on the other. If the shooter hit the bull's-eye, he saw the

---

day seldom passed without at least one general officer visiting Blackford's unit." It is very likely that General William T. Wofford was an observer during the time he was drawing up plans for his own sharpshooter battalion to be formed.

[22]Ray, Shock *Troops*, 45.

[23]W. S. Dunlop, *Lee's Sharpshooters or the Forefront of Battle: A Story of Southern Valor That Never Has Been Told Before* (1899; reprint, Dayton, OH: Morningside House, Inc., 1988) 22. According to Dunlop, the Enfield was tested along with the Austrian, Belgium, Springfield, Mississippi, and Minie rifles and was found to be more accurate and effective at longer distances, especially in the 600–900 yard range. See also Ray, *Shock Troops*, 46.

black side of the paddle. Whenever the shot hit anywhere else on the target, the white side was shown. This practice made it possible for a large number of men to fire at the same target and assess their skills instantly. Results were recorded to measure accuracy and progress. Any man who failed to improve his marksmanship was sent back to his regiment.[24]

In Wofford's Brigade and other Confederate units, sharpshooters were allowed to act more independently than conventional infantry. Whether skirmishing, in rifle pits, or on picket duty, they normally used their own judgment when circumstances required them to open fire. As accomplished marksmen, they had the shooting experience and as sharpshooters the tactical leeway to seek support for their rifle and exploit cover against enemy counter-fire.[25]

According to John Anderson Morrow, there were two basic types of sharpshooters in the Confederate army, "Whitworth sharpshooters" and "battalion sharpshooters." The Whitworth sharpshooters, named for the superb and very expensive[26] British-made long-range rifles they carried, were much smaller in number and typically operated independently. These men functioned primarily as snipers, although the term "sniper" was not used during the War Between the States. Like Blackford's Sharpshooter Battalion, the 3rd Georgia Sharpshooters were in latter group. Morrow further describes the role of battalion sharpshooters: "The battalion sharpshooters were essentially what would have been termed 'light infantry' of the previous century. They served as pickets, scouts, and advanced skirmishers. Often, they were handpicked men."[27] Another writer characterized the 3rd Georgia Sharpshooter Battalion as "an elite spearhead to lead...[Wofford's] already casehardened veterans." Like other battalion sharpshooter units, they were "specially trained for skirmish duty and for sniper harassment of the enemy." Yet another writer described the 3rd Battalion Sharpshooters ". . . like spikeheads of Toledo steel, under officers highly approved by General Wofford."[28] Other characteristics were noted by Gerald J. Smith:

> To increase the *élan* and promote the elite nature of these units, the "scouts" as they were known, were exempt from all onerous camp duty.

---

[24]For additional information on Blackford's sharpshooter training methods, see Ray, *Shock Troops*, 46–50.

[25]Major John L. Plaster, *Sharpshooting in the Civil War* (Boulder, CO: Paladin Press) 83.

[26]The estimated cost of a Whitworth long-range rifle was $1,200, a dear price to pay during this time.

[27]John Anderson Morrow, *The Confederate Whitworth Sharpshooters*, 2nd ed. (published by author, 2002) 7. The author noted that the term "sniper" originated in the 1800s with the British Army in India, where the snipe was a favorite game fowl.

[28]Dunlop, *Lee's Sharpshooters*, 17–23.

They messed and slept together and were never separated in action. Deployed, they were on the right of the line, in battle at the front, and in retreat, the rear guard.[29]

At the beginning, Wofford's new battalion was informally known as the "1st Georgia Sharpshooters." This designation was incorrect as there were already two Georgia sharpshooter battalions in the Western Theater that had been formed the previous year. The 1st Georgia Sharpshooter Battalion was organized in Savannah by Major Robert Houston Anderson in June 1862.[30] The unit served as part of Walker-Wilson-Stevens-Jackson Brigade in the Western Theater until the end of the war. Under General W. H. T. Walker, the 1st Battalion got its first taste of real combat operations in May 1863. The 2nd Georgia Sharpshooter Battalion was also organized in June 1862 and made up of men from three excess companies of the 5th Georgia Infantry Regiment along with one or two Alabama companies. They were called "Cox's Wildcats" after their first commander, Major Jesse J. Cox. By the time Wofford's sharpshooters were officially recognized, they were correctly designated the 3rd Georgia Sharpshooter Battalion.[31]

After impressive victories at Fredericksburg and Chancellorsville and the strengthening of its depleted ranks, the Army of Northern Virginia was poised for further engagements with their adversaries. The time had arrived for the Army of Northern Virginia to take decisive action with a second full-scale invasion of the North.

---

[29]John D. Young, "A Campaign with Sharpshooters," in *The Annals of the War: Written by Leading Participants, North and South* (1879; reprint, Gettysburg, PA: Civil War Times, 1974) 270; Gerald J. Smith, *One of the Most Daring of Men: The Life of Confederate General William Tatum Wofford*, vol. 16 of Journal of Confederate History Series, ed. John McGlone (Murfreesboro, TN: Southern Heritage Press, 1997) 65–66.

[30]Stewart Sifakis, *Who Was Who in the Civil War* (New York: Facts on File Publications, 1988) 12. Anderson was a West Point graduate (1857) from Savannah. He was a staff officer with General William H. T. Walker's Brigade when the 1st Georgia Sharpshooter Battalion was formed in June 1862. Anderson later commanded the 5th Georgia Cavalry and a brigade in Allen's Division, Wheeler's Cavalry Corps of the Army of Tennessee. He had the unique distinction of serving as an artillery officer, an infantry line and staff officer, and a regimental and brigade cavalry officer during the war.

[31]Russell K. Brown, *Our Connection With Savannah: A History of the 1st Battalion Georgia Sharpshooters* (Macon: Mercer University Press, 2004) 1–3.

11

Raid on the Ironworks

True consistency, that of the prudent and the wise, is to act in conformity with the circumstances.

—John C. Calhoun

After the victory at Chancellorsville, General Lee faced a serious dilemma. The Army of Northern Virginia lacked the provisions and equipment to adequately provide for the defense of the Southland. Virginia had been ravaged by war for more than two years and was beginning to resemble a wasteland. If the army remained in Central Virginia, it faced continued shortages of food, clothing, shoes, and fodder for its horses and mules. Beyond fodder, Lee's army had run out of other necessary supplies and equipment, including horseshoes, wagons, forges, anvils, hammers, and the steel to make to make other hardware. During the winter and spring, out of necessity, Lee had to scatter his mounted units, including many artillery batteries. To complicate matters, the Confederate government pressured Lee to send Pickett's Division to reinforce Pemberton's Command at Vicksburg.[1]

Given the perilous situation, Lee made a bold decision. He would lead the Army of Northern Virginia, including Pickett's Division, north of the Mason-Dixon Line into Pennsylvania. This strategic move would provide the opportunity to keep his army intact, draw Hooker's army out of Virginia and away from Richmond, and forage liberally for food, fodder, and equipment. There was also the possibility of a peace dividend, given the increased anti-war feelings that grew out of Lincoln's unpopular Conscription Act of March 1863.

As the Army of Northern Virginia began its march north toward Pennsylvania in June 1863, there was an air of excitement and anticipation among the men of the 16th Georgia, the newly-formed sharpshooter battalion, and the rest of their comrades in the Army of Northern Virginia. Almost everyone believed that this would be the campaign that would establish the independence of the Southern states. It was the Confederate "high tide." Despite the many shortages, the Army of Northern Virginia was at its zenith, full of confidence that it was both tough and efficient. Many of the soldiers felt

---

[1]Kent Masterson Brown, *Retreat From Gettysburg: Lee, Logistics, & the Pennsylvania Campaign* (Chapel Hill: University of North Carolina Press, 2005) 14–16.

that they would drive the Yankees into the Atlantic Ocean, capturing Washington as they advanced.[2]

The 3rd Battalion Sharpshooters and the regiments of Wofford's Brigade left their camps along the Rappahannock on 3 June and started the march to Culpeper Court House. By 8 June, Longstreet's and Ewell's corps had reached their destination where Jeb Stuart's cavalry was concentrated.[3] On the following day Stuart and his forces repulsed a surprise attack by two divisions of Union cavalry under Brigadier General Alfred Pleasanton at nearby Brandy Station. It was the largest all-cavalry battle of the war, and the Yankees made a credible showing, fighting Stuart's forces to a standstill before falling back.

The northward advance resumed on 10 June. Five days later Longstreet received orders to move out to two mountain passes on the east side of the Blue Ridge Mountains near the Virginia hamlet of Upperville. By 19 June units of Longstreet's Corps occupied Ashby's Gap and nearby Snicker's Gap.[4] Turning west through the mountain passes, his troops then crossed the Shenandoah River and once again turned northward, marching down the Shenandoah Valley with banners flying. Friendly crowds at Berryville and Martinsburg greeted the soldiers as they advanced toward the Potomac River. In each town along the route, ladies, waving from their porches, provided fresh bread, milk, and other delicacies to the men in uniform as they marched by. By the time the army reached the banks of the Potomac River, the men were well shod, having collected shoes in every town through which they passed.[5]

On 26 June the 16th Georgia and the other regiments of McLaws's Division waded across the Potomac at Williamsport, Maryland. The crossing was facilitated by the low water level and the men forded the river without difficulty.[6] Once all the troops had crossed the river, a ration of whiskey was

---

[2]"Letter from Major-General Henry Heth of A. P. Hill's Corps, A. N. V. to Rev. J. Wm. Jones, D. D. Secretary southern Historical Society," *Southern Historical Society Papers* (hereafter cited as *SHSP*) 4 (July–December 1877): 152.

[3]*The War of the Rebellion: A Compilation of the Official Records of the Union and Confederate Armies* (70 vols. in 128; Washington, 1880–1901), ser. I, vol. 27, pt. 2, 293, 305, 357. Hereafter cited as *OR*. See also Major-General Lafayette McLaws, "Gettysburg," *SHSP* 7 (January–December 1879): 64.

[4]*OR*, ser. I, vol. 27, pt. 2, 306; E. Porter Alexander, *Military Memoirs of a Confederate: A Critical Narrative* (1907; reprint, Dayton, OH: Press of Morningside Bookshop, 1977) 374.

[5]Fitzgerald Ross, *Cities and Camps of the Confederate States* (Urbana: University of Illinois Press, 1958) 31.

[6]Lafayette McLaws to Emily Allison McLaws (nee Taylor), niece of Zachary Taylor, 28 June 1863, Lafayette McLaws papers, ms. 472, Southern Historical Collection, University of North Carolina, Chapel Hill; John G. Oeffinger, ed., *A Soldier's General: The Civil War Letters of Major-General Lafayette McLaws* (Chapel Hill: University of North Carolina Press, 2002) 192.

issued to ease the discomfort of excessive dampness and raise the spirits of the men. From the Potomac Longstreet's Corps proceeded to Chambersburg, Pennsylvania, before stopping to rest while waiting for further developments.[7] The 16th Georgia and the remainder of McLaws's Division made camp about a mile past the town. While it was of no concern to Lee's Army at that time, Gettysburg lay a mere twenty-five miles to the east.

During the time they were in Chambersburg, the Confederate soldiers went on a shopping spree. Daily purchases were made from the lush local gardens. They cleared all the merchandise from the shelves in the town shops and paid for it with Confederate greenbacks and "promissory notes."[8] A number of Wofford's men took advantage of the lush, fertile farmland that surrounded the prosperous community. As Marcus Green of Phillips's Legion recorded in his diary on 28 June, "I got plenty of good brandy and chickens, butter, load of bread, and cherry last night."[9] Another member of Phillips Legion, John Barry, wrote his sister that "we had plenty [to eat] while in Pennsylvania, such as chickens, sheep and apple butter in abundance."[10] A member of the 3rd South Carolina in Kershaw's Brigade wrote of his displeasure (or envy) of his Georgia compatriots, "Last night [June 27] Wofford's Brigade of this division stole so much that they could not carry what rations they drew from the commissary."[11] James L. Lemon of the 18th Georgia was aware of his brigade's reputation, noting, "Our boys [are] fierce foragers, the best I think in the army and the entry into the enemy's country offered the greatest temptations to them to practice these skills with reckless abandon."[12]

Five days after reaching Chambersburg, General McLaws was ordered to move his division closer to Gettysburg. About 2:00 P.M. on 30 June the division arrived at Greenwood, a small village in the South Mountain pass about fifteen miles west of Gettysburg. Here the men bivouacked under orders to resume their march at 8:00 the next morning.

---

[7]*OR*, ser. I, vol. 27, pt. 2, 358; Alexander, *Military Memoirs*, 347; D. Augustus Dickert, *History of Kershaw's Brigade* (1899; reprint, Wilmington, NC: Broadfoot Publishing Company, 1990) 229.

[8]Dickert, *Kershaw's Brigade*, 229.

[9]Bradley M. Gottfried, *Brigades of Gettysburg: Union and Confederate Brigades at the Battle of Gettysburg* (Cambridge, MA: Da Capo Press, 2002) 419.

[10]John Barry to his sister, 25 July 1863, in John Alexander Barry papers, Southern Historical Collection, University of North Carolina, Chapel Hill; Mills Lane, ed., *"Dear Mother: Don't Grieve About Me. If I get Killed, I'll Only be Dead": Letters from Georgia Soldiers in the Civil War* (Savannah, GA: The Beehive Press) 258.

[11]The letter was written by Corporal Tally Simpson (Gottfried, *Brigades of Gettysburg*, 419); James Lile Lemon, *Feed them the Steel! Being the Wartime Recollections of Captain James Lile Lemon Company A, 18th Georgia Infantry C.S.A.* (Acworth, GA: printed by Mark H. Lemon, 2008) 44.

[12]Lemon, *Feed them the Steel*, 44.

The following day, Wofford's men received orders to cook three days' rations and be prepared to march. Before departing with the rest of his brigade, Captain Simmons received word of an independent assignment in command of his sharpshooter company.[13] He and his men were ordered to break off from the main column and proceed to an ironworks about nine miles northeast of Greenwood. Simmons was given the discretion to destroy the ironworks, confiscate any supplies that could be of use to the Army, and rejoin his brigade at Gettysburg. Under the rules of war the ironworks constituted a proper military objective with numerous precedents. Only a week before, Confederate General Jubal Early had ordered the burning of the nearby Caledonia Ironworks. That factory was owned by Thaddeus Stevens, a man Simmons described as the "bitterest and most unrelenting hater of the South in the United States Congress."[14] These facilities were very important to the Federal government as a large amount of war materials were manufactured there.

On the second of July, Captain Simmons and his sharpshooters proceeded cautiously through the Pennsylvania countryside, past the burned Caledonia Ironworks, to the vicinity of the unguarded ironworks. When they arrived he led his company to the office of the owner, a man named Archer, and announced his intention to burn the works. Archer vigorously protested the possible destruction of his property. He argued that the order should not be carried out, claiming that he was a Virginian, a Southern sympathizer, and the brother of James Jay Archer, a brigadier general in Ambrose Powell Hill's III Corps of the Army of Northern Virginia. General Archer was a native of Maryland, graduated from the College of New Jersey in 1835 (renamed Princeton University in 1896), and studied law at the University of Maryland. Like many other high ranking officers in the War Between the States, he fought in the Mexican War.[15]

Apparently unknown to both Archer and Captain Simmons, on the previous day the owner's brother participated in the opening attack that sparked the Battle of Gettysburg.[16] That morning General Archer led his brigade of seasoned Alabama and Tennessee troops at McPherson's Woods, south of the

---

[13]Byrd, *Them Brave Georgians*, 171.

[14]Ibid. After Stevens's iron works were burned by General Jubal Early's Confederates in June 1863, the *Charleston Mercury* celebrated the act as "punishment for his [Stevens's] enormous crimes against the happiness of the human race" (Eric Ethier, "The Union's Savage Politician Who Fought with Sarcasm and Wit," *America's Civil War* 21/4 [September 2008]: 23). Ethier writes that the *New York Herald* described Stevens as the "Mephistopheles of Congress."

[15]Stewart Sifakis, *Who Was Who in the Civil War* (New York: Facts on File Publications, 1988) 15.

[16]In William Simmons's recollection of the incident, there is no mention of whether he or Mr. Archer knew about General James J. Archer's capture the preceding day at Gettysburg (Byrd, *Them Brave Georgians*, 172–75).

Chambersburg Pike. There he and a large number of his men were surrounded and captured by several regiments of the infamous Union "Iron Brigade." Archer's right flank was turned by the 19th Indiana and the 24th Michigan and caught in murderous enfilade. As Archer's men made a hasty retreat, the Iron Brigade came after them. Archer was captured by a burly Irishman named Patrick Maloney, a private of the 2nd Wisconsin Infantry Regiment.[17] A first-hand account of the action and outcome was written by Benjamin Haskins, a Tennessean in Archer's Brigade:

> Upon the opening of the fight on the first day, our old brigade…was sent in to develop the Yankee line of battle, which we did in fine style and drove them to town. Having no support on either flank, the first we knew the enemy had closed upon our rear and were popping away at our backs. Of course we had to surrender. [After they were captured] General Archer and 100 of his men were sent to Forts McHenry and Delaware where they stayed only a short while and finally landed at Johnson's Island. He [Archer] remained there until sometime in 1865, when on account of bad health, he obtained a special exchange and went south, but was never able to take charge of the brigade again, and died…about the close of the war. God never made a truer or braver man.[18]

Back at the Archer Iron Works, the owner's claims of Southern sympathies did not move Captain Simmons, but the man's blood relationship to General James J. Archer certainly did. The young captain knew of General Archer and some of the facts of his career[19] (including his graduation from the College of New Jersey and service in the Mexican War), so he asked the general's brother a number of questions to determine whether he was telling the truth about his kinship. All of Archer's answers squared with Captain Simmons's knowledge of the general, so he began to consider other alternatives than burning down the ironworks.

For several minutes Simmons weighed his options and then announced his decision. He informed Archer that the ironworks would not be destroyed, but all of his horses and wagons would be taken for the Army of Northern Virginia. Archer was furious! He repeated all of his objections and insisted that any confiscation of his property would be an outrage.

---

[17] After he was captured, General Archer was taken to General Abner Doubleday, a former comrade in the Regular Army, who greeted him with a certain lack of sensitivity: "Good Morning, Archer," said Doubleday, "I am glad to see you." Replied Archer: "Well, I am *not* glad to see you by a damned sight."

[18] Benjamin Haskins, "Gen. Jas. J. Archer," *Confederate Veteran* 2/11 (November 1894): 355. The date of Archer's death was 24 October 1864.

[19] F. S. Harris, "Gen. Jas. J. Archer," *Confederate Veteran* 3/1 (January 1895): 18.

Captain Simmons was not swayed. Instead he told Mr. Archer that an ardent Southern sympathizer such as he claimed to be ought to be glad to make such a small "contribution" to the Confederacy.

Still protesting, Archer saw nothing small about the price he was about to pay, but Simmons remained steadfast in his demands. The owner continued to argue, but to no avail. He had woefully misjudged the firmness of Captain Simmons. After he had heard enough, Simmons stopped the conversation abruptly and told Archer that if he uttered another word, the ironworks would be burned to the ground. That was the last straw. Archer relented and Simmons directed his men to hitch up the horses and wagons and get underway to rejoin the army at Gettysburg. Within one hour of their arrival, the sharpshooter detachment was hurrying to the Confederate lines with more than thirty draft horses and a number of wagons.[20] It was a good day's work, but much more was in store for the 3rd Georgia Sharpshooters and their intrepid leader, William E. Simmons. It was the afternoon of 2 July 1863. The Battle of Gettysburg was raging.

---

[20]Byrd, *Them Brave Georgians*, 174.

12

The Peach Orchard and Wheat Field

That best portion of a good man's life;
his little, nameless, unremembered acts
of kindness and love…
                                        —William Wordsworth

While Captain Simmons and his detachment were "negotiating" with Mr.
Archer for his horses and wagons, the 16th Georgia and the rest of McLaws's
Division were on the final leg of their march to take up positions southwest of
Gettysburg. Departing at 6:00 A.M. on 2 July, they advanced toward Gettysburg
for a short distance before turning right down a country road and forming an
eight-mile long column *en route* to Black Horse Tavern to await further orders
while the artillery was brought up. The road to Gettysburg was hilly and narrow.
Confederate wounded and stragglers constantly impeded progress and the march
was slowed to a "snail's gait" at about two miles per hour or less.[1] By 10:00 A.M.
Hood's and McLaws's divisions of Longstreet's Corps had arrived at the tavern,
which was being used as a Confederate hospital to care for the soldiers who were
wounded the previous day.[2]

When the signal came later that morning, the long column moved out past
the tavern on a road leading eastward toward the Emmitsburg Road. As the
column approached the top of a hill, a Yankee signal station came into view on
Little Round Top. The column halted immediately and reversed its course.
Longstreet had been ordered to avoid exposing his corps to the enemy in
moving to his assigned positions.[3] The column backtracked past the Black
Horse Tavern and down a country road to Willoughby's Run, now a dried creek
bed.[4] They passed a school house below the Pitzer Farm, turned east toward
Emmitsburg Road and took their position towards the edge of some woods
about 600 yards from the road.

---

[1]D. Augustus Dickert, *History of Kershaw's Brigade* (1899; reprint, Wilmington,
NC: Broadfoot Publishing Company, 1990) 232.
[2]E. Porter Alexander, *Military Memoirs of a Confederate: A Critical Narrative* (1907;
reprint, Dayton, OH: Press of Morningside Bookshop, 1977) 388.
[3]Ibid., 391.
[4]J. B. Kershaw, Major-General, "Kershaw's Brigade at Gettysburg," in *Retreat from
Gettysburg*, vol. 3 of *Battles and Leaders of the Civil War* (1887; reprint, New York: Castle
Books, 1956) 333.

As the day wore on, the soldiers began to tire from the marching and the hot weather. Finally, in the early afternoon, the 16th Georgia and the other regiments of Wofford's Brigade reached their positions on Seminary Ridge close behind Barksdale's Mississippians. On their right were Semmes's and Kershaw's brigades. Still farther to the right, Hood's Division took up its positions facing Big and Little Round Top. There has been some disagreement concerning the alignment of Wofford's regiments, but most likely they lined up as was customary: from left to right—Phillips's Legion, Cobb's Legion, the 16th Georgia, 24th Georgia, and 18th Georgia, with the 3rd Georgia Sharpshooters out in front.[5]

For the next two hours, Wofford's men quietly listened to the distant noise of the battle. From Seminary Ridge where the brigade had been posted, a Confederate observer could see that enemy fire came from a portion of the Union battle line shaped like a "V." At the point of the "V" facing Seminary Ridge was a peach orchard located at the junction of the Emmitsburg Road and a country lane that led eastward towards Cemetery Ridge, where the main body of Union troops waited. One side of the "V" was defended by Union troops along the Emmitsburg Road. The other side of the "V" was protected by bluecoats in a battle line that strung out to the east through a nearby wheat field all the way to a wooded tangle of rocky hillocks known locally as the "Devil's Den." The Federal forces were made up of the III Corps under General Daniel Edgar Sickles.

That afternoon as the attack was about to begin, Captain Simmons and his command were about two miles west of Gettysburg, bumping down the dusty road in their captured wagons searching for their comrades. When they arrived behind the lines, it seemed to take an interminable length of time to find Major Raphael J. Moses, commissary officer of Longstreet's Corps. As soon as the major was located and the horses and wagons delivered, Captain Simmons and his men raced to the position where Wofford's Brigade was poised for battle.[6]

When Simmons's sharpshooter detachment finally reached its brigade on Seminary Ridge, their comrades were already in battle line formation. As usual,

[5]Gerald J. Smith, *One of the Most Daring of Men: The Life of Confederate General William Tatum Wofford*, vol. 16 of Journal of Confederate History Series, ed. John McGlone (Murfreesboro, TN: Southern Heritage Press, 1997) 81. Research by Madison Byrd suggests that the position of the regiments in Wofford's Brigade is established by Bachelder's map for the "Second Day's Battle." This map was compiled by John B. Bachelder from official reports, private letters and consultations on the battlefield (James Lile Lemon, *Feed them the Steel! Being the Wartime Recollections of Captain James Lile Lemon Company A, 18th Georgia Infantry C.S.A.* [Acworth, GA: printed by Mark H. Lemon, 2008] 46).

[6]Daniel M. Byrd Jr., *Them Brave Georgians*, manuscript, pg. 185, Gwinnett Historical Society Archives, Lawrenceville, GA (Fort Delaware Society Library, Delaware City, DE, also has a copy.).

General Wofford was "chafing at the bit" to lead his brigade into battle. He rode back and forth on his horse, dispatching courier after courier to General McLaws, asking to be advanced. Finally the command was given to advance, and Simmons and his sharpshooter detachment barely had time to take their positions in front of the brigade. Leading the brigade, the sharpshooters immediately advanced against the enemy's skirmishers and speedily drove them back to their battle line.[7] In that location a battery of seventeen enemy field guns was posted in the peach orchard, not far from a stone wall barn. As they advanced toward the orchard the Georgians came under long-range artillery fire. Colonel Goode Bryan, regimental commander of the 16th Georgia, witnessed a shell that exploded nearby, killing or wounding about thirty men.[8]

A member of the Troup Artillery stationed near Wofford's position observed the activity of the sharpshooters leading the brigade into battle:

> The skirmishers of both armies were actively engaged as we came into position, those of the enemy being some distance this side of the [Emmitsburg] road and making a determined stand to hold it. Very soon, however, they were driven back across the road upon their supports, and almost simultaneously with their withdrawal, our batteries opened fire upon the force in the peach orchard and field.[9]

The charging brigade was led by General Wofford and accompanied by General Longstreet. They soon caught up with the sharpshooters, and there was no stopping until the entire Union battery had been captured. A company of confederate artillerymen was sent in right behind Wofford's Brigade and successfully turned the artillery upon the fleeing bluecoats. So intent was General Longstreet in watching the progress of his two divisions that he rode ahead of Wofford's Brigade deep into the peach orchard, completely unmindful of his own safety, before turning back to the Emmitsburg Road.[10]

The peach orchard was the site of ferocious fighting on the second day of Gettysburg. The advancing Confederates encountered fierce opposition from General Dan Sickles's III Corps. Sickles had placed his 10,000 battle-tested veterans in the vicinity of the peach orchard by the Emmitsburg Road, a vulnerable position given the fact that he was separated from the main Union battle line by a considerable distance.[11] The initial onslaught was led by

---

[7]Ibid., 185–86.

[8]Smith, *One of the Most Daring of Men*, 86; Letter to Lafayette McLaws, 10 December 1877, McLaws papers, Southern Historical Collection, University of North Carolina, Chapel Hill (hereafter cited as McLaws papers).

[9]Smith, *One of the Most Daring of Men*, 82; John Stegeman, *These Men She Gave: Civil War Diary of Athens, Georgia* (Athens, GA: University of Georgia Press, 1964) 92.

[10]William Youngblood to James Longstreet, 5 September 1892, Longstreet papers, Southern Historical Collection, University of North Carolina, Chapel Hill.

[11]Battle maps suggest that the distance was as much as one mile.

Anderson's Brigade. Next came McLaws's brigades led by three of Kershaw's South Carolina regiments. A Georgia brigade under Brigadier General Paul J. Semmes followed Kershaw. In response, additional Union units were added in time to momentarily stop the advance of Semmes's Georgians. To the left, Brigadier General William Barksdale led his Mississippians across the Emmitsburg Road. Captain G. B. Lamar, Jr., McLaws's aide-de-camp, witnessed the charge and told his superior, "I never saw anything to equal the dash and the heroism of the Mississippians. His [Barksdale's] enthusiasm was shared by the men under his command."[12]

Despite the enthusiasm and élan of the advancing Confederates, they ran into stiff opposition from the Union forces more than twice their number. Just as the tide of battle seemed to be turning in favor of the North, Wofford's Brigade reinforced Semmes's men. The combined forces came down hard on the Union's right flank.

In the fierce fighting around the peach orchard, the Union III Corps would lose its commander. On horseback near his headquarters, Sickles was struck by a solid cannonball shot that left his right leg dangling below the knee by a few shreds of flesh. As aides helped him from his horse, Sickles calmly directed a drummer boy who was acting as a litter bearer to apply a tourniquet to his leg. Sickles then ordered his command turned over and sent out word to squelch a swiftly spreading rumor that he was dead. The wounded general then lit up a big Havana cigar and puffed it ostentatiously while being carried to the rear.[13] After his leg was amputated below the knee, Sickles directed that the shattered bones be sent to the Army Medical Museum in Washington, DC, where he visited them periodically for many years.

The Union's III Corps line was finally broken as the sun slowly sank to the west. The repulse of the Federal units in the peach orchard salient enabled Wofford's Georgians to push the Federals back even farther. Lieutenant Frank A. Haskell, an aide to Union Brigadier General John Gibbon, despairingly observed the Confederate onslaught, remarking, "The III Corps, after a heroic but unfortunate fight, is being literally swept from the field."

After passing through the peach orchard, Wofford re-formed his brigade and advanced down the Wheatfield Road with the sharpshooters in front, pressing the Yankees up and over a rocky hill. Ahead they saw thousands of Union soldiers in a large open wheat field desperately attempting to re-form their lines. This scene was vividly described by Captain James L. Lemon of the 18th Georgia, who was positioned on the right of the Wheatfield Road between the 24th Georgia and remnants of Kershaw's Brigade:

[12]John Purifoy, "The Splendid Valor Shown at Gettysburg July 2, 1863," *Confederate Veteran* 34/11 (January 1906): 17.

[13]W. A. Swanberg, *Sickles the Incredible* (New York: Charles Scribner's Sons, 1956) 216–18.

I looked to my left and saw our brigade marching with cool precision as if on parade. Gen'l Wofford ordered us to halt, dress, and then we fired a volley which fairly devastated those Yanks in our front who had been re-forming. With a piercing "Rebel" yell, we continued our advance into the field. A large force of Yankees moved out of the woods off to our right and moved to the left across our front. We fired several well-aimed volleys at them and pitched into them with a piercing yell. We caught them after a short distance and the most terrific hand-to-hand fighting occurred. Guns were fired [at close range] and then clubbed musket, bayonet, knives, and fists were employed. After the bloodiest struggle, we captured a stand of their colors belonging to a regiment of Michigan troops. We drove them down a slope to a small creek across which they bounded, fleeing up the rock hill to our right and front.[14]

As darkness descended on the evening of 2 July, Wofford's Brigade reached the foot of Little Round Top. Captain Simmons never forgot the struggle that took place on that day. When repeated volleys failed to drive the enemy back, he and his comrades engaged in close combat until the enemy's line was completely broken. At the end of the day, the Army of Northern Virginia held a large portion of the battlefield.

General McLaws described the attack by Wofford's Brigade as "brilliant."[15] Under heavy enemy fire, the brigade had moved steadily up to what seemed to be the very muzzles of the enemy's guns. Only 100 yards in front of the 16th Georgia had been an unattended Yankee battery of four pieces. The accurate fire of Simmons's sharpshooters had dropped its gunners. Members of the 16th Georgia were prepared to claim the guns as a prize of war, but their regimental commander, Colonel Goode Bryan, stopped them for fear that they would be captured.

In Bryan's account of the fighting, the 16th Georgia advanced farther than any regiment in Wofford's Brigade. At that point Wofford was determined to press on. He noted that, "there was no enemy either in front or on our right to cause us to fall back." But before the regiment could advance any further, he received orders by a courier from General Longstreet, who was close by. Seeing Longstreet some short distance to his rear, Wofford rode to him and asked that he not order the regiment to withdraw. Longstreet promptly refused Wofford's request. Rather than maintain the most forward position at the foot of Little Round Top, Longstreet ordered Wofford to move his brigade back to the relative security of the main Confederate battle line farther from the Union

---

[14]Lemon, *Feed them the Steel*, 46.
[15]Byrd, *Them Brave Georgians*, 191.

positions.[16] That night the 3rd Battalion Sharpshooters were thrown out on the skirmish line between the enemy and Wofford's Brigade.[17]

As soon as the new line was established, the sharpshooters were free for the first time to attend to their personal needs. In rotation, small groups of them searched for food and clean water to drink. When Captain Simmons's turn came, he was appalled at the carnage around him as he walked to the rear. In his own words, "The battlefield was literally strewn with the dead and wounded of both armies."[18]

By the light of a full moon, details sought out the dead and wounded. That evening, while checking on the fate of some of his friends, Simmons came across a Federal corporal giving aid to two of his officers who lay wounded on the ground. The young corporal, unmindful of his own safety, had remained with the officers long after the tide of battle had swept past. While Simmons admired the loyalty of the corporal to his officers, duty required him to send the corporal to the rear as a captive.[19]

The disabled officers knew that their aide was likely to be captured and sent to a Confederate prison. From the moment that Captain Simmons appeared, the officers begged him to allow the corporal to remain with them. Both officers were too badly injured to walk. They pointed out that Confederate details were giving priority to their own wounded. In the moonlight, hospital corpsmen could be seen taking wounded Southern soldiers to a stone barn[20] near the peach orchard. The officers pled that without the corporal to care for them, they would be left to die, likely caught between the opposing lines when the battle resumed the next day.

Simmons understood that what the officers said was true. The regular ambulance corps was overwhelmed by the large number of Confederate casualties and would not likely be able to attend to the needs of any wounded Union soldiers. Although he tried always to put such pictures out of his mind, he realized that he might be in same position as the Union officers in some future battle. Likely moved by empathy and compassion, he asked the names of the two officers. In later years, Simmons recalled that the younger of the two identified himself as Lieutenant Higgins and gave the name of his more

---

[16]Goode Bryan to Lafayette McLaws, 12 December 1877, McLaws papers; Smith, *One of the Most Daring of Men*, 89–90.

[17]Bradley M. Gottfried, *Brigades of Gettysburg: Union and Confederate Brigades at the Battle of Gettysburg* (Cambridge, MA: Da Capo Press, 2002) 422.

[18]Byrd, *Them Brave Georgians*, 193.

[19]Daniel M. Byrd Jr., *Them Brave Georgians*, manuscript, Gwinnett Historical Society archives, Lawrenceville, GA pg. 194 (Fort Delaware Society Library, Delaware City, DE, also has a copy.).

[20]This was most likely the stone barn belonging to the Rose family, about 700 yards south of the Peach Orchard.

seriously wounded companion as Captain Meade. Both men were attached to a Union Zouave regiment in Sickles III Corps.[21]

In his memoirs, William Simmons never revealed what exactly caused him to comply with their request, but he directed some of the sharpshooters accompanying him to carry the two Union officers to the stone barn. To show their appreciation, the officers asked for Simmons's name and address. They told him that if he were ever captured he should let them know and they would do their best to return his consideration and kindness. As the detail began to carry off the wounded officers, Lieutenant Higgins took off his sword and belt and, with further expressions of gratitude, presented them to Simmons. The young Confederate captain was both surprised and appreciative. After thanking Lieutenant Higgins for the weapon, he wished both Federal officers Godspeed and left to attend to his own personal needs and those of his company.

The peach orchard and much of the battlefield may have belonged to the Confederates after the second day of fighting, but the tide of battle would turn in favor of the Union army on the following day.

On the morning of 3 July, Wofford, apparently still upset from being recalled the previous evening, dispatched his sharpshooters back into the woods to probe the enemy. Soon the battalion became engaged in a hot exchange of fire with the enemy pickets. The brigade was then formed in the line of battle, and advanced for a short distance and placed to the right and rear of the sharpshooters. While awaiting further orders, Simmons and his comrades observed generals Lee and Longstreet ride up for a conference with General Wofford.[22] After a brief discussion, Wofford was asked if his brigade should renew a full-scale attack. He responded that the enemy was reinforced and had bolstered their already strong defensive positions. No advantage could be gained without being strongly supported. The decision was made not to launch a large

---

[21]Gottfried, *Brigades of Gettysburg*, 219–22; see Byrd, *Them Brave Georgians*, 193–95. Many years after his service in the Confederate army, William Simmons recounted to his nephew and grand nephew the episode in his memoirs and mentioned the names of the wounded officers and their unit. The passage of time likely clouded his memory with regard to the names of the two Union officers and their regiment. He recalled that the men were from the 3rd New York Zouaves, but this recollection is incorrect because that regiment was not engaged at Gettysburg on 2 July 1863. Simmons never mentioned the name of the corporal, but according to service records and other reference sources, the three Union soldiers were probably from the 73rd New York Regiment, nicknamed the "Second Fire Zouaves," of the Excelsior (2nd) Brigade under the command of Colonel William Brewster. The 73rd New York was organized by Dan Sickles in fall 1861. At Gettysburg, the Excelsior Brigade was attached to General Andrew Humphreys's 2nd Division of Sickles's III Corps. On the second day of the battle, the regiments of the Excelsior Brigade were positioned along the Emmitsburg Road. The 73rd New York was positioned directly in the path of Barksdale's Charge.

[22]Byrd, *Them Brave Georgians*, 196.

scale attack.[23] In Wofford's mind, the window of opportunity had closed overnight.

Although most of McLaws's Division rested on the third day of the battle, the 3rd Battalion Sharpshooters kept busy on the skirmish line. Throughout the day, the noise of the skirmish fighting around the Wheatfield "almost resembled that of a regular brigade," according to a solider in the 2nd Pennsylvania Reserve Infantry.[24] The Confederates who remained in the thick of the fighting belonged to Wofford's and Benning's brigades. Many in the skirmish line came from Wofford's talented sharpshooters who were positioned in Rose's Woods. At that location a number of the Georgia marksmen "treefrogged," that is, climbed into high branches and sniped at their foes from a higher vantage point. Throughout the morning and afternoon they killed or wounded a number of Union soldiers.[25] Despite the fear and chaos they caused, the Southerners had their hands full, especially when it came to dealing with the 1st Pennsylvania Rifles, widely known as the "Bucktails."

The exertions of the battle the day before had taken their toll on Wofford's men, and they rested along with the other brigades in McLaws's Division. After 11:00 A.M., except for the incessant fire of the sharpshooters and skirmishers, everything remained relatively quiet until 1:00 P.M. when more than 100 pieces of Confederate artillery opened fire against the Federal lines. McLaws's exhausted troops kept their muskets loaded, but no orders came for them to move out. Later in the afternoon, they watched and listened to the slaughter from their vantage point on the battlefield.

After the disastrous "Pickett's Charge," McLaws's troops were ordered to retire to Seminary Ridge, the location from where they had begun their attack just twenty-four hours earlier. When the division began to withdraw from the battlefield a group of Federal skirmishers advanced on the Confederates' position. Lieutenant Colonel Nate Hutchins ordered the 3rd Sharpshooter Battalion to remain behind and stave off the enemy. The sharpshooters had been heavily engaged over the past two days and were now called upon to protect the Confederate withdrawal. With resolute spirit the 3rd Battalion Sharpshooters and detachments from other brigades counter charged and drove the advancing Federal skirmishers beyond the peach orchard. The attacking

---

[23]Lemon, *Feed them the Steel*, 47.

[24]Evan Morrison Woodward, *Our Campaigns: The Second Pennsylvania Reserve Volunteers* (Philadelphia: J. E. Porter, 1865) 214. See also Timothy J. Orr, "'Sharpshooters Made a Grand Record This Day': Combat on the Skirmish Line at Gettysburg on July 3," in *The Third Day: The Fate of a Nation, July 3, 1863* (Gettysburg: Gettysburg National Military Park, 2010).

[25]Orr, "Sharpshooters," 69.

force occupied the Emmitsburg Road and remained at that location until the morning of 5 July.[26]

---

[26]Byrd, *Them Brave Georgians*, 197. Based on an account by William Simmons.

13

Retreat from Gettysburg

One must never lose time in vainly regretting the past or complaining
against the changes which cause us discomfort, for change is the
essence of life.

—Anatole France

After suffering a major setback on the third day of battle at Gettysburg, General
Lee carefully withdrew his Army with Union forces in slow pursuit. On 6 July,
Longstreet's Corps moved to Hagerstown, Maryland, to protect the army's
wagon train, which was seriously threatened by Yankee cavalry. The soldiers set
up camp two miles outside of town on the Sharpsburg Turnpike and remained
at that location until 10 July.[1]

The stop in Hagerstown was the first time in several days that Captain
Simmons had the opportunity to take stock of himself and his former regiment.
Colonel Goode Bryan, for nearly two years the commander of the 16th Georgia,
had been assigned as the immediate successor to General Paul Semmes. Semmes
had been killed as he led his brigade in the initial charge across the Emmitsburg
Road on the second day at Gettysburg. To succeed Bryan, the respected and
popular Lieutenant Colonel Henry P. Thomas was placed in command of the
16th Georgia.

With the promotion of Thomas, leadership of Simmons's old regiment
remained in good hands. The new regimental commander was fifty-three years
old and a native of Franklin County, Georgia. He attended Franklin College
(the University of Georgia), having graduated in 1832. His classmates included
Howell Cobb, Alexander H. Stephens, and William H. Crawford. Thomas was
an excellent scholar and graduated second in his class behind Stephens. Four
years later he served as an officer in the Creek Indian War. The following year
he married Ellen E. Burroughs and became a successful lawyer and planter in
Gwinnett County. Thomas spent many years in public service as ordinary of the
county and as a member of the Georgia Senate and House of Representatives. In

---

[1]*The War of the Rebellion: A Compilation of the Official Records of the Union and
Confederate Armies* (70 vols. in 128; Washington, 1880–1901), ser. I, vol. 27, pt. 2, 361
(hereafter cited as *OR*). For an excellent first-hand account of the retreat, see John D.
Imboden, Brigadier General, C. S. A., "The Confederate Retreat from Gettysburg," in
Retreat from Gettysburg, vol. 3 of *Battles and Leaders of the Civil War* (1887; reprint, New
York: Castle Books, 1956) 425–28.

1860 he served as a delegate to the Democrat Conventions in Charleston, South Carolina, and Baltimore, Maryland.[2] The good news of Colonel Thomas's promotion was tempered by the loss of a number of men in Captain Simmons's sharpshooter battalion and former regiment in the Battle of Gettysburg. Of the more than 100 casualties from the 16th Georgia, nine men were killed, including the color bearer who was shot as the regiment advanced through the peach orchard. An additional fifty-two men were wounded and forty-six were captured, including Major James S. Gholston, one of the original company captains of the regiment. Among the fatalities of the 3rd Sharpshooter Battalion was Private William M. Adair of Simmons's sharpshooter Company C. Adair had joined the Gwinnett Volunteers in Lawrenceville on the same day as Simmons. Two other sharpshooters from Company E, Private Jasper N. Beck and 1st Sergeant Jessie G. Ginn, were killed in the skirmishing at Gettysburg on 3 July. Later in the month Private James A. Davidson of Company C was killed at Hagerstown during the retreat.[3]

In taking stock of their personal and military situations, many of Wofford's Georgians felt that the campaign was a blunder and that some general would be made the scapegoat. In a letter to his wife soon after the Battle of Gettysburg, Lafayette McLaws echoed their sentiments and pinned the blame squarely on his superior, General Longstreet. He wrote,

> I think the attack was unnecessary and the whole plan of battle a very bad one. Genl Longstreet is to blame for not reconnoitering the ground [on the second day of battle] and for persisting in ordering the assault when his errors were discovered. During the engagement he was very excited, giving contrary orders to everyone, and was exceedingly overbearing.

In unflattering language, McLaws described his superior and West Point classmate as "a humbug, a man of small capacity, very obstinate, not at all chivalrous, exceedingly conceited and totally selfish." He concluded the letter by adding that the men in his division were "very much fatigued and foot sore, but not disheartened."[4]

---

[2]James C. Flanigan, *History of Gwinnett County, Georgia*, vol. 1 (1943; reprint, Lawrenceville: Gwinnett Historical Society, 1995) 351–52.

[3]According to service records, in addition to the four fatalities during the first week of July, there were three sharpshooters wounded: Private James William Reagan of Company A, Private Marcus L. Vandivier of Company B, and Private Samuel B. Lowry of Company E. Twelve sharpshooters were captured at Gettysburg, including Reagan and Lowry, privates L. J. Belk and George W. Parker of Company A, W. V. York of Company B, John T. Clark of Company C, M. V. York of Company E, 2nd Sergeant John W. Manning, and privates Joshua P. Stephens, Zachariah P. Heaton, John J. Howard, and James A. Carter of Company F.

[4]Major-General Lafayette McLaws to Emily Allison McLaws (nee Taylor), niece of Zachary Taylor, 7 July 1863, McLaws papers; John G. Oeffinger, ed., *A Soldier's*

The calm of the Hagerstown Camp was interrupted on 10 July by a report of advancing enemy troops accompanied by a large body of cavalry. Throughout the day the 3rd Battalion Sharpshooters, along with Cobb's and Phillips's infantry legions and the Troup Artillery, held the Union forces in check, driving the skirmishers back to their reserves. This bold action prevented the Federals from determining the position of Lee's Army and bought some time for the retreating Confederates to shore up defensive positions.[5]

The pursuing Federal army continued to trail their adversaries cautiously, catching up with Lee's army at Funkstown, Maryland, a few miles south of Hagerstown. By that time the Confederates had thrown up some temporary trenches, giving Meade an opportunity to offer battle, but while there was some fighting there was no real battle of importance. The 3rd Battalion Sharpshooters were engaged at both Hagerstown and Funkstown.[6]

The Confederate fortifications were placed in a line from Downsville to the Conococheague River. The line was not entrenched a moment too soon. On 12 July the enemy's skirmishers came into view, darting from one place of cover to the next. Captain Simmons and the sharpshooters carefully watched the stealthy approach of the enemy. When the bluecoats came within fairly close range, the Georgians took careful aim and fired. For the next few minutes, as Captain Simmons described it, he and his sharpshooters had some "pretty serious fighting" on their hands. The enemy skirmishers soon withdrew to a more protected line.[7]

Lee kept his army in defensive positions until a pontoon bridge could be constructed to allow his men to cross over the Potomac River into Virginia. The Confederates were in a very vulnerable spot, but the Federal army was badly crippled from the fighting at Gettysburg.

The night of 14 July was the last evening Captain Simmons would spend in Maryland on the retreat. That evening the soldiers of the 3rd Sharpshooter

---

General: The Civil War Letters of Major-General Lafayette McLaws (Chapel Hill: University of North Carolina Press, 2002) 195–97.

[5]John Stegeman, These Men She Gave: Civil War Diary of Athens, Georgia (Athens, GA: University of Georgia Press, 1964) 95; Gerald J. Smith, *One of the Most Daring of Men: The Life of Confederate General William Tatum Wofford*, vol. 16 of Journal of Confederate History Series, ed. John McGlone (Murfreesboro, TN: Southern Heritage Press, 1997) 94.

[6]According to service records, two sharpshooters from the 3rd Battalion were among the casualties at Hagerstown, MD, on 11 July 1863: Private James A. Davidson of Simmons's Company C was killed in action, and Private John William of Company A was wounded. Two sharpshooters from Company A were captured at Funkstown, MD: Private Levi D. Henderson on 11 July and Private Hugh L. White on 12 July.

[7]Daniel M. Byrd, *Them Brave Georgians*, manuscript, pg. 204–206, Gwinnett Historical Society Archives, Lawrenceville, GA (Fort Delaware Society Library, Delaware City, DE, also has a copy.).

Battalion were placed on the picket line to repel any sudden attack from the Union forces. At that time, Captain Simmons was not aware that General Lee would move out the last of his army that night under cover of darkness. When daybreak came, Simmons dispatched a courier to find out why no relief had been sent.[8] The courier returned to inform Simmons that the Confederate army had moved on to the river crossing. The officer in charge had neglected to send word to the picket forces in time to join the rest of the army for the river crossing.

As soon as he learned that his detachment had been left behind, Simmons and his men quietly abandoned their positions and headed for the river. Fortunately there was a heavy mist to restrict visibility during the early morning hours. Once safely out of earshot they raced towards the river. According to Simmons, the road was knee deep in mud and at times so impassable that the men had to run through the bordering woods and ravines.

Shortly before reaching the Potomac the sharpshooters spotted a small detachment of cavalrymen in the distance, but they were not able to determine if they were friend or foe. Simmons and his forces kept quietly under cover while scouts were sent out to determine the identity of the cavalry unit. They were soon relieved to find out that the cavalrymen were part of the Confederate rear guard. When they reached the river, they learned that virtually all of the Southern army had crossed over safely and had hastily thrown up some breastworks, covered with brush, on the other side. Simmons and the sharpshooters quickly made the river crossing and joined the Confederate forces on the southern shore.[9]

Early the next morning Longstreet's Corps resumed its march and went into a camp on the banks of Mill Creek, east of Bunker Hill, in what is now the state of West Virginia.[10] There, the men rested until 20 July when the corps completed a one-day march to Millwood, a small community in the Shenandoah Valley. Their mission was to cross the Shenandoah River and take Ashby's Gap in order to cover future movements of the army. The Federals, however, had already seized the gap and held a commanding position on the banks of the Shenandoah. Because the river was at flood stage, Longstreet was forced to move to Front Royal, Virginia, in hopes of effecting a crossing there.

After another day's march and the hurried construction of pontoon bridges, Longstreet's men began to cross the Shenandoah at midnight on 21 July. Once the crossing was completed, Wofford's Brigade was ordered to disperse the enemy's cavalry at the foot of the mountain at Chester's Gap and capture his artillery. After a light skirmish, Wofford's men forced the Yankee cavalry to retreat and the gap was secured.[11] Longstreet's remaining troops

---

[8] Ibid., 206–208 (based on an account by William Simmons).
[9] Ibid., 206–207.
[10] *OR,* ser. I, vol. 27, pt. 3, 1006.
[11] *OR,* ser. I, vol. 27, pt. 2, 362.

passed through the gap and continued the march to Culpeper Court House, arriving on 24 July.

By early August, the Army of Northern Virginia had found good camps in the rolling country bordered by the Rapidan River. The 3rd Sharpshooter Battalion and 16th Georgia were located at Waller's Tavern, which was about half way between Orange Court House and Hanover Junction.[12] Once again, Virginia hospitality was showered on the soldiers, and many young officers, including Captain Simmons, enjoyed the companionship of young ladies at dances in the evening and at picnics and riding parties by day.[13]

Throughout August and the early days of September, the army was strengthened in materiel, and its ranks once again swelled with new recruits and returning convalescents. The camp was a welcome respite after the fierce fighting at Gettysburg and the difficult retreat in July. Despite the period of relative inactivity and the comfortable accommodations of camp, the seasoned veterans of the Army of Northern Virginia knew there would be further clashes with the enemy in the days to come.

---

[12]Byrd, *Them Brave Georgians*, 209.

[13]G. Moxley Sorrel, *Recollections of a Confederate Staff Officer*, ed. Bell Irvin Wiley (Wilmington, NC: Broadfoot Publishing Company, 1995) 174–75.

14

Deployment to Chattanooga

Most roads lead men homewards.
My road leads me forth.

—John Masefield

In early September camp rumors began to surface that Longstreet's Corps would be sent to Tennessee to reinforce the faltering Confederate forces under General Braxton Bragg. The Army of Northern Virginia would take the defensive while Longstreet's men were absent.[1] The rumors were confirmed when the first of Longstreet's command left the camps along the Rapidan River for Richmond, their initial stop *en route* to Tennessee. Simmons and his fellow Georgians were elated by the news. Tennessee was much closer to home, and even if furloughs could not be secured, a trip by train would be a welcome relief from the interminable marches of the past.

On the evening of 7 September, Wofford's Brigade received orders to prepare rations for three days and march to Hanover Junction where the men would board railroad cars for their deployment to Tennessee. At Hanover Junction they were joined by the other regiments under General McLaws, and by 11 September they were on their way by rail to Richmond and points south.[2]

During a brief stay in Richmond, Captain Simmons noticed the changes that the war had brought about. Few families had escaped bereavement. Honor guards daily brought home the last remains of comrades for interment or for placement on southbound trains to be carried to their final resting places. The women of the city, called on so often to appear in mourning, had abandoned colorful dresses as being in bad taste.[3]

The troops were not allowed to dawdle in Richmond. Each day trains were starting on a journey to Atlanta that would take up to one week. Travel time depended on the route followed and the luck in making connections. Due to the war, it was not possible to take a more direct route through eastern Tennessee. Only two options were available: one route required going by way of

---

[1]Douglas Southall Freeman, *Lee's Lieutenants: A Study in Command*, vol. 3 (New York: Charles Scribner's Sons, 1944) 222.

[2]Daniel M. Byrd, *Them Brave Georgians*, manuscript, pg. 210–11, Gwinnett Historical Society Archives, Lawrenceville, GA (Fort Delaware Society Library, Delaware City, DE, also has a copy.).

[3]Robert Stiles, *Four Years Under Marse Robert* (New York: Neale Publishing Company, 1910) 119, 294.

Wilmington, North Carolina, a distance of about 700 miles. A second route went through Charlotte, North Carolina, and was seventy miles longer. Both alternatives required passage on at least six railroads and involved several changes in cars due to the different gauges of track.[4]

Although it was preferable to a long march, the trip by train was much more unpleasant than the train rides William Simmons had taken in the past. He commented in his diary that the "freight cars [were] fitted up with plank seats, and the men were packed in like sardines."[5] Since the weather was uncomfortably hot, the riders used axes and knives to cut away all but the framework of the boxcars. This made the trip more comfortable for the men and gave them an opportunity to view the passing scenery.

Through the Carolinas and Georgia, Simmons and his comrades passed by hundreds of bystanders along the roadside. The soldiers cheered when they saw young women waving handkerchiefs and flags at the passing trains and hats thrown in the air by boys and old men. Along the way they were provided with tasty delicacies, pushed into the cars by young ladies at every stop.[6]

At midnight on 18 September, after seven grueling days in transit, Simmons's train pulled into Atlanta.[7] Early the next morning the men boarded the cars of the Western and Atlantic Railroad and headed toward Chattanooga, 120 miles northwest of Atlanta. As the train lumbered toward its destination, a desperate struggle broke out along Chickamauga Creek, a meandering stream in Georgia, just south of Chattanooga. There General Braxton Bragg's Army of Tennessee opposed a formidable Union force under the command of General William S. Rosecrans.

The train reached Ringgold, Georgia, the evening of 20 September. The 115-mile trip from Atlanta had taken an agonizing thirty-two hours.[8] By that time the Confederate army had won a victory at the Battle of Chickamauga.

---

[4]Robert C. Black III, *The Railroads of the Confederacy* (Chapel Hill: University of North Carolina Press, 1952) 185.

[5]Byrd, *Them Brave Georgians*, 213.

[6]G. Moxley Sorrel, *Recollections of a Confederate Staff Officer*, ed. Bell Irvin Wiley (Wilmington, NC: Broadfoot Publishing Company, 1995) 182.

[7]E. Porter Alexander, *Military Memoirs of a Confederate: A Critical Narrative* (1907; reprint, Dayton, OH: Press of Morningside Bookshop, 1977) 448–49; Black, *Railroads of the Confederacy*, 189. The deployment required the use of seven different railroads for Captain Simmons and the 3rd Battalion Sharpshooters: Virginia Central, Richmond & Petersburg, Petersburg, Wilmington & Weldon, Wilmington & Manchester, South Carolina, and Western & Atlantic.

[8]William R. Montgomery of Company F, 3rd Battalion Georgia Sharpshooters wrote in his diary, "Arrived at Ringgold, GA on the night of the 20th of September. Took up our march for the battlefield. Joined our Corps [at Chickamauga] on the 21st" (George Montgomery Jr., *Georgia Sharpshooter: The Civil War Diary and Letters of William Rhadamanthus Montgomery* [Macon: Mercer University Press, 1997] 26).

Although Longstreet arrived before the battle began, some of his brigades did not reach their destination in time to engage in the fighting. Among the late arrivals were Simmons's 3rd Battalion Sharpshooters and most of Wofford's Brigade. They reached the battlefield on 21 September to learn that they had just missed one of the bloodiest battles of the war. Two days before they arrived, the right wing of Bragg's army attacked Rosecrans without decisive results. The next morning a strong attack by Bragg's left wing, led by General Longstreet, broke the Union line. The northern forces had been driven from the field and were in retreat toward Chattanooga.

The day they arrived on the battlefield, Wofford's late arrivals were assigned to picket duty on the LaFayette Road near Rossville, Georgia. This location was just south of the Tennessee state line near a gap in Missionary Ridge where a large number of Union forces had retreated from the Chickamauga battlefield. Lieutenant William R. Montgomery of Company F, 3rd Battalion Sharpshooters, recorded in his diary that they "Followed on after the yanks some six miles [and] had a heavy skirmish at the foot of Lookout Mountain." On that day Private David Richardson of Montgomery's sharpshooter company was killed.[9]

When the troops had taken up their picket positions, Captain Simmons joined General Wofford for a conference. The two officers sat on their horses and viewed the ground over which the Yankees had retreated. As recorded by Simmons, they were soon joined by General Nathan Bedford Forrest, who rode up on horseback with one of his aides.[10] Forrest tried to convince General Wofford that he should immediately send his brigade through the gap and occupy Chattanooga. He told the two Georgians that the enemy was evacuating the city "as hard as they could go" and that there were no Federal soldiers there.

General Wofford was more cautious and did not believe that an assault on Chattanooga was the best course of action at that time. Before he could fully explain his reasons for declining Forrest's proposal, a group of Yankee sharpshooters some 200 yards distant began to fire at the four officers from behind a shanty. After taking cover Wofford suggested that General Forrest was mistaken about the enemy's whereabouts. Forrest replied that the men doing the shooting were likely Union stragglers, left behind without regular troops to support them. To illustrate his point, Forrest turned to his aide and shouted,

---

[9]Montgomery, *Georgia Sharpshooter*, 26. Before joining the 3rd Georgia Sharpshooter Battalion, Private Richardson served in Company B [Dalton Guards] of Phillips Legion Infantry Battalion. At the formation of the sharpshooter battalion, he was assigned to Company F.

[10]The encounter with General Forrest is a re-write of an account by William Simmons. According to Daniel M. Byrd, although Simmons did not identify Forrest's aide by name, it was likely Major Charles W. Anderson, assistant adjutant and inspector general of Forrest's Cavalry Brigade (Byrd, *Them Brave Georgians*, 218).

"Follow me." The two officers charged at full speed into a steady enemy volley, captured five Yankee sharpshooters, and brought them back. The only casualty was Forrest's magnificent dappled gray horse, which was shot squarely through the fleshy part of the neck. Simmons described the action as "a daring and brilliant feat, one that no man of ordinary courage and intrepidity would have undertaken."[11]

After the prisoners had been sent to the rear under guard, the discussion continued between the two generals. Wofford persisted in his refusal to advance toward Chattanooga. He pointed out that Chattanooga would be defensively untenable from their side of the Tennessee River and would never be a desirable base for operations if General Bragg intended to invade Tennessee. None of General Forrest's arguments, it seemed to Captain Simmons, would have justified taking the responsibility for committing the army for such an objective. Moreover, neither General Longstreet nor General McLaws had authorized the advance.

General Forrest would not be deterred. Without support he sent his troopers against the enemy in the gap. Though his main force was stopped, one of his cavalry regiments bypassed the enemy and advanced within three miles of Chattanooga, taking positions on Missionary Ridge. That night Forrest continued his crusade. He confronted Braxton Bragg and urged a full-scale advance northward. When Bragg was adamant in his refusal, Forrest could scarcely contain his fury.

On the following day, 22 September, infantry under Generals Wofford and Kershaw began to replace Forrest's intrepid cavalrymen. The 3rd Georgia Sharpshooter Battalion took its position in the march at the head of Wofford's Brigade. Late in the afternoon, when within two miles of Chattanooga, they deployed in skirmish formation and covered the front of the brigade. Soon after his men selected sentry positions, Captain Simmons spotted a full Federal brigade and one battery of artillery as if on reconnaissance. He passed orders to the sharpshooters to hold their fire until the enemy came within 100 yards. They tensely waited until the Federals were about 100 yards away and then opened a destructive fire, reloading and shooting as rapidly as possible. The Union soldiers wavered and fell back.

Efforts of the officers of the Federal brigade to rally their men soon stopped the retreat and turned the brigade about for a second charge. Simmons's sharpshooters "guyed" their disorganized adversaries and dared them to resume the fight. Their challenge was soon accepted. Again the sharpshooters opened up with a continuous fire. This murderous volley mowed the enemy down. The Union soldiers turned on their heels again, despite rallying commands, and did not stop until safely back in Chattanooga. This skirmish was one of several

---

[11]Byrd, *Them Brave Georgians*, 217–219 (re-write of an account by William Simmons).

between the rear guard of the retreating Union forces, and elements of Wofford's and Kershaw's Brigades.[12]

This or a similar encounter was described by Captain James L. Lemon of the 18th Georgia:

> On the 22nd of September, we caught up with the Yankee rearguard and drove them with style into the city. We halted on the heights overlooking the city and commenced digging in and laying siege to the place. It took some days for all our army to come up and position itself, but soon we were all up and had fairly surrounded the Yanks, except to the north.[13]

After a final skirmish on 24 September, the Federals were driven completely wthin the lines around Chattanooga.[14] On that day Sergeant Eli P. Landers of the 16th Georgia described the sporadic fighting that had taken place near the area where Simmons' sharpshooters were posted:

> There has been some very hard fighting since our Virginia army had arrived here but our brigade has not been in no big fight yet, more than skirmishing. Our troops has been very successful so far. We have drove the enemy some eight or ten miles and cleared them off of Georgia soil, killing a great many of them and taking many prisoners. Our [Army of Northern] Virginia troops fights like tigers up here in the West. They say they are going to show them the lick it is done with but I think the Western boys [Confederate soldiers in the Army of Tennessee] is all right. They [the Union forces] are not as bad whipt as we heard they was. They all seem to be in good entrenchments. They are well fortified and we are in the line of battle, both parties near each other. It is thought that if we can't flank their position some way that we will have to charge them out of their works and if we do it will be done with great slaughter on our side. There is no other chance for they have got good cannon and rifle works.[15]

Early on the morning of 27 September, Captain Simmons received a report that two Union officers were riding with a white flag of truce towards the position held by the 3rd Battalion.[16] When the officers arrived, they introduced

---

[12]Ibid., 220–21.

[13]James Lile Lemon, *Feed them the Steel!* Being the Wartime Recollections of Captain James Lile Lemon Company A, 18th Georgia Infantry C.S.A. (Acworth, GA: printed by Mark H. Lemon, 2008) 52.

[14]William R. Montgomery recorded in his diary that the sharpshooters were engaged in "heavy skirmishes" on 22 and 24 September 1863 (Montgomery, *Georgia Sharpshooter*, 26–27).

[15]Eli P. Landers to Susan Landers, 24 September 1863, in Elizabeth Whitley Roberson, *In Care of Yellow River* (Fort Lauderdale: Venture Press, 1994) 138.

[16]*The War of the Rebellion: A Compilation of the Official Records of the Union and Confederate Armies* (70 vols. in 128; Washington, 1880–1901), ser. I, vol. 30, pt. 1, 203

themselves as Colonel Joseph C. McKibben and Captain Brown, members of General Rosecrans's staff. Captain Simmons asked the men why they carried the flag of truce. Colonel McKibben explained that they wished to obtain permission to send medicines and bandages to the wounded Yankee soldiers in Confederate hands and to recover their wounded soldiers who remained on the field.[17] The precipitous Federal retreat had not allowed adequate time to minister to the wounded or evacuate the main Union hospital at Crawfish Springs, which was now inside Southern lines. Simmons observed in his journal that Colonel McKibben was a "courtly gentleman." He asked the two officers to dismount and to remain at ease while he sent the message to brigade and division headquarters.[18]

While the officers waited for a response to the Union request, McKibben asked Simmons, "What command fought our troops the other evening at this position?"

"Why do you ask?" inquired Simmons.

"Well," answered McKibben, "we knew that it was not any of Bragg's regular troops from the accuracy and rapidity of their fire."[19]

When Simmons stated that the only troops engaged were his comrades in the six sharpshooter companies of the 3rd Battalion, McKibben was astonished. A handful of Confederate sharpshooters had stopped an entire Union infantry brigade in its tracks. McKibben replied, "We also knew, for the same reasons, when Longstreet's Corps struck our lines at Chickamauga. No western (Confederate) troops have ever attacked so rapidly and effectively."

The three officers continued their conversations until 10:00 A.M. when General Bragg's reply was received, consenting to the request. Later that day Union hospital wagons with doctors and medical supplies passed through the lines, returning shortly with the wounded from the battlefield and the Crawfish Springs Hospital.[20]

Years later when Simmons recalled Colonel McKibben's comparison of western soldiers with those of the Army of Northern Virginia, he wrote,

---

(hereafter cited as *OR*); Montgomery, *Georgia Sharpshooter*, 27. Montgomery wrote in his diary on 27 September that it was "All quiet today. The Yanks sent us a flag of truce, a dispatch to Gen. Bragg. The flag remained from 10 o'clock A.M. to 4 P.M."

[17] *OR*, ser. I, vol. 30, pt. 1, 225.

[18] Byrd, *Them Brave Georgians*, 222, based on an account by William Simmons.

[19] Ibid., 223.

[20] It was estimated that 1,750 wounded Union soldiers were returned, but 750 remained behind when Rosecrans refused to release an equal number of Confederate prisoners (*OR*, ser. 1, part 1, 205, 225). In his diary for 29 September, Montgomery noted that the "Yankees carried about 1,000 wounded through our lines" (Montgomery, *Georgia Sharpshooter*, 27).

The soldiers composing the Army of Northern Virginia were not any braver or more intrepid fighters than those in the western armies, but decidedly more dangerous and effective on the battlefield, which was solely due to their superior training. As an illustration, the Virginia army was taught not to shoot without taking aim, and never to that above the knee, as a low shot happening to strike the ground is sure to ricochet and probably be effective, whereas not five bullets out of every thousand ever hit anything but the air, and it is never advisable to aim above the crotch at any time.[21]

After the limited action outside Chattanooga, Wofford's men were not concerned with the rigors of battle for several weeks. The regiments remained in their positions along lines on the Chattanooga side of Missionary Ridge while the 3rd Battalion Sharpshooters were situated at the base of Lookout Mountain at Camp Lookout, only one-half mile from the outskirts of the besieged city.[22] The Southern strategy was to lay siege to Chattanooga and starve the enemy into submission.

---

[21]Byrd, *Them Brave Georgians*, 224 (from William Simmons's recollections).
[22]Montgomery, *Georgia Sharpshooter*, 93–96.

15

Assault on Fort Sanders

High station in life is earned by the gallantry with which
appalling experiences are survived with grace.
—Tennessee Williams

In putting the Union forces under siege at Chattanooga, Confederate leaders
were hopeful that the Union army would be forced to surrender or face
starvation. The bitter irony of the situation was that, after a couple of weeks, the
Confederate forces experienced significantly greater supply and subsistence
problems than their adversaries under siege. One rebel soldier from the Orphan
Brigade wrote in his journal, "Our rations were nothing but beef pickled in a
very strong brine, and cornbread. Our supply of food was so meager that we
actually suffered from pangs of hunger."[1] According to Sam Watkins, a private
in the Army of Tennessee, "Many soldiers lived on parched corn, picked out of
the mud and dirt under the feet of horses."[2]

Captain Simmons and his comrades in General Wofford's Brigade did not
fare any better than their counterparts from Tennessee. The brigade's larder was
empty for days at a time. In early October, hopes were raised when the men
learned that the brigade commissary officer, Major John C. Griffis, was able to
secure a large quantity of corn meal. Captain Simmons and 2nd Lieutenant
Joseph W. Barrett were appointed to a Board of Survey by General Wofford to
examine the meal and report on its condition. Barrett was a young officer from
Polk County, Georgia who was in Phillips Legion Infantry Battalion prior to his
selection to serve in the 3rd Georgia Sharpshooters. Unfortunately, the meal was
not edible. As Simmons noted in his diary, he and Lieutenant Barrett carefully
examined 216 pounds of meal and found it unfit for use.[3] With food so scarce,
the meal likely was infested with weevils and mold to have been rejected.

---

[1]A. D. Kirwan, ed., *Johnny Green of the Orphan Brigade: The Journal of a Confederate
Soldier* (Lexington: University of Kentucky Press, 1955) 105.

[2]Sam Watkins, *Company Aytch, or A Side Show of the Big Show*, M. Thomas Inge,
ed. (1882; reprint, New York: Plume Books, 1999) 91. William Montgomery of the 3rd
Battalion Sharpshooters complained of short rations in his diary entry of 28 September
1863. The following month, 22 October he wrote, "Almost starved for something good
to eat" (George Montgomery Jr., *Georgia Sharpshooter: The Civil War Diary and Letters of
William Rhadamanthus Montgomery* [Macon: Mercer University Press, 1997] 27–29).

[3]Simmons service records, in Byrd, *Them Brave Georgians*, 226.

The Confederates continued to starve while the Union rested comfortably and well-fed in Chattanooga after re-establishing their supply lines. Nearby, a Tennessee soldier wrote, "In all the history of the war, I cannot remember of more privations and hardships than what we went through at Missionary Ridge."[4] In the midst of the suffering and boredom there was an event that helped to lift the spirits of the demoralized Confederate forces and suggested that their wretched conditions would improve. On 9–10 October, President Jefferson Davis came to visit the army for a series of conferences with top military leaders in the field.[5] In honor of the president's visit, every soldier brought out his least shabby uniform to give the chief executive the best reception possible.[6]

Despite their efforts to look their best for President Davis, many of the soldiers at the review could not suppress the discomfort of their empty stomachs. A Tennessee soldier later wrote about the experience:

> When Jefferson Davis and his great retinue of staff officers and play-outs passed by at full gallop, cheers [from the soldiers at the review] greeted them with the words, "Send us something to eat, Massa Jeff. Give us something to eat, Massa Jeff. I'm hungry. I'm hungry!"[7]

Accompanying President Davis on the visit was John C. Breckenridge, the man William Simmons and the *Lawrenceville News* had supported for president of the United States in the election of 1860. Breckenridge was now a major general with an excellent reputation as a military leader. With him rode Captain Fitzgerald Ross, an Englishman who had served with the Austrian Hussars. In stark contrast to the Southern soldiers in their drab, tattered rags, Ross was resplendent in his full uniform, described as a "sky blue tunic, skin tight trousers, tasseled boots and a handsomely curved saber hanging on gold cords."[8]

After the president's two-day visit, the army returned to its routine. During this period of inactivity many of the men renewed their requests for furloughs that before had been uniformly rejected. This time a small number of requests were approved, and Captain Simmons was among the few who were granted leave. This would be his first visit home since his sick furlough in June 1862.

To get back to Lawrenceville, Simmons caught a ride on a mule wagon to Ringgold, Georgia. From that location, he took another slow-moving train to Atlanta and made the final 25-mile leg of the journey by mule wagon back home. Despite the hardships of war, his homecoming was a joyous event. There

---

[4]Watkins, *Company Aytch*, 89–90.
[5]G. Moxley Sorrel, *Recollections of a Confederate Staff Officer*, ed. Bell Irvin Wiley (Wilmington, NC: Broadfoot Publishing Company, 1995) 191.
[6]Ibid., 196.
[7]Watkins, *Company Aytch*, 90.
[8]Sorrel, *Recollections of a Confederate Staff Officer*, 197.

was a new member of the family awaiting his return, a one-year-old brother named Terrell, born in September 1862, a few months after Simmons's last visit home.[9]

Captain Simmons's leave slipped by rapidly, and soon he was on his way back to join the 3rd Georgia Sharpshooter Battalion. When he returned, he was informed that one of his fellow officers, Major Phillip E. Davant, had been promoted to lieutenant colonel and assigned to the 38th Georgia Regiment.[10] Although Simmons and the other five captains in the sharpshooter battalion were eligible for promotion, General Wofford chose to delay the selection of a replacement for Davant.

After Simmons returned from leave, weather conditions worsened. Cold rains continued for days at a time and the roads became impassable. To add to the hunger and misery, many men, lacking blankets and adequate shelter, fell ill.

On 3 November General McLaws received orders to proceed to Knoxville as part of Longstreet's command and engage the Union forces holding the city.[11] Their destination was about 120 miles northeast of Chattanooga. The following day the division marched to Tyner's Station on the East Tennessee & Georgia Railroad to board train cars for Sweetwater, sixty miles away. At Tyner's Station they were joined by Hood's Division under the command of Brigadier General Micah Jenkins. Hood was recovering from a wound he had received at Chickamauga. Combined, the two infantry divisions totaled about 10,000 men. In addition, the command included five brigades of cavalry under General Joseph Wheeler.[12]

As the Confederate forces prepared for the next leg of their journey, arrangements began to fall apart. There was neither adequate transportation nor sufficient food and equipment for the time required to move all of the troops to Sweetwater. The men of Wofford's Brigade, now under the command of

---

[9]Simmons service records, in Byrd, *Them Brave Georgians*, 229–31. Simmons's service records do not indicate the exact dates for his 1863 furlough and are also in error. He is shown on furlough for September and October, but this information is incorrect because he was present at least until 5 October 1863, the date that he served on the Board of Inquiry while in camp near Chattanooga. It is therefore reasonable to conclude that his furlough took place sometime between 6 October and 3 November, the day his brigade began the march toward Knoxville.

[10]*Compiled Service Records of Confederate Soldiers Who Served in Organizations from the State of Georgia*, microcopy 266, RG 109, National Archives and Records Administration, Washington, DC. The date of Davant's promotion is taken from William Simmons's service record.

[11]The War of the Rebellion: A Compilation of the Official Records of the Union and Confederate Armies (70 vols. in 128; Washington, 1880–1901), ser. I, vol. 31, pt. 1, 455 (hereafter cited as OR).

[12]E. Porter Alexander, *Military Memoirs of a Confederate: A Critical Narrative* (1907; reprint, Dayton, OH: Press of Morningside Bookshop, 1977) 480–81.

Lieutenant Colonel Nathan L. Hutchins Jr., were among the first to arrive in Sweetwater on 6 November. Once again, the train trip was an ordeal for Captain Simmons and his comrades. The men made the cold, windy journey in open cars. A disgusted passenger who rode on the first train remarked, "The railroad was of heavy [steep] grades and the engines light powered. When a hill was reached the long train would be instantly emptied—platforms, roofs, doors, and windows—of our fellows, like ants out of a hill, who would ease things by trudging up the dirt road and catching on again at the top." As an added task the soldiers had to carry water from roadside creeks and chop fence rails to supplement the insufficient water and wood for the engines.[13]

It took six more days for the shuttling trains to transport the rest of the troops to Sweetwater. From there Wofford's Brigade continued their journey through East Tennessee by way of Philadelphia to Loudon, finally reaching that destination at daybreak on 14 November. They remained there for a day while pontoon bridges were thrown across the river under the cover of darkness. The next day they continued their march to Lenoir's Station, about thirty miles from Knoxville. It took another three days to reach their destination. During the final leg of the journey there were numerous skirmishes with the Union forces, which fell back to the fortifications surrounding Knoxville.[14] The Federals were commanded by General Ambrose E. Burnside, who had led the Army of the Potomac at Fredericksburg the previous year.

Confederate forces took up positions on the outskirts of Knoxville. McLaws's Division was deployed to the west of the city, with Wofford's Brigade assigned positions on the left. As usual the 3rd Battalion Georgia Sharpshooters were assigned to scouting and picket duty. When Captain Simmons had an opportunity to observe the enemy's fortifications, he concluded that if the Confederates were to gain possession of the town it would take "some hard fighting because the place was strongly fortified with trenches and redoubts."[15] These strong fortifications consisted of a series of forts, well positioned on prominent heights circling the north side of the town. Knoxville was situated on the north bank of the Holston River, then a major tributary of the Tennessee River. Three creeks flowing through the valleys between the heights had been dammed up and were flooded, making it difficult to storm the Federal forts,

---

[13] Sorrel, *Recollections of a Confederate Staff Officer*, 200–201; Alexander, *Military Memoirs*, 481.

[14] According to service records, one of the unfortunate mishaps during the advance took place on 17 November 1863. Private S. Jasper Mitchell of the 16th Georgia, one of the original members of the Hutchins Guards, was captured. Mitchell had been seriously wounded at Crampton's Gap the previous year. Despite the amputation of a leg, he returned to duty as soon as he had recovered and carried out his duties as best his handicap would permit.

[15] Simmons's personal recollections, in Byrd, *Them Brave Georgians*, 237.

which were connected by a series of rifle pits.[16] The most imposing feature of the Federal defenses was Fort Sanders, named in honor of Burnside's recently slain cavalry chief, Brigadier General William P. Sanders. Sanders had been mortally wounded on 18 November in a skirmish on Kingston Pike west of Knoxville. He died the next morning. Sanders was a cousin of Jefferson Davis and the only Southern-born Union general killed in the Civil War.[17]

Fort Sanders was situated on a hill of considerable height at the northwest corner of Knoxville. It had been partially constructed by Confederate forces in the early months of the war and named Fort Loudon. The remaining work was completed by the Union engineers under the supervision of Major Orlando M. Poe. Fort Sanders formed a salient, which extended northwest of main defenses. The structure had earthen walls thirteen feet high and was fronted by a twelve-foot-wide ditch up to eight feet in depth.[18]

On 25 November Kershaw's Brigade advanced against a line of Union skirmishers west of Knoxville. Backed by Alexander's artillery, the South Carolinians drove the skirmishers from their advanced position. McLaws's Division moved up quickly and began constructing a line of rifle pits extending north from the Holston River to a point beyond the northwest bastion of Fort Sanders. After their arrival the Confederates forces dug in and waited for orders to storm the fortifications at Knoxville. Kershaw's Brigade was positioned on the right near the river and Humphreys's Mississippians were next in line. Wofford's Brigade, now under the command of Colonel S. Z. Ruff of the 18th Georgia, held down the left.[19] Colonel Ruff joined Lieutenant Colonel Hutchins in supervising the construction of rifle pits to be occupied by the 3rd Georgia Sharpshooters and other detachments. On that day the men of the 3rd Battalion were in the thick of the fighting as noted by Lieutenant W. R. Montgomery in a letter to his aunt in Georgia:

> We are now seeing what you might call a hard time & have a little fighting every day. We Sharp Shooters are in front all the time from 100 to 500 yards of the Yankies. We keep up a prettie heavy fire all the time, take a shot whenever a Yankie shows his head. Day before yesterday [25 November] the 2nd Michigan Regiment charged & flanked our rifle pits & drove our battalion back for a while, but we soon rallied, charged, and drove them back. The brigade was in the rear, too far to help us, and [we] had a prettie hard fight for a while. Our little battalion only has about 130 men for duty. We whipped and drove back one whole regiment of "Yanks"

---

[16]OR, ser. I, vol. 31, pt. 1, 492.

[17]Digby Gordon Seymour, *Divided Loyalties: Fort Sanders and the Civil War in East Tennessee*, 3rd ed. (Knoxville: East Tennessee Historical Society, 2002) 122–23.

[18]Alexander, *Military Memoirs*, 483; Seymour, *Divided Loyalties*, 147. Some observers estimated that the ditch was up to ten feet deep.

[19]OR, ser. I, vol. 31, pt. 1, 483.

capturing about sixty. Our loss was only two killed and three badly wounded, one from our company.[20]

This was a time of great hardship for the men of Longstreet's command. The weather was cold and misty, and food was scarce. A large number of the Confederate soldiers did not have shoes or adequate winter clothing. At night, lying on the frozen ground, those who were able to sleep hovered close together in spoon-fashion.[21]

Finally on 28 November after a two-week siege, General Longstreet ordered an attack on Fort Sanders the next day at dawn. Wofford's Georgians were chosen to lead the assault on the left of the northwest bastion of the fort with the 16th Georgia in front. General Humphreys's Brigade was selected for the assault on the right with three regiments of Bryan's Georgia Brigade close behind.[22] During the night Captain Simmons's 3rd Battalion Sharpshooters engaged in the fighting to capture the Union rifle pits closest to Fort Sanders. There they remained on duty through the long, wretched hours of freezing temperature and fine mists, waiting for daylight when they were to open fire and signal the start of the attack.[23]

At 6:00 A.M. with the first sign of light, the signal was given for the sharpshooters to open fire and the storming columns to advance with fixed bayonets. Longstreet issued orders that no one fire except for the sharpshooters in the newly captured rifle pits. During the charge on Fort Sanders the 3rd Georgia Sharpshooters poured a continuous fire into the fort's enclosures to prevent the use of cannon and keep the defenders pinned down.[24] According to Captain D. Augustus Dickert, a young officer in Kershaw's Brigade, "So carefully was this order observed that not a gun was loaded in three brigades that were ordered to storm the fort."[25]

---

[20]William R. Montgomery to Aunt Frank, 27 November 1863, in Montgomery, *Georgia Sharpshooter*, 98.

[21]James Lile Lemon, *Feed them the Steel! Being the Wartime Recollections of Captain James Lile Lemon Company A, 18th Georgia Infantry* C.S.A. (Acworth, GA: printed by Mark H. Lemon, 2008) 52.

[22]*OR*, ser. I, vol. 31, pt. 1, 491; Seymour, *Divided Loyalties*, 152.

[23]Seymour, *Divided Loyalties*, 154.

[24]William R. Montgomery to Aunt Frank, 27 November 1863, in Montgomery, *Georgia Sharpshooter*, 98. According to service records for the battalion, several sharpshooters were killed or wounded prior to the assault on Fort Sanders, but no casualties were recorded for 29 November. Private Noah H. Stewart of Montgomery's Company F was killed on 24 November. The wounded included Sergeant William J. Hainey on 17 November, Sergeant Joseph X. Beauchamp on 19 November, privates Archer J. Whitehead and Lewis Jasper Yearwood on 24 November, and Private T. R. Huff on 27 November.

[25]D. Augustus Dickert, *History of Kershaw's Brigade* (1899; reprint, Wilmington, NC: Broadfoot Publishing Company, 1990) 310.

Through the mist and the dim light, the assaulting columns moved quickly across an open space toward the fort, but soon became entangled in telegraph wire that the enemy forces had strung across the tree stumps and tangled branches placed in their path. There was great confusion as soldier after soldier stumbled over the well concealed wire placed close to the ground.[26]

The defenders took advantage of the situation to fire both with musket and canister into the halted lines. Despite the heavy fire the Confederate soldiers rose up and continued to press on with battle flags proudly unfurled. A Northern correspondent observed that the Confederates were stunned for a moment by the torrent of canister and lead poured upon them, but they never hesitated as they advanced on Fort Sanders.[27]

Once the wires were cleared away the line of attackers encountered abatis, which the Yankees had placed just in front of their works. Some of the assaulting party took axes and chopped away the limbs to provide several gaps for the soldiers. This caused a funnel effect, and the assaulting forces became a disorganized mob without alignment.[28] The men quickly reached the ditch in front of the fort and began a futile attempt to climb up the walls. Thinking the depth was shallow, most blindly leapt into the ditch in the dim light. To their surprise they realized that the ditch was much deeper, with an average depth of eight feet. Once in the ditch the men were confronted by a steep-sloped, ice-covered wall rising more than sixteen feet. The frozen walls were created earlier by the defenders by pouring water down the sides of the fort and the freezing rain that fell the preceding day.[29] This made it nearly impossible for the Confederate infantry to scale the walls, and hundreds of men were trapped in the ditch within easy range of the Union soldiers. Without scaling ladders, men climbed on each other's shoulders in a futile attempt to reach the top of the slippery walls.[30]

In the dim light of early morning, Captain Simmons and the sharpshooters watched in horror from the rifle pits as the attackers dropped from sight. A murderous fire rained down on the Confederates in the deep ditch and men fell by the scores. A few soldiers managed to reach the top of the wall, but nearly all who made it were instantly shot down. Observers noted that three battle flags were planted on the parapet, those of the 13th and 17th Mississippi and the

---

[26]E. Porter Alexander, Brigadier-General, C. S. A., "Longstreet at Knoxville," in *Retreat from Gettysburg*, vol. 3 of *Battles and Leaders of the Civil War* (1887; reprint, New York: Castle Books, 1956) 749.

[27]Seymour, *Divided Loyalties*, 158.

[28]Lemon, *Feed them the Steel*, 53.

[29]Alexander, *Military Memoirs*, 488.

[30]Orlando M. Poe, Brevet Brigadier-General, U. S. A., "The Defense of Knoxville," in *Retreat from Gettysburg*, 743; Seymour, *Divided Loyalties*, 161.

16th Georgia. In the desperate hand-to-hand combat, the 16th Georgia color bearer surrendered the flag to J. S. Manning of the 29th Massachusetts.[31]

As the battle raged, more lives were lost when the Federal artillery commander had his men prepare cannon shells with three-second fuses and toss the shells over the parapet to land among those trapped in the ditch.[32] William Osborne of the 29th Massachusetts was an eye witness to the early morning attack on the fort by the soldiers of the 16th Georgia:

> The Confederates, led by fearless officers, crowded the ditch, and crossing it on each other's shoulders, began to ascend the bank. One of their standard-bearers came running up and planted his colors upon the parapet. He had hardly performed his deed of daring, when one of our soldiers shot him through the heart, and he fell forward into the works. Inspired by the example of their color bearer, a large body of the Confederates, led by a gray-haired old officer [most likely Colonel Henry P. Thomas of the 16th Georgia], with wild shouts made a dash up the bank. At this moment, four companies of the [Union] regiment came running into the fort, and ranging themselves along the parapet, opened a deadly fire upon the assaulting party. The gray old leader, while waving his sword and shouting to his men to come on, was shot dead. Many of his brave followers suffered the same fate, and the handful of survivors fell hurriedly back into the ditch.[33]

Only a handful of the attackers made it over the wall without being killed or wounded. One such individual was 2nd Lieutenant Thomas W. Cummings of Simmons's old regiment, the 16th Georgia.[34] With great gallantry Lieutenant Cummings rushed up to the fort with a dozen of his men and pushed his way through a gun embrasure into the fort. There he demanded the surrender of the Union defenders. While the Yankees loudly cheered him for his audacity, he and his men were soon made prisoners of war.

Captain James L. Lemon was another of the assaulting force who was somehow able to scale the icy walls of Fort Sanders. Being trapped in the deep ditch, he looked up to see his comrades attempt to scramble up the outer slope

---

[31] *Hallowed Banners: Historic Flags in the Historic Georgia Capitol Collection* (Atlanta: Georgia Secretary of State, 2005) 15. Manning received the Congressional Medal of Honor for the capture.

[32] Alexander, *Military Memoirs*, 488; Alexander, "Longstreet at Knoxville," 749.

[33] William H. Osborne, *The History of the Twenty-Ninth Regiment of Massachusetts Volunteer Infantry in the Late War of the Rebellion* (Boston: Albert J. Wright, 1877). See also Seymour, *Divided Loyalties*, 159–60. Colonel Henry P. Thomas was fifty-four years old when he led his regiment in the assault on Fort Sanders.

[34] Cummings served as regimental adjutant and likely volunteered to accompany Colonel Henry Thomas, the regimental commander, in the assault.

of the fort, only to slide back down. He quickly thought of an ingenious way to reach the top of the wall:

Somewhere in the midst of this mayhem, I seized upon an idea and, drawing my sword, began to busy myself at cutting small holes or steps into the ditch and up the slope. Then, climbing up to the base of the parapet, I plunged my sword into the earthen slope above my head and pulled myself almost to the top. Others below saw my design and, using bayonets and Bowie knives, began to do likewise until about twelve men had joined me on the slope.[35]

One of the men Captain Lemon witnessed scaling the wall was his regimental commander Colonel S. Z. Ruff, who had taken the regimental colors from a wounded ensign. Colonel Ruff was in command of Wofford's Brigade on that fateful morning. Captain Lemon noted that his superior was using the staff of the colors to pull his way up the icy wall. While urging his men to follow him, Colonel Ruff was shot in the chest and died instantly as he fell back into the ditch. The men of the 18th Georgia mourned the loss of their colonel as they would the loss of a father or brother.[36]

After Colonel Ruff was shot, Captain Lemon and the handful of men at his side entered the fort and surprised the first rank of defenders who leapt down from the parapet. The attackers were instantly met by a "volley of musketry" from within the fort. Lemon was shot through the neck just below the jaw, with the ball exiting just in front of his left ear. The wound was not fatal, and the young officer became a captive.[37]

The attacking forces remained in the deep ditch for nearly twenty minutes, unable to reach the enemy and unwilling to retreat. The ditch was filling with dead and dying soldiers. Major Goggin of General McLaws's staff rode back to inform Longstreet of the situation.[38] After realizing the futility of the assault, Longstreet ordered a retreat.[39] Without panic the regiments withdrew and

---

[35]Lemon, *Feed them the Steel*, 53.

[36]James Madison Folsom, *Heroes and Martyrs of Georgia: Georgia's Record in the Revolution of 1861* (Macon: Burke & Boykin, 1864) 17.

[37]Lemon, *Feed them the Steel*, 53–54. For his courage and example at Fort Sanders, Captain Lemon would be awarded the Confederate Medal of Honor, the only recipient from his regiment. Today, Captain Lemon's medal is on permanent public display at the National Medal of Honor Museum in Chattanooga, TN (Greg S. Clemmer, "My Duty to My Country Is Done, Mine to My Family Remains," in *Valor in Gray: The Recipients of the Confederate Medal of Honor* [Staunton, VA: Hearthside Publishing Company, 1998] 341).

[38]J. B. Boothe, "The Siege of Knoxville and Its Results," *Confederate Veteran* 22/6 (June 1914): 266.

[39]James Longstreet, *From Manassas to Appomattox: Memoirs of the Civil War in America* (1896; reprint, New York: Barnes & Noble, 2006) 432.

reformed a short distance from the fort, awaiting orders. None came for a renewed attack.[40]

The assault on Fort Sanders lasted less than thirty minutes, but it had a profound effect on all who were there on that cold November morning. One observer was the artillery commander of Longstreet's Corps, Edward Porter Alexander, who said, "Nowhere in the War was individual example more splendidly illustrated than on that fatal slope and in that bloody ditch."[41]

After Longstreet abandoned hope for taking Fort Sanders, the leading surgeon and his staff went under a flag of truce to the ditch to attend to the wounded and remove the dead. There they found the lifeless body of Colonel Henry P. Thomas, the respected regimental commander of the 16th Georgia, sitting in an upright position facing the enemy.[42] Simmons was devastated at the loss of his friend and neighbor. He learned that while leading his regiment in an attempt to scale the icy walls, the brave and determined colonel fell, surrounded in death as he had been in life by the soldiers of the 16th Georgia. On that morning the regiment lost twenty-seven men.[43]

For the most part, Longstreet's men were neither demoralized by the outcome of the Battle of Knoxville nor shaken in their confidence in themselves and their general. They rejected the claim that Longstreet was a "horrible failure" and presented solid arguments that neither they nor their commanders were solely to blame for the defeat. The soldiers were furnished little or no subsistence, camp equipment, or winter clothing when they departed from Chattanooga for the arduous journey to Knoxville. All overcoats and heavy clothing had been left in Virginia, never to return to the front again.[44] There were no scaling ladders to overcome the steep, icy walls.[45] Moreover, the size of

---

[40]*OR*, ser. I, vol. 31, pt. 1, 490.

[41]Alexander, "Longstreet at Knoxville," 749.

[42]*OR*, ser. I, vol. 31, pt. 1, 465, 491, 497. Colonel Thomas was able to scale the steep walls of Fort Sanders and was killed in the hand-to-hand fighting before falling into the ditch from the parapet. The defenders of the fort, "the 29th Massachusetts carried hatchets as side arms, and the colonel of the 16th Georgia fell victim to one during the intense fighting..." (*Hallowed Banners*, 15).

[43]According to service records and other reference sources, there were twelve soldiers from the 16th Georgia Infantry Regiment killed at Knoxville on 29 November 1863, including Colonel Henry P. Thomas, Captain Henry C. Nash Jr., privates Joseph M. Arthur, Warren H. Chronic, Elijah J. Herring, Joseph J. Key, John W. R. Kidd, John T. Kirkus, Isaac B. Simmons, Jack Tankersley, Samuel M. Whitworth, and J. R. Wood. Eleven more were wounded. Two soldiers from the 3rd Battalion Sharpshooters were wounded: privates Monroe Wagnon and George S. Owens.

[44]Dickert, *Kershaw's Brigade*, 316–17.

[45]Years after the war, Boothe wrote that "With scaling ladders the entry into the fort and its speedy capture would have been comparatively easy, but without them the gallant stormers at its base were as impotent as the foolish king who stood upon the

Longstreet's force was only one-half that of the Union army they confronted throughout the region during the campaign.[46]

Regardless of these shortcomings, it was also a fact that Longstreet's forces had been repulsed at Knoxville. The Confederates suffered heavy losses[47] during the assault on Fort Sanders and did little damage to the enemy.

Perhaps the greatest disappointment among the men was that they were not able to penetrate the strong defenses of the city and claim the spoils of victory. On the day before the assault, General Archibald Gracie had ridden through his Alabama brigade to lift the spirits of his cold and disheveled men. To motivate them to put forth their utmost in the coming battle, he frequently pointed toward Fort Sanders and remarked, "There are shoes over there, boys," likely inspiring visions of warm, comfortable Yankee brogans in the minds of his barefoot soldiers.[48] Unfortunately, their utmost was not enough.

---

seashore and commanded the waters to cease their ebb and flow" (Boothe, "The Siege of Knoxville and Its Results," 266).

[46]G. Moxley Sorrel observed that General Bragg underestimated the size of the Union Forces in East Tennessee and soon pulled back Wheeler's "powerful body" of Cavalry, which consisted of four brigades and horse artillery (Sorrel, *Recollections of a Confederate Staff Officer*, 200).

[47]Of the four brigades of McLaws's Division engaged in the East Tennessee Campaign, Wofford's Brigade sustained the greatest losses, with 48 killed, 121 wounded, and 81 missing. Overall, there were 250 casualties between 4 November and 5 December (Alexander, *Military Memoirs*, 492).

[48]Lewellyn Shaver, A History of the Sixtieth Alabama Regiment, Gracie's Alabama Brigade (Montgomery, AL: Barrett and Brown, 1867) 24–27.

16

Another Bitter Winter

Difficulties strengthen the mind, as labor does the body.
—Seneca

In reflecting on the ill-fated assault on Fort Sanders, Longstreet realized that his forces remained in a very precarious position. With the cold hand of winter upon them, inadequate clothing and very little food, their position at Knoxville was not tenable. Longstreet soon learned about other developments that made the situation even worse. A dispatch revealed that General Bragg had suffered a severe defeat at Missionary Ridge and was in full retreat at Dalton, Georgia,[1] forty miles south of Chattanooga. In addition, a letter being carried by a captured Union courier indicated that Federal reinforcements were on their way to relieve Burnside and break the siege of Knoxville.[2] Longstreet became aware of another barrier to his return when he received word that the road to Dalton was closed.[3]

Given the dire situation, Longstreet realized that it would be foolish to attempt to join Bragg's forces. Such a move would require taking a circuitous route through the mountains in the dead of winter without adequate provisions. Moreover, the roads in upper Georgia were deemed impracticable during the winter months. Instead, Longstreet decided to move in the opposite direction. He sought a position away from Knoxville that would place his command closer to Virginia.

On 2 December 1863 orders were issued to raise the siege and begin a march to the northeast. Confederate wagon trains moved out on the next day and Wofford and Kershaw's Brigades departed the following night in a severe rainstorm.[4] For Captain Simmons and his comrades, it was another miserable march through the cold black of night over muddy roads deeply rutted by the wagon trains ahead. For some time before leaving Knoxville the only source of footwear had been moccasins made from the still warm hides of freshly

---

[1]E. Porter Alexander, *Military Memoirs of a Confederate: A Critical Narrative* (1907; reprint, Dayton, OH: Press of Morningside Bookshop, 1977) 489.

[2]*The War of the Rebellion: A Compilation of the Official Records of the Union and Confederate Armies* (70 vols. in 128; Washington, 1880–1901), ser. I, vol. 31, pt. 1, 462, 499. Hereafter cited as OR.

[3]Alexander, *Military Memoirs*, 489–90.

[4]Ibid., 490.

slaughtered cattle. When these wore out the soldiers continued marching shoeless in the freezing mud.[5]

One of those freezing soldiers in McLaws's Division recalled his experience with hand-made leather moccasins on the march in early December.

I was a luckless barefooted boy—a boy who had never before undertaken to construct a pair of rawhide moccasins. But necessity is said to be the mother of invention; and after I had incased my feet in the warm plush of a piece of Tennessee ox or cowhide made into moccasins by my own hands, I was highly complemented by my comrades on the neatness of my job. To those who have had no experience with moccasins it may be revealed that such footwear is not adapted to wet weather. [After fording two streams] mine were large enough to be pulled upon the feet of a good-sized elephant.

After crossing a third stream, the young soldier discarded his saturated moccasins and continued to march barefooted on the frozen ground.[6]

On the afternoon of 5 December, Longstreet's men reached Bain's Crossroads, where they were joined by General Robert Ransom with reinforcements from Virginia, which had been intended for the Battle of Knoxville. The combined forces continued their march the next day, arriving at the Blevins farm near Rogersville, Tennessee, on 9 December. They were now about fifty miles from Knoxville.[7] Fortunately for the half-starved Confederates, the country around Rogersville abounded with provisions. Foraging parties were sent out through the countryside and returned with wagonloads of food, including the first flour the troops had tasted in days. Quickly the impression spread, perhaps as a result of wishful thinking, that winter quarters would be established at Rogersville. Many men began to build shelters for protection against the severe weather.[8]

At Rogersville, Captain Simmons and his comrades of McLaws's Division were reluctant witnesses to one of the most heart-rending scenes of the war. In an unguarded moment, a backwoods soldier had forgotten his oath of duty in his yearning for home and family and deserted. He was soon apprehended and returned to his regiment. The soldier was then court-martialed and sentenced to

---

[5]D. Augustus Dickert, *History of Kershaw's Brigade* (1899; reprint, Wilmington, NC: Broadfoot Publishing Company, 1990) 316, 318.

[6]J. B. Boothe, "The Siege of Knoxville and Its Results," *Confederate Veteran* 22/6 (June 1914): 266.

[7]*OR*, ser. I, vol. 31, pt. 1, 462–63, 494.

[8]Dickert, *Kershaw's Brigade*, 318. The fine location near Rogersville was not meant to be home for long. Burnside, emboldened by the prospect of strong reinforcements nearing Knoxville from the southwest, moved out a large detachment to pursue the Confederates. This caused Longstreet to withdraw and seek winter quarters in a more remote and defensible location.

die before a firing squad. For several days, the condemned man sobbed in his tent, consoled only by his young son, who had come over the mountains to spend the last moments with his father.

The soldier's execution was chronicled by Captain D. Augustus Dickert, a staff officer in Kershaw's Brigade:

> At 9:00 A.M. on the execution date the four brigades of McLaws's Division were lined up on three sides of a broad plateau. A detail of thirty men, all with powder in their rifles but only 15 minie balls, stood at parade rest facing a stake at the eastern end of the ground. After the condemned man and his little son marched past the entire division, the pathetic soldier was blindfolded and tied to the stake. The stoic lad moved off to the right. The officer in charge began to give the command, but before he could finish, the condemned man cried out "fire." The squad responded and, with a convulsive shudder, the deserter fell to the ground.[9]

After their brief stay at Rogersville and a skirmish with Federal forces at Bean's Station[10] on 14 December, Longstreet's Corps moved into winter quarters on the east bank of the Holston River by the little hamlet of Russellville, not far from Morristown, Tennessee.[11] Flat bottom boats ferried the troops across the river. Only two companies at a time could cross the river by pulling on a rope tied on the opposite bank. A blinding sleet storm covered the ropes with a layer of ice, freezing the hands of the ill-clad soldiers. When all were safely across, the various brigades selected campsites and the soldiers were soon busy improvising shelters to protect themselves from the cold weather. Since only a small number of tents were available, groups of soldiers fastened three tents together to provide a roof and three sides opening on to a roaring fire. In the bitter sub-freezing weather, the soldiers slept under their thin

---

[9]Ibid., 319–21. According to courts martial records for Wofford's Brigade, no soldier was executed for desertion, suggesting that the executed soldier was from another brigade. Overall, of the seventeen men in Wofford's Brigade who were court martialed for desertion, seven were sentenced to hard labor, three were fined or had their pay stopped, three were acquitted, two were "drummed out of the service," and two were to be executed, but the sentence was "not conclusively carried out." A much larger number deserted and either took the oath of allegiance to the Union, were not heard of again, or not court martialed. According to service records and other sources, out of the 3rd Battalion Sharpshooters *not* court martialed, there were twenty-one deserters (eleven of whom took the oath of allegiance to the United States), about 6 percent of the total number in the battalion. The desertion rate was much lower in the 16th Georgia Infantry Regiment, with thirteen deserters, a rate of less than 1 percent.

[10]Lieutenant Colonel N. L. Hutchins Jr., acting commander of Wofford's Brigade, reported that the brigade was not engaged at Bean's Station.

[11]Dickert, Kershaw's Brigade, 325.

blankets with their feet stretched out to the fires that they constantly fed from an ample supply of wood.[12]

Soon after settling into winter quarters, General Longstreet issued an order that caused a great deal of controversy among the soldiers under his command. On 17 December, without providing an adequate explanation, Longstreet relieved General Lafayette McLaws from further duty with the army, ordered him to Augusta, Georgia, and placed his division under the command of his senior brigadier, General Joseph Kershaw.[13] When the news broke on the following day, Captain Simmons and his comrades were all mystified at the decision. Longstreet and McLaws were fellow Georgians who had been classmates at West Point. Longstreet's order relieving McLaws indicated that his subordinate had displayed a lack of confidence throughout the campaign.[14]

Subsequently, Longstreet accused McLaws of poor leadership in the assault on Fort Sanders at Knoxville, and more specifically, not properly advancing the sharpshooters when the assault on Fort Sanders began on the night of 28 November. It is likely that the news did not sit well with Captain Simmons and the men who made up the sharpshooter battalion. No one could comprehend why such a charge was made since all of the sharpshooters had advanced that night past the enemy's rifle pits and firmly established a new line within easy range of the fort.[15]

Longstreet also charged that General McLaws failed to "organize a select body of men to lead the assault." This caused great dismay and indignation among the survivors who led the ill-fated bayonet charge at Fort Sanders. Most agreed that these fine men were as well commanded as any that could be found anywhere to lead the assault. Finally, Longstreet charged that General McLaws assaulted the fort at a point where the ditch was impassable, that he failed to provide ladders, and that the "west side" of the fort could be entered with little delay.[16]

The resolution of the charges against General McLaws was long delayed. The court martial heard the charges and issued its findings the following spring, which resulted in a sixty-day suspension for the accused. Shortly after the sentence was handed down, President Davis dismissed all charges.[17]

---

[12]G. Moxley Sorrel, *Recollections of a Confederate Staff Officer*, ed. Bell Irvin Wiley (Wilmington, NC: Broadfoot Publishing Company, 1995) 210; Dickert, *Kershaw's Brigade*, 326–27.

[13]*OR*, [ser. I, vol. 31?] pt. 1, 497–98; James Longstreet, *From Manassas to Appomattox: Memoirs of the Civil War in America* (1896; reprint, New York: Barnes & Noble, 2006) 442–44. The notification came in the form of Special Order Number 27, sent by Lieutenant Colonel G. Moxley Sorrel, Longstreet's assistant adjutant-general.

[14]Longstreet, *From Manassas to Appomattox*, 443–44.

[15]*OR*, ser. I, vol. 31, pt. 1, 501.

[16]Ibid., 504.

[17]Ibid., 506.

After McLaws departed for Georgia, the men of Longstreet's Corps returned to their routines of winter camp. Fortunately food was abundant in the rich farmland around Morristown. Supplies hidden by the farmers were scouted out by foraging details and overflowing wagons returned to camp daily. With adequate food, fuel, and shelter, the soldiers turned to supplying themselves with better clothes and footwear.[18] Several handlooms in the country supplied cloth and newly developed shoemaking talent turned rawhides into tanned leather and then into comfortable shoes. Two men from the 3rd Battalion Sharpshooters, William A. Doster and J. S. Franks, were assigned to work as shoemakers.[19] The 24,000 men under General Longstreet looked forward to an enjoyable rest, something they had not known for many long months. While all of this domestic activity was going on, the soldiers did the best they could to celebrate Christmas and bring in the New Year.

With the removal of General McLaws there was little doubt that the command of the division would be given to Joseph Kershaw, the senior brigadier in Longstreet's Corps. Kershaw was greatly admired for his steady courage and military aptitude. His official appointment was delayed until February while he was on leave. During Kershaw's absence General Wofford was given command of the division.[20] Lieutenant Colonel N. L. Hutchins Jr. became acting commander of Wofford's Brigade until Kershaw returned from leave in February 1864.[21] Captain William Simmons filled in as acting commander of the 3rd Battalion Sharpshooters during this time.

With the coming of the New Year, the weather grew more severe. The cavalry had the most difficulty, playing a constant game of hide-and-seek with the Union cavalry over rough mountain trails, which were almost impassable due to the ice. For many weeks, camp life for Simmons and his comrades consisted of little more than a daily survival against the elements.

In addition to the challenges faced by Longstreet's command, there was the matter of soldier morale. Many of the men had signed on for three years of service in spring 1861 and assumed that their terms of enlistment were soon to expire. Captain Simmons realized that the Army of Northern Virginia was in a precarious position, so he took decisive action to bolster the resolve of his men and set an example for the rest of Longstreet's command.

On 12 February, while in camp at New Market, Tennessee, Simmons called a meeting of the 3rd Battalion Sharpshooters to decide on a course of action in view of the approaching expiration of service. He appointed Captain

---

[18]Longstreet, *From Manassas to Appomattox*, 445.

[19]Throughout the months in the winter camps, shoe production reached the level of 100 pairs per day.

[20]Sorrel, *Recollections of a Confederate Staff Officer*, 228; *OR*, ser. I, vol. 32, pt. 3, 737; *OR*, ser. I, vol. 32, pt. 2, 641.

[21]*OR*, ser. I, vol. 32, pt. 2, 802.

John W. King to preside and Captain Garnett McMillan to act as secretary. When the sharpshooters gathered for the meeting, Simmons presented a preamble and resolution he had written that was read to the men. The preamble stated that the Union "was persistent in waging a war of conquest and subjugation against the Confederate States." Given the situation, the resolution read, "we hereby tender our services…and express our unalterable determination never to lay down our arms so long as the foot of an armed enemy presses the soil of our country…." (see Exhibit 4 in the Appendix). The resolution was met with a unanimous adoption and forwarded to the secretary of war, Lieutenant General Longstreet, General Wofford, and a number of Georgia newspapers.[22]

Throughout the winter months there were a number of skirmishes with the enemy, most notably at Dandridge, Tennessee, which is located about thirty miles northeast of Knoxville on the French Broad River.[23] On 14 January, a large Union force advanced toward the left flank of the Confederate line. The Confederates were in a favorable position and stood their ground rather than give up their winter camp. On the following day the Confederate infantry began to march toward Dandridge. McLaws's Division, now under the command of General Wofford, took up positions along the Morristown-Strawberry Plains Road to meet the enemy and reinforce other units of the Army.[24]

Shortly after dark, while Wofford's forces awaited further instructions, the troops nearer Dandridge executed a flanking movement to their right and forced the Federal forces to retreat. The next morning Wofford and the other commanders on the Strawberry Plains Road were ordered to pursue the retreating Federals, but the warmer weather had turned the roads into a muddy quagmire that bogged down the pursuit. The main body of Union soldiers made it back to Knoxville, but not before the Confederates captured some stragglers and seized ammunition and a grand haul of 800 cattle and 31 wagons.[25]

After the action at Dandridge the soldiers returned to their winter camp. Lieutenant William R. Montgomery of Company F, 3rd Battalion Sharpshooters, wrote about the ordeal in a letter to his aunt in Georgia:

> We just got in last night from a 3 days march through rain, snow, and mud, and by the way a little hard fighting. Had to stay out 3 nights without any covering [in the snow] save the wide expanded arch of Heaven, which you may imagine was by no means pleasant. It is enough to make tears come from the eyes of the most hardened soul to see our brave

---

[22]"Action of the Third Georgia Battalion of Sharpshooters," *Augusta Weekly Chronicle & Sentinel*, 16 March 1864. A complete copy of the resolution appears in the Appendix as Exhibit 4.

[23]Sorrel, *Recollections of a Confederate Staff Officer*, 213.

[24]*OR*, ser. I, vol. 32, pt. 2, 556.

[25]Longstreet, *From Manassas to Appomattox*, 450–53; *OR*, ser. I, vol. 32, pt. 2, 653.

men marching through the mud & snow almost naked and barefooted. In my company, we have but 5 or 6 men with shoes.[26]

In February Longstreet's cavalry units were transferred to Georgia, and Kershaw's Division was later relocated to camps close to Greenville, Tennessee, farther from Knoxville.[27] While the new camps were behind a more defensible line, the miserable weather and shortage of food and clothing did nothing to endear the location to the troops. A seasoned veteran from Alabama described winter 1863–1864 as the "hardest winter that we had ever experienced." With expressive simplicity, he said,

> It rained, sleeted, and snowed so much that the earth became so full of water that a little stomping around our campfire would cause the water to rise. It would rise on us at night in our beds, and everywhere our hipbones rested water would come to the surface. Ditching around our tents done no good. A good supply of wheat straw gave some relief, but that would only be temporary.[28]

Fortunately for the half-starved and tattered men of Longstreet's command, there were no more major confrontations with the enemy for the rest of the winter.

The threadbare uniforms of the soldiers offered little protection against the cold. As the frigid weather persisted in March, General Longstreet begged Confederate authorities in Richmond for help, but no uniforms or blankets could be provided. Fortunately Longstreet's adopted state was able to respond. On 22 March, the quartermaster general of Georgia arrived in Greenville with 3,000 suits of clothing for Georgia's destitute sons in the field.

Captain Simmons was overjoyed at the sight of the uniforms. As soon as the clothing could be unpacked and arrangements made for distribution, he requisitioned clothing for his men in the sharpshooter battalion and obtained Lieutenant Colonel Hutchins's approval. In addition to jackets, shirts, and pants, the Georgians received underwear, socks, shoes, hats, and blankets. To add a full measure, their beloved home folks had included pens, paper, and envelopes. Captain Simmons noted in his journal that he received five-quire

---

[26]William R. Montgomery to Aunt Frank, 19 January 1864, in George Montgomery Jr., *Georgia Sharpshooter: The Civil War Diary and Letters of William Rhadamanthus Montgomery* (Macon: Mercer University Press, 1997) 100. Of the men who wore shoes, Montgomery said, "Some of them wear mockersons made of rawhide" (100).

[27]*OR*, ser. I, vol. 32, pt. 2, 802.

[28]W. A. McClendon, *Recollections of War Times by an Old Veteran while Under Stonewall Jackson and Lieutenant General James Longstreet* (1909; reprint, Tuscaloosa: University of Alabama Press, 2010) 223.

letter paper, one bottle of ink, one bunch of envelopes, thirteen pens, one penholder, and one pencil.[29]

Not long after the clothing, blankets, and stationery were distributed, the division's base of operations was moved to Bristol on the Tennessee-Virginia border. While in the Bristol camps, Simmons learned that he had been selected as the new major for the 3rd Battalion, Georgia Sharpshooters. The position had been open since October 1863 when Major P. E. Davant was promoted to lieutenant colonel and given command of the 38th Georgia Infantry Regiment.[30] On 2 April 1864 General Wofford wrote to the inspector general in Richmond to recommend Simmons for promotion. General Kershaw endorsed his approval two days later and forwarded the recommendation to General Longstreet's headquarters. After several delays, the recommendation was finally approved, but Simmons would not receive official notification of his promotion for another two months.

---

[29]Simmons Diary, Box 19 Drawer 78 Georgia Department of Archives and History, Morrow, Georgia, in Daniel M. Byrd, *Them Brave Georgians*, manuscript, pg. 269, Gwinnett Historical Society Archives, Lawrenceville, GA (Fort Delaware Society Library, Delaware City, DE, also has a copy.).
[30]Simmons service records, ibid., 268–69.

17

Back to the Wilderness

I can't say I was ever lost, but I was bewildered once for three days.

—Daniel Boone

After a brief stay in Bristol, Longstreet received orders to rejoin General Lee and the Army of Northern Virginia. The first troops left by rail on 12 April for Charlottesville, Virginia. Up to 1,500 men were moved each day on the trains shuttling back and forth between the two cities. By 21 April all of Longstreet's Corps were assembled in Charlottesville for the march to new camps near Gordonsville, about twenty miles to the northeast.[1]

Longstreet's I Corps arrived at the Gordonsville camps in a deplorable state. Supplies were brought in as quickly as possible and recruiting was stepped up to help fill the depleted ranks.[2] The soldiers were placed under strict camp discipline, with the majority of their waking hours devoted to drilling, cleaning, and repairing weapons and equipment and answering surgeons' calls.

On 29 April, in the midst of the frenzied preparations, General Robert E. Lee arrived at the Gordonsville camps. He desired to return the affection that Longstreet's men felt for their commander-in-chief by holding a grand review and inspection. In anticipation of the visit, hair was cut, uniforms brushed and mended, boots and shoes greased, and battered hats given a "lick and a promise."[3] For Captain Simmons and the long-suffering soldiers of Longstreet's I Corps, there was a genuine rebirth of spirit and pride to go hand-in-hand with

---

[1] *The War of the Rebellion: A Compilation of the Official Records of the Union and Confederate Armies* (70 vols. in 128; Washington, 1880–1901), ser. I, vol. 36, pt. 1, 1054; pt. 2, 940; vol. 51, pt. 2, 855. Hereafter cited as *OR*.

[2] According to service records, during late winter and early spring 1864, at least twelve recruits and transfers were assigned to the ranks of the depleted 3rd Georgia Sharpshooter Battalion. Company A: Corporal E. J. Slaughter, and privates C. W. Cunningham and N. T. Thomas; Company B: Private James Jackson; Company C: privates John Carter, James S. Ferguson (transfer from Company B of the 16th Georgia), and W. F. Phillips; Company D: Private Moses W. Young; Company E: privates James S. Cotton and Alexander E. Shaw; and Company F: privates J. W. Dawson and Levi J. Stewart.

[3] D. Augustus Dickert, *History of Kershaw's Brigade* (1899; reprint, Wilmington, NC: Broadfoot Publishing Company, 1990) 340.

their admiration for General Lee.[4] D. Augustus Dickert of Kershaw's South Carolina Brigade wrote about the review to illustrate the special bond between the men and their commander-in-chief.

The 29th of April was a gala day for the troops of Longstreet's Corps, at camp near Gordonsville. They were there to be reviewed and inspected by their old and beloved commander, General R. E. Lee. Out a mile or two was a very large field, of perhaps 100 acres or more in which we formed in double columns. The artillery stationed on the flank fired thirteen guns, the salute to the commander-in-chief, and as the old warrior rode out into the opening, shouts went up that fairly shook the earth. Hats and caps flew high in the air, flags dipped and waved to and fro, while the drums and fifes struck up "Hail to the Chief." General Lee lifted his hat modestly from his head in recognition of the honor done him, and we know the old commander's heart swelled with emotion at this outburst of enthusiasm by his old troops on his appearance. The command was broken into columns of companies and marched by him, each giving a salute as it passed.[5]

The commanding officer of Longstreet's artillery, General E. Porter Alexander, was also a witness to the event. Writing more than forty years after the review, he vividly recalled the sight of General Lee upon Traveler, at the head of his staff, emerging on the parade ground to a thundering artillery salute and the rebel yell and cheers of his men. That afternoon Alexander felt a wave of sentiment sweep over the field and noted that "All felt the bond which held them together. There was no speaking, but the effect was as of a military sacrament."[6]

The review was the last ever held by General Lee. It had a profound effect on Captain Simmons and the rest of Longstreet's Corps. In less than one week they would reunite with the Army of Northern Virginia to engage a Union army more than twice their size. Their adversary, the mighty Army of the Potomac, continued under the command of General George Gordon Meade, accompanied by Union commander Ulysses S. Grant, and posed the most serious threat to Richmond since the beginning of the war. The two armies would be locked in conflict for the next six weeks with hardly any break in the action.

The first move was made by the Northern forces, now numbering over 120,000. At midnight on 3 May 1864, the Federals left their camps for the lower fords of the Rapidan River. Early movements indicated that the Army of

---

[4]Daniel M. Byrd, *Them Brave Georgians*, manuscript, pg. 273, Gwinnett Historical Society Archives, Lawrenceville, GA (Fort Delaware Society Library, Delaware City, DE, also has a copy.).

[5]Dickert, *Kershaw's Brigade*, 340–41.

[6]E. Porter Alexander, *Military Memoirs of a Confederate: A Critical Narrative* (1907; reprint, Dayton, OH: Press of Morningside Bookshop, 1977) 403.

the Potomac was advancing toward Richmond once again. This action marked the start of the Overland Campaign. At that time Longstreet's Corps was positioned at Mechanicsville, several miles north of Richmond.

The next afternoon divisions under Kershaw and Field began a circuitous forty-eight mile march from Mechanicsville to meet up with other Confederate divisions to the south of the Rapidan and make a stand against the Union army. The site of the coming battle was to be remembered as the Wilderness, a wild, tangled forest of stunted trees, covering about fifteen square miles between Orange Courthouse and Fredericksburg. It was a foreboding place, mostly covered by thickets, dense undergrowth and swamp mire. Passing through the Wilderness were two parallel roads, the Orange Turnpike and the Orange Plank Road. Almost perpendicular to these two roads through the nearly impassable wilderness was the Germana Plank Road, which ran from the fords of the Rapidan in a southeast direction to connect with Brock Road, a direct route to Spotsylvania Court House.

For their first major battle of 1864, William Simmons and the 3rd Battalion Georgia Sharpshooters were under the command of their able leader, Lieutenant Colonel N. L. Hutchins Jr. They remained in Wofford's Brigade along with the 16th, 18th, and 24th Georgia Infantry Regiments, and Cobb's and Phillips' Legion Infantry Battalions. The 16th Georgia was now led by B. Edward Stiles, who was promoted to lieutenant colonel and given command of the regiment after Colonel Henry Thomas was killed at Knoxville.[7]

The 3rd Georgia Sharpshooters left Gordonsville at 4:00 P.M. on 4 May and marched toward Fredericksburg until 11:00 P.M. After only a few hours rest, the battalion arose at 4:00 A.M. and marched all day. As evening approached, they encountered a force of Union soldiers and drove them back several miles before retiring for a short rest.[8]

Promptly at 12:30 A.M. on 6 May the 3rd Battalion Sharpshooters and the rest of Wofford's Brigade resumed their march. By dawn they had reached Parker's Store on the Orange Plank Road.[9] For the previous two days Wofford's men had served as a rear guard for the immense I Corps wagon train.[10] They had covered the last ten miles in six hours on the night time march. The men were exhausted from the forced march and lack of sleep, but they had no time to recover before being pressed into battle. The battle-hardened Georgians were rushed forward from the rear by General Longstreet himself. When they arrived

---

[7]Stiles was a native of Habersham County, Georgia, and led Company E (Cobb Infantry) of the 16th Georgia before his promotion.

[8]George Montgomery Jr., *Georgia Sharpshooter: The Civil War Diary and Letters of William Rhadamanthus Montgomery* (Macon: Mercer University Press, 1997) 48.

[9]*OR*, ser. I, vol. 36, pt. 1, 1034; Alexander, *Military Memoirs*, 498.

[10]*OR*, ser. I, vol. 36, pt. 1, 1061.

at the front, they found the Confederate forces locked in a death struggle with the enemy along the Plank Road.[11]

Wofford's Brigade was placed in a position on the right flank of the battle line to the right of the Orange Plank Road.[12] They made their way as quickly as possible through the tangled undergrowth and dense thickets of dwarf saplings, past their comrades of Kershaw's Division, and lined up next to General G. T. Anderson's Georgia Brigade. Positioned nearby were General Mahone's Brigade of Virginians and General A. P. Hill's III Corps.[13]

When Wofford returned to report that his brigade was ready, he joined a conference of generals mapping bold plans for a flanking movement. General Martin Luther Smith, chief engineer of the army,[14] had studied the enemy's lines and was reporting that the left flank was exposed and could easily be turned.[15] This information was also reported to Wofford by the 3rd Battalion Sharpshooters, who had been scouting the area. The scouts confirmed that "the enemy's extreme left was very near, hanging as it were in the air."[16] In addition, they had discovered the grade of an unfinished railroad which ran almost parallel to the Orange Plank Road. After sizing up the situation, Wofford suggested that a column move through the protection of the thick forest until it reached the unfinished railroad cut. From this point, the attacking force could roll the left of the enemy's line while Longstreet's other brigades drove straight ahead into the disorganized ranks.[17] Longstreet consented and the proposed flanking attack was ordered with the personal approval of General Lee. Colonel G. Moxley Sorrel, Longstreet's chief of staff, relayed the orders to the three generals (Wofford, Mahone, and Anderson) whose commands were to undertake the

---

[11]Dickert, *Kershaw's Brigade*, 347; *OR*, ser. I, vol. 36, pt. 1, 1061.

[12]A. J. McWhirter, "Gen. Wofford's Brigade in the Wilderness," *Atlanta Journal*, 21 September 1901, 2; Fred L. Ray, *Shock Troops of the Confederacy: The Sharpshooter Battalions of the Army of Northern Virginia* (Asheville, NC: CFS Press, 2006) 203.

[13]Dickert, *Kershaw's Brigade*, 348; G. Moxley Sorrel, *Recollections of a Confederate Staff Officer*, ed. Bell Irvin Wiley (Wilmington, NC: Broadfoot Publishing Company, 1995) 232; *OR*, ser. I, vol. 36, pt. 1, 1090.

[14]*OR*, ser. I, vol. 33, 1287.

[15]Sorrel, *Recollections of a Confederate Staff Officer*, 231; *OR*, ser. I, vol. 31, pt. 1, 1055.

[16]*Atlanta Southern Confederacy*, 15 June 1864; Gerald J. Smith, *One of the Most Daring of Men: The Life of Confederate General William Tatum Wofford*, vol. 16 of Journal of Confederate History Series, ed. John McGlone (Murfreesboro, TN: Southern Heritage Press, 1997) 111, 201. Gerald Smith suggests that the unidentified writer of the article must have been one of Wofford's staff officers. He (Smith) also asserts that Wofford suggested Longstreet's flank attack.

[17]*OR*, ser. I, vol. 36, pt. 1, 1062.

flanking movement. Sorrel remained to coordinate the units in the dense woods.[18]

Under the thick cover of the Wilderness forest, studded with briars and tangled vines, the three brigades made their way to the bed of the unfinished railroad and slipped up on the unsuspecting Union forces. About noon, with the sharpshooters leading the way, the three brigades swooped down on the Union soldiers, taking them completely by surprise. In the heat of battle dry leaves caught fire, which began to spread as the Yankees fled in confusion.[19] It turned into a complete rout. Two Union brigades gave way under the initial onslaught and raced pell-mell to better-protected positions near the Plank Road.[20]

The flanking attack was described by Corporal Andrew J. McWhirter of Company C, 3rd Georgia Sharpshooters. On that day, the company was led by Captain Charlton H. Strickland, a Gwinnett County native who had previously served with William Simmons in the Hutchins Guards of the 16th Georgia.

> Captain Strickland gave the command to charge at the very top of his voice. The boys raised the old rebel yell and went on them like a duck on a June bug. Some few of them ran, throwing down their guns as they went; some lay flat on the ground. The Yankees had another line of temporary works, and they made another stand. The Johnnies made no halt at all, and the enemy fled before them as they had done a short time before.[21]

The surprise attack was a brilliant maneuver. Wofford's Brigade, including the 16th Georgia and the 3rd Sharpshooter Battalion, were stationed on the right, with Anderson's Georgians in the center and Mahone's Virginians on the left.[22] Wofford's Brigade, being the farthest to the east, was able to get behind the Union left flank, which was now surrounded on three sides. While the three brigades pursued the retreating Federals, the other brigades of Longstreet's I

---

[18]Sorrel, *Recollections of a Confederate Staff Officer*, 232; OR, ser. I, vol. 36, pt. 1, 1061, 1091; James Madison Folsom, Heroes and Martyrs of Georgia: Georgia's Record in the Revolution of 1861 (Macon: Burke & Boykin, 1864) 19.

[19]Sorrel, *Recollections of a Confederate Staff Officer*, 232; OR, ser. I, vol. 36, pt. 1, 1091; General William F. Perry, "Reminiscences of the Campaign of 1864 in Virginia," *Southern Historical Society Papers* (hereafter *SHSP*) 7 (January–December 1879): 59.

[20]Sorrel, *Recollections of a Confederate Staff Officer*, 286.

[21]McWhirter, Wofford's Brigade, 2.

[22]OR, ser. I, vol. 36, pt. 1, 1052; Richard M. Coffman and Kurt D. Graham, *To Honor These Men* (Macon: Mercer University Press, 2007) 202. The authors place Wofford's Brigade in the center, with Mahone on the left and Anderson on the right. The changes in position may have taken place after deployment and prior to the flank attack.

Corps attacked head-on, advancing on both sides of the Plank Road with a fair degree of success.[23] The tide of the battle was turning in the favor of the South. The Southerners surged to the north, pushing the Federals up the Brock Road past its intersection with the Plank Road. Through the dense undergrowth the Confederates carried everything before them until the enemy retreated behind breastworks on Brock Road from which they had advanced early that morning.[24]

With the success of the flanking attack, Longstreet immediately planned a similar maneuver before the Union forces could recover from the morning's disaster. The plan called for the Southern troops on the right and left of the Brock Road to break the enemy's line. In the meantime, General Smith was to take Wofford's Brigade and other available troops to lead another flanking attack further to the east.[25]

Later in the afternoon the second flanking movement was initiated. Wofford's Brigade marched south in an attempt to encircle the Union left flank. The men had only gone a short distance when the attack was unexpectedly called off. Soon, Captain Simmons and his fellow Georgians received the news that General Longstreet had suffered a serious wound[26] and two of his staff officers had been killed. At the same location, General Micah Jenkins was mortally wounded along with Captain Alfred E. Doby of Kershaw's staff and his orderly. In the confusion of battle the 12th Virginia had become separated from its command. Upon attempting to return to rejoin its brigade, Longstreet's party was mistaken for the enemy in the dim light. Shots were fired in the dense, smoking forest, and Longstreet and the other three officers were cut down before anyone could stop the unfortunate exchange.[27] The tragic accident took place a short distance from where Stonewall Jackson was killed by friendly fire at the Battle of Chancellorsville one year earlier.[28]

Sometime between 3:00 P.M. and 4:00 P.M. Wofford received orders to reinforce the battered troops of Fields's Division, positioned to the left of the Plank Road.[29] Led by the sharpshooters, Wofford's reinforcements arrived just in time to breach a hole that had been opened in the Confederate battle line and drive back the Union forces. Colonel William F. Perry of the 44th Alabama

---

[23]James Longstreet, *From Manassas to Appomattox: Memoirs of the Civil War in America* (1896; reprint, New York: Barnes & Noble, 2006) 482–83.

[24]*OR*, ser. I, vol. 36, pt. 1, 1091; Sorrel, *Recollections of a Confederate Staff Officer*, 289.

[25]Longstreet, *From Manassas to Appomattox*, 563.

[26]Edward Steere, *The Wilderness Campaign* (New York: Bonanza Books, n.d.) 405–406. Longstreet took a minie ball through the throat and shoulder.

[27]*OR*, ser. I, vol. 36, pt. 1, 1062; Sorrel, Recollections of a Confederate Staff Officer, 290; Longstreet, From Manassas to Appomattox, 483–84.

[28]Sorrel, *Recollections of a Confederate Staff Officer*, 237–38.

[29]Perry, "Reminiscences of the Campaign of 1864 in Virginia," 60–61.

reported that "[Wofford's Georgians]...swooped down upon the enemy in the midst of their exultation and confusion and swept them away like chaff." He added, "The enemy disappeared like an apparition."[30] Once again, Wofford's men had helped to turn the tide of battle. The Confederate line was restored and the enemy returned to the positions held before the attack began.[31]

Nightfall of 6 May closed the Battle of the Wilderness and marked another successful repulse of the Union army's efforts to drive on to Richmond. Of the 3rd Georgia Sharpshooter Battalion, the casualties included one killed and nine wounded. Six of the wounded were from Captain Simmons's Company C.[32] Grant had lost nearly 18,000 men killed, wounded, and missing. Confederate casualties exceeded 10,000.[33] Despite the greater number of casualties, Grant was steadfast in his determination to continue as the aggressor and press his war of attrition on to the Confederate capital.

That evening, before retiring, Grant told Henry Wing, a correspondent who was about to depart for Washington, to file his story on the battle. Grant added, "If you see the President, tell him, from me, that whatever happens, there will be no turning back." The following day, Wing would pass on Grant's words in person to President Lincoln and several members of his cabinet.[34] Grant would be true to his promise.

---

[30]Ibid., 62.

[31]*OR*, ser. I, vol. 36, pt. 1, 1062.

[32]According to service records and other reference sources, Major Henry H. Smith was killed on 6 May 1864. Smith was a member of the Hiwassee Volunteers (Company D) of the 24th Georgia before his promotion to the battalion staff. Those wounded on 6 May included 1st Sergeant Thomas P. Nelms, and privates John Carter, Samuel Davis, James S. Ferguson, William B. Owens and W. F. Phillips of Company C; Private John A Brooks of Company E; and Sergeant James H. Cheek and Private J. W. Dawson of Company F.

[33]Noah Andre Trudeau, *Bloody Roads South: The Wilderness to Cold Harbor, May–June 1864* (Boston: Little, Brown and Company, 1989) 341. Trudeau listed Union casualties for the Wilderness (5 May to 7 May 1864) as 14,283 killed or wounded and 3,383 captured for a total of 17,666. The numbers were computed by Bryce Suderow, using Frederick H. Dyer's *Compendium of the War of the Rebellion* (Des Moines: Dyer Pub. Co., 1908) and tables contained in *OR*.

Trudeau indicates that casualty figures for Confederate forces "have been newly computed by Alfred Young and are based in part on casualty lists found in contemporary Confederate newspapers and on service records of Lee's soldiers" (341). Young also used Dyer's *Compendium* and tables contained in the *OR*. Young's estimate was 8,949 killed or wounded and 1,881 captured, a total of 10,830 casualties. Other estimates are lower.

[34]Trudeau, *Bloody Roads South*, 117.

18

Slaughter at the Bloody Angle

To persevere, trusting in what hopes he has, is courage. The coward despairs.

—Euripides

On the day following the Battle of the Wilderness the exhausted men of Longstreet's Corps remained in comparative safety behind heavily entrenched lines while the two armies engaged in light skirmishes and probing attacks. The men were likely preoccupied with thoughts of their wounded corps commander, General James Longstreet. Late in the afternoon word was passed down the chain of command that General Lee had ordered Major General Richard Heron Anderson to assume temporary leadership of Longstreet's Corps.[1] William Simmons and his comrades were likely pleased with the announcement. Anderson was the second senior major general in the Army of Northern Virginia behind Lafayette McLaws, who had recently been acquitted of charges growing out of the attack on Fort Sanders the previous year. That evening the order was given for General Anderson to move the I Corps to Spotsylvania Court House, twelve miles southeast of the Wilderness. Federal activity clearly indicated that Grant's forces were moving in that direction in an attempt to slip by Lee's right flank.

By the middle of the night the 16th Georgia and other regiments in the I Corps were underway, engaged in a frantic race against the Army of the Potomac. Their objective was to stay between the Union army and Richmond. The route taken was over a new military road that was hacked out of the wilderness earlier that day by men under General William Pendleton, Lee's artillery chief.[2] The night was dark and filled with shadows cast by brush fires along the route.[3] One of the corps staff officers, G. Moxley Sorrel, soon to become a brigadier general, described the eerie scene witnessed along the way: "The brush and undergrowth had taken fire from the musketry, and the flames and smoke were obscuring everything. The numerous parties out for burying the

---

[1]G. Moxley Sorrel, *Recollections of a Confederate Staff Officer*, ed. Bell Irvin Wiley (Wilmington, NC: Broadfoot Publishing Company, 1995) 239.

[2]Noah Andre Trudeau, *Bloody Roads South: The Wilderness to Cold Harbor, May–June 1864* (Boston: Little, Brown and Company, 1989) 125.

[3]E. Porter Alexander, *Military Memoirs of a Confederate: A Critical Narrative* (1907; reprint, Dayton, OH: Press of Morningside Bookshop, 1977) 509.

dead and gathering the wounded were greatly impeded and many wounded must have perished, hidden in that awful burnt tangle."[4]

That night Captain Simmons and the 3rd Georgia Sharpshooters and other sharpshooter units from the I Corps were given the arduous assignment of marching between the advancing Confederate column and the Union lines further to the left. In this position, the sharpshooters provided a continuous scouting force to prevent any accidental collision with the enemy.[5]

The Confederate forces reached Spotsylvania Court House on 9 May in the early hours of the morning. By the time they arrived, heavily massed Union infantry was challenging General Fitzhugh Lee's Cavalry Brigades. A mile away, Rosser's Cavalry Brigade was being driven out of Spotsylvania by a Union cavalry division under General Phillip Sheridan.[6] In response, General Anderson quickly split his forces and sent each half to reinforce the two beleaguered Southern cavalry generals. Wofford's and Bryan's brigades were sent to the aid of General Rosser. They arrived at the courthouse in the nick of time and began a successful flanking attack against the Union cavalry. The Confederates quickly seized the advantage and poured a volley into the enemy's ranks, driving them back to the safety of the Union lines. Later that morning, the two brigades were joined by Bratton's South Carolina Brigade of Fields's Division, which had arrived after an exhausting night march from the Wilderness Battlefield and taken positions to the rear of the Union line at the Court House.[7] The two Confederate lines pressed down hard on the Yankees from both directions. The Union forces were driven from the little town and retreated back up the road over which they had advanced earlier in the day.[8]

The race for Spotsylvania Court House had been won by the Georgians and South Carolinians in a photo finish, but there was little time to rest and regroup. Soon Wofford's Brigade was dispatched to positions north of the court house where Kershaw's and Humphreys's brigades had been engaged since early that morning. They were joined by reinforcements from Bryan's and Bratton's brigades.[9] The Georgians under Wofford and Bryan were positioned to the left of Kershaw's line, and Bratton's men were placed on the right side. For the next

---

[4]Sorrel, *Recollections of a Confederate Staff Officer*, 239–40.

[5]John D. Young, "A Campaign with Sharpshooters," in *The Annals of the War: Written by Leading Participants, North and South* (1879; reprint, Gettsyburg, PA: Civil War Times, 1974) 275.

[6]Alexander, Military Memoirs, 511; The War of the Rebellion: A Compilation of the Official Records of the Union and Confederate Armies (70 vols. in 128; Washington, 1880–1901), ser. I, vol. 36, pt. 1, 1027. Hereafter cited as OR.

[7]Ibid., 1065.

[8]Ibid., 789.

[9]Ibid., 1065; Alexander, *Military Memoirs*, 511.

three hours the men rested under a hot May sun. It was a welcome respite after nearly twenty-four hours of continuous marching and fighting.[10]

Sometime around 5:00 P.M., an advancing enemy interrupted the slumber of Wofford's Georgians.[11] The force of the attack was directed to the extreme right of the Confederate line and Wofford's men were not under fire. It was nightfall before the results were known. A large force of the enemy had almost succeeded in flanking the right of Kershaw's Division, but Rodes's Division of Ewell's Corps had arrived from the Wilderness in time repel the assault and drive the enemy back to their line.[12]

On the next day, Simmons and the sharpshooters were placed in advance of Anderson's line to watch the enemy. Their comrades in the rear began erecting a formidable line of defense to the north of Spotsylvania Courthouse. They strengthened their log and earth breastworks by the hour as countless skirmishes took place nearby. By the late afternoon the Confederate front resembled a ragged V, with flanks bent back to meet attacks from either left or right and a strong salient in the center protruding northward. At the apex the Southern lines were heavily fortified with artillery and shielded by a heavy abatis of felled trees with their branches sharpened and pointed toward the attackers. It was at this location that the fiercest fighting of the battle would soon take place. The site would be called the "Mule Shoe," with the pointed tip referred to as the "Bloody Angle."

Captain Simmons and the sharpshooters spent much of the next two days in front of the lines from secure positions, keeping up a sniping fire on anyone who showed himself along the Federal lines. They were positioned to the left (west) of the Mule Shoe ahead of Wofford's Brigade.

On the afternoon of 10 May the battle heated up again as the Union forces advanced toward the well-entrenched Southern positions. Much of the fighting was concentrated on the left side of the Mule Shoe salient and along the Confederates' left flank where General Fields and his brigades were entrenched, including Wofford's Georgians and the other brigades of Kershaw's Division.[13] There were upwards of a dozen attacks by Union forces as reported by an eyewitness, who noted that while fresh troops were poured into almost every charge, the same men remained on the Confederate line throughout the day.[14]

---

[10]*OR*, ser. I, vol. 36, pt. 1, 1065, 1071.

[11]Alexander, *Military Memoirs*, 512.

[12]*OR*, ser. I, vol. 36, pt. 1, 1071.

[13]Alexander, *Military Memoirs*, 511.

[14]Stiles noted that the Southerners were "so full of fight and fun after repelling the first advance that they leaped upon the breastworks and shouted to the retiring Federals to come a little closer next time, but were so weary and worn and heavy by that evening that they could scarcely be roused to meet the charging enemy" (Robert Stiles, *Four Years Under Marse Robert* [New York: Neale Publishing Company, 1910] 253).

The entrenched soldiers repelled each wave of bluecoats with strong support from Confederate Artillery, firing volley after volley of canister and inflicting severe losses.[15] As night approached, the Union column again burst upon Anderson's line, but the results were disastrous to the Yankees.[16] Although some of the enemy's soldiers scaled the Southern breastworks, few were able to use their bayonets before they were shot down within the fortified line. Later that night, there were other feeble attacks that were easily repelled. When the smoke had finally cleared, there were heavy Union losses and relatively few Confederate casualties.[17] Of the 3rd Battalion Sharpshooters, two men were killed and one wounded.[18]

The following day, 11 May, Grant planned to launch another frontal assault, but was held back by a dramatic change in the weather. The extreme heat was replaced by uncomfortably cold weather followed by heavy wind, rain, and hail. Throughout the day the 3rd Georgia Sharpshooters and the other units of the I Corps kept up a steady fire on the enemy's lines. A Confederate sharpshooter officer described the intensity of the fighting at close range between the sharpshooters of both sides:

> The Federal sharpshooters were in our immediate front, and displayed an animus of vindictive spite, which the boys in gray were not slow to reciprocate. The perpetual cry of their deadly rifles...from every tree and bush and boulder spurted fire and smoke and death...aroused in the Confederate sharpshooters a glow of patriotic ardor which could be restrained only by the most peremptory orders.[19]

While Simmons and the sharpshooters were keeping busy, Grant came to the conclusion that the Mule Shoe salient was the most vulnerable part of Lee's defensive formation. He decided to attack with overwhelming numbers and use his best corps under Major General Winfield Scott Hancock to lead the advance. To bolster the assaulting forces, Grant ordered several brigades of Wright's VI Corps to join Hancock. Combined, these units totaled 20,000 Union infantrymen, who were moved to positions directly opposing the salient. Another 40,000 soldiers were to attack the formation from each side. Grant's

---

[15]Alexander, *Military Memoirs*, 515; W. S. Dunlop, *Lee's Sharpshooters or the Forefront of Battle: A Story of Southern Valor That Never Has Been Told Before* (1899; reprint, Dayton, OH: Morningside House, Inc., 1988) 51–53; *OR*, ser. I, vol. 51, pt. 2, 911.

[16]Alexander, *Military Memoirs*, 515.

[17]Ibid.; *OR*, ser. I, vol. 36, pt. 1, 911.

[18]According to service records, on 10 May Private John H. Cook of Company D and Private Martin N. Wall of Company E were killed, and 3rd Corporal William Phillip Cosby of Simmons's Company C was wounded.

[19]Dunlop, *Lee's Sharpshooters*, 53–54.

objective was to split the Confederate army in half, leaving Lee's force no choice but scatter or face destruction.[20]

The cold temperatures and driving rain continued throughout the night and into the next day. The ground became a sea of mud and standing water collected on the battlefield where the two armies opposed each other. But these conditions did not deter General Ulysses S. Grant. Early on the morning of 12 May, after the heavy rain had slowed to a drizzle, he unleashed the might of the Army of the Potomac against Lee's Army of Northern Virginia. His men quickly overwhelmed the Confederate picket line and surged toward the Mule Shoe. The battle raged throughout the day with the most intense fighting taking place at the Bloody Angle, first assaulted by Hancock's crack II Corps. In the initial charge the bluecoats crashed over the top of the salient and captured a large number of men from General Edward Johnson's Division. Lee ordered a counterattack led by General John B. Gordon of Rodes's Division that halted the enemy advance and pushed the enemy back to the upper portion of the salient.[21] The South Carolina brigade of Samuel McGowan also played an important role in stemming the Union assault. The unit was called up by General Lee to seal a breach in the Mule Shoe and hold off the enemy until a second defensive line could be constructed.[22] In the afternoon, more reinforcements from Wofford's Brigade and other brigades from Kershaw's Division were moved up to the Mule Shoe to stem the tide.[23] They were positioned on the left side of the salient and soon joined with Rodes's brigades in the hand-to-hand fighting. In many places the forces were fighting from opposites of the same earthworks, just a few feet apart.[24]

Throughout the day the slaughter continued in the falling rain. Many wounded men suffocated in the mud and drowned in the flooded trenches. Here and there the firing ceased for moments as bodies were flung outside the trenches so the infantrymen could gain a footing to continue firing. The volume of fire was unprecedented in the history of warfare. Pack mules, each carrying 3,000 rounds of ammunition, brought a continuous supply of cartridges to the Federal lines. Large oak trees were chopped down by the hail of lead and came

---

[20]Gordon C. Rhea, "Mule Shoe Redemption," *Confederate Veteran* 65/5 (September/October 2007): 20.

[21]Gerald J. Smith, *One of the Most Daring of Men: The Life of Confederate General William Tatum Wofford*, vol. 16 of Journal of Confederate History Series, ed. John McGlone (Murfreesboro, TN: Southern Heritage Press, 1997) 116.

[22]Rhea, "Mule Shoe Redemption," 23, 50.

[23]Diary of the First Army Corps. JPBIV indicates this is part of *Them Brave Georgians*, so perhaps Diary of the First Army Corps, in Byrd, *Them Brave Georgians*.

[24]Fred L. Ray, Shock Troops of the Confederacy: The Sharpshooter Battalions of the Army of Northern Virginia (Asheville, NC: CFS Press, 2006) 209.

crashing onto the huddled ranks below. So many bullets hit some corpses that they simply fell apart.[25]

While the terrible struggle at the Bloody Angle was in progress, other Confederate troops dug a new line across the bottom of the mule shoe about one mile to the rear of the embattled trenches. After midnight Captain Simmons and the rest of Wofford's Brigade withdrew to the new position and later returned to their original position on the Confederate line to the left of the Mule Shoe.[26]

Despite countless assaults by Union forces, the Confederate lines held. The Battle of Spotsylvania was over by the end of the day. In the two primary days of fighting, 10 and 12 May, close to 6,000 of Lee's men had been killed or wounded and 4,000 had been captured. Grant's toll was equally devastating— 11,000 killed, wounded, or captured.

Once again Captain William Simmons and the stalwart Georgians of the 3rd Sharpshooter Battalion and 16th Regiment had been in the thick of one of the bloodiest engagements of the war. Miraculously they only sustained light casualties. Of the regiment, seven men were killed and four others were wounded or captured. The sharpshooter battalion lost one killed and six wounded.[27] As he reflected on the outcome of the battle, Madison Byrd wrote,

On the records of the regiment, alongside the Sunken Road, Bloody Lane, and the Peach Orchard, the Georgians could now inscribe the "Bloody Angle." With the utmost modesty, however, the anonymous author of the "Record of Events" for the 16th Georgia merely noted, "Moved to Spotsylvania C. H. where we were engaged on the 10 and 12 successfully." They were indeed "successfully engaged" [in holding back the Union army]. General Lee personally praised the gallantry of the soldiers of Anderson's Corps in a letter written shortly after May 12. General Anderson issued a bulletin to the Corps quoting General Lee's flattering praise for the valiant conduct of the Corps, but modestly refrained from mentioning General Lee's appreciation for his [Anderson's] own masterly handing of the I Corps during the battle. Captain Simmons, by the grace

---

[25]For a detailed account of Hancock's assault of the Mule Shoe Salient on 12 May 1864, see John Cannan, *Bloody Angle*, Battleground America Guides (South Yorkshire, England: Leo Cooper, n.d.).

[26]E. M. Law, Major General, C. S. A., "From the Wilderness to Cold Harbor," in *The Way to Appomattox*, vol. 4 of *Battles and Leaders of the Civil War* (1887; New York: Castle Books, 1956) 134.

[27]According to service records and other sources, the 3rd Battalion Sharpshooters suffered seven casualties on 12 May at Spotsylvania. Private W. B. Kimbro of Company B was killed in action. Six sharpshooters were wounded, including Private William J. Hill of Company A; privates John Solomon Goodwin and Elijah Walraven of Company E; and sergeants Joseph Curtis England and Robert M. Wood, and Private John M. Henderson of Company F.

of a kind and loving God, had once more been spared. In his memoirs, he proudly listed the battle of Spotsylvania among those in which he had participated.[28]

After the battle of Spotsylvania, the Confederate forces remained in their positions for several days. It was a welcome rest for the weary soldiers. Only the 3rd Battalion Sharpshooters and other skirmishers of Kershaw's Division saw any activity during the lull in action. They soon discovered that the Union forces had abandoned their breastworks and were once again attempting a flanking movement to get between the Southern Army and Richmond. Another race was about to begin, much like that from the Wilderness to Spotsylvania Court House.

On the morning of 21 May the sharpshooters and the 16th Georgia began a quick-time march of thirty miles to the North Anna River near Hanover Junction, arriving at noon on the following day. Not long after their arrival Captain Simmons and his comrades heard the news that General Jeb Stuart, the Army's brilliant cavalry leader, had been mortally wounded at Yellow Tavern on 19 May.[29] They later learned that the man credited with killing General Stuart was Private John Huff of the 5th Michigan Cavalry, a forty-eight-year-old former sharpshooter. Huff, in turn, was killed one week later at Haw's Shop in a skirmish with units of General Wade Hampton's Cavalry Division.[30] Unknown to all, Simmons and his men would meet up with Huff's cavalry regiment in the Shenandoah Valley later that year.

From 23 May through 26 May, the troops waited in their trenches on the south side of the North Anna for another major assault from the Army of the Potomac.[31] Skirmishing continued each day with varying intensity, but the expected all-out attack never came. On the afternoon of 26 May, Federal skirmishers advanced with considerable strength but were beaten back by the 3rd Battalion Sharpshooters and other units from the brigades of Bryan, Bratton, and Ramseur. By the early hours of 27 May, the enemy was nowhere to be found. It became obvious that another flanking movement was underway and another race was beginning.[32]

---

[28]Daniel M. Byrd Jr., *Them Brave Georgians*, manuscript, Gwinnett Historical Society archives, Lawrenceville, GA, pg. 310 (Fort Delaware Society Library, Delaware City, DE, also has a copy.).
[29]D. Augustus Dickert, *History of Kershaw's Brigade* (1899; reprint, Wilmington, NC: Broadfoot Publishing Company, 1990) 364; A Private of the 6th Virginia Cavalry, "The Death of General J. E. B. Stuart," in *The Way to Appomattox*, vol. 4 of *Battles and Leaders of the Civil War*, 194.
[30]Gregory Jaynes, *The Killing Ground: Wilderness to Cold Harbor* (Alexandria, VA: Time-Life Books, 1986) 149.
[31]Law, "From Wilderness to Cold Harbor," 135–36.
[32]Ibid.

19

A Well-deserved Promotion

> What one has, one ought to use; and whatever he does, he should do with all his might.
>
> —Cicero

On 27 May Anderson's I Corps began a double time march to head off the Union forces that were attempting a flanking movement to the east. The Confederates covered twenty-eight miles in two days and took up positions to the east of Richmond to defend against possible approaches to the Confederate capital. For several days, every soldier was busy building a semi-circular fortified line that ran for about eight miles from Atlee's Station on the northwest to a point near Bethesda Church on the southeast.[1]

When the defensive line was completed, the army learned that the Federals were flanking toward Cold Harbor, a dusty crossroads just fifteen miles northeast of Richmond. The tiny community was a key location for the area since five roads intersected there. Once again the Confederate forces had to quickly relocate to remain between the Army of the Potomac and Richmond.

The fighting began on 1 June 1864, a day when the temperature rose to nearly 100 degrees.[2] The battle raged for three days as Grant threw assault after assault against the Confederates' defensive positions without making a significant breach in the lines. Once again Captain Simmons and the sharpshooters were in the thick of the action. The battalion was placed in the middle of the Confederate line along with the rest of Anderson's Corps. On their left were newly-arrived reinforcements under General Breckenridge and the III Corps led by General A. P. Hill. To the right were the divisions of the II Corps, under the temporary command of General Jubal Early. The line now extended past Bethesda Church towards Cold Harbor.[3] The enemy continued its flanking movement and Anderson's soldiers were ordered to change places in

---

[1]E. Porter Alexander, *Military Memoirs of a Confederate: A Critical Narrative* (1907; reprint, Dayton, OH: Press of Morningside Bookshop, 1977) 533; The War of the Rebellion: A Compilation of the Official Records of the Union and Confederate Armies (70 vols. in 128; Washington, 1880–1901), ser. I, vol. 51, pt. 2, 974. Hereafter cited as OR.

[2]Robert K. Krick, *Civil War Weather in Virginia* (Tuscaloosa: University of Alabama Press, 2007) 132. The temperature reached 92 degrees by 2:00 P.M. in Washington, DC.

[3]*OR*, ser. I, vol. 51, pt. 2, 974; Alexander, *Military Memoirs*, 535–36.

the line with Early's troops and then push to the right as quickly as possible to connect with reinforcements from Richmond under the command of General Hoke.[4] Later on, A. P. Hill's Corps and Breckenridge's command would be repositioned to anchor the right of the Confederate line.

Early on 1 June, Kershaw's Brigade and the reinforcements under Hoke attempted to attack the Union left wing before the enemy could entrench, but due to serious blunders the attacking forces were completely repulsed. The Confederates began to entrench along the line where they had been stopped and there was skirmishing and sharpshooting throughout the day.[5] Around 6:00 P.M. the enemy launched an attack on the newly-established Confederate line. The assault was checked except for a gap between Wofford's Brigade and Hoke's Division. At that point there was a thickly-wooded ravine that had prevented construction of a continuous line of breastworks. The ravine jutted out toward the Union line, allowing the enemy to approach free of detection during the attack. The advance was led by the 6th Maryland (US) and the 138th Pennsylvania.[6] By the time they were discovered, the Yankees had approached the rear of Wofford's Brigade.[7]

General Wofford immediately responded by pulling his men back and directing their fire into the ravine, which was now crowded with Union soldiers. General Hoke also pulled his line back to help seal the breach. Soon, Confederate reinforcements arrived to connect the broken ends with a line resembling a horseshoe. By nightfall most of the lost ground was retaken and the enemy soon withdrew. Casualties for the 3rd Battalion Sharpshooters were light (one killed, three wounded, one captured), but a large number of soldiers from Wofford's Brigade were captured.[8]

The break in the defensive line was described by Captain Charles H. Sanders of Phillips Legion Infantry Battalion:

---

[4]E. M. Law, Major General, C. S. A., "From the Wilderness to Cold Harbor," in *The Way to Appomattox*, vol. 4 of *Battles and Leaders of the Civil War* (1887; New York: Castle Books, 1956) 138.

[5]Alexander, *Military Memoirs*, 536.

[6]Ernest Furgurson, *Not War But Murder: Cold Harbor, 1864* (New York: Vintage Books, 2000) 104–105.

[7]Alexander, *Military Memoirs*, 537–38; Law, "From the Wilderness to Cold Harbor," 138.

[8]According to service records and other sources, those wounded on 1 June included Private John A. Winborn of Company A, 4th Corporal Robert C. Little of Company B and Private James Talbot Crawford of Company E. Private Winborn was also captured. Private William W. Berry of Company D was killed on the same day, but the location is not recorded in his service record. The 16th Georgia had fifty men captured, three killed, and nine wounded on that day.

On the right of our brigade, there was about a hundred Yanks or maybe three hundred in the line that was not occupied by any troops thus, though we did not know, and it was a great oversight on our part. We were fighting away, when all at once a perfect shower of bullets came from behind, for the Yankees [were] advancing in as from the rear and a line of them was also advancing from the front. There was only one thing to do. We all saw that we had to get out of that place and quick, too. The order for retreat was given and away we went.[9]

By the morning of 2 June, the opposing lines were drawn up close to each other. Throughout the day there was heavy skirmishing and cannonading, but there was no major attack. About 4:00 P.M. the oppressive heat and dust of the past four days gave way to a violent rain storm. As soon as darkness came, the Confederates laid out a new and stronger defensive line on higher ground behind the ravine.[10] The most intense fighting of the battle took place in the early hours of 3 June when the Union VIII Corps under General William F. Smith advanced on the entrenched brigades of Kershaw's Division. The long, thin Confederate lines were ready for the enemy. The center of the attack was headed in the direction of the gap held by Wofford's Georgians, now reinforced by other troops.[11] Waves of Union soldiers scrambled over the abandoned Confederate positions, aiming towards the newly constructed line. With a steady aim, the imperiled Confederate veterans fired volley after volley at the attacking mass of men. A battle-hardened observer "[said of]…the terrible havoc that met the assaulting column, 'I never in all the bloody conflicts that I had been in, saw such a destruction of human lives. They literally piled on top of one another, often the dead would hold down the wounded and vice versa'."[12] The brunt of the action was over in an hour, but intermittent fighting continued until 8:00 A.M. In all, fourteen assaults were made and repulsed. The dead and wounded Federals piled in front of the lines numbered at least 7,000, while the Confederates suffered about 1,500 casualties.[13]

---

[9]Charles Sanders to his Deany [Sanders], 5 June 1864, in "Collection of Confederate Letters," drawer 186, box 31, Georgia Department of Archives & History, Morrow, GA; Mills Lane, ed., *"Dear Mother: Don't Grieve About Me. If I get Killed, I'll Only be Dead": Letters from Georgia Soldiers in the Civil War* (Savannah, GA: Beehive Press) 296. Captain Sanders led Company A (Lamar Infantry) of Cobb's Legion Infantry Battalion.

[10]*OR*, ser. I, vol. 36, pt. 1, 87.

[11]Law, "From the Wilderness to Cold Harbor," 139.

[12]W. A. McClendon, *Recollections of War Times by an Old Veteran while Under Stonewall Jackson and Lieutenant General James Longstreet* (1909; reprint, Tuscaloosa: University of Alabama Press, 2010) 211.

[13]Alexander, *Military Memoirs*, 540. E. P. Alexander indicated that the Confederate losses on 3 June were never reported. The *Confederate Medical and Surgical*

The Battle of Cold Harbor had ended, as had the fifth and last campaign in the "On to Richmond" drive by the Federal forces in 1864.[14] Exhausted Confederate survivors remained in their trenches for the next ten days. For nearly a month the two armies had been in continuous fighting or in preparation for battle. When the infantry and artillery were not locked in conflict, sharpshooters' fire from both sides kept every soldier pinned down. It had been a miserable campaign, but Confederate morale was high. The Southerners had repelled their adversaries every time they attacked.[15]

On the morning of 13 June the Union forces withdrew from their trenches. Initially there was no indication of where the enemy was going, but later reports indicated that Grant was moving toward Petersburg, a strategic transportation hub on the south bank of the James River twenty-three miles south of Richmond. At that location five railroads converged from all directions.

There was no fighting or marching on 15 June, so Captain Simmons made the most of the day. He recorded in his diary that his trousers had become so worn and tattered that they hardly deserved the name of trousers. Because of the constant marching and skirmishing, he had been unable to supply himself with a pair. Fortunately Captain Phillips, the brigade quartermaster, had come upon a supply. When Simmons learned that trousers were available, he secured a requisition form, which required advance approval of Colonel Hutchins. This form must have been a source of amusement to both officers since it had been confiscated from the Yankees. With a stroke of the pen Simmons substituted a "C" for the "U" in U.S. Army. Colonel Hutchins endorsed his approval and Captain Simmons became the proud owner of a new pair of pants. When he picked up his prized possession from the quartermaster, he wrote on the doctored form "one pair pants—Price (12.00) Lincoln Dollars."[16] One might wonder if Simmons was serious, or just making light of the situation.

By 17 June it became clear that the Union army was nearing Petersburg. Kershaw's Division left that night to help shore up the defenses around the city. The reinforcements arrived in Petersburg the following morning about sunrise. By that time the streets were already lined with townspeople waving banners and handkerchiefs, cheering the newly arriving defenders. The seasoned veterans

---

History of the War (estimates that 1,200 were wounded and 500 missing from 1 June to 12 June 1864, *Confederate Medical and Surgical History of the War*. J. J. Woodward, *Medical History*, part 1, vol. 1 of *Confederate Medical and Surgical History of the War* (Washington, DC: Government Printing Office, 1870).

[14]Law, "From the Wilderness to Cold Harbor," 142.

[15]Ibid., 143; D. Augustus Dickert, *History of Kershaw's Brigade* (1899; reprint, Wilmington, NC: Broadfoot Publishing Company, 1990) 376–77.

[16]Simmons service records, in Byrd, *Them Brave Georgians*, 322.

soon replaced the handful of regulars and militia who had been mustered to defend their homes.[17]

Not long after Kershaw's men occupied their newly dug trenches behind an older series of breastworks, the first Union attack began. When the enemy advanced to the abandoned trenches they were halted by a hail of gunfire from the new line. There were three more attacks made at the same point that afternoon, but all were easily beaten back.[18]

For the next few days the men of the 16th Georgia worked side by side with other soldiers to improve the trenches and construct a labyrinth of deep narrow walkways connecting buildings and bomb shelters for protection against the Union artillery. While their comrades labored with pick and shovel, Simmons and the 3rd Battalion were constantly involved in sharpshooting, day and night. Soon it became apparent that Grant had changed his tactics to lay siege to Petersburg rather than continue with frontal assaults.[19]

On 23 June, after a week in the trenches, Kershaw's Division was ordered to proceed at once to Chaffin's Bluff on the north side of the James River. This action was in response to reports of Union movements north of the James. To surprise the enemy General Lee directed Kershaw to lead his men out of Petersburg undetected and as rapidly as possible.[20]

The division moved out at daybreak, avoiding roads to keep from being spotted and not stopping until reaching the James River. After crossing the river the soldiers marched all night through brush, bogs and briars until they finally reached Chaffin's Bluff. Before them lay Deep Bottom, a large swamp of timber and underbrush. On the opposite side of Deep Bottom was an entrenched force of Federals, supported by gunboats at anchor on the James.[21]

On 26 June Kershaw's Division made a futile attempt to storm the defenses in a daring nighttime raid. Realizing the Confederates were greatly outnumbered,[22] General Lee immediately ordered General Anderson to provide reinforcements. Two days later, after Anderson's four brigades were pressed into battle, the tide turned and the Confederates gained the upper hand. With the assistance of General Fitzhugh Lee's Cavalry, the Union forces abandoned their positions and crossed back over the river. The Confederates captured artillery

---

[17]Dickert, *Kershaw's Brigade*, 380; P. G. T. Beauregard, General, C. S. A., "Four Day of Battle at Petersburg," *The Way to Appomattox*, vol. 4 of *Battles and Leaders of the Civil War* (1887; New York: Castle Books, 1956) 543.

[18]Beauregard, "Four Days of Battle at Petersburg," 543–44.

[19]Alexander, *Military Memoirs*, 560; Dickert, *Kershaw's Brigade*, 386–87.

[20]*OR*, ser. I, vol. 40, pt. 3, 795–96.

[21]Dickert, *Kershaw's Brigade*, 389.

[22]*OR*, ser. I, vol. 40, pt. 3, 808; Union forces included three divisions of the II Corps plus cavalry.

and took seventy-five prisoners before returning to Petersburg at the end of the following month.

On 30 July there was "skirmishing nearly all the day." Colonel Hutchins was severely wounded by shrapnel from an artillery shell.[23] Command of the 3rd Sharpshooter Battalion was once again in the hands of Captain William Simmons.

When Simmons and the sharpshooters returned to Petersburg on the last day of July, the main topic of conversation was the savage "Battle of the Crater" that had taken place the day before. On that day the Union forces had set off an underground explosion at dawn that created a huge crater in the Confederate breastworks. After the smoke and dust had cleared, thousands of Yankees had poured into the open hole. By afternoon, the Confederates mounted a determined counterattack. Lining the rim of the crater, soldiers in gray fired down on the Federals like fish in a barrel. Witnesses observed that the Union soldiers were packed so closely in the crater that many could not reload or fire their rifles. By nightfall there were more than 4,000 Union casualties.[24]

While all the talk about the explosion was taking place, Simmons learned that his recommended promotion as major of the sharpshooters had finally been approved in Richmond. On 21 July the War Department entered the last endorsement on General Wofford's recommendation dated 4 April 1864 when his brigade was in Greenville, Tennessee. The promotion was dated back to September 1863, the month Major Davant was promoted to lieutenant colonel and given command of the 38th Georgia Infantry Regiment.[25]

After a week of relative inactivity at Petersburg, selected brigades from Anderson's I Corps, including the 16th Georgia and the 3rd Sharpshooter Battalion, were given orders to leave Petersburg and march to an undisclosed destination. Despite the uncertainty shared by the men of Wofford's Brigade, there was a general feeling of relief in being able to leave the besieged city and its confining breastworks and trenches. On 6 August the soldiers were transported by train from Chester's Station to Mitchell's Station, near Culpeper, Virginia. There they were to be joined by wagon trains, artillery, and General Fitzhugh

---

[23]Diary of Private James A. Reynolds, Company K, 16th Georgia Infantry. Entry for 30 July 1864. A photocopy is in the possession of Richmond National Battlefield Park, transcribed by Robert E. L. Krick. Reynolds enlisted in the Ramsey Volunteers on 10 March 1862 and served until he was captured at Sailor's Creek on 6 April 1865. His diary was dropped on the battlefield of Cedar Creek, 19 October 1864, and picked up by a Union Soldier.

[24]A thorough description of the action at the Petersburg Crater is covered in ch. 23 of Dickert, *Kershaw's Brigade,* 386–416, documenting several eye-witness accounts.

[25]Simmons service records, in Byrd, *Them Brave Georgians,* 330.

Lee's Cavalry.[26] The men sensed that they were on an important mission knowing that General Anderson was personally accompanying the command. It would prove to be a fateful event for Major Simmons and many of the men in his sharpshooter battalion.

---

[26]G. Moxley Sorrel, *Recollections of a Confederate Staff Officer*, ed. Bell Irvin Wiley (Wilmington, NC: Broadfoot Publishing Company, 1995) 256; Dickert, *Kershaw's Brigade*, 417.

20

The Major's Last Battle

The ideal man bears the accidents of life with dignity and grace, making the best of circumstances.

—Aristotle

It was not until 11 August that the wagon trains, artillery and cavalry arrived at Mitchell's Station to join the expedition.[1] Soon after sunrise on the following morning, Anderson's command began the march northward to Culpeper, Virginia. After a four-hour rest the column resumed the march and turned to the northwest. With the change in direction, the men soon realized that their destination was most likely the Shenandoah Valley where General Jubal Early's II Corps was attempting to drive Sheridan's Union forces out of the region.[2]

On the third day of their deployment, after passing through the town of Flint Hill, the soldiers crossed the Blue Ridge Mountains at Chester's Gap. Before them lay the incomparable Shenandoah Valley, known as the "bread basket of the South." Rising above the valley in the distance they observed the northern end of Massanutten Mountain, an unusual land formation that split the valley into two distinct parts. On either side of the mountain, separate forks of the Shenandoah River flowed until they merged above the old hamlet of Front Royal. From that point the Shenandoah flowed in a northerly direction until it emptied in to the Potomac. Early that afternoon, Wofford's Brigade made camp near the village between the farm of S. B. Gardner and the home of Dr. Charles Eckardt, the local music teacher.[3] Late in the evening, Dr. Eckhart called on General Wofford's headquarters, where he requested and received a guard of three men to ensure the security of his home.[4]

Sunday afternoon, 14 August, was both a memorable and enjoyable time. All the dust and grime of the recent march were washed off in the clear, blue waters of the Shenandoah. After a refreshing bath many of the men were welcomed at the bountiful tables of loyal Southern families. Nearly all of the

---

[1] *The War of the Rebellion: A Compilation of the Official Records of the Union and Confederate Armies* (70 vols. in 128; Washington, 1880–1901), ser. I, vol. 42, pt. 2, 1213. Hereafter cited as OR.

[2] *OR*, ser. I, vol. 42, pt. 2, 1161.

[3] Diary of Marcus B. Buck, Confederate Museum, Front Royal, VA. Buck was one of the most prominent landowners in the area. Cited hereafter as Buck Diary.

[4] Diary of Dr. Charles Eckardt, Confederate Museum, Front Royal, VA. Cited hereafter as Eckardt Diary.

local residents did their best to contribute to the comfort and pleasure of the Confederate soldiers. One private in the 16th Georgia Infantry Regiment noted that we are "now in quiate [quiet] camps with plenty to eat encircled with as warm friends as we could wish."[5] The Buck family entertained from 75 to 100 hungry soldiers. Nearby, the Richardson family held an open house. Dr. Eckardt also received friends of the three pickets furnished by General Wofford.[6]

Unknown to Major Simmons, the enjoyable time in Front Royal would be his last respite for many long months. Everyone sensed that a major battle was imminent. On 15 August, a Union cavalry brigade and infantry were sighted several miles north of Front Royal at Cedarville.

On the following day Simmons and his men were refreshed by a much needed morning rain shower.[7] Around noon there was a report that four more Union cavalry brigades were moving along the North Fork of the Shenandoah toward Cedarville. The sighting was made by Captain J. H. Manning, the I Corps Signal Officer, from an observation station in the middle field of the Buck Farm.[8] The dense clouds of dust raised by the cavalry were visible from miles away. The news was ominous. If Union forces were allowed to fortify the northern bank of the Shenandoah, they could control the vital route through the valley northward to Winchester and block Confederate efforts to cross the river. Control of this area would provide the Federals a strong artillery position on Guard Hill, which was located above the road to Winchester. After sizing up the situation, General Anderson ordered General Wofford's Georgians and a brigade of Virginia cavalry and horse artillery under the command of General W. C. Wickham to seize Guard Hill and protect the nearby fords across the river.[9]

Wickham's Brigade advanced down the Winchester Pike and over the narrow neck of land separating the two forks of the Shenandoah. One of Wickham's regiments, the 2nd Virginia, crossed the Shenandoah further downstream to guard the approaches along the river. The 3rd Sharpshooter Battalion advanced further downstream to lead the way for Wofford's Brigade in a flanking movement to the right.[10]

As soon as Wickham's troopers were across the forks of the river, the command to charge was given and the Confederate cavalry dashed straight

---

[5]Diary of Private James A. Reynolds, Company K, 16th Georgia Infantry. Entry for 14 August 1864. A photocopy is in the possession of Richmond National Battlefield Park, transcribed by Robert E. L. Krick. Cited hereafter as Reynolds Diary.

[6]Diaries of Buck and Eckardt, as previously noted, along with diarists Miss Sue Richardson and Letitia Blackmore, Confederate Museum, Front Royal, VA.

[7]Reynolds Diary, 16 August 1864.

[8]Buck Diary; G. Moxley Sorrel, *Recollections of a Confederate Staff Officer*, ed. Bell Irvin Wiley (Wilmington, NC: Broadfoot Publishing Company, 1995) 117.

[9]Diary of the First Army Corps, in Byrd, *Them Brave Georgians*, 336–38.

[10]Ibid., 338.

toward Guard Hill. The startled Federal pickets offered token resistance before retreating to a safer position down the turnpike. Wickham's Virginians cleared Guard Hill and took possession of high ground on each side of the pike where a bridge spans a stream called Crooked Run. The artillery was brought up the steep embankment and positioned to fire at the advancing Union cavalry coming from the north. The enemy put up stiff resistance but were driven back further.[11]

Emboldened by success, General Wickham ordered his troopers to charge. The cavalry rode forward but were soon stopped by overwhelming numbers, bolstered by the recent arrival of the Union First Cavalry Brigade of General Wesley Merritt's Division. Wickham's troopers withdrew to stronger defensive positions at Guard Hill and the higher ground along a small stream called Crooked Run.[12]

Major Simmons, now in command of the 3rd Georgia Sharpshooters, led Wofford's Brigade into battle.[13] When the battalion was some distance ahead of the main force, they reached a shallow ford on the Shenandoah three miles north of Front Royal, about one and a half miles downstream from where the North and South Forks join together. A short distance below the ford, Crooked Run empties into the Shenandoah River.

When Simmons and the sharpshooters arrived at the river, they saw several mounted Yankee videttes on the opposite bank. The horsemen took one quick look at the gathering troops, and galloped away without firing a shot. Major Simmons rode into the river, with his battalion following on foot, later noting that the river had fallen to a level no more than waist deep due to a drought in recent weeks. Once the sharpshooters were safely across the river, they began to

---

[11]*OR*, ser. I, vol. 43, pt. 1, 439, 473; Wesley Merritt, Major-General, U. S. V. Brigadier General, U. S. A., "Sheridan in the Shenandoah Valley," in *The Way to Appomattox*, vol. 4 of *Battles and Leaders of the Civil War* (1887; New York: Castle Books, 1956) 502.

[12]*OR*, ser. I, vol. 43, pt. 1, 473.

[13]Filed with the personal papers of Nathan L. Hutchins Jr., 16th Georgia Regiment are the originals of letters from Nathan L. Hutchins Jr. to J. M. Goggin dated 23, 25, 27 April 1863 and 11 May 1863 (in *Compiled Service Records of Confederate Soldiers Who Served in Organizations from the State of Georgia*, microcopy 266, RG 109, National Archives and Records Administration, Washington, DC). As previously noted, Major William E. Simmons became acting commander of Wofford's Sharpshooter Battalion after Lieutenant Colonel N. L. Hutchins Jr. was wounded on 30 July 1864. Hutchins's service record does not indicate the location where he was wounded, but it likely took place when the sharpshooters were returning to Petersburg from the action at Deep Bottom. Hutchins took a bullet in the shoulder and was treated at Hospital #4 in Richmond. He was granted a forty-day furlough on 24 August and subsequently returned to lead the sharpshooters sometime around the end of September 1864.

hear the distant sound of artillery and gunfire to the west.[14] The action at Guard Hill[15] was underway.

A short distance ahead, across open fields, Simmons could see the saplings and dense undergrowth lining the banks of Crooked Run. Riding forward, he soon located a place where the sharpshooters could easily wade across the creek. The young major and his horse splashed their way through the shallow waters of the stream, beckoning the men to follow. Once across, he sent his horse to the safety of the rear.

As quickly as possible, Simmons formed his battalion in a skirmish line along the northern bank of Crooked Run, about one-half mile from Winchester Pike. He assumed that if the sharpshooters could reach the pike, they would be on the flank of any Federal forces approaching Guard Hill. The skirmish line moved out promptly and struck the enemy's forward line of dismounted cavalry troopers from General George Armstrong Custer's 1st Brigade. The Union line was driven back, offering only slight resistance as it fell back to a second position some 200 yards to the rear. The cool-headed sharpshooters steadily advanced, taking cover only long enough to ram new charges in their rifles. Then the Georgians poured a salvo into the second line, which like the first was easily driven off.[16]

As the Union cavalry were retreating from their second position, Major Simmons saw something that must have made his heart leap in terror. In the distance, stretched out before him, was a great host of Federal cavalry racing across the Winchester Pike in full battle array, with swords glittering and battle flags waving in the August breeze. In later years, Simmons recalled that he saw what appeared to be about 10,000 Federal horsemen.[17]

In view of the overwhelming size of the Union force, discretion clearly dictated a withdrawal. Simmons quickly dispatched a courier to General Wofford, warning him to hold the brigade on the south side of the Shenandoah River. The general himself returned with the courier to confer with the major. Together the two officers cautiously sought a better observation point. In the distance a light field artillery battery was firing in their direction. The challenge of Federal guns seemed to stir the General's blood to fighting heat. Turning to his subordinate, Wofford said, "Cavalry will not fight infantry. We are going to

---

[14]Byrd, *Them Brave Georgians*, 339.

[15]The North referred to the engagement as the Battle of Cedarville. See General Wesley Merritt's account in "Sheridan in the Shenandoah Valley," 502–503.

[16]Byrd, *Them Brave Georgians*, 342.

[17]*OR*, ser. I, vol. 43, pt. 1, 439. D. M. Byrd Jr. noted that there were five regiments in Custer's First Brigade that "[moved] to the right of the [Guard] Hill to act in concert with the dismounted men." Byrd wrote, "It is unlikely that Major Simmons could have seen the Federal Second Brigade, then busy meeting the charge of Wickham's Cavalry near Guard Hill" (*Them Brave Georgians*, 342–43).

capture that battery. Hold your position until I get the brigade across the river and into battle line, and then advance at once."[18]

The young major was concerned with the course of action that General Wofford had outlined. Simmons knew that Sheridan's cavalry was operating in the Valley and that they were among the elite fighters of the Union army. Within the bounds of military propriety, he sought to reason with his commanding officer, saying, "I think you are going to make a bad mistake. There is a strong possibility that the brigade will be destroyed." Wofford disagreed. There was nothing Simmons could do. "I am a soldier," he said as the general prepared to depart, "and stand ready to obey your command."[19]

Keeping an eye on the Union forces, but also watching in the direction of the river, Simmons readied his men to advance as directed by his superior. As soon as Wofford's Brigade[20] waded boldly into the river, the sharpshooters moved forward. Something was strangely wrong, however. Once again, the Federal line fell back and Simmons sensed that there would be an ambush. The brigade charged up the banks of Crooked Run and across the open high ground along the stream. A wild, enthusiastic rebel yell died in their throats as a deadly fire was poured into their solid ranks by a large contingent of Sheridan's dismounted cavalrymen. Soon it became apparent that the bluecoats had purposely allowed the Georgians to approach within short carbine range before they opened fire.[21]

Further disaster awaited the exposed Georgians. Simmons hardly had time to shout "Rally by the fours" before a mounted battalion of the 1st Michigan Cavalry rode through the ranks of the 3rd Battalion.[22] The signal was to guard against a cavalry charge with groups of men standing back-to-back facing in four directions. There was no stopping or slowing the driving Union cavalrymen.

---

[18]Ibid., based on an account by William Simmons.

[19]Ibid.

[20]According to Gerald J. Smith (*One of the Most Daring of Men: The Life of Confederate General William Tatum Wofford*, vol. 16 of Journal of Confederate History Series, ed. John McGlone [Murfreesboro, TN: Southern Heritage Press, 1997] 129) and Richard M. Coffman and Kurt D. Graham (*To Honor These Men* [Macon: Mercer University Press, 2007] 234), the action at Guard Hill included Cobb's Legion Infantry Battalion, the 16th and 24th Georgia Infantry Regiments, and the 3rd Battalion Sharpshooters from Wofford's Brigade. Phillips Legion Infantry Battalion remained behind. There was no mention of the 18th Georgia Infantry Regiment. However, according to service records, the 18th Georgia was also involved, given that at least twelve men from among five different companies in the 18th Georgia were killed, wounded, or captured in the fighting that took place near Front Royal on 16 August 1864.

[21]General Wesley Merritt reported to Sheridan that the Georgians were "allowed to approach within short carbine range before opening fire" (*OR*, ser. I, vol. 43, pt. 1, 439).

[22]Jeffrey D. Wert, *The Controversial Life of George Armstrong Custer* (New York: Simon & Schuster, 1996) 173.

They hardly paid any attention to the widely placed sharpshooters as they galloped across the field in pursuit of the main body of Wofford's Brigade.

Simmons looked back in horror at the melee caused by hundreds of charging horsemen, which now included troopers from the 7th Michigan. Wofford's Brigade was flanked at both ends of the battle line, with the Confederate soldiers in a wild scramble to escape capture. Throughout the ranks the soldiers raced to get out of the way of the galloping horses and deadly, slashing swords. Hundreds of Confederate infantrymen were driven into the river, while others fell wounded and dead. A bullet felled Wofford's bay mare and the general barely escaped capture after falling into the river. The wildest confusion reigned. The brigade was decisively and completely routed. Later, Simmons would learn that many of his comrades of the 3rd Battalion and 16th Georgia Regiment would be numbered as casualties in the Battle of Guard Hill.[23] Seventeen members of his battalion and old regiment were killed or wounded and fifty-nine were captured on that disastrous day. Overall, 150 prisoners were taken from Wofford's Brigade.

The battle was described by Floyd Jordan, a young private from the 24th Georgia, one of six Jordan family members who saw action at Guard Hill. All of the family served in Company A (Independent Volunteers) from Banks County. In a letter to his uncles, he wrote about the incident:

> Our boys got into a severe fight with the Yankie Calvary on the 16th of this month…about one hour before the sun went down, our boys charged the Yankie's calvary for about half a mile through an open corn field and got within 40 or 50 yards of them when there was a flank movement made and the enemy flanked around our left and got in our rear, and caused us to fall back in a most confused condition. There was a force of [Confederate] calvary posted on our left flank to protect us, and they gave away at the sight of the enemy as usual, and caused all the brigade to get flanked….[24]

As he watched the debacle, Major Simmons began to think about the safety of his sharpshooters. The situation was desperate, more perilous than it had been at Crampton's Gap when he and his men were separated from their

---

[23] According to service records, there were substantial losses to Wofford's 3rd Sharpshooter Battalion. Two men were killed, four wounded, and fifty were captured. The sixteenth of August was a disastrous day for the Jordan family. Allen C., Thomas W. and Newton Jordan of the 24th Georgia, Company A were captured and sent to prison. All three died in captivity. Allen and Thomas died of Variola at Elmira in February 1865. Newton died of disease on the steamer USS "Northern Light" in October 1864. Most likely his death occurred in transit from Point Lookout Prison to Elmira (Floyd Jordan to Thomas and Lovice Jordan, 19 August 1864, in Allen C. Jordan Family papers, Hargrett Rare Book & Manuscript Library, University of Georgia, Athens).

[24] Edward G. Longacre, *Custer and His Wolverines: The Michigan Cavalry Brigade 1861–1865* (Conshohocken, PA: Combined Publishing, 1997) 244.

regiment and narrowly escaped. Here, however, the sharpshooters did not yet have the protective cover of darkness to elude the enemy. In the pandemonium and confusion of battle, Major Simmons weighed his alternatives. On his right Federal forces remained in force astride the Winchester Pike and along the banks of the river, closing those avenues of escape. Another possibility was to race toward the heights on the left where Wickham's artillery was posted, but to reach that point, Simmons and his men would have to dodge a large number of Union cavalrymen who had skulked out of the fighting and lagged behind the main Union force.

Before he could make a decision, fifteen or twenty of the Union skulkers charged the sharpshooters who remained on the open battle field. As he drew his pistol, Major Simmons shouted orders down the line for the men to withhold their fire until commanded, then fire and throw down their weapons and surrender. Without a moment to spare the sharpshooters aimed their rifles at the advancing Federal horsemen. At a second shouted command, Major Simmons and his sharpshooters fired their last bullets for the Southland, then dropped their weapons to the ground and quickly raised their hands.

The Georgians were deadly marksmen. Their final volley killed seven of the charging Yankee cavalrymen, all shot down within a few yards of Simmons. One of the horsemen, obviously enraged by the loss of his comrades, wildly slashed out with his saber at the young major in retaliation. Simmons sidestepped the intended blow and drew his sword in defense. The horseman wheeled around and charged again, swinging and cutting. Stroke after stroke was parried, but the cavalryman's saber landed heavier blows. Simmons's sword was shattered to the hilt, and he sustained a wound to his elbow.

In the midst of the fracas, a Union cavalry officer saw what was happening and galloped up in time to witness the scene. He ordered the cavalryman to stop the attack and denounced the assault as a cowardly act, without excuse. The cavalryman protested and informed the officer that the major (Simmons) was responsible for the death of seven cavalrymen by giving the command to fire when there was no chance of escape.

The explanation did not alter the command. If the trooper struck another blow, the Federal officer swore that he would shoot his subordinate on the spot. Simmons breathed a little easier and uttered a silent prayer of thankfulness. He was no doubt struck by the irony of having his life saved by the combination of a Union sword from Gettysburg and an intervening Yankee cavalry officer. The broken sword that likely saved his life was the one given to him by the wounded Union officer whom Simmons had treated with respect and provided shelter at the Battle of Gettysburg. The wound to Simmons's elbow was the only injury that he ever received during the time he served in the Confederate army.

It was a tragic day for Major Simmons and his comrades as witnessed by Major James Harvey Kidd, who commanded a cavalry regiment assigned to Custer's Michigan Cavalry Brigade. Edward G. Longacre, an authority on the

Union cavalry in the Civil War, described the debacle based on Kidd's recollections.

The Rebel [cavalry] neutralized, Custer turned to confront a phalanx of foot troops making for his left flank via a ford across Crooked Run. Again he dosed the enemy—part of Kershaw's command—with shells from [Captain Dunbar R.] Ransom's battery, then ordered a dismounted advance…. Attacking out of a ravine that shielded them from enemy view, the Fifth Michigan opened on the enemy line with such effect that, according to James Kidd, "the head of Kershaw's column was completely crushed." Minutes later the Rebels were returning to the ford on the double. To help them along, a mounted battalion of the First Michigan under Angelo Paldi galloped past the Fifth and slammed into Kershaw's rear, cutting down luckless footmen and capturing almost 150 of them. Custer's casualties numbered close to fifty. By day's end, Custer was minus one of his golden locks, shorn by a stray bullet, but otherwise in excellent condition as well as high spirits.[25]

Custer's hair loss from the stray bullet was noted by a sergeant of the 1st Michigan, who recalled that, as was Custer's habit, he rode along the brigade's line to "encourage the men."[26] If the bullet that grazed his head had been an inch or two to the right, the young cavalry general would likely have been killed. The following day, Sheridan described the action and mentioned Custer's near miss in a brief dispatch to his Chief of Staff.

August 17, 1864

General Merritt's division of cavalry was attacked yesterday afternoon on [the] north side of the Shenandoah by Kershaw's Division, of Longstreet's Corps, and Wickham's and Lomax's Brigades of cavalry. After a very handsome cavalry fight the enemy were badly beaten, with a loss of two stand of colors, 24 officers, and 276 men prisoners. Most of the prisoners are from Longstreet's Corps and Kershaw's Division. The cavalry made some handsome saber charges, in which most of the prisoners were captured. General Custer made a very narrow escape. Devin's and Custer's Brigades were engaged.[27]

P. H. Sheridan, Major-General

---

[25]James H. Kidd, *Personal Recollections of a Cavalryman with Custer's Michigan Cavalry Brigade in the Civil War* (1908; reprint, Iona, MI: Sentinel Printing Co., 1997) 376–77; Wert, *Controversial Life of George Armstrong Custer*, 173.
[26]Wert, *Controversial Life of George Armstrong Custer*, 173.
[27]*OR*, ser. I, vol. 43, pt. 1, 19.

21

Captured and Imprisoned

> I have learned from experience that the greater part of our happiness
> or misery depends on our dispositions and not on our circumstances.
>
> —Martha Washington

As darkness was closing on the battlefield, Simmons's captors escorted him to the headquarters of General Custer. In later years, the major recalled that while there, he was received with "courtesy and kindness." Madison Byrd noted, "Neither officer left a record of what was said, but a feeling of mutual respect must have developed." After their encounter, Custer furnished Simmons with a mount and an orderly to accompany him to the office of the Federal provost marshal in Harpers Ferry.[1]

The next day, while Simmons and the orderly rode north to Harpers Ferry, Sheridan implemented orders from Ulysses Grant to inflict widespread destruction throughout the Shenandoah Valley. In his instructions, Grant had written, "Nothing should be left to invite the enemy to return." Sheridan dispatched units of his cavalry, led by Brigadier General Alfred Torbert, to burn the fields and farm structures, destroy farm implements, kill the livestock, and set the slaves free. There were two primary reasons for the order. Inflicting widespread destruction on civilian property would severely cripple the region's ability to feed the Confederacy. More specifically, Grant wanted to "make the Valley untenable for the raiding parties of the rebel army." His primary focus was Virginia's Loudon County, the sanctuary of Lieutenant Colonel John Singleton Mosby and his mounted partisans.[2]

After his arrival at the provost marshal's office on 17 August, Simmons learned that his next stop would be the Old Capitol Prison, a brick building in the shadow of the partially completed capitol in Washington.[3] The structure was erected in 1817 after the original capitol building had been destroyed by the British during the War of 1812. In later years, the building was remodeled as a

---

[1]Daniel M. Byrd Jr., *Them Brave Georgians*, manuscript, Gwinnett Historical Society archives, Lawrenceville, GA, pg. 349 (Fort Delaware Society Library, Delaware City, DE, also has a copy.).

[2]Joseph Wheelan, "The Burning," *America's Civil War* 12 (November 2012): 41–42. Adapted from Wheelan's *Terrible Swift Sword: The Life of General Philip H. Sheridan* (Cambridge, MA: Da Capo Press, 2012).

[3]Byrd, *Them Brave Georgians*, 350. Simmons's name appears on roll 45, sheet 8 of Prisoners Captured at Front Royal by General Sheridan during August 1864.

fashionable boarding house. During the war, conditions were much more modest, as the boarding house was transformed into a Union prison. The prisoners' rooms contained bunks like those on canal boats, one above the other, about eighteen inches apart. Iron bars covered the windows. While he was at the Old Capitol Prison, Simmons began to record in his diary the names of comrades from Georgia who had died from a multitude of diseases and battle wounds.[4]

William Simmons's stay at the Old Capitol Prison was to be a short one. He arrived at the facility on 21 August and departed in less than one week. On 27 August, Simmons and a large group of Confederate officers were taken under guard by rail to Baltimore, where they changed trains and continued to New Castle, Delaware. From the railroad station the captured officers marched about one mile through the town, down to the wharf. They were then taken by boat to Pea Patch Island, situated in the middle of Delaware Bay that separates New Jersey and Delaware.[5] For the next eleven months, Fort Delaware Prison would be Simmons's dismal home.

Fort Delaware was originally constructed on Pea Patch Island to control the navigation of the Delaware River. After the war's start, the United States used it to hold political and naval prisoners. In 1862, to handle the growing number of Confederate prisoners, the Federals built shed barracks inside the fort to house 2,000 men. During the period of exchange under the cartel of 22 July 1862, the fort served as a way station for officers and enlisted men en route to City Point, Virginia. With the breakdown of the cartel in 1863, the Federal authorities designated Fort Delaware as a regular prison depot and built barracks outside the walls of the original fort to hold an additional 5,000 prisoners.[6]

When the prisoners arrived Simmons saw a depressing sight. Pea Patch Island, well-named for its size, covered only 178 acres at the head of Delaware Bay, about five miles south of New Castle, Delaware. On the desolate island, only a small area of fifty-two acres was habitable, and there the marshy ground stayed continually wet. Most of the high ground was occupied by the fort. Over the remaining soggy forty-five acres, Federal prison authorities had placed the shed barracks. Each building was constructed of rough lumber and measured about 300 feet by 150 feet. Inside each of the barracks buildings, partitions divided the space into large rooms or "divisions." The divisions were

---

[4]Byrd, *Them Brave Georgians*, 351. Register no. 304, part 783, page 498 of the Old Capitol Prison gives August 21 as the date of commitment (NARA).

[5]Byrd, *Them Brave Georgians*, 352.

[6]For a more in-depth account of Fort Delaware's construction and early history, see Dale Fetzer and Bruce Mowday, *Unlikely Allies: Fort Delaware's Prison Community in the Civil War* (Mechanicsburg, PA: Stackpole Books, 2000) 1–30. Also see Brian Temple, *The Union Prison at Fort Delaware: A Perfect Hell on Earth* (Jefferson NC: McFarland & Company, Publishers, 2003) 3–9.

honeycombed with multi-decked bunks, separated by four-foot walkways, with only enough space near the center for a single upright stove.[7]

Like prisoners on both sides of the War Between the States, William Simmons endured harsh conditions at Fort Delaware. During his incarceration, the prison held nearly 10,000 Confederate inmates within its walls. Officers and enlisted men were sent to separate facilities, but no matter the rank of the inhabitants, conditions at the prison were abominable. During the course of the war more than 30,000 men were imprisoned there.

Fort Delaware was unique among northern prisons in the makeup of its prison population. Within its walls it housed Confederate officers (including sixteen generals) of all ranks as well as enlisted men. Less than a week before Major Simmons arrived, 600 Confederate officers held at Fort Delaware were sent South with the implication that all would be exchanged. They were first sent to an open prison stockade on Morris Island just outside Charleston, where they were used as human shields against artillery fire from their own army. They were later taken to Hilton Head, South Carolina, and Fort Pulaski outside Savannah. During their ordeal only fifty of the officers were exchanged, and forty-four died in captivity. Those who remained were taken by ship back to Fort Delaware in spring 1865. Among the survivors was 1st Lieutenant Milton M. Mosley, Company B, 3rd Battalion Sharpshooters. Lieutenant Mosley had been captured at Spotsylvania on 12 May 1864.[8]

There were also a number of Union soldiers imprisoned at Fort Delaware.[9] In addition, political prisoners from both sides of the Mason-Dixon Line were confined on the swampy island. One political prisoner, Dr. Isaac W. K. Handy,

---

[7] *The War of the Rebellion: A Compilation of the Official Records of the Union and Confederate Armies* (70 vols. in 128; Washington, 1880–1901) (hereafter cited as *OR*), ser. II, vol. 6, 281; "Diary of Captain Robert E. Park, of the Twelfth Alabama Regiment," *Southern Historical Society Papers* (hereafter *SHSP*) 3/1 (January 1877): 43. Park's diary is continued in several *SHSP* volumes. Park gives an eye-witness description of the prison and the life of its inmates during the time that William Simmons was confined. At the time of his imprisonment, Park was a lieutenant. See also D. Augustus Dickert, *History of Kershaw's Brigade* (1899; reprint, Wilmington, NC: Broadfoot Publishing Company, 1990) 461–66. In his account of prison life, Dickert includes the recollections of a fellow officer, Lieutenant U. B. White, a sharpshooter officer in Kershaw's Brigade who was imprisoned at Fort Delaware following his capture at Cedar Creek in October 1864.

[8] Muriel Phillips Joslyn, *Immortal Captives: The Story of 600 Confederate Officers and the United States Prisoner of War Policy* (Gretna, LA: Pelican Publishing, 2008) 290–91. See also Judge Henry Howe Cook, "The Story of the 600," *Confederate Veteran* 5/5 (May 1897): 219–20.

[9] Jocelyn P. Jamison, *They Died at Fort Delaware: Confederate, Union and Civilian* (Wilmington: Fort Delaware Historical Society, n.d.) 85–88. According to Ms. Jamison, who based the information on a compilation of records from the National Archives, 110 Union soldiers and 39 civilians died while imprisoned at Fort Delaware.

was kept for fifteen months without being formally charged or given a trial. Handy was a native of Washington, DC, and a Presbyterian minister who pastored a church in Hampton, Virginia. He was visiting his wife's family and friends in Delaware when he was overheard making sympathetic remarks about the South in table conversation at a private gathering. After several days and numerous exaggerations, he was denounced as "a notorious Rebel and a dangerous man" and arrested.[10]

"It is useless to attempt a description of the place," declared Georgia native Robert Emory Park, an officer of the 12th Alabama who was incarcerated at Fort Delaware. "A respectable hog would have turned up his nose in disgust at it." The meat and bacon available to both officers and enlisted men were described in letters and journals as "rusty and slimy"—and the other fare was no better. Park declared that "the soup at Fort Delaware came with white worms, half an inch long." It was a standing joke, he wrote, "that the soup was too weak to drown the rice worms and pea bugs, which, however, came to their death by starvation."[11]

One of the biggest complaints was the poor quality of water that was made available to the prisoners. The water that was used for cleaning came from ditches and the bay and was polluted by the fort's own sewage. Drinking water brought in by boat from nearby Brandywine Creek was marginally less noxious. Complaints of dampness in a prison barely above sea level were endemic. In July 1863 several barracks sank into the mud or threatened to tip over.

Under such conditions, ill health, including typhoid fever, was to be expected. In September 1863, 327 men died out of a total prison population of 8,822. The following month smallpox broke out, yet the U.S. Commissary general of prisoners rejected the complaint even of the surgeon general that the fort was not a suitably healthy prison site. The monthly death toll did decline in 1864 despite an increased prison population of more than 9,000 men. Because a large number of literate, vocal officers of all ranks were among the prisoners, conditions at Fort Delaware elicited frequent denunciations by the Confederate government and newspapers.

The miserable conditions at Fort Delaware were compounded during the rainy season. To avoid the mud and slush churned up during rainy weather, prisoners used the narrow plank walks connecting the various barracks, mess hall, and privy. Any prisoner using the walkways was under the constant observation of guards walking along parapets on the high fences that separated the pens of the officers from those of the enlisted men. Fifteen feet from the

---

[10]Isaac W. K. Handy, *Imprisoned for Conscience Sake: Fifteen Months at Fort Delaware* (1874; reprint, Harrisonburg, VA: Sprinkle Publications, 2005) 5–9.

[11]"Diary of Captain Robert E. Park."

fence was the "dead line." Prison rules stipulated that any prisoner crossing that mark would be shot without warning.[12]

When William Simmons was first imprisoned at Fort Delaware, the ranks of prison guards were mostly made up of inexperienced militiamen. Many of these men were unfit for their positions and were often cruel in their treatment of the officers held in captivity. In contrast, the prisoners at Fort Delaware were usually accorded much better treatment by veteran Union regiments assigned to prison guard duty. Prison inmates soon learned to distinguish between the raw militiamen and the veterans. As Lieutenant McHenry Howard of the 1st Maryland Infantry (CS) recalled, it "was like the difference between bad and good weather." Imprisoned at Fort Delaware in 1864, Howard had ample opportunity to observe the behavior of the 157th Ohio Militia Guard, a green regiment assigned to garrison duty at the camp. The militiamen's conduct toward the prisoners, he wrote, "was atrocious, devilish in the apparent desire to insult and practice small cruelties." The guards regularly confiscated personal possessions of the prisoners and opened fire on them at the slightest provocation.[13]

On the other hand, when the Ohio Militia was replaced by the veteran 6th Massachusetts Infantry Regiment, Howard related, "the cursing and other abusive conduct immediately stopped. They behaved to us in a soldier-like and I may say gentlemanly manner and often spoke contemptuously of the actions of their predecessors."[14]

Next to the harsh treatment from the militia guards, the prisoners of Fort Delaware most detested the food and sanitary conditions of their new home. The dismal mess hall was a long, dark room, containing one pine table on which food was placed twice a day. No knives, forks, or spoons were provided. Rations were scanty, and the men were always hungry. For breakfast they were allowed one slice of bread, often stale, and weak coffee. The second meal of the day consisted of bean soup, bread, and a small piece of salted meat, or boiled beef when available. Even for Confederates who had become inured to minimum and infrequent rations, prison allowances were downright minuscule.[15] Ordinary, well-bred, courteous officers pushed and scuffled for a place at the table, then gulped down the meager portions, which they had grabbed for like so many dogs.

The "sanitary" facilities were woefully inadequate. Wells could not be sunk in the marshy ground occupied by the officers' pen. Water, of doubtful

---

[12]Dickert, *Kershaw's Brigade*, 462.

[13]McHenry Howard, *Recollections of a Maryland Confederate Soldier and Staff Officer Under Johnston, Jackson, and Lee* (1914; reprint, Dayton, OH: Morningside Bookshop, 1975) 317.

[14]Ibid., 326–27.

[15]Dickert, *Kershaw's Brigade*, 465.

cleanliness, had to be brought from Brandywine Creek in hogsheads and dipped out with tin cups, coffee pots, and buckets. Occasionally, when this source of water was low, the officers were forbidden to draw water for baths or even to wash their hands and faces. Their only alternative was the filthy water in a ditch that ran through the pen. This brackish water was usually covered with green scum. The men stood along the banks, pushing back the scum in order to take their baths. The men downstream bathed in water used by their neighbors and thrown back into the ditch.

The privy was located on the beach, fifty yards from the nearest barracks and clearly in sight of Delaware City. Not even the constant wash of sea water could keep it disinfected and remove the waste of 9,000 men. It was not large enough for the number of prisoners, and its seats and floors stayed dirty and vile-smelling from constant use. Diarrhea and dysentery were so prevalent that the men often had to wait in line for an hour or longer to use the facility. Infection and disease could hardly be avoided.[16]

With such woefully inadequate and unsanitary facilities, the officers were forced to organize some form of self-government to minimize their trials and tribulations. Each of the sixteen divisions elected a "chief" who was responsible to the prisoners for the operation of the division. The chief kept a roll of the inmates, rotated assignments for housekeeping details, reported names of sick men, presided at division meetings and mediated any disputes arising among the officers.

For the prisoners of Fort Delaware there were a number of diversions to break the boredom and routine of prison life, including many forms of gambling that were tolerated in certain divisions. Any book, magazine, or out-of-date newspaper was a prized possession. Novels and histories allowed the men to momentarily forget their wretched existence. Others studied modern languages to divert their minds from their hopeless surroundings.[17] A number of books were sent to the prison by sympathetic Baltimore ladies. The *Philadelphia Inquirer*, the only newspaper the prisoners were allowed to buy, cost ten cents, a dear price for the mostly penniless officers and enlisted men. Each copy made the rounds of the divisions.

Mail call represented the high point of the day if a prisoner was fortunate enough to receive a letter. Each division had at least one postmaster. Daily he carried the prisoners' unsealed letters to prison authorities for inspection and returned shortly with censored incoming mail.[18] Correspondence with Northern acquaintances or comrades in other prisons was permissible, but letters southward had to be smuggled out of the prison through the kindness of any

---

[16]R. R. Stevenson, *The Southern Side; or, Andersonville Prison* (1876; reprint, New Market, VA: John M. Bracken Publishing, 1995) 164, 258.

[17]Dickert, *Kershaw's Brigade*, 464.

[18]Ibid., 462.

man fortunate enough to be exchanged. Occasionally a boat under a flag of truce would bring some mail from the South.

When the division postmaster returned from his daily trip, every man would gather around him. Some personal touch from the outside world would cause the filth and suffering to be forgotten momentarily. Absolute silence prevailed while the postmaster called out the names of lucky recipients. Here and there eyes sparkled with pleasure, while the disappointed turned away dejectedly. Soon the latter would stop gathering around the postmaster.

None of these moments of escape could erase for long the abject misery and wretchedness of prison life that Major Simmons and his fellow prisoners endured. The hunger and emptiness wore down the pride and self-respect of many a cultured man. Prisoners ate the repulsive food as the only alternative was starvation. When the floors were swept, prisoners seized and devoured pieces of bread crusts and stale scraps of food that formerly they would not have fed such to farm animals. Some of the half-starved prisoners even resorted to eating rats and mice.[19]

There was an alarmingly frequent occurrence of deaths by smallpox, pneumonia, fever, dysentery, and various other diseases. Shortly after he arrived, William Simmons purchased a small notebook in which he wrote the names and ranks of 248 Georgians who died and the causes of their deaths. Methodically he recorded the names and causes of death for other departing soldiers. Among the saddest entries were those of the fifteen soldiers of the 16th Georgia who died as a result of illness. Chronic diarrhea led the list, followed by smallpox and typhoid fever. Other causes of death were officially assigned, but only once did complications from a battle wound claim a Georgian.[20]

One Georgia native, Private Isaac A. Reed of Company H, 7th Georgia Infantry Regiment, summarized the prison's gamut of privations, sufferings and cruelty:

"When I had recovered from wounds enough to travel," he wrote, "I thought I had suffered about all that a human could suffer to live, but when I reached Fort Delaware I began to realize that marches, battles and wounds were not to be compared to the suffering of a prisoner at that miserable place. My first suffering at the old fort was hunger that I can never describe. It was beyond anything that I had ever before endured, for a wounded man requires more food than a sound man. My next trouble was smallpox. I was removed to the hospital where that disease was being treated, and where men died daily on my right and left. I surely felt relieved to get out of that awful place, but then I was sent back to the barracks, barefooted and almost destitute of clothes. While in this condition all of

[19]Stevenson, *The Southern Side*, 258; Dickert, *Kershaw's Brigade*, 465–66.
[20]Simmons diary, drawer 19, box 78, Georgia Department of Archives and History, Morrow, GA; Byrd, *Them Brave Georgians*, 358.

the prisoners in my ward were ordered out and packed back next to the bay to be searched. The ground being covered with snow, I tried to fall in the rear so that I could be among the first to get back, when that unfeeling Sergeant, whom we boys called old 'Hike-out' came up, gave me a lick on the head and said, 'close up.' But I was helpless and could only obey orders, step out with bare feet into the snow and suffer."[21]

Over the course of the war the terrible climate, unsanitary conditions and overcrowding took their toll on the underdressed, undernourished prison population. Of the approximately 32,000 men held at one time or another on the island, more than 2,400 of those who died were ferried across the Delaware and buried at Finn's Point, New Jersey, thus earning Fort Delaware the name "Andersonville of the North." Other remains were interred on the island, and some were sent south for burial.

Despite suffering and privations, some sort of day-to-day existence had to be pieced together by Major Simmons and his fellow inmates. To divert their minds from their troubles, many new and pleasant acquaintances were made. A great many imprisoned officers secured autograph books and collected the names, organizations, and home addresses of newly acquired friends. Using the same book in which he had recorded the deaths of Georgians, Simmons secured the autographs of many of his old and new friends. Five of his subordinate officers of the 3rd Battalion provided their signatures as a memento of prison friendships. Four of them had also been captured at Front Royal and had made the same trip from Harper's Ferry to prison with Major Simmons, including Captain John F. Martin, Lawrenceville, Georgia; Lieutenant Payson L. Ardis; Lieutenant Delona Bunt, Lithonia, Georgia; and Lieutenant John E. Shelton, Acworth, Georgia. The other, Captain M. P. Crumley, a native Georgian from Augusta, arrived at the prison about six weeks later. He had been captured by Sheridan's forces in October 1864 at the Battle of Cedar Creek in the Shenandoah Valley.[22]

A. B. Cain, Captain of the Flint Hill Grays (16th Georgia), one of the first Gwinnett County companies, also supplied his signature. Captain Cain had enlisted as a private in spring 1861. He was captured at Front Royal with Major Simmons. Three officers from Cobb's Legion placed their signatures in

---

[21]Isaac A. Reed, "Old Vet's Experiences at Fort Delaware," in *Reunion of Confederate Soldiers*, vol. 2 32–33. A copy exists at the Georgia Department of Archives and History, Morrow, GA.

[22]Simmons diary, in Byrd, *Them Brave Georgians*, 360–61; *Compiled Service Records of Confederate Soldiers Who Served in Organizations from the State of Georgia*, microcopy 266, RG 109, National Archives and Records Administration, Washington, DC.

Simmons's book along with officers of twelve additional Georgia regiments.[23] Captain S. Yates Levy of Savannah, one of the first to sign, added an original piece of poetry titled "A Prayer for Peace."

William Simmons did not restrict his autograph collecting to Georgians. There were signatures from officers of every state of the Confederacy except Florida. Two natives of Maryland also signed his book. In later years, each name in his book awakened some pleasant recollection to partially alleviate the many terrible memories of prison life that he would always carry. Lieutenant Robert E. Park, a meticulous prison diarist, recorded events involving seventeen of the officers who signed Simmons's book.[24]

During their captivity, William Simmons and Brigadier General Rufus Barringer became friends. Like the young major, General Barringer had been captured by Sheridan's Cavalry late in the war. The incident, which took place after the fall of Petersburg, was the result of a Yankee trick. While Barringer was trying to lead remnants of his North Carolina Cavalry Brigade to safety, an overwhelming force of Sheridan's men appeared in their front. Off to the side, the general related, he saw what appeared to be a group of Confederate horsemen and he quickly led his men in that direction. To his dismay, what he thought to be friends turned out to be a squad from the 15th New York Cavalry, dressed in Confederate uniforms as a decoy. He and his men soon became captives.

Simmons also befriended Brigadier General R. L. Page of Clarke County, Virginia. General Page was one of the most colorful officers in the prison. Nicknamed "Ramrod" and "Bombast" in the United States Navy, General Page resigned his commission as a commander when Virginia seceded and accepted the same rank from the Confederacy.[25] After building naval works on the James and Nansemond rivers and participating in several naval battles, he became a brigadier general in the Confederate army. As the ranking officer in the defense of Mobile Bay during August 1864, General Page was compelled to surrender in the face of a combined Federal land and sea attack. Both Page and his inspector general, Captain R. T. Thom, signed Simmons's autograph book.

Another officer who signed his autograph was Brigadier General Robert R. Vance, commander of the department of Western North Carolina. An elder brother of North Carolina's wartime governor, Zebulon Vance, General Vance organized a company of soldiers when the war began. He was later promoted to Colonel to lead the 29th North Carolina Infantry and became commanding

---

[23]James C. Flanigan (*History of Gwinnett County, Georgia*, vol. 1 [1943; reprint, Lawrenceville: Gwinnett Historical Society, 1995] 244–45) lists the names of several prisoners who signed Simmons's diary.

[24]"Diary of Captain Robert E. Park."

[25]Ezra J. Warner, *Generals in Gray* (Baton Rouge: Louisiana State University Press, 1959) 226.

officer of Rains's Brigade upon the death of General James E. Rains. Vance began serving his sentence at Fort Delaware in January 1864. For Simmons's book, he contributed two poems, which attributed to him and all the officers a deep longing for their native South as well as a burning desire to see the beautiful ladies at home.

In his diary Simmons noted that ladies were allowed to visit relatives in the prison. Unfortunately, most of the prisoners were hundreds or more than a thousand miles from their loved ones and were not able to visit with their female family members. The resourceful major did not let distance and separation get the better of him and his fellow prisoners. As noted in J. C. Flanigan's *History of Gwinnett County*,

> One day Simmons asked one of his fellow prisoners to introduce him to a young lady as his cousin, which he did. The major then invited the lady to come again and instructed her to tell her lady friends to call with the admonition that they should be sure to ask for "Cousin William." They did so, and soon he had a continuous stream of ladies calling on him. He introduced his "cousins" to his fellow inmates, and in this manner made prison life more pleasant. His diary contains over two pages of the names of these ladies, written in their own hand.[26]

In April 1865 *The Prison Times* made its appearance at Fort Delaware.[27] The publication was written in pen and ink, and a limited number of copies were passed around among the prisoners. The newspaper included a wide variety of articles, poems, advertisements, different accounts of prison life, and a directory of division and club officers.[28] It was "published" by Captain J. W. Hibbs of the 13th Virginia Infantry.

The little pleasures afforded by the prison newspaper and the visits of Major Simmons's lady cousins could not erase for long the anxiety the captured officers felt when they heard bad news from the battlefield. Arriving prisoners brought confirmation of some disaster previously reported in the *Philadelphia Inquirer*.

Not long after William Simmons became a prisoner at Fort Delaware, he learned that Atlanta had fallen to Sherman's army on 2 September 1864. Later

---

[26]Flanigan, *History of Gwinnett County*, 1:245; Handy, *Imprisoned for Conscience Sake*, 84, 90, 118, 123, 158, 237. One of the "cousins" who signed Simmons's autograph book was Miss Julia Jefferson of New Castle, DE. The lady is mentioned six times in Dr. Handy's prison diary, beginning on 25 August 1863. Later in the year Handy wrote, "A box came from Miss Julia Jefferson, with clothing to be distributed among sundry prisoners. The articles are accompanied by a good lot of peaches and sweet potatoes for my own comfort. This faithful almoner and her associates ought ever to be remembered by the boys from 'Dixie.'"

[27]Byrd, *Them Brave Georgians*, 365.

[28]Ibid., 365–66.

that autumn he grieved over the news of Sherman's March to the Sea and the widespread burning and destruction throughout the heart of Georgia. He was anxious for the safety of his mother and father and his beloved brothers and sisters, who remained at home. He prayed for their deliverance and hoped that his father had hidden the printing presses of the *Lawrenceville News* in a safe place so the Union army would not destroy them.[29]

According to the *Inquirer*, nothing seemed to stop Sherman. The account of his march through their native state was especially heartbreaking to the Georgia prisoners. Throughout the winter the bad news continued as the Confederate army dwindled in manpower and resources. In early April the prisoners learned of the evacuation of Richmond and Petersburg. This event had been feared for some time but never openly discussed.

Despite the bad news, most Confederate prisoners at Fort Delaware did not lose faith. The men were confident that General Lee would somehow be able to join forces with General Johnston's army in North Carolina and continue the fight against the Union army.

On 10 April 1865 Simmons and his fellow captives were stunned to learn of Lee's surrender at Appomattox the previous day. In utter disbelief, man after man whispered the awful news to his friends.[30] On that day Lieutenant Park eloquently poured out his emotions by making the following entry in his diary:

No human tongue, however eloquent, no pen, however gifted, can give an adequate description of our dismay and horror at the heart-rending news. The sudden, unexpected calamity shocked reason and unsettled memory. The news crushed our fondest hopes. On every countenance rests the shadow of gloom, on every heart the paralyzing torpor of despair. We move about, or sit on our beds, silent, almost motionless, in the speechless agony of woe, in the mute eloquence of unutterable despair. After four long weary years of battle and marches, of prayers and tears, of pain and sacrifice, of wounds and woe, of blood and death, such an ending of our hopes, such a shocking disappointment, is bitter, cruel, and crushing.[31]

---

[29]Ibid., 367.

[30]Dickert, *Kershaw's Brigade*, 467.

[31]"Diary of Captain Robert E. Park, of the Twelfth Alabama Regiment," *Southern Historical Society Papers* (hereafter *SHSP*) 3/5 and 3/6 (May–June 1877): 244.

22

The Prisoners' Oath

Fall seven times, stand up eight.
—Japanese Proverb

With General Lee's surrender at Appomattox, the prison guards adopted a kinder policy toward the captives. Unfortunately this lasted only a few days. On the morning of 15 April the prisoners woke up to the news that President Lincoln had been assassinated.[1] Most of the Confederate prisoners were shocked at the news and subdued, but a handful reacted with cheering and celebration. This display so angered the prison commandant, General Albin Schoepf, that he ordered the artillery of the fort to be turned on the prisoners' pen and instructed the guards to fire on any prisoner showing pleasure at the news.

After the surrender of Lee's Army of Northern Virginia, the Union authorities began to seriously consider the matter of prisoner release. The process was initiated despite the fact that Confederate forces under three generals were still actively engaging the Union army. Prisoners who had sworn allegiance to the United States before Lee's surrender received preferential treatment in the prison. For these men, taking the oath was a certain ticket to their release.[2]

On 24 April Captain G. W. Ahl, aide to Commandant Schoepf, ordered all imprisoned Confederate officers to line up. The men were informed that they would be polled to state if they were willing to take the oath of allegiance as the price for liberty. That day a large portion of the captives indicated that they would take the oath, but there were several hundred holdouts.[3] Several days later the prisoners were given a second opportunity to announce their intentions. Hundreds more changed their minds after hearing that General Joseph E. Johnston had surrendered his army to Sherman in North Carolina. After a third offer to make a public proclamation on 30 April, there were only 165 officers,

---

[1] Brian Temple, *The Union Prison at Fort Delaware: A Perfect Hell on Earth* (Jefferson, NC: McFarland & Company, 2003) 142.

[2] Daniel M. Byrd Jr., *Them Brave Georgians*, manuscript, Gwinnett Historical Society archives, Lawrenceville, GA pg. 370 (Fort Delaware Society Library, Delaware City, DE, also has a copy.).

[3] Simmons in his memoirs stated that "a large majority of the prisoners took the oath." Park, on the other hand, gives the result for seven officers only, stating that "900 out of 2,300 swore allegiance" ("Diary of Captain Robert E. Park, of the Twelfth Alabama Regiment," *SHSP* 3 [January–June 1877]: 243).

including William Simmons, who steadfastly refused to take the oath of allegiance.[4]

Each time that an officer swallowed his pride and answered in the affirmative, a clerk would record the officer's name and secure pertinent information concerning rank, regiment, place of residence, physical description, and a brief history of the oath. As soon as possible a roll was prepared in alphabetical order, which set forth in appropriately-headed columns the information supplied by the officers.[5] When the roll was completed, the officers would be taken under guard from the pen to the fort and lined up for the oath of allegiance ceremony. While each man raised his right hand, one of the prison officials would read the oath out loud. Hands lowered, the officers then filed past a clerk's desk, signed the roll, and were sent on their way.

For Major Simmons and the other officers who refused to take the oath, such an action would be swearing against their consciences. No oath could be taken "freely and voluntarily" if it was the price of release from that miserable prison. The holdouts insisted that only a mean and cowardly despotism would force a self-respecting man to perjure himself. Twice the obstinate group petitioned the authorities to banish them, but each time their requests were indignantly refused.[6] The remaining prisoners roundly condemned the Federal government for repeatedly offering the insulting oath when it was obvious that the words "freely and voluntarily" would never be accepted. They remained steadfast, knowing that the armies of generals Taylor and Kirby Smith were still fighting, and President Jefferson Davis was at large.

The authorities were outraged, particularly by the audacity of the holdouts requesting banishment. There was even some speculation that they would be hanged if they persisted in their obstinate resistance or that the conditions of their imprisonment would become worse.

In May the prisoners who still refused to take the oath held a lengthy meeting.[7] The entire garrison of Federal officers and several of their wives came to see what the Confederate holdouts would do. General Rufus Barringer was the first speaker. He urged his fellow officers to accept the oath and go home. He even intimated that the men might be banished from the country if they persisted in their refusal.

---

[4]D. Augustus Dickert, *History of Kershaw's Brigade* (1899; reprint, Wilmington, NC: Broadfoot Publishing Company, 1990) 467.

[5]Prison roll 186, sheet 3, Record Group 109, National Archives and Records Administration, Washington, DC.

[6]Byrd, *Them Brave Georgians*, 378.

[7]Simmons identifies the location as a "great mess hall" (Byrd, *Them Brave Georgians*, 378). Lieutenant Park wrote in his diary that a meeting was held in Division 22 ("Diary of Captain Robert E. Park," 250). Both likely wrote about the same meeting based on the similarity of their reports.

When General Barringer concluded, the crowd remained quiet. A dropped pin could be heard across the room. Suddenly, shouts of "Fellows!" rang out. Captain John R. Fellows[8] then rose to address the men. He was a brilliant orator who, though originally from New York, had served on the staff of General Beall in Arkansas. Everyone knew from previous conversations that he was the best spokesman to defend the position of those who would not submit. He began by saying, "General Barringer says if we do not tamely submit, we shall be banished from the country. What is banished but set free from daily contact with the things we loathe? Banished? We thank you for it. It would break our chains."[9]

Loud applause repeatedly interrupted Captain Fellows. Simmons noted that each time the captain resumed his oration, it was on a more soul-stirring note. Fellows urged his comrades to remain faithful to the bitter end and closed with a challenge obviously directed to the prison authorities, "They threaten to hang us unless we add perjury to perfidy. If they will, let them hang! The moment they do, the gallows will become next in holiness to the cross."[10]

Fellows's inspiring words "bought down the house." Officers, women spectators waving handkerchiefs, and Union soldiers all joined in a demonstration. One private, yelling so as to be heard above the tumult, said, "If you hang these men, you'll have to get another garrison." The resolution was adopted by a unanimous vote.[11]

Instead of being sent to the fort dungeon or the gallows, as they had expected, the prisoners were given all the privileges of Pea Patch Island. Federal soldiers on guard were even required to salute the Confederate officers as they did their own superiors. In other respects, life in prison continued as usual.

One memorable event took place on 20 May 1865. That day the Prison Benevolent Association presented one of its most entertaining concerts. The high point of the program was an original composition in minstrel dialect, sung to the tune of "Swamps of the Louisiana Low Lands, Low." Simmons recounted that the song, "In de Prison of Fort Delaware, Delaware," was sung with "great effect...for the relief of indigent officers." Obviously intrigued with the

---

[8]A fellow prisoner, Lieutenant Charles F. Crisp of the 10th Virginia Infantry, said that Fellows was a "'good deal of an orator' who used to make a speech to the boys once and sometimes twice a day at the time we were discussing the advisability of taking the oath of allegiance to the United States." He added that "Fellows appealed to the prisoners not to take the oath as long as there was an army in the field." Fellows was captured in June 1863 at the capture of Port Hudson, and spent two years at Fort Delaware (Charles Crisp, "True to Their Oaths," *Confederate Veteran* 5/3 [March 1897]: 119).
[9]"Diary of Captain Robert E. Park," 250.
[10]Byrd, *Them Brave Georgians*, 374.
[11]Brian Temple, *The Union Prison at Fort Delaware*, 145–46.

composition's lyrical references to prison life, Simmons copied the words of the song in his autograph book.[12]

Throughout the month of May the prisoners learned of defeat after defeat for their beloved South. By the middle of the month General Taylor had surrendered and President Davis had been captured. Toward the end of the month, General Edmund Kirby Smith surrendered all his forces in the Trans-Mississippi Department. The final "surrender" took place on 23 June 1865 when Confederate Brigadier General Stand Watie agreed to a cease fire at Doaksville, Choctaw Nation, Indian Territory. These events convinced a number of the remaining prisoners that further resistance was hopeless. With some reluctance, they notified the commandant's office that the oath would no longer be refused if offered.

During the month of June the overall prison population dropped dramatically, going from a total of 7,126 present on 1 June to a total of only 110 by the end of the month.[13] By that time, there were only eighty-two Confederate officers, including William Simmons, who remained steadfast in their refusal to take the oath. The young major and the others vowed that they would never take the oath "freely and voluntarily" if taking it was a condition of their release. The band of eighty-two settled down to a waiting game with the Federal government.

One summer morning William Simmons was fishing at the riverbank when a prison guard came up to him to see if he had caught any fish. In the ensuing conversation, Simmons learned that the private was from a New York Zouave regiment. Remembering the incident that took place at Gettysburg, Simmons asked the young man if he knew the whereabouts of Captain Mead and Lieutenant Higgins. The private informed him that Mead was dead, but Higgins was now a colonel of the regiment and stationed on the island. Simmons was delighted to hear this news. He promptly sent Higgins a note, and in a very short time, Higgins appeared. It was an emotional meeting. Both men had vivid recollections of their encounter at Gettysburg, but it had been dark and neither would have recognized the other. Simmons still had the sword belt that was given to him and took great pleasure in returning it to Colonel Higgins. Likewise, Higgins was very happy to get it back as a memento. He then escorted the young major to his regimental headquarters, introduced him to his officers, and offered his assistance.

---

[12]Byrd, *Them Brave Georgians*, 365; Simmons diary, drawer 19, box 78, Georgia Department of Archives and History, Morrow, GA.

[13]The population included twenty-eight Union soldiers and political prisoners in addition to the eighty-two Confederate officer holdouts (Dale Fetzer and Bruce Mowday, *Unlikely Allies: Fort Delaware's Prison Community in the Civil War* [Mechanicsburg, PA: Stackpole Books, 2000] 152–53).

Although the two officers had only met twice, the Union officer must have formed a favorable opinion of William Simmons. Only the major's decision to have Higgins and his fellow officer carried to a safe resting place and allow their faithful corporal to remain with them spared his life at Gettysburg.[14] But now on Pea Patch Island the major's stubborn convictions, and those of the other eighty-one Confederate officers, were standing in the way of their release and the Union colonel's discharge from military service.

Into the summer the Confederate holdouts persisted in their refusal to sign the oath of allegiance as it was written. Finally on 24 July 1865, the stalemate ended. By order of prison authorities the words "freely and voluntarily" were stricken from the oath. No time was wasted in having a clerk prepare the final roll. All eighty-two officers raised their right hands and swore allegiance to the nation they had taken up arms against. They lined up, without regard to rank or alphabetical order, and filed past the clerk's desk. General Page was first, followed by General Barringer. Major Simmons was fifty-sixth in line. Each man filled in the required information and signed his name.[15] One prisoner who was not among the holdouts on that day was Captain John R. Fellows, who had been released on parole the previous month. In later years, Fellows said that he had never taken the oath and told General Schoepf that he owed his allegiance to the Confederate government.[16]

The time had finally come for William E. Simmons to begin the long journey back to his home in Georgia.

---

[14]Byrd, *Them Brave Georgians*, 377–78.

[15]Prison roll showing the names of officers who took the revised oath of allegiance at Fort Delaware 24 July 1865, roll 186, sheet 3, Record Group 109, National Archives and Records Administration, Washington, DC.

[16]Crisp, "True to Their Oaths," 119.

Chapter 23

Home at Last

Let your hook be always cast. In the stream
where you least expect it, there will be a fish.
—Ovid

With transportation furnished from Fort Delaware prison by the Federal government, William Simmons soon reached his home in Lawrenceville. Like most all of the returning Confederate soldiers, he found ruin and devastation everywhere. Sherman's men had plundered Gwinnett County before embarking on their March to the Sea. His father's cotton mill, the Lawrenceville Manufacturing Company, had been destroyed by fire in 1864, with Sherman's soldiers getting credit for the torch.[1] Half of the wealth of Gwinnett County was lost and the plantation gave way to the small farm. The Freedman's Bureau, an agency set up by the Federal government, cared for freed slaves as a relief organization and supervised their work. Federal soldiers were stationed in the county under military rule to enforce the new laws.[2] The old order had changed completely. No longer were there the familiar guideposts to foretell the future. All the resoluteness and strength of character that the young Confederate had shown during four years of war were needed to face the uncertainties of the time to rebuild his future.[3]

Soon after he returned home, Simmons began studying law in his father's office. He also helped to dig up the printing presses and type fonts of his newspaper that had been buried on a family farm under a plowed field when it became clear that Sherman's troops would destroy everything in their march across Georgia during the final months of 1864. The presses and equipment were carefully exhumed and reconditioned by their owner, and as soon as he located a supply of newsprint, the *News* resumed publication.

Meanwhile other veterans had also returned home to begin their lives anew in Gwinnett County and the surrounding area. Of the Gwinnett soldiers[4] who

---

[1]James C. Flanigan, *History of Gwinnett County, Georgia,* vol. 1 (1943; reprint, Lawrenceville: Gwinnett Historical Society, 1995) 248.

[2]Ibid., 1:246.

[3]Daniel M. Byrd Jr., *Them Brave Georgians,* manuscript, Gwinnett Historical Society archives, Lawrenceville, GA pg. 382 (Fort Delaware Society Library, Delaware City, DE, also has a copy.).

[4]Included are Companies H (Flint Hill Grays) and I (Hutchins Guards) of the 16th Georgia, and Company F (Gwinnett Independent Blues) of the 24th Georgia.

had served with Simmons in the Wofford/DuBose Brigade, forty remained in Federal prisons after Lee surrendered. From these men and other veterans who returned home, Simmons found out what had happened to his old regiment and sharpshooter battalion after he had been captured at Front Royal in August 1864. He learned that after the disastrous fight at Guard Hill, his sharpshooter battalion had continued to serve for another month in the Shenandoah Valley under General Wofford, brigade commander; General Kershaw, division commander; and General Anderson, corps commander. On 14 September his comrades, on orders from General Lee, left the valley by way of Front Royal to bolster the Army's main positions near Richmond. Kershaw's Division, including the 16th Georgia Infantry Regiment and 3rd Sharpshooter Battalion, progressed no further south than Culpeper before they were ordered back to the Shenandoah Valley. General Wofford, still feeling the effects of his injury from the fall off his horse the previous month, remained behind.[5]

On 18 October, Wofford was granted sick leave and returned to Georgia. As soon as he was able, he traveled to Cassville where he witnessed the devastation of his home town and surrounding area. Most of the homes and all business buildings (including his law office) were burned by Sherman's men when they advanced toward Atlanta. Food and farm stock had been confiscated, adding to the suffering of the people who remained. To add to the misery, the North Georgia region was mostly lawless. Deserters from both sides roamed the countryside, stealing at will, and many guerilla bands operated in the area. Wofford was greatly concerned about the dire situation and directly appealed to President Davis to take measures to stop the devastation and ease the suffering. He returned to brigade headquarters briefly in December and continued on to Richmond to meet with the Confederate president and request assignment to North Georgia.[6]

For more than two months after the debacle at Guard Hill, Wofford's Georgians were engaged in futile attempts to drive Federal forces from the Valley, including the Battle of Cedar Creek in October.[7] In mid-November, Kershaw's Division rejoined General Longstreet, who had returned to duty the previous month. The ugly wound that the General had received in the battle of

---

[5]Gerald J. Smith, *One of the Most Daring of Men: The Life of Confederate General William Tatum Wofford*, vol. 16 of Journal of Confederate History Series, ed. John McGlone (Murfreesboro, TN: Southern Heritage Press, 1997) 130.

[6]Ibid., 130–33.

[7]According to service records, eight sharpshooters were among the casualties at Cedar Creek: Private John Bellah of Company F was killed; 1st Corporal John O. Collins of Company C, and 4th Sergeant George B. Crumley of Company B were wounded; and six were captured, including Crumley, 1st Corporal L. M. Mann, and Private P. T. Smith of Company A; privates Jeremiah Mize and William P. Durham of Company E: and Corporal Arthur J. Barrett of Company F. Crumley was imprisoned at Fort Delaware, and the others were sent to Point Lookout.

the Wilderness had left him partially paralyzed, but he was anxious to resume his command. About that time General Anderson was given command of a 4th Corps, made up of four brigades.

After he returned, Longstreet assumed command of all forces north of the James River, with the responsibility of protecting the roads to Richmond against any advance of the enemy. The 16th Georgia was placed in defensive lines on the outskirts of the capital city and remained there with other troops under General Kershaw until Richmond was evacuated.

In January 1865, upon the approval of Governor Brown of Georgia, General Wofford was released from service with the Army of Northern Virginia to assume the position of military commander in North Georgia. Like Wofford, the governor was desperate to put a stop to the bushwhackers and the guerillas of both armies who terrorized the area after their respective commands had moved on. To succeed Wofford as brigade commander, General Lee appointed Dudley McIver DuBose, formerly a colonel in the 15th Georgia. A native of Tennessee, DuBose was educated at the University of Mississippi and at the Lebanon Law School in his native state. In 1860, after practicing law for several years in Tennessee, he moved to Augusta, Georgia. The following year, he entered service as a lieutenant with the 15th Georgia. As the son-in-law of General Robert Toombs of Washington, Georgia, he was well-connected in both military and political circles.[8] After the War, DuBose served in the U.S. House of Representatives from 1871 to 1873.[9]

During the final months of the war, a number of vacancies occurred among the officers of Simmons's regiment and battalion that were never filled. When no one was named to succeed Lieutenant Colonel Stiles, command of the regiment was given to one of the captains. Similarly, when the sharpshooter battalion's Lieutenant Colonel Hutchins and most of its other officers were captured at the Battle of Sailor's Creek[10] on 6 April 1865, the ranking lieutenant led the sharpshooters. At the time of Lee's surrender at Appomattox three days later, the highest-ranking officer of the 3rd Georgia Sharpshooter Battalion was Assistant Surgeon R. B. Dennis.[11]

---

[8]Stewart Sifakis, *Who Was Who in the Civil War* (New York: Facts on File Publications, 1988) 192.

[9]Charles Edgeworth Jones, "Confederate Brigadiers in Congress," *Confederate Veteran* 5/10 (October 1897): 529.

[10]In addition to Lieutenant Colonel Hutchins, the captured officers included Captain Newton Napoleon Gober, Lieutenant John S. Cook, 2nd Lieutenant Young A. Cole, 1st Lieutenant Martin V. Jackson, Captain John W. King, 1st Lieutenant William Cabell Muse, 1st Lieutenant T. B. Slaughter, and 1st Lieutenant James H. Williams. Of this group, all but Lieutenant Cook were captured at Sailor's Creek. See also "The Fighting at Sailors Creek," *Confederate Veteran* 5/10 (October 1897): 448–52.

[11]"Paroles of the Army of Northern Virginia," *Southern Historical Society Papers* 15 (January–December 1887): 171.

The road to Appomattox was a tragic path for the Army of Northern Virginia. Early in March 1865, General Lee had recognized that continual defense of an ever-lengthening line south of Petersburg was impractical. In a last desperate gamble, the general ordered an attack on Fort Stedman, a part of the Federal line. The assault was initially successful, but soon the overpowering weight of the Union forces pushed the Confederates back to their previous positions in the trenches near Petersburg. The end was clearly in sight.

On the night of 2–3 April the Army of Northern Virginia evacuated its trenches and began a withdrawal that was destined to end at Appomattox Court House. On that very night, Richmond was burned and the 16th Georgia and the 3rd Battalion Sharpshooters broke through the flames to join the main body of the army. On 6 April, Lee's army suffered a crushing defeat at Sailors Creek. That day, most of the remaining sharpshooters were captured in the vicinity of Sailors Creek and the nearby communities of Farmville, High Bridge, and Burkeville.[12]

Sensing the outcome of the battle, General Kershaw advised those of his men who were able, to escape. He then surrendered a large part of his division while about 200 of his men eluded capture and joined the remnant of the army heading west toward Appomattox. It was there on 9 April 1865 that General Lee finally surrendered. With him at the end were fifty-one members of the 16th Georgia Infantry Regiment and twenty-six members of the 3rd Georgia Sharpshooter Battalion.[13] Those tenacious survivors of death and disease were the diehards of a proud infantry regiment numbering at one time nearly 1,000 men and an elite battalion of sharpshooters organized with an original complement of over 300 marksmen.

In conversations with his friends who had survived the war and returned home, Major Simmons relived the agony of military capitulation and endured the pervasive humiliation of Reconstruction. Unlike some veterans, however, he never permitted himself to brood over the past and what might have been. He recognized excessive resentment and bitterness as a self-defeating indulgence that would waste energy otherwise needed to help rebuild his own life and that of his beloved Southern homeland.

---

[12]According to service records, at least fifty men from the 3rd Georgia Sharpshooter Battalion were captured on 6 April 1865. The battalion was likely over-extended and very disorganized given that twenty men were captured at Sailor's Creek, fifteen at Farmville, fourteen at High Bridge, and one at Burkeville. All were sent to Northern prisons.

[13]"Paroles of the Army of Northern Virginia," 171, 173, 174. There were seventeen Gwinnett County soldiers from DuBose's Brigade among the parolees at Appomattox. They included Private Peyton Randolph Hutchins of the 3rd Battalion Sharpshooters, eight from the 24th Georgia Infantry Regiment (Gwinnett Independent Blues), and eight from the 16th Georgia Infantry Regiment (Flint Hill Grays and Hutchins Guards).

After learning the fate of his regiment, Simmons resolved to make the most of his life and put the horrible experiences of the war and his captivity behind him. He cast his lot with the future. Soon he resumed his quest to become a lawyer, and after a relatively short period of intense study, he was admitted to the bar in 1866 at the March term of the Gwinnett Superior Court.[14]

Less than one month after he began practicing law, Simmons filed his first case at the April term of court in nearby Dekalb County. He listed his first five cases in the signature book he kept while imprisoned at Fort Delaware. Those cases were soon closed, and he received fees paid him from three of his clients, which netted him a grand total of $85.00. From this modest beginning, his practice grew steadily. Within two years he had a larger docket in his own county than any other lawyer.

The young lawyer's ability and determination no doubt contributed to his initial success at the bar, but his family name, widespread popularity, and war record also helped to attract many clients. To his acquaintances he was "the Major," a handsome young Confederate veteran, greatly admired for his wartime sacrifices. For the rest of his life he would always be respectfully and affectionately addressed by the title he had earned as a Georgia sharpshooter officer in the Army of Northern Virginia.[15]

During spring 1867 the Georgia General Assembly enacted a law creating courts in the various counties of the state to have jurisdiction in all misdemeanor cases, as well as certain civil cases. For each court the judge and solicitor were to be selected by popular vote. An election for filling the positions was called to be held about six weeks after adjournment of the March term of the superior court. The first announced candidate for the position of solicitor in Gwinnett County was a lawyer with sixteen years' experience at the bar. The job was an attractive one; the successful candidate could continue to practice in all other courts. Simmons immediately "shied his castor into the ring, and the battle was on," as he noted in his memoirs.

Simmons's opponent attacked him upon the grounds of incapacity as a lawyer, given that he had been admitted to the bar only a short time before the election. However, the young man more than made up for his lack of experience with his personal charisma, sterling reputation, and effective campaigning. He triumphed over his more experienced candidate by carrying every precinct in the county, including an 800-vote majority in the Lawrenceville District.[16]

Not long after his election, the Major turned his attention toward an attractive young lady in town. As recorded by a family friend, "He began to pay

---

[14]Byrd, *Them Brave Georgians*, 386.
[15]Ibid.
[16]Ibid., 387–88.

court to Miss Mary Ambrose, one of the beauties of the county."[17] When he marched off to war, William Simmons had been unaware of the then twelve-year-old girl, who was the oldest daughter of George Washington and Mary Ann (*nee* Wood) Ambrose. Mary's father was successful merchant and the owner of several large farms. Now, with the war over, "Miss Molly" was a charming lady of nineteen, and William Simmons was one of the town's most eligible bachelors."

Molly Ambrose was acknowledged to be the pick of the belles of Gwinnett County. Vivacious and intelligent, the young lady often received admiring glances from many young officers home from the war. She was the living fulfillment of soldier dreams while in camp, on the march, and in prison.[18]

As he began to focus his attention on Mary Ambrose, there is no doubt that William Simmons recalled a tragic incident that had taken place a couple of years before that involved Mary and her older brother, Charles. One day in December 1866, Charles Ambrose accompanied his sister to the Lawrenceville town square. While they were in front of the apothecary on Perry Street, several young men gathered around to pay their respects to seventeen-year-old Mary. One of the men in the group was William M. Orr, a young man of twenty-three, who lived in the Lawrenceville District and had served in the Hutchins Guards of the 16th Georgia Infantry Regiment.[19] Rather that complimenting "Miss Molly," Orr startled everyone present by making unflattering remarks about the young lady and her family. Charles Ambrose immediately confronted Orr and demanded that he retract what had been said. Orr refused and sarcastically repeated his remarks. An argument ensued, and Charles opened fire with his revolver. Orr dropped to the ground, severely wounded. Hours later he died from the gunshot wound.

That night, under the cover of darkness, Charles Ambrose left town and never returned except for a couple of furtive, unannounced visits with his relatives in the small hours before daylight. The next day he was charged with murder.[20] Two days after the incident, Orr's body was laid to rest in the

---

[17]Ibid., 388.

[18]Ibid.

[19]According to his service records and Census information, Private William M. Orr was likely well-known to William Simmons, given that both had grown up in Gwinnett County and had served in Company I (Hutchins Guards) of the 16th Georgia Infantry Regiment. Orr was one of only six men from his regimental company who were paroled at Appomattox ("Paroles of the Army of Northern Virginia," 174).

[20]Robert S. Davis Jr., *The Georgia Black Book: Morbid, Macabre & Sometimes Disgusting Records of Genealogical Value*, vol. 1 (Easley, SC: Southern Historical Press, 1982) 160. In the nineteenth century, Georgia governors offered rewards through proclamations for the arrest of felons who had fled justice. The proclamations abstracted are from Record Group 1-2-3, Georgia Department of Archives & History, and found in the Governor's Proclamation Book for the years 1854–1869. According to state records,

Lawrenceville City Cemetery.[21] The community grieved over the tragic shooting of William Orr. Mary Ambrose was upset by the incident and the departure of her older brother, to whom she was very close.

As Mary Ambrose approached her twentieth birthday, William Simmons stepped up to fill the void in her life. From the very start, a deep and abiding relationship developed between the young lady and the Major. Their friendship grew into a mutual affection that led to matrimony.[22] On 16 December 1869, they exchanged vows before the Reverend J. L. King, pastor of the Fairview Presbyterian Church in Lawrenceville.[23] It was the first day of nearly sixty-two years of married life for the newlyweds.

---

the shooting took place on 28 December 1866 and was officially classified as murder, with Charles Ambrose named as the perpetrator and William M. Orr named as the victim (entry 75). In his manuscript, D. M. Byrd Jr. incorrectly identified the perpetrator of the offensive remarks as "a young man named Bates." Bates is also incorrectly mentioned in Cecile Richards, *Wherever You Go: The Life of Jane Heard Clinton, Indian Territory Bride* (New York: iUniverse, 2003) 24, which was based on information from Byrd, *Them Brave Georgians*, 388–89.

[21]Joseph P. Byrd IV, "The Saga of Charles Ambrose-Clinton," Part I, Gwinnett Historical Society, *The Heritage Quarterly* 39/1 (Spring 2010): 11. According to the U.S. Census of 1860, the Orr family consisted of William M. Orr (17), his mother Mary (40), and sisters Sara Caroline (20), Eber (Evelyn? 14), and Emer (Emma? 6). William's father, James M. Orr, was a blacksmith who died in 1858. The previous year, William's sister, Sara Caroline Orr, married Nathan L. Hutchins Jr., who would become William Simmons's commanding officer in the 3rd Georgia Sharpshooters five years later.

[22]Byrd, *Them Brave Georgians*, 389.

[23]Simmons Family Bible. Copies of the birth, death, and marriage pages are in the possession of the author.

24

The Young Legislator

The work praises the man.
—Irish Proverb

The serenity of the young couple's married life was in marked contrast to the spirit of the times when they were married. As a new decade approached, Georgia remained in the grip of Reconstruction with a Federal provisional governor, Rufus B. Bullock, in control of the civil government. During the early years of Reconstruction, Bullock, who was originally from New York, fought to retain his control of Georgia and to that end opposed the return of the state to the Union. A major setback to Bullock's ambitions finally came on 15 July 1870 when the U.S. Congress readmitted Georgia and permitted more open elections to be held.

Bullock's actions encouraged William Simmons to become actively involved in political life.[1] The young major had lost none of his passion for politics during the long years of war and imprisonment. He was strongly opposed to Governor Bullock and longed to take an active role in the rebuilding of his state. In August 1870 Simmons attended the Democrat Party state convention as one of seven delegates from Gwinnett County.

Early in October of 1870, in a last ditch effort to retain power, Bullock forced a law through his Reconstruction legislature that provided for the first post-war elections and at the same time created election machinery designed to perpetuate his control of the government. Since no registration lists of voters were available, Bullock provided in his law that every person, black or white, must be given a ballot. In addition the law allowed for the polls to remain open for three days. With this provision, Bullock hoped to convey a sufficiently large number of repeat voters from place to place to assure the outcome of the election in his favor.

In Gwinnett County, three tickets were formed to run in the election of 1870. The Democrat convention nominated Major William Simmons and Captain John H. Jones for the State House of Representatives. Some prominent

---

[1]Daniel M. Byrd Jr., *Them Brave Georgians*, manuscript, Gwinnett Historical Society archives, Lawrenceville, GA 389–91 (Fort Delaware Society Library, Delaware City, DE, also has a copy.). Madison Byrd's accounts of Simmons's political career are based partly on information passed down to him by William Simmons, and partly by his father, Dan M. Byrd Sr., who was raised by William and Mary Simmons and was the Major's law partner in the early days of his career.

men in the county were disappointed over their failure to be nominated for the office and entered the race on an independent ticket. The Republicans also put up a slate of candidates. Two years before, the Republicans had carried Gwinnett County, electing Dr. Johnson Matthews and Wiley R. Bracewell to the Constitutional Convention, which framed the new Georgia constitution. In the 1870 election, Matthews was again the Republican candidate. In an action that was completely unexpected, Matthews put the name of William Simmons on the Republican ticket. When he discovered this ploy on the day of the election, Simmons asked Matthews in the presence of a large crowd why he had placed his name on the ballots, knowing that he (Simmons) was a loyal and uncompromising Democrat. Matthews replied that, "Everybody knows you are going to be overwhelmingly elected." The outcome was never in doubt. That day, Simmons won a resounding victory, receiving all but 176 of the votes (from Republicans and Democrats alike) cast in Gwinnett County.[2]

One week before the Georgia legislature met, Governor Bullock stepped down from his position and absconded to New York. He was replaced by Benjamin Conley, a Republican, who was president of the Senate and *ex-officio* governor. Bullock clearly foresaw the end of his corrupt political reign, during which he had plundered the Georgia treasury to pay for large gifts for his friends.

The General Assembly of 1871–1872 was one of the most important in the history of Georgia, and there were a great many prominent men in both houses. William Simmons was made a member of the judiciary committee and given a number of other important assignments. One of his fellow committee members was Garnett McMillan of Habersham County, who was a close friend and staunch political ally. McMillan entered service as a 2nd lieutenant in his father's company (McMillan Guards) of the 24th Georgia and later commanded Company B of the 3rd Georgia Sharpshooters.[3] The legislature faced the monumental task of reorganizing the government and unraveling all of the financial chicanery and plundering of the Bullock administration. Representative Simmons was in full accord with efforts to clean up the mess left by the Reconstruction government, but his high sense of propriety would not let him go to the extremes advocated by many of his peers. He strenuously fought against the efforts to oust Governor Conley on the grounds that such a move would be both revolutionary and set a bad precedent. He supported an alternative bill providing for a special election. The bill finally became law despite the veto of the governor, who obviously did not want to go through

---

[2]Byrd, *Them Brave Georgians*, 390.

[3]Lucian Lamar Knight, *Georgia's Bi-Centennial Memoirs and Memories*, 4 vols. (published by the author, 1931) 1:328–30. McMillan was a graduate of Emory & Henry and a brilliant lawyer who studied under his father, who was a member of the Georgia Senate in the 1850s along with James P. Simmons.

another campaign. The special election was held in December 1872 with the selection of James M. Smith, then speaker of the house.

During Simmons's term in the state legislature, there were twenty-seven Negro members of the House. A resolution was made by Representative Dunlap Scott to expel them on the grounds that they had failed to pay taxes for the year preceding their election. There was a very strong sentiment favorable to such an action among the members, but Simmons led the fight against it. He argued that because their election was legal, such an action would most likely result in another imposition of Reconstruction for the state. Soon a vote was called, and the resolution was defeated by a very small majority. Simmons's forces had prevailed against formidable opposition. On the day the vote was taken U.S. Senator Thomas F. Bayard[4] of Delaware was on the floor of the Georgia statehouse. He was very impressed with the debate and eventual result, and he personally expressed his gratitude to Simmons at the outcome because the issue was of great importance to the South.

The young legislator's moderation had its limits, however. He drew the line when it came to unfair proposals to restore the government to the majority of Georgians at any cost. While the General Assembly was in session, Robert E. Park, Simmons's acquaintance from Fort Delaware, asked him to sponsor a bill changing the form of county government of Meriwether County, Georgia. In the election of 1870, the Republican Party had captured the county, but Republican representatives refused to introduce the bill that the grand jury of Meriwether County wanted to have passed. Simmons gladly complied with the request of his fellow prisoner of war. Madison Byrd wrote about this incident in his manuscript based on information passed on by his great uncle.

> Years later [Simmons] told of his experience in guiding the bill through the State House of Representatives. "The two Republican members from that county were very indignant because of the introduction of the bill and fought its passage." While the Major was speaking for the measure, one of the Meriwether representatives interrupted him to inquire who was representing Meriwether. Was it "The gentleman from Gwinnett or the elected Representatives from Meriwether County?" Caustically Simmons replied, "I am representing the worth and intelligence of your county. You and your colleague were sent here by the Negroes and scalawags. I was elected to succeed both of you by the Grand Jury of your county."[5]

The bill went through the legislature like a whirlwind. In his anger, one of the Meriwether Republicans rushed over to the Major and declared that he "was

---

[4]Thomas F. Bayard was one of five members of his family to serve Delaware in the U.S. Senate. He was preceded by James A. Bayard, Richard H. Bayard, and James A. Bayard Jr. His son, Thomas F. Bayard Jr., served in the U.S. Senate in the 1920s.

[5]Byrd, *Them Brave Georgians*, 392, based on Simmons's personal recollection.

insulted by the denunciation." Undaunted, Simmons stood up to his adversary and challenged him to do something about the claimed insult. The offended representative meekly returned to his seat after hearing Simmons's response, and nothing more came of the confrontation.

During his tenure in the Georgia House of Representatives, William Simmons was actively involved in a number of important debates and legislative acts. One of the most notable involved the operation of the Western & Atlantic Railroad. During the Bullock regime, the legislature leased the Western & Atlantic to the Joseph E. Brown Company at a rental rate of several thousand dollars per month, which was regularly paid to the state. A faction, backed by former Confederate general Robert Toombs, drafted a bill to repeal the legislation and return the railroad to the state for operation. After the bill was introduced, Toombs remained at the capitol to use his power and influence to ensure passage of the measure.

Rising to the challenge Simmons again led the opposition to the bill and delivered the main speech opposing its passage. Addressing the legislature he traced the history of the railroad from its construction up to the present. He reminded his colleagues that over the years that the railroad had been operated by the state of Georgia, it had lost over one million dollars and had brought revenue into the state treasury in only two years. Simmons stressed that no railroad should be a toy for state politicians because the people chosen to run the railroad are typically selected on the basis of political patronage rather than their ability, character, or experience. Once again Simmons's forces prevailed, and a narrow majority defeated the bill.

Of all the legislative battles in which the Major participated, the most important involved the introduction of a bill establishing the method of borrowing money on property and declaring the rights of lender and borrower. Prior to 1871 the Georgia Supreme Court had ruled that the widow of a borrower was entitled to homestead and dower rights in land mortgaged by her deceased husband and that the value of these rights had to be given to her even if the borrower sold the land to collect the amount owed. These rulings effectively prevented poor Georgians from borrowing money on their land to rebuild homes, barns, and business establishments. Simmons's law transferred absolute title to the lender at the time the loan was made and required the courts to rule that the lender continued to have all rights in the land until the debt was paid. This method of borrowing money, called a deed to secure debt, allowed Northern capital to be safely invested in the state and aided greatly in the state's economic rebirth. This act was later codified in Section 330t of the State Legal Code of 1911.

At the end of the 1871–1872 General Assembly, Governor James M. Smith tendered to William Simmons the position of judge of the Western

Judicial Circuit.[6] The Major courteously declined the offer, explaining to the governor that he had made up his mind never to hold another political office and instead intended to devote his life to the practice of law. Later on, Simmons was asked to reconsider and accept the nomination to represent Georgia's 6th Congressional District in the U.S. House of Representatives.[7] There was widespread support for Simmons, particularly from his many backers in Gwinnett County, one of whom praised his character and qualifications in a letter published in the *Atlanta Constitution*:

[Gwinnett County] has many who would honor the position [U.S. representative], and among the number, none are more worthy than Major Simmons. He has shown himself a prudent, wise and skillful legislator—bold and aggressive in securing the welfare of his people—fearless and defiant in the denunciation of crime, peculation, and fraud—evincing throughout his political course tact and sagacity rarely equaled in one of his years. Though cosmopolitan in character, with a heart pulsating in unison to the wellbeing and honor of the entire people of Georgia and the South, the peculiar interests of his District would find in him a zealous advocate and fearless champion.[8]

William Simmons must have been flattered by such praise, but once again he graciously declined. His brief fling as an elected representative was over, and William Simmons welcomed the opportunity to focus on his law practice in Lawrenceville.

---

[6]The Western Circuit of Georgia included eight counties in the northeastern region of the state: Clarke, Franklin, Gwinnett, Habersham, Hall, Jackson, Rabun, and Walton (James C. Flanigan, *History of Gwinnett County, Georgia, 1818–1960*, vol. 2 [1959; reprint, Lawrenceville: Gwinnett Historical Society, 1999] 46).

[7]"Major William E. Simmons for Congress in the 6th Congressional District," *Atlanta Constitution*, 23 July 1872; "Major William E. Simmons for Congress," *Atlanta Constitution*, 1 August 1872; "Democratic Meeting in Gwinnett—Hon. W. E. Simmons Recommended for Congress," *Atlanta Constitution*, 8 September 1872, 1.

[8]"Major Wm. E. Simmons for Congress," *Atlanta Constitution*, August 1, 1872.

25

Family and School Ties

He did it with all his heart, and prospered.
—2 Chronicles 31:21

William and Mary Ambrose Simmons were happily married for sixty-two years, but they never had any children of their own. They were loving "surrogate" parents for several nieces and nephews, in particular the children of Mary's older brother, Charles.

After the incident with William Orr on the courthouse square, Charles Ambrose left Lawrenceville and traveled to Texas. Sometime after his arrival in spring 1867, he changed his surname to Clinton and began working as a cattle hand on the legendary Chisholm Trail. During fall 1871 or early spring 1872, while returning to Texas through Indian Territory on the Shawnee Trail, he stopped at a settlement called Okmulgee, the new capital of the Creek Indian Nation. There he met Louise Atkins, a mixed-blood Creek citizen, who was a teacher in the local boarding school. They soon fell in love and were married in 1873 by Samuel Checote, the principal chief of the Creeks and an ordained Methodist minister. Two years later Charles and Louise left Okmulgee to establish the Half Circle (S) Ranch[1] on Duck Creek, near the settlement of Twin Mounds, about twenty-five miles south of present day Tulsa, Oklahoma. Their first home was a three-room cabin with a lean-to kitchen. It was commonly called the "Last Chance Ranch" because it was the last chance for a hungry traveler to obtain a splendid home-cooked meal from Louise Clinton before venturing into the wilds of Indian Territory.[2]

---

[1]The "S" in the ranch's name stood for Severs, Clinton's mentor and employer. Frederick Ballard Severs was one of the first white settlers in the Creek Nation. He came to Indian Territory to teach at a mission school and later worked at a trading post run by his uncle, Hagerman Shields. Like Charles Ambrose Clinton, Frederick Ballard Severs fought for the Confederacy in a cavalry regiment. Severs was an officer (and the only white) in the Creek Mounted Rifles, led by Principal Creek Chief Samuel Checote. After the war, Severs established a prosperous mercantile business in the Creek Nation capital of Okmulgee and started a cattle ranch near Muskogee in the Creek Nation (Federal Writers Project Collection Manuscripts, box 23, folder 4, Oklahoma Historical Society Archives, Oklahoma City, OK; Frederick B. Severs Collection, Oklahoma Historical Society Research Division, Oklahoma City, OK).

[2]Fannie Brownlee Misch, "Cattle Led the Way," *Tulsa World*, 3 January 1965. This excellent article provides a wealth of information about the pioneer life of Charles and

The Clintons prospered in their new home, and Charles became a successful rancher. Several years later, when the railroad came to the Creek Nation, Charles and Louise established a second ranch close to the rail line. Their new home was in Red Fork, a small town on the Arkansas River. In the 1920s, Tulsa annexed Red Fork, and it was there, sometime around 1884, that Charles and Louise built a home for their growing family, which included three sons, Fred, Lee, and Paul, and a daughter, Vera.[3]

In 1888, Charles Clinton died while in Hot Springs, Arkansas. He was only forty-one years old. Louise was devastated by the loss of her husband and concerned as to how she would manage the ranch and raise four children. After hearing of his brother-in-law's untimely death, William Simmons assumed responsibility for the education and welfare of his niece and nephews. As soon as they were old enough to board, the Clinton children were brought to Georgia for their education. All three boys attended school at Young Harris, and Vera Clinton graduated from Wesleyan College in Macon, Georgia. When school was not in session, the children stayed with William and Mary Simmons in their spacious home in Lawrenceville.

The school the boys attended was located in the picturesque Brasstown Valley of the North Georgia Blue Ridge Mountains. It was chartered in 1887 by the Methodist Church and named in honor of Judge Young I. Harris of Athens, Georgia. When the Clinton boys were first enrolled, there were no housing facilities for students on the campus. William Simmons had a large home constructed next to the school grounds to be used as a student housing for his three nephews and other students.[4] After his nephews finished their studies at Young Harris, Simmons donated the home to the college.[5]

While at they were in the Collegiate Department at Young Harris, the two eldest sons, Fred and Lee, met the women they would later marry. Fred was introduced to Jane Carroll Heard of Elberton, Georgia, when she came to the college at commencement to visit a friend. Miss Heard was from one of the most prominent families in Georgia.[6] Jane was a direct descendant of Stephen

---

Louise Clinton in the Creek Nation, Indian Territory. The late Mrs. Misch was a close friend and colleague of Angie Debo, a noted historian of Oklahoma and the Creek Nation of Indian Territory. Both ladies were well acquainted with Louise Clinton and her four children.

[3]See Joseph P. Byrd IV, "The Saga of Charles Ambrose-Clinton, Part 2; 4-part series," Gwinnett Historical Society, *The Heritage Quarterly* 39/2 (Summer 2010): 44–47. Additional information on the Clinton family appears in *The Heritage Quarterly* 39/3 (Fall 2010) and 39/4 (Winter 2010).

[4]Cecile Richards, *Wherever You Go: The Life of Jane Heard Clinton, Indian Territory Bride* (New York: iUniverse, 2003) 25.

[5]Byrd, "The Saga of Charles Ambrose-Clinton," *Gwinnett Heritage Quarterly* 39/4 (Winter 2010): 107.

[6]Richards, *Wherever You Go*, 23–24.

Heard, a brigadier general in the Revolutionary War, governor of Georgia, and a personal friend of George Washington.[7] Jane's father was James Lawrence Heard, who was an infantry colonel in the Confederate army and served in the Georgia legislature. Her mother, Melissa Harper Heard, was one of the first graduates of Wesleyan College in Macon.[8]

About the same time his older brother began courting Jane Heard, Lee Clinton made the acquaintance of Susan Merrill, a lovely Young Harris student from Jasper, Georgia. Susan's father, Sherman Morton Merrill, had been a major in the Union army and served as a chaplain during the Civil War. After the war, Major Merrill returned to the South from his home in Iowa and settled in Pickens County, Georgia, which had long been a hotbed of resistance to secession.

After completing their education in Georgia, William and Mary's three nephews and niece returned to Indian Territory and settled in Tulsa, then not much more than a dusty crossroads across the Arkansas River from the Clinton Ranch in Red Fork. All four remained in Tulsa and became prominent citizens of Indian Territory and the state of Oklahoma.[9]

Soon after arriving in Tulsa with his young bride, Fred Clinton began a medical practice in partnership with Dr. J. C. W. Bland. Four years later the partners financed the drilling of the first production oil well in Red Fork, Creek Nation.[10] The well was located on the Dawes Commission land allotment of Sue A. Bland, Dr. Bland's Creek wife. The gusher came in on 25 June 1901 and ignited the oil boom that eventually led to Tulsa becoming renowned as the "Oil Capital of the World" throughout the first half of the twentieth century. The Sue A. Bland no. 1 well was still producing after nearly fifty years. Although he could have chosen to become wealthy off the oil discovery, Fred Clinton was more concerned about the future economic development of Tulsa. He continued his medical practice and was instrumental in establishing the Indian Territory Medical Association and the Oklahoma Medical Association. After statehood,

---

[7]Stephen Heard was a Revolutionary War hero and the patriarch of one of Georgia's most prominent families. He served as provisional governor of Georgia in 1780. See James F. Cook, *Governors of Georgia, 1754–2004*, 3rd ed. (Macon: Mercer University Press, 2005); Richards, *Wherever You Go*, 8–14.

[8]Angie Debo, "Jane Heard Clinton," *Chronicles of Oklahoma* 24/1 (Spring 1946): 20.

[9]In 1996, the year Tulsa celebrated its centennial, both Dr. Fred Severs Clinton and Jane Heard Clinton were honored posthumously as two of Tulsa's most prominent citizens during its first century.

[10]Kenny Franks, et al., *Early Oklahoma Oil: A Photographic History, 1859–1936*, number 2 in The Montague History of Oil Series (College Station: Texas A & M University Press, 1981) 32–36.

Dr. Clinton opened the first hospital in the area and built the first fireproof office building in downtown Tulsa, a five-story "skyscraper."[11]

Fred Clinton's wife, Jane, became the undisputed "Matron of the Arts" in Tulsa. Three years before Oklahoma statehood, she was president and a founding member of the Hyechka Club, which was created to "advance the interest and promote the culture of music in Tulsa, and for the mutual improvement of its members." Within a short period of time, she began to bring opera and symphonic music to Tulsa and organized a chorus that made its debut in 1911 in a performance with the New York Symphony Orchestra. In 2004, the club celebrated its 100th anniversary.[12] For nearly fifty years until her death in 1945 she labored tirelessly to support arts and civic organizations in her adopted city.

Fred Clinton's younger brother, Lee, was a prominent banker, real estate investor, and president of the Tulsa Stock Yards. Fred's sister, Vera Clinton, married James Hugh McBirney, founder and president of the National Bank of Commerce in Tulsa. Along with Fred Clinton, McBirney was a founding member of the International Petroleum Exposition and Congress, which opened in 1923. McBirney came to Indian Territory in 1897 from Kansas to pitch for the city baseball team and work for the Tulsa Banking Company. He was the acknowledged "Dean of Oklahoma Bankers" for nearly a half century until his death in 1944. In the early years of statehood, Vera McBirney became the first female bank director in the state of Oklahoma.[13] Paul, the youngest Clinton sibling, left Young Harris to return to Red Fork and help manage the Clinton Ranch. He later graduated from Henry Kendall College, which later became Tulsa University, and was a well-known Tulsa businessman, successful in real estate and ranching. For all of the Clinton children, their accomplishments in life and many contributions are in no small measure due to the love and nurturing they received from their Uncle William and Aunt Mary Simmons as well as their devoted mother, Louise, who never remarried.

William and Mary were also close to the Byrd family of Lawrenceville. Mary's younger sister Georgia married Joseph P. Byrd in 1879. The couple had ten children, nine of whom survived infancy. All were favorites of their aunt and uncle, especially the third child, Daniel Madison Byrd. Dan's son, Madison,

---

[11]See Dr. Fred S. Clinton, "The Indian Territory Medical Association," *Chronicles of Oklahoma* 26/1 (Spring 1948): 23–55; "The Beginning of the Oklahoma State Hospital Association," *Chronicles of Oklahoma* 22/3 (Fall 1944): 337–53; "First Hospitals in Tulsa," *Chronicles of Oklahoma* 22/1 (Spring 1944): 1–28.

[12]Fred S. Clinton, "*Hyechka* Club," *Chronicles of Oklahoma* 21/4 (1943):351–52. See Richards, *Wherever You Go*, 46–50.

[13]Dr. Fred S. Clinton, "James Hugh McBirney (1870–1944)," *Chronicles of Oklahoma* 22/3 (Fall 1944): 1–5.

grew up in Lawrenceville next door to the Simmons's home and wrote of the special relationship William and Mary had with their "children":

> [William and Mary Simmons had] feelings like those of proud parents and, later on, indulgent grandparents. For while they had no children of their own, the childhood attachment of a nephew resulted in a "son" they loved as much as if the appealing little boy had been their own. [My father] Dan was one of the oldest of ten children born to Mrs. Simmons' younger sister, Georgia, who had married a successful farmer and merchant. Dan's grandfather, for whom Dan had been named, was also a prosperous farmer, long time member of the County Court, and one of the county's leading citizens.

With the approaching arrival of each successive baby in the younger sister's family, the older children were "farmed" out to visit relatives in the little village. Young Dan was always assigned to his Aunt Mary and Uncle William. He thoroughly enjoyed their personal, undivided attention during these visits and often would beg his Aunt Mary, after he was returned to his large family, to be allowed to spend the night with her or go to the farms with his uncle. The guileless lad intuitively felt the longing of his aunt and uncle for the son they had been denied.[14]

After one of his many brothers and sisters was born, Dan M. Byrd was allowed to stay with his Aunt Mary and Uncle William. For the rest of his life, his home was with them. They raised him as their only son, educated him at the University of Georgia, and shared his joys and problems. When he was admitted to practice law, there was never any doubt that he would become the Major's partner. To their home, he brought his bride[15] and in their home his two sons played, not as great-nephews but as grandchildren.

In 1893, after an absence of more than thirty years, William Simmons got back into the newspaper business. He formed and chartered a stock company under the name of the Lawrenceville Publishing Company and remained actively engaged in the venture for many years .[16]

The next year, Simmons was offered any state position within the appointive powers of Governor William Yates Atkinson. As one of Governor

---

[14]Daniel M. Byrd Jr., *Them Brave Georgians*, manuscript, Gwinnett Historical Society archives, Lawrenceville, GA pg. 396–97 (Fort Delaware Society Library, Delaware City, DE, also has a copy.).

[15]The "bride" of Dan M. Byrd Sr. was Nanaline ("Nancy") King, granddaughter of Reverend J. L. King, the minister who married William and Mary Simmons in 1869.

[16]Mary Frazier Long, *About Lawrenceville* (Madison, GA: Southern Lion Books, 2008) 324. In January 1915, William Simmons leased the paper to L. M. Bird and V. L. Hagood for a term of five years. The *News-Herald* continued publication under a number of different owners until the 1960s when it was combined with two other weeklies into one publication, the *Gwinnett Daily News*.

Atkinson's top campaign advisors, the Major asked only one favor; for the Governor to appoint one of the defeated candidates, Clement Anselm Evans, formerly a general in the Confederate army, to the newly established Prison Commission. The governor granted Simmons's request, and Evans served faithfully for many years.[17] In 1914 newly formed Evans County, Georgia, was named in honor of General Evans.

After Simmons rejected Governor Atkinson's offer of a state position, the governor insisted that he accept an appointment to of the Georgia University Board of Trustees. To be of service to his beloved home state was a responsibility that the Major could not refuse. From the date of his appointment on 4 June 1896[18] until 1927, successive governors recognized the Major's contributions and reappointed him as an at-large member of the Board of Trustees.

Throughout his life, William Simmons was a self-described "rabid, uncompromising Democrat." He was "ever ready to "take up the cudgel for the Democrat Party and his personal friends."[19] Over the years Cotton Tom Watson was a frequent visitor to the Major's home. Simmons admired his friend's writing and intellectual powers, but he did not agree with most of Watson's populist theories. When populism was at its height, the Major was in great demand as a stump speaker in opposition to it. He spoke in many Georgia counties under the sponsorship of the state Democratic committee.

On numerous occasions, Simmons was a delegate to the Georgia and National Democrat Conventions and held important committee assignments. He was chosen as an elector in three presidential elections, voting twice for President Grover Cleveland and once for President Woodrow Wilson. Simmons always boasted that he had the "good luck never to suffer a defeat at the polls."[20]

For more than three decades William Simmons was an influential member of the University Board of Trustees. When he was appointed, the University of Georgia was barely able to scrape by financially, with only token support from the Georgia legislature. Tuition was free, and the institution had to rely primarily on Federal funds and gifts from outside benefactors to survive. Leaders and interest groups throughout Georgia complained that the university was a "hotbed of vice and sin" and did not serve the state well.[21] In addition, there was strong opposition from the denominational colleges in Georgia, led by Warren Akin Candler, a prominent Methodist minister and editor of the *Wesleyan*

---

[17]Byrd, *Them Brave Georgians*, 394.

[18]*Atlanta Constitution*, 5 June 1896. William Simmons succeeded Dr. H. V. M. Miller, who had recently died.

[19]Byrd, *Them Brave Georgians*, 395.

[20]Ibid.

[21]Thomas G. Dyer, *The University of Georgia: A Bicentennial History 1785–1985* (Athens: University of Georgia Press, 1985) 133.

Christian Advocate, who championed the superior moral tone of Christian education. At the age of thirty, Candler had become the president of Emory College, Simmons's alma mater.[22] The newly appointed trustee now found himself now at odds with the legislature he had once served and the college from which he had graduated nearly forty years prior.

The turn of the century marked a decisive turning point in the history of the University of Georgia. In 1898, Chancellor William Boggs was forced to resign after a decade of weak leadership. One year later the vacant position was filled by Walter Barnard Hill, an alumnus of the university (Class of 1870) and a prominent Methodist layman. Hill's election proved to be a stroke of genius. He had the support of Governor Atkinson, the university Board of Trustees, the general public (Hill was a teetotaler), and even Warren Candler. The new chancellor worked tirelessly to expand the physical plant, improve academic standards, and convert the school into a true university in the early years of the Progressive Era.[23]After six years, Hill's hectic schedule and work habits took their toll. He died in December 1905 of pneumonia and exhaustion at the age of fifty-four.[24]

The successor to Walter Hill was David C. Barrow, who was dean of the Franklin College of Arts and Sciences at the university. He became acting chancellor at Hill's death, and served for nearly twenty years until his resignation in 1925. Barrow continued down the path forged by Hill and was successful in securing greater financial support and upgrading expanded academic offerings for the university.

In the critical growth years under Chancellor Barrow, William Simmons served as chairman of the finance committee. He worked diligently to ensure adequate funding and resources for the university system and often butted heads with the Georgia legislature and the smaller public colleges in the state. In 1917, when pressed by the Georgia Normal and Industrial College in Milledgeville for a greater share of the money allocated by the Smith-Lever Fund coming from federal government, he responded by adding clarity and perspective to the university's funding that appeared in the *Atlanta Constitution*.

> No state having a university of its own appropriates so little for its maintenance as Georgia does to hers. The trustees of the university feel a deep interest in every school in its system, and never leave anything undone that they can do to build all of them up, always co-operating with the local authority of each in procuring appropriations from the legislature.[25]

---

[22]Ibid., 143.
[23]Ibid., 163.
[24]Ibid., 162.
[25]William E. Simmons, "The University and the Georgia Normal and Industrial College," *Atlanta Constitution*, 7 August 1917, 4.

At commencement exercises on 1 June 1919, the University of Georgia expressed its appreciation of Simmons's service by conferring upon him the honorary degree of Doctor of Laws. As the degree was being presented, Chancellor David Barrow said, "In view of the distinguished service you have rendered the state and the University of Georgia system, the conferring of this degree brings no additional honor to you, but you honor it."

Two years later the university trustees and those of branch colleges were challenged by a bill introduced in the state senate that would replace the present organization with a single Board of Seven Regents. Once again, William Simmons authored a response that was printed in the *Atlanta Constitution*. He reminded the readership that this was a bad idea, especially from the standpoint of economy and representation:

> The purpose of the [current] law making chairmen of the boards of trustees of the branch colleges ex-officio [allows for] capable men to fill such an important position. But the salary of the Board of Regents alone would nearly double the amount now being paid to all of the trustees of all of the schools referred to.

> The people of Georgia are too intelligent and liberty-loving to tamely submit to the setting up of such a politico-educational oligarchy as this wild-cat scheme provides for, under which they would have no voice in their educational institutions, even including the common schools, and those aiding in it are making a record that must be faced later on.[26]

Simmons further asserted that "The University of Georgia, proper, Franklin College, has 1,175 students on its campus, and would soon have 5,000 if provided with the necessary dormitory facilities, equipment, and other essential buildings for their accommodation."[27]

William Simmons continued serving on the board of trustees until 1927. By that time, he was well into his eighties and needed to slow down. With the coming of a new decade, his health began to fail and he became somewhat absent-minded. A relative remembered that occasionally the Major ate an entire meal at home without removing his hat. He added that out of deference to the Major, no one wished to bring it to his attention.

William Simmons continued to serve his community and state until his final days. He served as president of the Gwinnett County Fair and three terms as an unpaid member of the Lawrenceville City Council. Finally, on 29 January 1931, as he approached his ninety-second year, the old soldier died peacefully in his home in Lawrenceville. His devoted wife, Mary, followed him five years later on 18 December 1935. In the words of their great nephew, Madison Byrd,

---

[26]"Col. [Major] Wm. E. Simmons Appeals to Legislature for Fair Play for the University System," *Atlanta Constitution*, 27 July 1921, 8.

[27]Ibid.

"Hand in hand they lived full lives as Christian citizens, ever-mindful of the responsibilities accompanying their material good fortune and personal happiness."[28]

---

[28]Byrd, *Them Brave Georgians*, 397.

Afterword

In reflecting on the extraordinary life of William E. Simmons, I am profoundly affected by the content of his character and the depth of his convictions in all he endeavored to do. Although he died twelve years before I was born, I feel a kinship and affinity that is difficult to express. Despite these feelings of inadequacy, I would like to share my thoughts on the traits that the man embodied.

Above all, William Simmons represented the highest ideals of the Southern gentleman. He never wavered in his steadfast loyalty to the South despite great adversity and suffering. Perhaps this was helped along by his native stubborn nature. He truly believed that the Southern cause was just and worth sacrificing his life to defend. From the day that he enlisted in the Army, he made it clear that he and his comrades in the Gwinnett Volunteers would serve "for the duration of the war," not just for a few months or even years. Though he was actively involved in local, state, and national politics, he stuck to his Confederate roots and never accepted a war pension from the federal government.

At Fort Delaware Prison he and eighty-one other officers faced the prospect of being hanged or banished from the United States for refusing to sign their name to an oath that they could not abide by in good conscience. These men made this choice despite that thousands of Confederate prisoners of war at Fort Delaware had already taken the oath and were released to return to their homes and families. It was not an easy decision for Major Simmons to remain in prison after the surrender of the Confederate army. There is no doubt that his family desired to have him return home as soon as possible. Moreover, he understood that with his release he could fulfill his long-held dream of becoming a lawyer like his father and perhaps resurrect the newspaper that he had successfully launched at the age of nineteen. Still, he persisted until his conscience was clear and there was unanimous agreement among the last eighty-two officers held at Fort Delaware.

William Simmons's life was a model of service. He gave selflessly to his community, to Georgia, and to its two principal institutions of higher learning. Into his late eighties, he continued to serve as a trustee of both the University of Georgia and the Georgia Institute of Technology. As a state representative in the Georgia Assembly, he helped to guide Georgia as it struggled to make the difficult transition from Reconstruction to take its place as the "Empire State" of the New South.

William Simmons showered love and generosity on his family. Although he and Mary never had children of their own, he was "father" and "grandfather" to numerous nephews and nieces. He provided the support and nurturing for the four Clinton children who were left without a father in 1888. I believe he respected his brother-in-law's defense of Mary's honor, despite the unfortunate fact that he took the life of another man. William Simmons made certain that all four Clinton children received a proper education and were adequately prepared for adulthood. Throughout their school years he opened his home to them and provided a safe haven during the time they were nearly a thousand miles from their mother in Indian Territory. He also provided for the education of his nephew, Dan M. Byrd, at the University of Georgia, and was both his mentor and law partner.

The Major's generosity was matched by his courage. As an infantry officer in the 16th Georgia Infantry and 3rd Battalion Georgia Sharpshooters, he led his men into some of the most fiercely contested battles of the Civil War. He witnessed the terrible carnage at Bloody Lane at Sharpsburg, the Sunken Road at Fredericksburg, the Peach Orchard and Wheat Field at Gettysburg, and the Bloody Angle at Spotsylvania. His bravery in the Shenandoah Valley at Guard Hill was unquestioned, and his escape from the battlefield at Crampton's Gap was nothing short of miraculous.

In addition to his obvious pride in his home state, I am certain that the Major was proud of his position as an officer in the Army of Northern Virginia. He was privileged to serve under some of the greatest Confederate generals of the Civil War. Like many of his peers, he expressed great admiration for his commander-in-chief, General Robert E. Lee; I Corps commanders, James Longstreet and Richard H. Anderson; and division commanders, Lafayette McLaws and Joseph Kershaw. He maintained close relations with, and an abiding respect for, his command officers and fellow Georgians, Howell Cobb, Thomas R. R. Cobb, and William T. Wofford.

In commanding his regimental company and sharpshooter battalion, William Simmons demonstrated great leadership throughout the war. His loyalty to the Southern cause was clearly demonstrated in the wording of the resolution that was adopted by his battalion in February 1864.

In contrast to the pride he expressed in his roots and affiliations, William Simmons was always modest about his many notable achievements in life. There are numerous examples of how he expressed his pleasure at the accomplishments and good fortunes others rather than merely acknowledging his own.

Finally, William Simmons was always compassionate and fair toward others. This is apparent in the way he treated the two wounded Union officers at Gettysburg when he allowed their corporal to care for them rather than detaining him as a prisoner of war. Perhaps the Major was influenced by the actions of the sympathetic young Confederate sergeant, Richard Kirkland, whom he witnessed ministering to the wounded and dying Union soldiers near the Sunken Road at Fredericksburg. Some years later, as a state representative, Simmons risked rebuke and ridicule from many of his peers for his determined opposition to legislation that would have unfairly removed twenty-seven Negro legislators from the Georgia Assembly.

Though he has been gone for more than eighty years, I believe there is much that is timeless and enduring about the life and character of William E. Simmons. He was a gallant Georgian who will forever live in my memory.

Exhibit 1

Acceptance Letter of Commissions by Officers of
the Gwinnett Volunteers

Lawrenceville, Georgia
June 4, 1861
General Henry C. Wayne
Dear Sir:
The undersigned, commissioned officers of the "Gwinnett Volunteers," in obedience to your orders, hereby inform you of their acceptance of the positions to which they have been elected by said company, and commissioned by the Governor.

Our company is now full and will be prepared to leave for the seat of war so soon as their uniforms are complete, which will be about two weeks from this time—a large portion of them now being made. We cannot procure the Georgia buttons anywhere unless you are able to furnish us with them—if so, would you be so kind as to forward us immediately 91 dozen of the larger size…and 42 dozen of the smaller size for sleeves, etc.

Our company will be encamped for the next two weeks, and at the expiration of that time we desire to leave for the war, and hereby tender to the Governor our services for the war.[1]

Can the state furnish us with swords? If not, where can we find them?

Very respectfully, your obedient servants,

Henry P. Thomas, Captain
N. L. Hutchins, Jr., 1st Lieutenant
W. E. Simmons, 2nd Lieutenant
John A. Mitchell, 3rd Lieutenant

"Gwinnett Volunteers"

---

[1]Emphasis original to letter.

Exhibit 2

Letter from D. Madison Byrd Jr. to J. P. Byrd III Regarding
the Military Records of Major William E. Simmons, CSA

1001 Connecticut Avenue, N.W.
Washington 6, D.C.
June 10, 1960

Mr. Joseph P. Byrd, III
President
Oil Field Equipment Corporation
Rocky Mountain Arsenal
Denver, Colorado

Dear Joe:

The National Archives has just delivered the first (but largest) of two orders of prints of documents dealing with the military career of Uncle William. I ordered only a single copy, thinking that I would make additional copies in this office on our verifax machine. You are now in a position to decide whether you would like me to place an order for you for Xerox prints from National Archives, or whether you are content with the verifax copy, or whether you would like micro prints made from the State of Georgia. I am sending a complete set of verifax prints made from my Xerox prints. When the prints were made, a couple of entries from other files mistakenly drifted in and, therefore, you will have an opportunity to judge the relative quality of all three methods of reproduction.

Now, a word about these records. After the Federal forces captured Richmond, they brought all of the Confederate records to Washington and placed them in the "Rebel Archives" of the War Department. As some subsequent date, the War Department began cataloging and indexing these records. To that end, envelopes and cards were printed with legends that would be applicable to large bodies of men; for instance, a series of envelopes were printed with legends for the 16th Georgia Infantry and carried blank spaces for the insertion of specific information about each soldier as to his name, rank, and company. Into these envelopes were placed index cards which show each time that soldier's name appeared in any of the various Confederate books. For example, a copyist of the register of General Hospital No. 4 of Richmond,

Virginia, for May 30, 1863, found that Uncle William was a patient at that time and that he was returned to duty of June 2, 1863. The copyist then made an index card which had printed on it the legend identifying the register of the hospital. These cards were all numbered on the reverse side and that number was entered on the front of the envelope for the particular soldier. Each of the original records can be inspected at the National Archives Building. For example, as to Uncle William's stay in the hospital, if you asked for "Confederate Archives, Chapter 6, File N. 178, page 10," there you will find Uncle William's name as a patient in the hospital. In similar fashion, the regimental returns and rosters for various dates likewise can be inspected for verification of the index cards, pictures of which are being sent to you.

As you will notice, two of the index cards show Uncle William's promotion from Lieutenant to Captain and from Captain to Major. The first of these refers you to 245/H Appointments 1863 and to the personal papers of Nathan L. Hutchins. By request, I was shown a large book, about half the size of a normal desk top, which was the appointment book for 1863. Then, by turning to the tab for the letter "H" and looking at entry No. 245, you can find the date of Hutchins' appointment and the general by who he was recommended, and the general finally making the appointment. This entry on Hutchins also shows that the papers relating to his appointment are filed in Hutchins' envelope.

In similar fashion, I looked at the appointment book for 1864 under the letter "S" at entry No. 59, which shows in book 1-157 that Uncle William was recommended for promotion to Major on March 8, 1864 by General Wofford, and that this recommendation was approved by General Longstreet on March 24, 1864, as shown by a still further volume entitled "Endorsement Book 239."

The papers filed in Hutchins' envelope are the additional documents which I have ordered and not yet received. These documents consist of two letters, dated April 25, 1863, and April 28, 1863, written by General Wofford on blue stationery. These letters detail Wofford's reasons for forming the 3rd Battalion Georgia Sharpshooters and attach the present strength by companies of his brigade; and, second, a list of the names of the officers and men selected for the 3rd Georgia Battalion. As to Uncle William, Wofford wrote that he proposed to promote him from Lieutenant to Captain and that Uncle William was "a young officer of fine education and attainments, distinguished in battle for coolness and courage."

I am afraid my money is going to run out before I can get pictures of everything I would like to have. For example, there are other records which show the original officers of the 16th Regiment, the personalized names of the various companies, and some few squibs as to activities of various companies in the 16th Regiment. Some of these other records, for which I have not yet placed an order, identify Camp Bryan as located at Upper Grafton, York County, Virginia, and Camp Lamar as being near Yorktown, Virginia. Still other records show the requisitions for rifles and clothes for the men in the 16th Regiment and the various leaves of absence of Howell Cobb to serve as Speaker of the House in Richmond, and the dates that Uncle William's superior officers were promoted or changed.

I am currently making a list of all names found in Uncle William's journal, kept during his imprisonment at Fort Delaware, and hope that I will have an opportunity to check the career of some of these men so as to determine the specific identity of others who were captured at the same time with him.

Major Clark Howell writes, sadly, that Uncle William's biography was destroyed in the fire in the old *Constitution* Building.

If you want Xerox copies send me the verifax copies and $13.60 and I'll send both to the National Archives so they will know what documents to reproduce. If you'd like Xerox copies of all documents that I get, let me know.

D. M. Byrd, Jr.

p.s. A verifax copy of the first page of a bio written by Uncle William is also enclosed. I can't locate the original or a copy!

Exhibit 3

The Simmons Journal at Fort Delaware Prison

The journal that Major William E. Simmons kept at Fort Delaware Prison bears the date of 5 June 1865. It contains several war poems and the names of many of his fellow prisoners with their rank and address. Some of the Georgia officers are listed below, including four of William Simmons' fellow officers from the 3rd Battalion Georgia Sharpshooters: Lieutenant Delona Bunt, Captain M. F. Crumley, Lieutenant John E. Shelton, and Captain John F. Martin. A more complete list is documented in the *History of Gwinnett County, Georgia, Vol. II*, 244, 245.

C. M. Baldwin, Captain, Company G, Cobb's Legion, Madison, Georgia

Geo. W. Bartlett, Captain; Brigadier General Irenus Staff, Wheeler's Corps, Monticello, Georgia

W. H. Bennett, Captain, and A. C. S. Benning's Brigade, Army of Northern Virginia, Columbus, Georgia

Delona Bunt, Lieutenant, Company D, 3rd Battalion Georgia Sharpshooters, Lithonia, Georgia

M. F. Crumley, Captain, Company A, 3rd Battalion Georgia Sharpshooters, Augusta, Georgia

A. W. Gibson, Major, 45th Georgia Regiment, Knoxville, Georgia

Isaac Hardeman, Lieutenant Colonel, 12th Georgia Infantry Regiment, Army of Northern Virginia, Clinton, Georgia

Thomas W. Hooper, Colonel, 21st Georgia, Rome, Georgia

C. S. Jenkins, Captain, Company K, 64th Georgia Regiment, Dallas, Georgia

Charles H. Landers, Captain, Company A, Cobb's Legion, Covington, Georgia

J. C. McDonald, Major, 4th Georgia Cavalry, Waynesville, Georgia

John F. Martin, Captain, Company E, 3rd Battalion Georgia Sharpshooters, Lawrenceville, Georgia

Esquire S. Mitchell, Lieutenant, Company F, 45th Georgia Infantry, Clinton, Georgia

William L. Platt, Adjutant, 7th Regiment, Georgia Cavalry, Augusta, Georgia

C. S. Porter, Adjutant, Cobb's Legion, Madison, Georgia

John E. Shelton, Lieutenant, Company E. 3rd Battalion Georgia Sharpshooters, Acworth, Georgia

A. S. Talley, 1st Lieutenant, Co. A, 9th Georgia Battalion, Atlanta, Georgia

The following is a partial list of William Simmons' lady visitors ("cousins") at Fort Delaware Prison. See *History of Gwinnett County, Georgia, Vol. I,* 245.

Miss Julia Jefferson, New Castle, Del.
Mary A. Timberlake, Box 36, Norfolk, Va.
Miss Bessie Barney, New Castle, Del.
Miss Lettie Spotwood, New Castle, Del.
Marion G. Howard, Baltimore, Md.
Miss Beulah S. Reese, Alexandria, Va.
Miss Julia Ogle, New Castle, Del.
Miss Virginia Harrison, Alexandria, Va.

Exhibit 4

Resolution to Continue Service to the CSA

Third Battalion Georgia Sharpshooters, ANV
Captain William E. Simmons, Acting Commander
February 12, 1864

Whereas, The government of the United States persists in waging a war of conquest and subjugation against the Confederate States, and by refusing to agree to an honorable and equitable adjustment of our present difficulties, leaves us no other alternative but to fight on for the accomplishment of the glorious and that we have pledged our lives, our honor, and our fortunes to achieve; and Whereas, the term of three years for which we volunteered our service in the Army of the Confederate States, therefore,

Resolved, That we hereby tender our services to the Hon. Secretary of War, for the war, and express our unalterable determination never to lay down our arms so long as the foot of an armed enemy presses the soil of our country – nor until we win an honorable peace and Independence.

Resolved, That we see nothing in the situation to discourage any man who is worthy to be a freeman, if our countrymen will all determine to discharge the duty that they owe to themselves, their country, and, above all, to their God, in this, the crisis of our struggle for Independence.

Resolved, That we appeal to those who are at home, and especially to the ladies – whose untiring devotion to our cause, and zealous efforts on our behalf have elicited our highest admiration and entitled them to our lasting gratitude – to drive the skulkers and unauthorized absentees back to the army by heaping upon them the indignant scorn their baseness merits.

Resolved, That a copy of these resolutions be forwarded to the Hon. Secretary of War – to Lieut. General Longstreet and Brig. General Wofford, and that the Georgia papers be requested to publish the same.

John W. King, President
Garnett McMillan, Secretary

Exhibit 5

William E. Simmons Obituary
Lawrenceville News Herald

LAWRENCEVILLE, Ga., February 5, 1931 Major William E Simmons, former solicitor-general of the old western circuit, and one of Georgia's distinguished pioneers, died Thursday at noon at his home here following an illness of three months. He was 91 years of age.

His services were conducted Saturday afternoon from the residence on Clayton Street, with Dr. Wallace Rogers, of Atlanta, Dr. J. R. King of Decatur, and Rev. W. W. Cash of the local Methodist church presiding. Interment was in Shadowlawn Cemetery.

Major Simmons resided in Lawrenceville for more than ninety years on the property that has been in the Simmons family for more than a century. He was the son of the late Rev. James P. Simmons, who was also a lawyer, and Eliza Terrell Simmons. He was born August 26, 1839.

Major Simmons had always taken an active interest in religious and public affairs and had served the Methodist church as steward and as [manager[1]] of the camp ground. He was a liberal donator to every worthy cause, and will be greatly missed.

Major Simmons was one of the most influential and prominent men of the state and a lawyer of wide reputation.

He graduated from Emory College with degree of A. B. in 1858. He unexpectedly entered the field of journalism when his father advanced money to some parties to establish a newspaper in the town, named the *Lawrenceville News*. Operators of the paper failed to pay for the plant and his father made him a present of it to do as he pleased with it, either run or sell it. Major Simmons found that finding a suitable purchaser of a county newspaper plant was not an easy matter, and was forced to become an editor and publisher in order to keep it a growing concern, at 19 years of age, and the venture was successful.

When the national democratic convention at Baltimore failed to make a nomination and adjourned to re-convene at Charleston, which resulted in a split and the nomination of two presidential candidates, Breckenridge and Douglas, the *News* vigorously espoused the cause of Breckenridge as it had been fighting the latter's views on slavery in the territories from the start.

When it became evident that Lincoln would be elected president, the *News* advocated secession as the only safe and honorable course left to the south.

---

[1]This word is illegible in the original, but it may be "manager."

When secession had been accomplished and war was inevitable, Major Simmons volunteered in the first company organized in Gwinnett county, and was chosen second lieutenant, and later during the was elevated to the rank of major for his gallantry on the battlefield.

He took part in the following engagements: Yorktown, Petersburg, South Mountain, first and second battles of Fredericksburg, Sharpsburg, Chancellorsville, the Wilderness, Spotsylvania, Gettysburg, Funkstown, Cold Harbor, Gaines Mill, Hanover Junction, Malvern Hill, Culpepper Court House, Chattanooga, Knoxville, and (Front) Royal. At the battle of South Mountain, at which he was commanding Company I, 16th Georgia Regiment, his company lost 27 of 35 men he carried into the fight. Major Simmons, during the fighting, received one bullet through his hat brim, and 14 through his clothes. In the great and bloody battle of Sharpsburg, he went into the fight with his five men and came out alone, as all five of his command were killed. This and scores of other war hazards he went through without a serious injury.

Major Simmons was captured near the end of the war. He was first sent to the Old Capitol prison at Washington and later to Fort Delaware, where he remained until several months after the surrender of the Confederate armies.

With the surrender of Lee's army, all prisoners were offered liberty upon taking the oath of allegiance to the United States, which a large majority of the prisoners did and were sent home. When Johnston surrendered a few weeks later, the remainder of them, with the exception of 82 among them Major Simmons, refused to do so upon the ground that General Kirby Smith, commanding the trans-Mississippi forces, had not surrendered. All privates and officers below the rank of major took the oath upon the surrender of General Johnston's army, but these 82 still refused, despite threats of "hanging."

In August 1865, the federal government agreed to strike the "freely and voluntarily" amendment from the oath and all of the 82 men took it.

After the war Major Simmons began studying law in his father's office and was admitted to the bar at the March term of Gwinnett superior court, 1867. Six weeks later he was elected solicitor-general. In 1870, he was elected to the general assembly by one of the largest majorities ever accorded a candidate.

On December 16, 1869, he and Miss Mary Ambrose were married. Miss Ambrose was the daughter of the late Mr. and Mrs. Washington Ambrose. They celebrated their sixty-first anniversary last year.

Major Simmons took much interest in politics, both local and national, he being an uncompromising democrat, and fought hard for their principles. In his eighty-ninth year, during the 1928 campaign for president, he was active in behalf of the democratic ticket.

He was interested in sports, listening to all of the baseball games during the summer that were broadcast. He was also fond of football and was propped in bed to listen in on the game the day that Georgia beat New York University.

For 32 years Major Simmons served as trustee of the University of Georgia and was also a trustee of Georgia Tech for twelve years. His advancing years made it necessary for him to resign, he informed the governor in 1927, at which time he was the senior member of the board. He succeeded the late United States Senator H. V. M. Miller on the board.

In conferring the LLD degree on Major Simmons in 1919 at the University of Georgia, Chancellor David Barrow said, "In view of the distinguished service you have rendered the state and the University of Georgia, the conferring of this degree brings no additional honor to you, but you honor it."

In 1905 Major Simmons was president of the Gwinnett county fair when the Gwinnett county exhibit won the $1,000 prize for the display of farm products at the state fair in Atlanta.

Major Simmons is survived by his widow; one brother, Col. Terrell Simmons, of Atlanta; Col. Daniel M. Byrd of Decatur, a nephew of Mrs. Simmons, whom they reared, and a number of other nephews and nieces.

Pallbearers were: L. R. Martin, Scott Candler, E. L. Cain, William Akers, James T. Williams, Grady Vaughan, Thomas W. Mitchell, and Courtland S. Winn. Members of the Lawrenceville Bar Association and faculty of the University of Georgia acted as honorary pallbearers.

In speaking of Major Simmons as a business associate Mr. W. S. Witham, prominent Georgia banker, said: "Of the 75 partners I had in the banking business, located each in his own town and state, not one was more trustworthy than William E. Simmons. I have had many transactions with him in the past twenty-five years and have found him to be, in all commercial and social transactions, at home and abroad, prompt, accurate, accommodating and thoroughly reliable. He was a friend among many."

3rd Battalion Georgia Sharpshooters

Statistical Summary

Throughout the two years of its existence, at least 358 men served in the 3rd Georgia Sharpshooter Battalion. Of this number, fifteen officers and men served on the battalion staff. The men were fairly evenly divided among six companies, each with a total of about sixty soldiers.

Five companies were predominantly from one infantry regiment or battalion:

Company A 18th Georgia Infantry Regiment
Company B 24th Georgia Infantry Regiment
Company C 16th Georgia Infantry Regiment
Company D Cobb's Legion Infantry Battalion
Company F Phillips Legion Infantry Battalion
Company E 16th, 18th, and 24th Georgia Infantry Regiments and Phillips Legion Infantry Battalion.

Wofford's Sharpshooters came from a broad area of North Georgia, including company units from at least twenty-two different counties. Of the 316 sharpshooters for whom a home county is recorded, the largest concentration came from Cobb County. Combined, three of every ten (30.3 percent) were from one of three counties: Cobb, Cass (now Bartow), or Gwinnett.

Like their counterparts in the Confederate army, the men of the sharpshooter battalion were mostly young. Of the 122 men for which a year of birth is known, the average age at enlistment was 23.1 years and the median age was 22 years. Overall, the age at enlistment ranged from sixteen to forty-six. Nearly three-fifths (57.4 percent) of this group were in their twenties on the day they enlisted.

The sharpshooters were in the thick of the fighting as evidenced by the casualty rate. Of those who served, nineteen were killed in action and another six men died of wounds suffered in battle. Overall, about three in ten (103 or 29 percent) from the sharpshooter battalion were wounded in action, several two or more times.

During the two years the sharpshooter battalion was in existence, almost half (168; 47 percent) of the sharpshooters were captured. Of this group, most were apprehended at Front Royal on 16 August 1864 or Sailor's Creek on 6 April 1865. Another twenty deserted. Of those who were captured or deserted, eighteen took the oath of allegiance to the U.S. before the war ended and were either sent north or joined a U.S. military unit.

Prison took its toll on a large portion of the sharpshooters. A large majority of those captured were sent to Northern prisons. Of this group, three-fourths went to either Point Lookout (40 percent) or Elmira (35 percent). Most of the others were imprisoned at Fort Delaware or Johnson's Island. Of those who were sent to prison, fifteen died while incarcerated, mostly of sickness or disease.

Over the course of the war, many of the sharpshooters in the 3rd Battalion were afflicted by sickness or disease. In addition to the men who died in prison, an additional twenty-three died in camp or a hospital. The two most common causes of death were chronic diarrhea and variola (smallpox). Overall, the death rate from all causes was about 12 percent (43 of 358).

The 3rd Georgia Sharpshooters

The following roster summarizes the records of the soldiers who served in the 3rd Battalion Georgia Sharpshooters formed from the three regiments and two infantry battalions of General William T. Wofford's Brigade in spring 1863. The 358 soldiers are listed alphabetically by company, with officers at the head of the list. For each entry most information appears in chronological order. From compiled service records and other sources, there are numerous instances where there are two or more different spellings of a soldier's name. In those cases the most likely spelling is used. The information is maintained in a 358-record, 75-field data base to facilitate additional research analysis, with each individual assigned a unique number for reference and to distinguish one or more persons with the same name. The roster includes information for those men who served in the Confederate army *prior* to their transfer to the sharpshooter battalion. It also includes soldiers who were directly assigned to the sharpshooter battalion later in the war and those who were selected for the sharpshooter battalion but declined.

Information was obtained from the following sources, shown as 2-, 3- or 4-letter abbreviations for each soldier listed.

Baker, John William. *History of Hart County, Georgia*. 1933. Reprint, Hart Historical Society, 1951. (HHC)

Barrow, Hugh. *Private James R. Barrow and Company B of Cobb's Legion Infantry*. Carrollton, GA: self-published, 1996. (HB)

Bunch, Jack A. *Roster of the Courts-Martial in the Confederate States Armies*. Shippensburg, PA: White Mane Books, 2001. (CM)

Census of Confederate Soldiers—1905. (CCS)

Coffman, Richard M. and Kurt D. Graham. *To Honor These Men: History of Phillips Legion Infantry Battalion*. Macon: Mercer University Press, 2007. (PL)

Confederate Service Records. National Archives and Records Administration, Washington, DC. (SR)

Confederate State Roster (CSR)

Confederate Veteran. Monthly publication of the United Confederate Veterans and the sons of Confederate Veterans. (CV)

Cunyus, Lucy Josephine. *History of Bartow County, Georgia (formerly Cass)*. Revised reprint edition. Easley, SC: Southern Historical Press, 1988. (HBC)

Evans, Clement A., editor. *Georgia*. Vol. 7 of *Confederate Military History*. 1899. Reprint, Wilmington, NC: Broadfoot Publishing Co., 1987. (CMH)

Evans, Tad, compiler. *Milledgeville, Georgia, newspaper clippings from the Southern Recorder*. Vol. 11 (1862–1866). Savannah, GA: self-published, 1997. (MSR)

Flanigan, James C. *History of Gwinnett County, Georgia.* Vol. 1. 1943. Reprint, Lawrenceville, GA: Gwinnett Historical Society, 1995. (HGC)
———. *History of Gwinnett County, Georgia.* Vol. 2. 1959. Reprint, Lawrenceville, GA: Gwinnett Historical Society, 1999. (HGC)
Georgia United Daughters of the Confederacy. *Roster of Confederate Graves.* 9 vols and index. Atlanta, GA: 1995–2004. (UDC)
Henderson, Lillian, comp. *Roster of the Confederate Soldiers of Georgia, 1861–1865.* Volumes 1–4, plus index. Hapeville, GA: Longino & Porter, Inc., 1964. (LH)
Ingmire, Francis and Carolyn Ericson. *Confederate P.O.Ws: Soldiers and Sailors Who Died in Northern Prisons and Military Hospitals in the North.* Nacogdoches, TX: Ericson Books, 1984. (IE)
Ledford, Karen Ann Thompson, comp. *These Men Wore Grey: Genealogical, Military and Interment Records of Confederate Soldiers.* 8 vols. Toccoa, GA: self-published, 1998–2010. (TMWG)
Lyle, Thomas E., Larry O. Blair, Debra S. Lyle. *Organizational Summary of Military Organizations from Georgia in the Confederate States of America.* Marietta, GA: self-published, 1999. (OS)
Montgomery, George F. Jr. *Georgia Sharpshooter: The Civil War Diary and Letters of William Rhadamanthus Montgomery.* Macon: Mercer University Press, 1997. (GSS)
National Park Service. (NPS)
"Paroles of the Army of Northern Virginia." *Southern Historical Society Papers* 15 (January–December 1887): (SHSP)
Research Online. (RO)
Roster of Hutchins Guards, copy of roster accompanying a letter from Nathan Louis Hutchins Jr. to E. Porter Alexander. Lawrencville, GA: Gwinnett Historical Society Archives. (NLH)
Southern Watchman. Newspaper. Athens, GA. (SW)
Stallings, James E. Sr. *Georgia's Confederate Soldiers who Died as Prisoners of War 1861–1865...and Angels Did Attend and Comfort Them.* Macon, GA: Published by the author, 2009. (ST)
Turner, Nat, editor. *A Southern Soldier's Letters Home: The Civil War Letters of Samuel Burney, Army of Northern Virginia.* Macon: Mercer University Press, 2002. (BL)
Williams, Carol White, ed. *History of Greene County, Georgia.* Macon, GA: J. W. Burke Company, 1961. (HGC)
Wiltshire, Betty C. *Confederate Casualties of the War for Southern Independence.* Vol. 1. Carrollton, MS: Pioneer Publishing Co., 2008. (CCW)
Worthy, Marvin Nash. *History of Gwinnett County, Georgia, 1818–1893.* Vol. 3. Gwinnett Board of Commissioners, 1994. (HGC)

Please note that Confederate service records often contain misspellings, inaccurate and/or incomplete information and contradicting entries. In some cases the cards may show as many as three or more different spellings of names, enlistment dates, etc., for a specific individual. Given the probability of missing records, the following summaries are not collectively exhaustive. Additional details may be contained in the individual's service record and other sources researched that do not appear in the following summaries.

3rd Georgia Sharpshooter Battalion Roster

Battalion Commanders

Hutchins, Nathan Louis Jr. Enlisted for the war at Lawrenceville, Georgia (Gwinnett County), in the Gwinnett Volunteers (later, Hutchins Guards, formed 6 May 1861) 16 July 1861. 1st lieutenant, Company I, 16th Georgia Infantry Regiment. Promoted to captain. Transferred to take command of the 3rd Battalion Sharpshooters with the rank of lieutenant colonel, date of rank 10 June 1863. Succeeded Lieutenant Colonel A. W. Patton who was killed at the Battle of Chancellorsville. Wounded in the right shoulder 30 July 1864. Admitted to General Hospital #4, Richmond. Furloughed for forty days 24 August 1864. Battalion command relinquished to Major William E. Simmons until he was taken prisoner at Front Royal on 16 August 1864. Resumed command of the battalion on or before 29 September 1864. Captured at Sailor's Creek 6 April 1865. Oath of Allegiance indicates he was five feet seven inches, with dark complexion, dark hair, and dark eyes. Imprisoned at Johnson's Island; released 25 July 1865. Brother of Peyton Randolph Hutchins. Born in Lawrenceville, Georgia in 1835. Graduated from Emory College, Oxford, Georgia in 1855. Began law practice in 1857. Served three terms in the Georgia legislature.Western Circuit Superior Court Judge from 1882 until 1898. Died in Lawrenceville, Georgia, 8 June 1905. Buried in the Old Lawrenceville Methodist Church Cemetery. LH, HGC, GSS, NLH, SR, NPS, OS, CSR, CMH

Patton, A. H. Enlisted at Camp McDonald (Cobb County) 11 June 1861. Elected 2nd Lieutenant 26 June 1861 in Company C (Jackson Volunteers), 18th Georgia Infantry Regiment. Appointed adjutant of the 18th Georgia, 7 April 1862. Promoted to captain and appointed assistant adjutant general of Wofford's Brigade 17 February 1863. Recommended for promotion to lieutenant colonel and appointed commanding officer of the 3rd Georgia Sharpshooter Battalion 1 May 1863. Killed at Chancellorsville 6 May 6 1863. NLH, GSS, SR

Simmons, William E. Enlisted at Lawrenceville, Georgia (Gwinnett County), 16 July 1861. Elected 2nd lieutenant, Company I (Hutchins Guards), 16th Georgia Infantry Regiment. Promoted to 1st lieutenant. Transferred to Company C, 3rd Battalion Sharpshooters 8 June 1863. Promoted to captain, appointment date 17 June 1863 to take rank 5 June 1863. Promoted to major to take rank 18 September 1863. Captured at Front Royal 16 August 1864 while acting commander of the 3rd Battalion Sharpshooters. Committed to Old Capitol Prison, Washington, D. C. 21 August 1864. Transferred to Fort Delaware 27 August 1864; released 24 July 1865. Oath of Allegiance indicates he was five feet ten inches tall, with fair complexion, light hair, and blue eyes. Born 26 August 1839 in Lawrenceville, Georgia. Died 29 January 1931 in Lawrenceville, Georgia. Buried in Shadowlawn Cemetery, Lawrenceville, Georgia. LH, NLH, SR, NPS, OS, CSR, CMH

Battalion Staff:

Davant, Phillip E. Enlisted in Hartwell, Georgia (Hart County), 9 June 1861. Elected captain, Company B (Hart Volunteers), 24th Georgia Infantry Regiment 24 August 1861. Transferred to Company D, 3rd Battalion Sharpshooters 8 June 1863. Promoted to the rank of major 10 June 1863. Appointed lieutenant colonel to take rank 18 September 1863. Assignment to the 38th Georgia Infantry Regiment of General Clement A. Evans Brigade 1 October 1863. Captured at Spotsylvania 12 May 1864. Imprisoned at Fort Delaware; paroled 25 June 1864. Transferred for exchange to Hilton Head, South Carolina 26 June 1864 on the USS *Dragoon*. Returned to duty December 1864. Surrendered at Appomattox 9 April 1865. Roll at surrender indicates that he was five feet eight inches tall, with fair complexion, dark hair, and dark eyes. Born in Crawfordville, Georgia (Taliaferro County), March 1834. Died in Taylor County, Georgia, 9 October 1906. Buried at Butler Memorial Cemetery, Butler, Georgia (Taylor County). LH, HHC, SR, NPS, OS, CSR, CMH

Brengle, W. D. Commissioned September 1862 and assigned to General Hospital, Staunton, Virginia. December 1862, remained at Staunton General Hospital "Convalescent but still unfit for duty." Left Staunton for duty in the field. Appointed assistant surgeon, 3rd Battalion Sharpshooters June 1863. Captured at Gettysburg 5 July 1863. Sent to West's Buildings Hospital, Baltimore, Maryland 3 August 1863. Captured by the 8th Tennessee Infantry Regiment (U.S.) near Russellville, Tennessee 10 April 1864. Sent to Chattanooga 27 April 1864. Admitted to the Military Prison Hospital, Knoxville, Tennessee 4 May 1864. Returned to Duty 16 May 1864. Exchanged 28 September 1864 at Rough and Ready, Georgia. On roll dated January 1865. At Longstreet's Corps Infirmary near Richmond, 27 February 1865. Captured; paroled 25 April 1865. SR, NPS, CSR

Dennis, R. E. Assistant Surgeon, 3rd Battalion Sharpshooters. Surrendered at Appomattox 9 April 1865. SR, NPS, CSR

Dozier, L. F. Assistant Medical Officer, 3rd Battalion Sharpshooters. No later record. SR, NPS, CSR

Erwin, Joseph Bryan Enlisted at Camp McDonald (Cobb County), 25 June 1861. Private, Company C (Habersham Volunteers), Phillips Legion Infantry Battalion. Promoted to commissary sergeant in 1862. Transferred to the 3rd Battalion Sharpshooters. Surrendered at Appomattox 9 April 1965. Brother of Alexander S. Erwin of Phillips Legion Infantry Battalion. Born 15 January 1841. Died 1916. Buried in the Old Clarkesville Cemetery, Habersham County, Georgia. PL, NPS, CSR, SR

Farrill, Andrew Jackson Enlisted in Lawrenceville, Georgia (Gwinnett County), 16 July 1861. 2nd Sergeant, Company C, 3rd Battalion Sharpshooters. Detailed as commissary sergeant August 1864. Admitted to Jackson Hospital, Richmond for the treatment of pneumonia 4 January 1865. Returned to duty 20 January 1865. Surrendered at Appomattox 9 April 1865. Born 1836 in Georgia. Died 1913 in Newton, Georgia. HGC, SHSP, SR, NPS, CSR

Phillips, James Patton Enlisted in Company C, Phillips Legion Infantry Battalion 18 December 1861. Elected 2nd lieutenant 18 December 1861. Wounded in the leg at Fredericksburg 13 December 1862. Transferred to 3rd Battalion Sharpshooters 1 May 1863.Wounded at Chancellorsville 3 May 1863. Admitted to General Hospital #4, Richmond 4 May 1863. Returned to his command 19 May 1863. Promoted to captain and quartermaster, date of rank 25 June 1863. Inspection report dated 28 November 1864 shows him on duty at I Corps Headquarters (General Anderson) near Richmond. Shown as quartermaster in Anderson's Corps March 1865. No later record. Born in 1826. Died in 1918. Buried in the Phillips Family Cemetery (Farm Hill) near Clarkesville, Georgia. UDC, PL, SR, NPS, CSR

Strickland, Elisha W. Enlisted in the Gwinnett (County) Volunteers 16 July 1861. Private, Company I, 16th Georgia Infantry Regiment. Promoted to 1st sergeant. Transferred to the staff of the 3rd Battalion Sharpshooters with the rank of sergeant major. Acting battalion adjutant. Roll for 1 July 1864 shows him present. No later record. LH, HGC, NLH, NPS, CSR, SR

Williams, James H. Enlisted at White County, Georgia, 24 August 1861. Private, Company C (White County Marksmen), 24th Georgia Infantry Regiment. Transferred to the 3rd Battalion Sharpshooters. Promoted to 1st lieutenant, date of rank 29 June 1863. Battalion Adjutant. Captured at Sailor's Creek 6 April 1865. Imprisoned at Johnson's Island; released 20 June 1865. Oath indicates that he was five feet eight inches tall, with fair complexion, light hair, and blue eyes. LH, SR, NPS, CSR

Sharpshooter Company A

Company Officers:

Crumley, M. F. Enlisted at Camp McDonald (Cobb County), 26 June 1861. 3rd Lieutenant, Company B (Newton Rifles) 18th Georgia Infantry Regiment. Promoted to 1st lieutenant 2 August 1862. Transferred to Company A, 3rd Battalion Sharpshooters. Promoted to captain 5 June 1863. Captured at Cedar Creek 19 October 1864. Imprisoned at Fort Delaware; released 17 June 1865. Oath of Allegiance indicates that he was five feet eight inches tall, with dark complexion, dark hair and blue eyes. LH, NLH, SR, NPS, OS, CSR

Cook, John S. Enlisted in Cass (now Bartow) County, Georgia, 26 June 1861. Private, Company K (Rowland Infantry), 18th Georgia Infantry Regiment. Admitted to General Hospital, Farmville, Virginia 6 November 1862. Returned to duty 22 December 1862. Transferred to Company A, 3rd Battalion Sharpshooters 8 June 1863. Promoted to 5th Sergeant. Promoted to lieutenant. Captured at Farmville, Virginia (Sailor's Creek) 6 April 1865. Imprisoned at Point Lookout; released 10 June 1865. LH, SR, NPS, OS, CSR

Guinn, T. D. Enlisted at Camp McDonald (Cobb County), 11 June 1861. 2nd Sergeant, Company B (Newton Rifles), 18th Georgia Infantry Regiment. Wounded at

Cold Harbor 27 June 1862. Transferred to Company A, 3rd Battalion Sharpshooters 1 April 1863. Promoted to 2nd lieutenant: date of appointment 17 June 1863; to take rank 5 June 1863; date of confirmation 17 February 1864. Inspection Report dated 27 February 1865 states that he was "Absent with leave. Left camp February 8, 1865." No later record. LH, SR, NPS, OS, CSR

Enlisted Men:

Allen, J. R. Enlisted at Camp McDonald, Marietta, Georgia (Cobb County), 13 June 1861. Private, Company K (Rowland Infantry), 18th Georgia Infantry Regiment. Transferred to Company A, 3rd Battalion Sharpshooters 8 June 1863. Captured at Front Royal 16 August 1864. Imprisoned at Elmira; released 11 July 1865. LH, SR, NPS, CSR

Anderson, William B. Enlisted at Homer, Georgia (Banks County), 24 August 1861. Private, Company A (Independent Volunteers), 24th Georgia Infantry Regiment. Transferred to Company B, 3rd Battalion Sharpshooters 8 June 1863. Admitted to Howards Grove Farm Hospital, Richmond. On furlough of indulgence 31 August 1864. Transferred to duty in Athens, Georgia, 8 May 1865. Captured and paroled on 8 May 1865. LH, SR, NPS, CSR

Belk, H. C. Enlisted at Camp McDonald (Cobb County) 13 June 1861. Private, Company H (Rowland Highlanders), 18th Georgia Infantry Regiment. Transferred to Company A, 3rd Battalion Sharpshooters 8 June 1863. Admitted to Henningsen Hospital, Richmond 31 August 1863; returned to duty 7 September 1863. Admitted to Stuart Hospital, Richmond for treatment of chronic diarrhea 4 July 1864; returned to duty 20 July 1864. Captured at Front Royal 16 August 1864. Admitted to Old Capitol Prison 21 August 1864. Transferred to Elmira 28 August 1864; released 11 July 1865. Oath of Allegiance shows him to be six feet tall, with fair complexion, light hair and hazel eyes. LH, SR, NPS, CSR

Belk, L. J. Enlisted at Camp McDonald (Cobb County) 26 June 1861. Private, Company H (Rowland Highlanders). Wounded at 2nd Manassas 30 August 1862. Transferred to Company A, 3rd Battalion Sharpshooters 18 June 1863. Captured at Gettysburg 3 July 1863. Imprisoned at Fort Delaware 7 July 1863; released for exchange 1 February 1865; received at Boulware & Cox's Wharves 10 March 1865. LH, SR, NPS, CSR

Burnett, William P. Enlisted at Adairsville, Georgia (Cass County, now Bartow) 3 August 1861. Private, Company K (Rowland Infantry), 18th Georgia Infantry Regiment. Wounded at Sharpsburg 17 September 1862. Wounded at Cold Harbor 27 September 1862. Admitted to Camp Winder Hospital, Richmond 28 September 1862. Returned to duty. Transferred to Company A, 3rd Battalion Sharpshooters 8 June 1863 with the rank of 3rd corporal. Wounded at Chattanooga 23 September 1863. Promoted to 3rd sergeant in 1864. Captured at High Bridge, Virginia (Sailor's Creek) 6 April 1865. Imprisoned at Point Lookout; released 24 June 1865. Oath of Allegiance indicates that he was five feet six inches tall, with fair complexion, brown hair and gray eyes. LH, SR, NPS, CSR

Byers, J. W. Enlisted at Camp McDonald (Cobb County) 26 June 1861. Private. Transferred to Company A, 3rd Battalion Sharpshooters. Roll for 31 August 1864 indicates that he was absent without leave. No later record. SR, NPS, CSR

Conn, James M. Enlisted at Camp McDonald, Marietta, Georgia (Cobb County), 26 June 1861. Private, Company F (Davis Guards), 18th Georgia Infantry Regiment. Wounded at 2nd Manassas 30 August 1862. Transferred to Company A, 3rd Battalion Sharpshooters 8 June 1863. Captured at Petersburg 29 July 1864. Imprisoned at Elmira; released 7 July 1865. LH, SR, NPS, CSR

Cunningham, C. W. Enlisted at Bristol, Tennessee 28 March 1864. Private, Company A, 3rd Battalion Sharpshooters. Wounded in the right cheek, date and location not recorded. Admitted to Jackson Hospital 15 May 1864. Admitted to Jackson Hospital for treatment of chronic diarrhea 7 August 1864. Furloughed for thirty days 2 September 1864. Surrendered at Appomattox 9 April 1865. SHSP, SR, NPS, CSR

Dysart, James M. Enlisted at Camp McDonald (Cobb County) 11 June 1861. Private, Company H (Rowland Highlanders), 18th Georgia Infantry Regiment. Admitted to Camp Winder Hospital, Richmond for treatment of diarrhea 9 May 1862. Returned to duty 17 May 1862. Transferred to Company A, 3rd Battalion Sharpshooters 8 June 1863 with the rank of 4th sergeant. Demoted to private 1 June 1864. Pension records show he surrendered at Appomattox 9 April 1865. Born 1845 in Georgia. LH, SR, NPS, CSR

Ellis, J. P. Enlisted at Camp McDonald (Cobb County) 26 June 1861. Private, Company B (Newton Rifles), 18th Georgia Infantry Regiment. Wounded in the arm at Fredericksburg 12 December 1862. Admitted to Chimborazo Hospital #2, Richmond 15 December 1862. Transferred to Confederate Hospital, Danville, Virginia 23 December 1862. Returned to duty 18 January 1863. Transferred to Company A, 3rd Battalion Sharpshooters 8 June 1863. Killed in action at Winchester 1 October 1864. Born *ca.* 1838. LH, SR, NPS, MSR, CSR

Franks, J. S. Enlisted in Bartow County, Georgia, 22 February 1862. Private, Company K (Rowland Infantry), 18th Georgia Infantry Regiment. Transferred to Company A, 3rd Battalion Sharpshooters 8 June 1863. Detailed to McLaws Division as a shoemaker from January to May 1864. Promoted to 4th sergeant June 1864. Name appears on a receipt roll dated 27 November 1864. No later record. LH, SR, NPS, CSR

Gordon, Charles P. Enlisted at Camp McDonald (Cobb County) 13 June 1861. Private, Company H (Rowland Highlanders), 18th Georgia Infantry Regiment. Transferred to Company A, 3rd Battalion Sharpshooters 8 June 1863. Captured at High Bridge, Virginia 6 April 1865. Imprisoned at Point Lookout; released 27 June 1865. Oath of Allegiance indicates he was five feet six inches tall, with light complexion, auburn hair and blue eyes. LH, SR, NPS, CSR

Goree, John William Enlisted at Richmond, Virginia 20 September 1861. Private, Company B (Newton Rifles), 18th Georgia Infantry Regiment 20 September 1861.

Admitted to Camp Winder Hospital for treatment of diarrhea 4 July 1862. Returned to duty 12 July 1862. Transferred to Company A, 3rd Battalion Sharpshooters 8 June 1863. Wounded in left knee at Funkstown, Maryland 11 July 1863. Captured at Williamsport, Maryland 14 July 1863. Admitted to Seminary Hospital, Hagerstown, Maryland. Transferred to U.S. Hospital, Chambersburg, Pennsylvania 16 September 1863. Died from wounds 29 September 1863. LH, ST, SR, NPS, CSR.

Guinn, John Enlisted at Big Shanty, Georgia (Cobb County), 26 June 1861. Private. Discharged 28 October 1861. Reenlisted at Conyers, Georgia (Rockdale County), 22 February 1862. Private, Company B (Newton Rifles), 18th Georgia Infantry Regiment. Wounded in right leg at Cold Harbor 27 June 1862. Admitted to Chimborazo Hospital #2 6 October 1862. Transferred to Company A, 3rd Battalion Sharpshooters 8 June 1863. Admitted to Jackson Hospital, Richmond for treatment of dysentery 26 May 1864. Returned to duty 1 June 1864. Surrendered at Appomattox 9 April 1865. LH, SR, NPS, CSR

Henderson, Levi D. Enlisted at Camp McDonald (Cobb County) 19 June 1861. Private, Company K (Rowland Infantry), 18th Georgia Infantry Regiment. Transferred to Company A, 3rd Battalion Sharpshooters 8 June 1863. Captured near Williamsport, Maryland 11 July 1863. Imprisoned at Point Lookout. Took Oath of Allegiance to the U.S. Government on 25 January 1865 and enlisted in U.S. service. Oath of Allegiance indicates he was six feet tall, with dark complexion, brown hair and blue eyes. LH, SR, NPS, CSR

Hill, William J. Enlisted at Conyers, Georgia (Rockdale County), 22 February 1862. Private, Company B (Newton Rifles), 18th Georgia Infantry Regiment 22 February 1862. Transferred to Company A, 3rd Georgia Sharpshooters 8 June 1863. Wounded at Spotsylvania, 12 May 1864. Admitted to Stuart Hospital, Richmond 4 July 1864. Returned to duty 20 July 1864. Captured at Petersburg, 29 July 1864. Imprisoned at Elmira, released 14 June 1865. Oath of Allegiance indicates he was five feet nine inches tall, with florid complexion, light hair and blue eyes. Born *ca.* 1843. LH, SR, NPS, CSR

Hollyman, W. F. Enlisted at Camp McDonald, Marietta, Georgia (Cobb County), 26 June 1861. Private, Company A, 3rd Battalion Sharpshooters. Admitted to Jackson Hospital, Richmond for treatment of chronic diarrhea 9 August 1864. Furloughed for thirty days 14 August 1864. No later record. SR, NPS, CSR

Humphries, C. H. Enlisted at Camp McDonald (Cobb County) 26 June 1861. Private, Company B (Newton Rifles), 18th Georgia Infantry Regiment. Wounded near Fredericksburg 18 December 1862. Transferred to Company A, 3rd Battalion Sharpshooters 8 June 1863. Wounded at Chancellorsville 3 May 1863. Wounded at Chickamauga 19 September 1863. Wounded in the right leg in May 1864, location not recorded. Admitted to Jackson Hospital 28 May 1864. Admitted to Chimborazo Hospital, Richmond 17 September 1864. Furloughed for thirty days 21 September 1864. Absent, wounded at the end of the war. LH, SR, NPS, CSR

Jenkins, Eli Enlisted at Camp McDonald (Cobb County) 13 June 1861. Private, Company H (Rowland Highlanders), 18th Georgia Infantry Regiment. Wounded at Fredericksburg 18 December 1862. Transferred to Company A, 3rd Battalion Sharpshooters 8 June 1863. Wounded in the left hand at Chancellorsville 2 May 1863. Admitted to Chimborazo Hospital #2, Richmond 6 May 1864. Transferred to CSA Hospital, Lynchburg, Virginia 8 May 1864. Returned to duty. Wounded at Spotsylvania 12 May 1864. Captured at Burkeville, Virginia 6 April 1865. Imprisoned at Point Lookout; released 28 June 1865. Oath of Allegiance indicates he was five feet ten inches tall, with dark complexion, dark hair and hazel eyes. Born in Lincoln County North Carolina in 1843. LH, SR, NPS, CSR

Lawson, Jasper B. Enlisted at Camp McDonald (Cobb County) 13 June 1861. Private, Company F (Davis Guards), 18th Georgia Infantry Regiment. Transferred to Company A, 3rd Battalion Sharpshooters 8 June1863. Captured at Williamsport, Maryland July 12, 1863. Imprisoned at Point Lookout; released for exchange 18 February 1865; received at Boulware & Cox's wharves 20 February 1865. No later record. LH, SR, NPS, CSR

Ledbetter, Charles Enlisted at Camp McDonald (Cobb County) 28 June 1861. Private, Company K (Rowland Infantry), 18th Georgia Infantry Regiment. Wounded at Sharpsburg 17 September 1862. Admitted to Camp Winder Hospital, Richmond 28 September 1862. Furloughed for thirty days 3 October 1862. Transferred to Company A, 3rd Battalion Sharpshooters 8 June 1863. Roll dated August 1864 shows him in the hospital. No later record. LH, NPS, CSR, SR

Ledbetter, Daniel Enlisted at Camp McDonald (Cobb County) 28 July 1861. Private, Company K (Rowland Infantry), 18th Georgia Infantry Regiment. Wounded at 2nd Manassas 30 August 1862. Captured and paroled at Warrenton, Virginia 29 September 1862. Transferred to Company A, 3rd Battalion Sharpshooters 8 June 1863. Wounded in 1863. Roll dated August 1864 shows him absent without leave. No later record. LH, NPS, CSR, SR

Ledbetter, Richard Enlisted at Camp McDonald (Cobb County) 17 July 1861. Private, Company K (Rowland Infantry), 18th Georgia Infantry Regiment. Admitted to Camp Winder Hospital for treatment of diarrhea 10 July 1862. Returned to duty 14 July 1862. Captured and paroled at Warrenton, Virginia 29 September 1862. Transferred to Company A, 3rd Battalion Sharpshooters 8 June 1863 with the rank of 4th corporal. Wounded in 1864. Roll for August 1864 shows him on wounded furlough. No later record. LH, NPS, CSR

Ledbetter, William Enlisted at Griffin, Georgia (Spalding County), 3 September 1861. Private. Transferred to Company K (Rowland Infantry), 18th Georgia Infantry Regiment 14 November 1861. Admitted to Camp Winder Hospital, Richmond, 28 September 1862. Returned to duty 5 October 1862. Transferred to Company A, 3rd Battalion Sharpshooters. No later record. CSR, SR

Mann, L. M. Enlisted at Camp McDonald (Cobb County) 13 June 1861. Private, Company H (Rowland Highlanders), 18th Georgia Infantry Regiment. Transferred to

Company A, 3rd Battalion Sharpshooters 8 June 1863 with the rank of 1st corporal. Wounded at Chancellorsville 3 May 1863. Wounded at Chickamauga 19 September 1863. Captured at Stasburg, Virginia (Cedar Creek) 19 October 1864. Imprisoned at Point Lookout; released for exchange 28 March 1865; received at Boulware & Cox's Wharves 30 March 1865. No later record. LH, SR, NPS, CSR

Mcdonald, Robert F. Enlisted at Camp McDonald (Cobb County) 26 June 1861. 2nd Corporal, Company B (Newton Rifles), 18th Georgia Infantry Regiment. Wounded at Malvern Hill 1 July 1862. Transferred to Company A, 3rd Battalion Sharpshooters 1 April 1863 with the rank of 1st sergeant. Reduction in rank to private. Surrendered at Appomattox 9 April 1865. LH, SR, NPS, CSR

McMurray, John A. Private, Company A, 3rd Battalion Sharpshooters. SR, NPS, CSR

Miller, H. H. Enlisted at Camp McDonald (Cobb County) 26 June 1861. Private, Company B (Newton Rifles), 18th Georgia Infantry Regiment. Wounded in the hip at Cold Harbor 27 June 1862. Transferred to Company A, 3rd Battalion Sharpshooters 8 June 1863. Captured at Front Royal 16 August 1864. Committed to Old Capitol Prison, Washington, D. C. 21 August 1864. Transferred to Elmira 21 August 1864; released 16 June 1865. Oath of Allegiance indicates he was six feet tall, with fair complexion, Brown hair and blue eyes. Died 24 August 1917, Lithonia, Georgia. LH, SR, NPS, CSR

Morgan, Thomas J. Enlisted at Conyers, Georgia (Rockdale County), 15 February 1862. Private, Company B (Newton Rifles), 18th Georgia Infantry Regiment. Transferred to Company A, 3rd Battalion Sharpshooters 8 June 1863. Absent without leave August 1864. No later record. Born *ca.* 1836. LH, SR, NPS, CSR

Parker, George W. Enlisted at Camp McDonald (Cobb County) 26 June 1861. Private, Company B (Newton Rifles), 18th Georgia Infantry Regiment. Transferred to Company A, 3rd Battalion Sharpshooters 8 June 1863. Wounded and captured at Gettysburg 5 July 1863. Imprisoned at Fort Delaware. Released for exchange 1 February 1865; received at Boulware & Cox's Wharves 10 March 1865. Born *ca.* 1826. LH, SR, NPS, CSR

Phelps, William N. Enlisted at Conyers, Georgia (Rockdale County), 26 June 1861. Private, Company B (Newton Rifles), 18th Georgia Infantry Regiment. Wounded at Cold Harbor 27 June 1862. Captured at Sharpsburg 28 September 1862. Released for exchange from Fortress Monroe 1 November 1862. Received at Aiken's Landing 10 November 1862. Returned to duty. Transferred to Company A, 3rd Battalion Sharpshooters 8 June 1863. Admitted to General Hospital, Petersburg, Virginia 2 February 1864. Furloughed for thirty days 17 February 1864. On detached duty at Richmond hospital until August 1864. No later record. LH, SR, NPS, CSR

Reagan, James William Enlisted at Camp McDonald (Cobb County) 11 July 1861. Private, Company K (Rowland Infantry), 18th Georgia Infantry Regiment. Wounded in the hand at Fredericksburg 13 December 1862. Admitted to Chimbozaro Hospital #2,

Richmond 15 December 1862. Returned to duty 22 December 1862. Transferred to Company A, 3rd Battalion Sharpshooters 8 June 1863. Wounded and captured at Gettysburg 3 July 1863. Imprisoned at Fort Delaware; released 10 May 1865. Oath of allegiance indicates he was five feet seven inches tall, with light complexion, light hair and blue eyes. LH, SR, NPS

Rice, G. W. Enlisted at Camp McDonald (Cobb County) 15 July 1861. Private, Company K (Rowland Infantry), 18th Georgia Infantry Regiment. Transferred to Company A, 3rd Battalion Sharpshooters 8 June 1863 with the rank of 3rd Sergeant. Discharged 22 September 1864 with the rank of private. LH, SR, NPS, CSR

Richardson, S. J. Enlisted at Camp McDonald (Cobb County) 26 June 1861. Private, Company B (Newton Rifles), Company B, 18th Georgia Infantry Regiment. Wounded in the left hand at Chancellorsville 3 May 1863. Admitted to Chimbozaro Hospital, Richmond 28 May 1863. Transferred to Company A, 3rd Battalion Sharpshooters 8 June 1863. Transferred to CSA Hospital, Danville 16 June 1863. Returned to duty. Admitted to Jackson Hospital, Richmond 26 May 1864. Admitted to Jackson Hospital, Richmond 29 May 1864. Returned to duty 14 October 1864. Admitted to Jackson Hospital, Richmond 19 November 1864. Returned to duty 7 December 1864. No later record. LH, SR, NPS, CSR

Sims, Richard Simpson Enlisted at Conyers, Georgia (Rockdale County), 22 February 1862. Private, Company B (Newton Rifles), 18th Georgia Infantry Regiment. Transferred to Company A, 3rd Battalion Sharpshooters 8 June 1863. Wounded at Chickamauga 19 September 1863. Roll for August 1864, last on file, states that he was absent, wounded. No later record. LH, NPS, CSR, SR

Slaughter, E. J. Enlisted at Bristol, Tennessee 30 February 1864. 4th Corporal, Company A, 3rd Battalion Sharpshooters. Roll for June 1864 states we was absent with leave. No later record. NPS, CSR, SR

Slaughter, T. B. Enlisted at Camp McDonald (Cobb County) 26 June 1861. Private, Company K (Rowland Infantry), 18th Georgia Infantry Regiment. Wounded at Sharpsburg 17 September 1862. Admitted to CSA General Hospital, Farmville, Virginia 12 November 1862. Returned to duty 22 December 1862. Appointed 1st sergeant 3 May 1863. Transferred to Company A, 3rd Battalion Sharpshooters 8 June 1863. Promoted to 1st Lieutenant, date of rank 5 June 1863. Captured at Sailor's Creek 6 April 1865. Committed to Old Capitol Prison, Washington, D. C. 14 April 1865. Transferred to Johnson's Island 17 April 1865; released 20 June 1865. Oath of Allegiance indicates he was five feet ten inches tall, with dark complexion, dark hair and hazel eyes. LH, SR, NPS, OS, CSR

Smith, George T. Enlisted at Camp McDonald (Cobb County) 26 June 1861. Private, Company B (Newton Rifles), 18th Georgia Infantry Regiment. Transferred to Company A, 3rd Battalion Sharpshooters 8 June 1863. Captured at Farmville, Virginia (Sailor's Creek) 6 April 1865. Imprisoned at Point Lookout; released 20 June 20. Oath of

Allegiance indicates he was five feet eight inches tall, with dark complexion, brown hair and blue eyes. LH, NPS, CSR, SR

Smith, Joseph N. Enlisted at Camp McDonald (Cobb County) 26 June 1861. Private, Company K (Rowland Infantry), 18th Georgia Infantry Regiment. Wounded, captured, and paroled at 2nd Manassas 30 August 1862. Transferred to Company A, 3rd Battalion Sharpshooters 8 June 1863. Admitted to Chimborazo Hospital #2, Richmond 18 June 1863. Returned to duty 15 July 1863. Captured at Front Royal 16 August 1864. Committed to Old Capitol Prison, Washington, D. C. 21 August 1864. Transferred to Elmira 28 August 1864; released 30 June 1865. Oath of Allegiance indicates he was five feet eight inches tall, with florid complexion, light hair and blue eyes. LH, NPS, CSR, SR

Smith, P. C. Enlisted at Camp McDonald (Cobb County) 13 June 1861. Private, Company H (Rowland Highlanders), 18th Georgia Infantry Regiment. Admitted to CSA Hospital, Danville, Virginia 2 July 1862 for treatment of debilitas. Returned to duty 10 July 1862. Captured and Paroled at Warrenton, Virginia 29 September 1862. Transferred to Company A, 3rd Battalion Sharpshooters 8 June 1863. Captured in 1864, date and location not recorded. Roll dated January 1865 shows him "Absent, in hands of the enemy." No later record. LH, NPS, CSR, SR

Smith, William H. C. Enlisted on 10 April 1862. Private, Company K (Rowland Infantry), 18th Georgia Infantry Regiment. Wounded in the hip at Cold Harbor 27 June 1862. Admitted to General Hospital, Howards Grove Farm, Richmond 13 September 1862. Returned to duty 19 October 1862. Admitted to General Hospital #7, Richmond 24 October 1862. Furloughed November 1862. Returned to duty. Wounded at Fredericksburg 13 December 1862. Transferred to Company A, 3rd Battalion Sharpshooters 8 June 1863. On furlough 31 August 1864. No later record. LH, NPS, CSR, SR

Stansell, Richard A. Enlisted at Camp McDonald (Cobb County) 26 June 1861. Private, Company B (Newton Rifles), 18th Georgia Infantry Regiment. Transferred to Company A, 3rd Battalion Sharpshooters 8 June 1863. Absent, wounded 31 August 1864. No later record. Born *ca.* 1840. LH, NPS, CSR, SR

Stansell, William S. Enlisted at Conyers, Georgia, 13 August 1861. Private, Company B (Newton Rifles), 18th Georgia Infantry Regiment. Admitted to CSA General Hospital, Howard's Grove, Richmond for treatment of anemia 13 September 1862. Returned to duty 23 September 1862. Transferred to Company A, 3rd Battalion Sharpshooters 8 June 1863 with the rank of 2nd corporal. Captured at Farmville, Virginia (Sailors Creek), 6 April 1865. Imprisoned at Point Lookout; released 20 June 1865. Oath of Allegiance indicates that he was five feet nine inches tall, with dark complexion, dark brown hair and blue eyes. Born *ca.* 1843. LH, NPS, CSR, SR

Steadman, Albert W. Enlisted in Bartow County 26 April 1862. Private, Company K, 18th Georgia Infantry Regiment. Admitted to Chimborazo Hospital #3, Richmond for treatment of debility 4 October 1862. Furloughed for forty days 25 October 1862.

Returned to duty. Transferred to Company A, 3rd Battalion Sharpshooters 8 June 1863. Captured near Williamsport, Maryland 11 July 1863. Imprisoned at Point Lookout. Transferred for exchange at City Point, Virginia 16 March 1864. Returned to battalion. Captured at High Bridge, Virginia 6 April 1865. Imprisoned at Point Lookout; released 19 June 1865. Oath of Allegiance indicates he was five feet eight inches tall, with light complexion, light brown hair and gray eyes. LH, NPS, CSR, SR

Stowers, Hering H. Enlisted at Camp McDonald (Cobb County) 26 June 1861. Private, Company B (Newton Rifles), 18th Georgia Infantry Regiment. Transferred to Company A, 3rd Battalion Sharpshooters 1 May 1863. Wounded at Chickamauga 19 September 1863. Absent, wounded 31 August 1864. No later record. Born 1842 in Dekalb County, Georgia. LH, NPS, CSR, SR

Taylor, J. H. Enlisted at Conyers, Georgia (Rockdale County), 15 February 1862. Private, Company B (Newton Rifles), 18th Georgia Infantry Regiment. Transferred to Company A, 3rd Battalion Sharpshooters 8 June 1863. Wounded in the right thigh near Chattanooga. Admitted to Stuart Hospital, Richmond 6 June 1864. Transferred to Jackson Hospital, Richmond 7 June 1864. Furloughed for forty days 15 July 1864. Roll for August 1864 states he was absent, on wounded furlough. No later record. Born *ca.* 1838. SR

Thomas, N. T. Enlisted at Bristol, Tennessee 28 March 1864. Private, Company A, 3rd Battalion Sharpshooters. Roll for August 1864, last on file, states he was absent, in the hands of the enemy. No later record. NPS, CSR, SR

Thorn, Hezekiah G. B. Enlisted at Camp McDonald (Cobb County) 26 June 1861. Private, Company B (Newton Rifles), 18th Georgia Infantry Regiment. Admitted to Camp Winder Hospital, Richmond for treatment of parotitis 4 July 1862. Returned to duty 12 July 1862. Transferred to Company A, 3rd Battalion Sharpshooters 8 June 1863 with the rank of 5th Sergeant. Captured at Farmville, Virginia (Sailor's Creek) 6 April 1865. Imprisoned at Point Lookout; released 21 June 1865. Oath of Allegiance indicates he was five feet nine inches tall, with fair complexion, sandy hair and hazel eyes. LH, NPS, CSR, SR

Underwood, D. E. Enlisted at Camp McDonald (Cobb County) 26 June 1861. Private. Transferred to Company A, 3rd Battalion Sharpshooters. Roll for August 1864 states he was absent, on furlough. No later record. NPS, CSR, SR

Upshaw, James M. Enlisted on 13 June 1861. Private, Company H (Rowland Highlanders), 18th Georgia Infantry Regiment. Transferred to Company A, 3rd Battalion Sharpshooters 8 June 1863 with the rank of 2nd Sergeant. Promoted to 1st Sergeant in 1864. Captured at Front Royal 16 August 1864. Committed to Old Capitol Prison, Washington, D. C. 21 August 1864. Transferred to Elmira 28 August 1864; released for exchange 10 March 1865. Received at James River. No later record. LH, NPS, CSR, SR

Ward, John Enlisted at Camp McDonald (Cobb County) 13 June 1861. Private, Company H (Rowland Highlanders), 18th Georgia Infantry Regiment. Detailed as teamster on brigade duty 15 December 1861. Wounded at Seven Pines 1 June 1862. Transferred to Company A, 3rd Battalion Sharpshooters 8 June 1863. Roll for 31 August 1864, last on file, shows him absent without leave. No later record. LH, NPS, CSR, SR

White, Hugh L. Enlisted at Conyers, Georgia (Rockdale County), 15 February 1862. Private, Company B (Newton Rifles), 18th Georgia Infantry Regiment. Captured at Williamsburg, Virginia 6 May 1862. Imprisoned; sent to Fort Delaware 21 June 1862. Exchanged at Aiken's Landing 5 August 1862. Transferred to Company A, 3rd Battalion Sharpshooters 8 June 1863. Captured at Funkstown, Maryland July 12, 1863. Imprisoned at Point Lookout; released for exchange 1 November 1864. Received at Venus Point, Savannah River 15 November 1864. No later record. U.S. Prison Register indicates he was five feet nine inches tall, with dark complexion, black hair and black eyes. Born *ca.* 1838. LH, NPS, CSR, SR

Winborn, John A. Enlisted at Camp McDonald (Cobb County) 26 June 1862. Private, Company B (Newton Rifles), 18th Georgia Infantry Regiment. Wounded in thigh, date and location not recorded. Admitted to Chimborazo Hospital #1, Richmond 30 June 1862. Returned to duty 9 July 1862. Transferred to Company A, 3rd Battalion Sharpshooters 8 June 1863. Wounded and captured at Cold Harbor 1 June 1864. No later record. Service record shows he was absent without leave from 31 August 1863 to 1 March 1864 with no mention of wounding or capture at Cold Harbor. LH, NPS, CSR, SR

Wofford, William B. Enlisted at Camp McDonald (Cobb County) 13 June 1861. Private, Company H (Rowland Highlanders), 18th Georgia Infantry Regiment. Transferred to Company A 3rd Battalion Sharpshooters 8 June 1863. Absent, sick from 1 November 1863 to 1 March 1864. No later record. LH, NPS, CSR, SR

Worsham, William W. Enlisted at Camp McDonald (Cobb County) June 1861. Private, Company C (Jackson Volunteers), 18th Georgia Infantry Regiment. Admitted to Chimborazo Hospital #1, Richmond 18 November 1861. Returned to duty 28 November 1861. Admitted to Chimborazo Hospital #2, Richmond for treatment of ulcer on arm 4 May 1863. Transferred to CSA Hospital, Lynchburg, Virginia 7 May 1863. Returned to duty. Transferred to Company A, 3rd Battalion Sharpshooters 8 June 1863. Detailed as a teamster January and February 1864. Captured at Sailor's Creek 6 April 1865. Imprisoned at Point Lookout; released 22 June 1865. Oath of Allegiance indicates he was five feet six inches tall, with fair complexion, sandy hair, and gray eyes. LH, NPS, CSR, SR

Sharpshooter Company B

Company Officers:

Arnold, Medicus Franklin Enlisted at Clarkesville, Georgia (Habersham County), 24 August 1861. Private, Company K (McMillan Guards) 24th Georgia Infantry Regiment. Promoted to Captain to take rank 1 May 1862. A.C.S. for the 24th Georgia. Transferred to Company B, 3rd Battalion Sharpshooters 8 June 1863. Surrendered at Appomattox 9 April 1865. Buried in Fork Cemetery, Madison County, Georgia. Born 13 June 1827 in Wilkes County, Georgia. Died 13 February 1908 in Madison County, Georgia. LH, UDC, SR, NPS, TMWG, CSR, MP

Chandler, Elias H. Enlisted in Homer, Georgia (Banks County), 24 August 1861. Private, Company A (Independent Volunteers), 24th Georgia Infantry Regiment. Transferred to Company B, 3rd Battalion Sharpshooters. Promoted to 2nd lieutenant 5 June 1863. Absent without leave from 10 April 1864. Admitted to Jackson Hospital, Richmond 31 July 1864. Appears without remark on roll dated 31 August 1864. No later record. LH, SR, NPS, OS, CSR

McMillan, Garnett Enlisted 24 August 1861. 2nd Lieutenant, Company K 24th Georgia Infantry Regiment. Wounded in the face at Fredericksburg 13 December 1862. Transferred to Company B 3rd Battalion Sharpshooters. Promoted to Captain, date of rank 5 June 1863. Detailed to General Rains Staff August 1864. No later record. NLH, SR, NPS, OS, CSR

Moseley, Milton M. Enlisted 18 September 1861. Private, Company A (Independent Volunteers), 24th Georgia Infantry Regiment. Transferred to Company B, 3rd Battalion Sharpshooters. Promoted to 1st Lieutenant, date of rank 5 June 1863. Captured at the Wilderness 10 May 1864. Imprisoned at Fort Delaware 17 May 1864. Sent to Hilton Head, South Carolina 20 August 1864. Sent to Fort Pulaski, Georgia, date not recorded. Imprisoned, held captive 26 December 1864. Returned to Fort Delaware from Hilton Head, South Carolina; received 12 March 1865. Released 16 June 1865. Oath of Allegiance indicates he was six feet tall, with dark complexion, dark hair and hazel eyes. SR, IC

Enlisted Men:

Barnes, William W. Enlisted at Homer, Georgia (Banks County), 24 August 1861. Private, Company A (Independent Volunteers), 24th Georgia Infantry Regiment. Wounded at Crampton's Gap 14 September 1862. Transferred to Company B, 3rd Battalion Sharpshooters 8 June 1863. Captured at Front Royal 16 August 16, 1864. Imprisoned at Elmira; Paroled 20 February, 1865; received for exchange at James River 21 February 1865. Admitted to General Hospital, Howard's Grove 1 March 1865. No later record. Born 3 March or 13 May 1833; died 17 May 1925. Buried Hudson River Baptist Church Cemetery, Franklin County, Georgia. LH, SR, NPS, TMWG, CSR

Brown, John M. Enlisted at Hartwell, Georgia (Hart County), 24 August 1861. Private. Transferred to Company B, 3rd Battalion Sharpshooters. Admitted to Jackson Hospital, Richmond for treatment of dysentery 31 May 1864. Returned to duty 15 June 1864. Wounded in the left leg near Petersburg 20 June 1864. Admitted to Jackson Hospital, Richmond 21 June 1864. Died in hospital 2 July 1864. SR, NPS, CSR

Crumley, George B. Enlisted at Clarkesville, Georgia (Habersham County), 24 August 1861. Private, Company K (McMillan Guards), 24th Georgia Infantry Regiment. Admitted to Chimborazo Hospital #2, Richmond for treatment of debility 1 September 1862. Returned to Duty 30 September 1862. Transferred to Company B, 3rd Battalion Sharpshooters 8 June 1863. Promoted from ranks to 4th sergeant 15 June 1863. Wounded at Cedar Creek 19 October 1864. Absent, wounded 1 February 1865. No later record. LH, SR, NPS, CSR, HCH

Crumley, Sidney S. Enlisted Clarkesville, Georgia (Habersham County), 24 August 1861. Private, Company K (McMillan Guards), 24th Georgia Infantry Regiment. Admitted to Chimborazo Hospital #3, Richmond 9 September 1862. Returned to duty 16 December 1862. Transferred to Company B, 3rd Battalion Sharpshooters 8 June 1861. Promoted from ranks to 2nd corporal 14 June 1863. Absent, on furlough 1 February 1865. No later record. LH, SR, NPS, CSR, HCH

Foster, Virgil Enlisted Clarkesville, Georgia (Habersham County), 26 April 1863. Private, Company G (Hall Volunteers), 24th Georgia Infantry Regiment. Transferred to Company B, 3rd Battalion Sharpshooters 8 June 1863. Deserted 1 October 1863. No later record. LH, SR, NPS, CSR

Fryar, Willard F. Enlisted at Clarkesville, Georgia (Habersham County), 4 March 1862. Private, Company K (McMillan Guards), 24th Georgia Infantry Regiment. Admitted to Chimborazo Hospital #4, Richmond 30 October 1862. Returned to duty 8 December 1862. Transferred to Company B, 3rd Battalion Sharpshooters 8 June 1863. Captured at High Bridge, Virginia (Sailor's Creek) 6 April 1865. Imprisoned at Point Lookout; released 17 June 1865. Oath of Allegiance indicates he was five feet seven inches tall, with light complexion, light auburn hair and blue eyes. SR, NPS, CSR

Green, J. H. Enlisted in Lawrenceville, Georgia (Gwinnett County), 16 March 1863. Private, Company B, 3rd Battalion Sharpshooters. Roll dated February 1865 indicates he was absent without leave. No later record. SR, NPS, CSR

Hardy, Nathaniel B. Enlisted at Homer, Georgia (Banks County), 24 August 1861. Private, Company A (Independent Volunteers) 24th Georgia Infantry Regiment. Admitted to CSA Hospital, Danville, Virginia 29 June 1862. Returned to duty 28 August 1862. Admitted to Chimborazo Hospital #2, Richmond for treatment of hepatitis 5 June 1863. Transferred to Company B, 3rd Battalion Sharpshooters on 8 June 1863. Returned to duty 11 June 1863. Wounded at Front Royal 16 August 1864. Admitted to General Hospital #9 13 September 1864. Furloughed for sixty days 14 September 1864. On wounded furlough at the end of the war. LH, SR, NPS, CSR

Heath, John B. Enlisted at Nacoochee, Georgia (White County), 24 August 1861. Private, Company G (Hall Volunteers), 24th Georgia Infantry Regiment. Captured at Sharpsburg 16 September 1862; paroled 27 September 1862. Transferred to Company B,

3rd Battalion Sharpshooters 8 June 1863. Promoted to 3rd corporal 14 June 1863. Absent without leave 31 October 1863 to 31 August 1864. Reduction in rank to private. Roll dated 1 February 1865 states he was absent without leave. No later record. LH, SR, NPS, CSR

Hicks, James F. Enlisted at Hartwell, Georgia Hart (County), 24 August 1861. Private, Company B (Hart Volunteers), 24th Georgia Infantry Regiment. Admitted to Camp Winder Hospital #4 22 October 1862. Returned to duty 9 December 1862. Transferred to Company B, 3rd Battalion Sharpshooters 8 June 1863. Captured at Front Royal 16 August 1864. Committed to Old Capitol Prison, Washington, D.C. 21 August 1864. Transferred to Elmira 28 August 1864; released 21 June 1865. Oath of Allegiance indicates he was five feet nine inches tall, with dark complexion, dark hair and hazel eyes. LH, HHC, SR, NPS, CSR

Hurt, James L. Enlisted at Nacoochee, Georgia (White County), 24 August 1861. Private, Company G (Hall Volunteers), 24th Georgia Infantry Regiment. Admitted to Chimborazo Hospital #1, Richmond for treatment of typhoid fever 27 June 1862. Returned to duty 10 July 1862. Transferred to Company B, 3rd Battalion Sharpshooters 8 June 1863. Court Martial 4 May 1864; Absent without leave; sentenced to hard labor. Wounded 7 June 1864. Roll dated 31 August 1864, last on file shows him absent. No later record. Buried in Hazel Creek Baptist Church Cemetery, Clarkesville, Georgia. CM, SR, NPS, TMWG, CSR

Jackson, Francis M. Enlisted at Cleveland, Georgia (White County), 24 August 1861. Private, Company C (White County Marksmen), 24th Georgia Infantry Regiment. Transferred to Company B, 3rd Battalion Sharpshooters 8 June 1863. Promoted to 1st corporal from the ranks 14 June 1863. Roll dated 31 August 1864 shows him present. No later record. LH, SR, NPS, CSR

Jackson, James Enlisted at Richmond, Virginia 1 April 1864. Private, Company B, 3rd Battalion Sharpshooters. Admitted to Jackson Hospital, Richmond 24 July 1864 for treatment of acute diarrhea. Returned to duty 26 July 1864. Captured at Front Royal 16 August 1864. Committed to Old Capitol Prison, Washington, D. C. 21 August 1864. Transferred to Elmira 28 August 1864; released 21 June 1865. Oath of Allegiance indicates he was five feet six inches tall, with fair complexion, light hair and blue eyes. SR, NPS, CSR

Jackson, Jerdan A. Enlisted at Cleveland, Georgia (White County), 18 January 1862. Private, Company C (White County Marksmen), 24th Georgia Infantry Regiment. Transferred to Company B, 3rd Battalion Sharpshooters. Captured at Front Royal 16 August 1864. Committed to Old Capitol Prison, Washington, D. C. 21 August 1864. Transferred to Elmira 28 August 1864; released 21 June 1865. Oath of Allegiance indicates he was five feet eight inches tall, with florid complexion, dark hair and blue eyes. SR, CSR

Jackson, Martin V. Enlisted on 24 August 1861. Musician, Company B (Hart Volunteers), 24th Georgia Infantry Regiment. Transferred to Company B, 3rd Battalion

Sharpshooters 8 June 1863. Promoted to 1st Sergeant from the ranks 14 June 1863. Roll dated 1 February 1865 states he was transferred by promotion. LH, UDC, HHC, SR, NPS, CSR

Jerrels, Fritze M. Enlisted at Nacoochee, Georgia (White County), 4 March 1862. Private. Transferred to Company B, 3rd Battalion Sharpshooters. Roll dated 31 August 1864, last on file, shows him present. No later record. SR, NPS, CSR

Johnson, Daniel F. Enlisted at Hartwell, Georgia (Hart County), 24 August 1861. Private, Company B (Hart Volunteers), 24th Georgia Infantry Regiment. Transferred to Company B, 3rd Battalion Sharpshooters 8 June 1863. Admitted to General Hospital, Camp Winder, Richmond 3 August 1863. Returned to duty 11 August 1863. Wounded at Chattanooga 25 September 1863. Roll dated 30 January 1865 shows him absent without leave. No later record. LH, HHC, SR, NPS, CSR

Kimbro, W. B. Enlisted in 1861. Discharged 28 December 1861. Private. Re-enlisted at Lawrenceville, Georgia (Gwinnett County), 16 March 1862. Private, Company I (Hutchins Guards), 16th Georgia Infantry Regiment. Transferred to Company B, 3rd Battalion Sharpshooters 8 June 1863. Killed at Spotsylvania 12 May 1864. SR, NPS, CSR

Little, Robert C. Enlisted in White County, Georgia, 24 August 1861. Private, Company C (White County Marksmen), 24th Georgia Infantry Regiment. Transferred to Company B, 3rd Battalion Sharpshooters 8 June 1863 with the rank of 4th corporal. Wounded at Cold Harbor 1 June 1864. Captured at Greenville, South Carolina 23 May 1865; paroled 25 May 1865. LH, NPS, CSR (Service record missing for 3rd Battalion Sharpshooters)

Lowery, John N. Enlisted in Gwinnett County 24 August 1861. Private, Company F (Independent Blues), 24th Georgia Infantry Regiment. Transferred to Company B, 3rd Battalion Sharpshooters 8 June 1863 with the rank of 3rd sergeant. No later record. LH, NPS, CSR (No service record for 3rd Battalion Sharpshooters)

Maxwell, Elbert Thomas Enlisted in Hart County 24 August 1861. Private, Company B (Hart Volunteers), 24th Georgia Infantry Regiment. Transferred to Company B, 3rd Battalion Sharpshooters 8 June 1863. Wounded at Chattanooga 24 November 1863. Died from wounds 26 November 1863. According to his service records, he was five feet ten inches tall, with fair complexion, light hair and blue eyes. LH, HHC, SR, NPS, CSR

Mayes, Telemachus A. Enlisted at Homer, Georgia (Banks County), 24 August 1861. Private, Company A (Independent Volunteers), 24th Georgia Infantry Regiment. Transferred to Company B, 3rd Battalion Sharpshooters. Promoted to 3rd sergeant. Captured at Farmville, Virginia (Sailor's Creek) 6 April 1865. Imprisoned at Point Lookout; released 19 June 1865. Oath of Allegiance indicates that he was five feet five inches tall, with light complexion, auburn hair and blue eyes. SR, NPS, CSR

McDaniel, Sanford Enlisted at Lawrenceville, Georgia (Gwinnett County), 16 March 1862. Private, Company F, 24th Georgia Infantry Regiment. Transferred to Company B, 3rd Battalion Sharpshooters. Captured at Sailor's Creek 6 April 1865. Imprisoned at Point Lookout; released 29 June 1865. Oath of Allegiance shows him to be five feet ten inches tall, light complexion, brown hair and brown eyes. SR, NPS, CSR

Moise, A. Welborne Enlisted at Richmond, Virginia 10 December 1862. Private, Company D (Hiawassee Volunteers), 24th Georgia Infantry Regiment. Transferred to Company B, 3rd Battalion Sharpshooters 2 August 1863. Appointed Sergeant Major of 24th Georgia Infantry Regiment 30 April 1864. Returned to regiment. Elected 1st lieutenant of Company H (Currahee Rangers), 24th Georgia Infantry Regiment 1 December 1864. Surrendered at Appomattox 9 April 1865. LH, SR, NPS, CSR

Payne, Larkin C. Enlisted at Hartwell, Georgia (Hart County), 24 August 1861. Private, Company B (Hart Volunteers), 24th Georgia Infantry Regiment. Admitted to CSA Hospital, Danville, Virginia 15 May 1862. Returned to duty 28 May 1862. Transferred to Company B, 3rd Battalion Sharpshooters 8 June 1863. Admitted to Jackson Hospital, Richmond for treatment of chronic diarrhea 30 July 1864. Furloughed for thirty days 5 August 1864. Surrendered at Appomattox 9 April 1865. LH, UDC, HHC, SR, NPS, CSR

Payton, William M. Enlisted at Homer, Georgia (Banks County), 24 August 1861. Private, Company A (Independent Volunteers), 24th Georgia Infantry Regiment. Transferred to Company B, 3rd Battalion Sharpshooters 8 June 1863. Deserted; took Oath of Allegiance to the U.S. Government at Washington D.C. on 29 March 1865. Furnished transportation to Philadelphia, Pennsylvania. LH, SR, NPS, CSR

Phillips, James Enlisted in Hart County, Georgia, 24 August 1861. Private, Company B (Hart Volunteers), 24th Georgia Infantry Regiment. Transferred to Company B, 3rd Battalion Sharpshooters 8 June 1863. Deserted at Richmond 26 March 1865. Took Oath of Allegiance to the U.S. Government at Washington, D.C. 30 March 1865 and furnished transportation to Springfield, Illinois. LH, HHC, SR, NPS, CSR

Smith, George W. Enlisted at Homer, Georgia (Banks County), 1 January 1862. Private, Company A (Independent Volunteers), 24th Georgia Infantry Regiment. Admitted to Chimbozaro Hospital #1, Richmond for treatment of debility 1 September 1862. Returned to duty. Transferred to Company B, 3rd Battalion Sharpshooters 8 June 1863. Captured at High Bridge, Virginia (Sailor's Creek) 6 April 1865. Imprisoned at Point Lookout; released 20 June 1865. Oath of Allegiance indicates he was six feet one inch tall, with light complexion, brown hair and dark blue eyes. Born in Georgia in 1842. Buried in Harmony Baptist Church Cemetery, Homer, Georgia. LH, UDC, NPS, CSR, SR

Smith, James J. Enlisted at Cleveland, Georgia (White County), 24 August 1861. Private, Company C (White County Marksmen), 24th Georgia Infantry Regiment. Wounded in the chest at Malvern Hill 1 July 1862. Transferred to Company B, 3rd

Battalion Sharpshooters 8 June 1863. Killed in action at Front Royal 16 August 1864. LH, NPS, CSR, SR

Stephenson, William H. Enlisted at Hartwell, Georgia (Hart County), 24 August 1861. 4th Sergeant, Company B (Hart Volunteers), 24th Georgia Infantry Regiment. Transferred to Company B, 3rd Battalion Sharpshooters 8 June 1863. Admitted to Jackson Hospital, Richmond for treatment of chronic diarrhea 24 July 1864. Returned to duty 9 August 1864. Captured at Farmville, Virginia (Sailor's Creek) 6 April 1865. Imprisoned at Point Lookout; released 19 June 1865. Oath of Allegiance indicates he was five feet eight inches tall, with fair complexion, brown hair and hazel eyes. LH, NPS, CSR, SR

Trotter, Henry C. Enlisted at Nacoochee, Georgia (White County), 24 August 1861. Private, Company G (Hall Volunteers), 24th Georgia Infantry Regiment. Admitted to Chimbozaro Hospital #2, Richmond for treatment of pneumonia 18 February 1863. Returned to duty 30 March 1863. Transferred to Company B, 3rd Battalion Sharpshooters 8 June 1863. Promoted to 3rd corporal. Roll for 31 August 1864 shows him present. No later record. LH, NPS, CSR, SR

Vandivier, A. P. Enlisted at Nacoochee, Georgia (White County), 4 March 1862. Private, Company G (Hall Volunteers), 24th Georgia Infantry Regiment. Transferred to Company B, 3rd Battalion Sharpshooters 8 June 1863 with the rank of sergeant. Detailed as shoemaker from 1 January 1864 until 31 March 1864. Killed in action at Richmond 6 April 1865. LH, NPS, CSR, SR

Vandivier, Marcus L. Enlisted at Nacoochee, Georgia (White County), 24 August 1861. Private, Company G (Hall Volunteers), 24th Georgia Infantry Regiment. Admitted to CSA Hospital, Danville, Virginia for treatment of debilitas 2 July 1862. Returned to duty 4 July 1862. Admitted to Chimbozaro Hospital #4, Richmond 30 August 1862 for treatment of diarrhea. Returned to duty 22 October 1862. Transferred to Company B, 3rd Battalion Sharpshooters 8 June 1863. Wounded at Gettysburg 2 July 1863. Admitted to Chimborazo Hospital #4, Richmond. Roll dated 1 February 1865, last on file, shows him absent without leave. No later record. LH, NPS, CSR, SR

Vickery, William James Enlisted at Hartwell, Georgia (Hart County), 9 May 1862. Private, Company B (Hart Volunteers), 24th Georgia Infantry Regiment. Transferred to Company B, 3rd Battalion Sharpshooters 8 June 1863 with the rank of corporal. Wounded at Front Royal 16 August 1864. Promoted to corporal, date not recorded. Captured and paroled at Hartwell, Georgia, 18 May 1865. Pension records show that he was at home on wounded furlough at the end of the war. Born 1838 in Franklin County, Georgia. Died 28 December 1919. Buried in Hillcrest Church Cemetery, Bowman, Georgia. LH, UDC, NPS, CSR, SR

Wade, James C. Enlisted at Homer, Georgia (Banks County), 24 August 1861. Private, Company A (Independent Volunteers), 24th Georgia Infantry Regiment. Transferred to Company B, 3rd Battalion Sharpshooters 8 June 1863. Promoted to 5th Sergeant from the ranks 15 June 1863. Captured at High Bridge, Virginia (Sailor's

Creek) 6 April 1865. Imprisoned at Point Lookout; released 22 June 1865. Oath of Allegiance indicates he was five feet seven inches tall, with fair complexion, brown hair and gray eyes. Born 25 July 1841 in Georgia. LH, NPS, CSR, SR

Way, Benjamin Franklin Enlisted in Hart County, Georgia July 1861. Private, Company C (Hartwell Infantry), 16th Georgia Infantry Regiment. Discharged 21 August 1861. Re-enlisted at Hartwell, Georgia, 2 March 1862. Transferred to Company B, 3rd Battalion Sharpshooters 8 June 1863. Admitted to Jackson Hospital for treatment of chronic diarrhea 8 August 1864. Returned to duty 20 August 1864. Captured at Farmville, Virginia (Sailor's Creek) 6 August 1865. Imprisoned at Point Lookout; released 22 June 1865. Oath of Allegiance indicates he was five feet nine inches tall, with fair complexion, light brown hair and blue eyes. Born *ca.* 1828. Died 22 April 1914 in Palo Pinto County Texas. NPS, CSR, SR

West, B. C. Private, Company C (White County Marksmen), 24th Infantry Regiment. Transferred to Company B, 3rd Battalion Sharpshooters 8 June 1863. Surrendered at Appomattox 9 April 1865. LH, SHSP, NPS, CSR, SR

West, B. F. Enlisted at Cleveland, Georgia (White County), 13 March 1862. Private, Company C (White County Marksmen), 24th Georgia Infantry Regiment. Admitted to General Hospital #19, Richmond 21 December 1862. Returned to duty. Transferred to Company B, 3rd Battalion Sharpshooters. Wounded (gunshot in side and back) at Chancellorsville 3 May 1863. Admitted to General Hospital #18, Richmond. Furloughed for sixty days 13 June 1863. Returned to duty. Admitted to Jackson Hospital, Richmond 27 May 1864. Deserted from the hospital 25 June 1864. No later record. CSR, SR

West, James B. Enlisted at Cleveland, Georgia (White County), 24 August 1861. Private, Company C (White County Marksmen), 24th Georgia Infantry Regiment. Admitted to General Hospital, Howard's Grove, Richmond for treatment of diarrhea 4 November 1862. Returned to duty 29 November 1862. Transferred to Company B, 3rd Battalion Sharpshooters 8 June 1863. Admitted to Stuart Hospital, Richmond for treatment of chronic diarrhea 4 July 1864. Returned to duty 29 September 1864. Surrendered at Appomattox 9 April 1865. LH, CSR, SR

White, James Wiley Enlisted at Lawrenceville, Georgia (Gwinnett County), 24 August 1861. Private, Company F (Gwinnett Independent Blues), 24th Georgia Infantry Regiment. Admitted to Chimborazo Hospital #1 for treatment of debility 1 September 1862. Returned to duty 2 September 1862. Wounded at Sharpsburg 17 September 1862. Transferred to Company B, 3rd Battalion Sharpshooters 8 June 1863. Admitted to Jackson Hospital, Richmond for treatment of debilitas 28 May 1864. Returned to duty 11 June 1864. Promoted to corporal. Transferred to 14th Georgia Infantry Regiment 1 February 1865. LH, NPS, CSR, SR

Whitehead, Archibald J. Enlisted at Clarkesville, Georgia (Habersham County), 24 August 1861. Private, Company K (McMillan Guards), 24th Georgia Infantry Regiment. Musician. Wounded at Fredericksburg 13 December 1862. Transferred to

Company B, 3rd Battalion Sharpshooters 8 June 1863. Wounded at Knoxville 24 November 1863 and left behind. Captured at Knoxville 5 December 1863. Sent to Camp Chase 24 February 1864. Received at Louisville Military Prison 29 February 1864. Received at Camp Chase 19 March 1864. Transferred to Johnson's Island 13 September 1864; released 13 June 1865. Oath of Allegiance indicates he was five feet eleven inches tall, with fair complexion, dark hair and gray eyes. Born *ca.* 1840. LH, NPS, CSR, SR

Whitehead, McDonald Enlisted at Clarkesville, Georgia (Habersham County), 23 January 1862. Private, Company K (McMillan Guards), 24th Georgia Infantry Regiment. Captured at Crampton's Gap 14 September 1862. Imprisoned at Fort McHenry. Paroled November 1862. Returned to regiment. Transferred to Company B, 3rd Battalion Sharpshooters. Court Martial 29 February 1864. Charge not recorded. Assigned company punishment – docked six months' pay. Roll dated 1 February 1865 states that he deserted 19 October 1864. No later record. CM, CSR, SR

Whitfield, Henry Enlisted at Homer, Georgia (Banks County), 24 August 1861. Private, Company A (Independent Volunteers), 24th Georgia Infantry Regiment. Wounded at Crampton's Gap 14 September 1862. Transferred to Company B, 3rd Battalion Sharpshooters 8 June 1863. Absent, sick 31 August 1863. Roll dated 30 January 1865, last on file, shows him absent without leave. No later record. LH, NPS, SR

Witcher, Daniel H. Enlisted at Athens, Georgia (Clarke County), 11 July 1861. Private, Company A (Madison County Greys), 16th Georgia Infantry Regiment. Transferred to Company C, 3rd Battalion Sharpshooters with the rank of 4th Sergeant. Wounded at Deep Bottom 30 July 1864 with a shell wound to right hip and thigh. Admitted to Hospital #9, Richmond 31 July 1864; died of wounds 9 August 1864. HGC, NPS, CSR, SR

Woody, Peter L. Enlisted at Cleveland, Georgia (White County), 24 August 1861. Private, Company C, 24th Georgia Infantry Regiment. Transferred to Company B, 3rd Battalion Sharpshooters 8 June 1863. Admitted to hospital, name and date not recorded. Left hospital on 13 November 1863. Roll for 31 August 1864 shows he deserted. No later record. LH, NPS, CSR, SR

Yearwood, Bird Oliver Enlisted at Decatur, Georgia (Dekalb County), 20 September 1863. Private, Company B, 3rd Battalion Sharpshooters. Died 10 November 1863. SR, NPS, CSR

Yearwood, Lewis Jasper Enlisted at Clarkesville, Georgia (Habersham County), 23 January 1862. Private, Company K (McMillan Guards), 24th Georgia Infantry Regiment. Transferred to Company B, 3rd Battalion Sharpshooters. Wounded 24 November 1863. Died 25 or 26 November 1863. NPS, CSR, SR

York, W. V. Enlisted for the war at Nacoochee, Georgia (White County), 24 August 1861. Private, Company C (White County Marksmen), 24th Georgia Infantry Regiment. Transferred to Company B, 3rd Battalion Sharpshooters. Captured at

Gettysburg, 5 July 1863. Imprisoned at Fort Delaware; released on parole 1 February 1865. No later record. SR, NPS, CSR

Sharpshooter Company C

Company Officers:

Muse, William Cabell Enlisted at Athens, Georgia (Clarke County), on 11 July 1861. Private, Company A (Madison County Grays), 16th Georgia Infantry Regiment. Transferred to Company C, 3rd Battalion Sharpshooters 8 June 1863 with the rank of 1st lieutenant. Captured at Sailor's Creek 6 April 1865. Imprisoned at Johnson's Island; released 19 June 1865. LH, SR, NPS, OS, CSR

Simmons, William E. Enlisted at Lawrenceville, Georgia (Gwinnett County), 16 July 1861. Elected 2nd lieutenant, Company I (Hutchins Guards), 16th Georgia Infantry Regiment. Promoted to 1st lieutenant. Transferred to Company C, 3rd Battalion Sharpshooters 8 June 1863. Promoted to Captain, appointment date 17 June 1863 to take rank 5 June 1863. Promoted to Major to take rank 18 September 1863. Captured at Front Royal 16 August 1864 while Acting Commander of the 3rd Battalion Sharpshooters. Committed to Old Capitol Prison, Washington, D. C. 21 August 1864. Transferred to Fort Delaware 27 August 1864; released 24 July 1865. Oath of Allegiance indicates he was five feet ten inches tall, with fair complexion, light hair and blue eyes. Born 26 August 1839 in Lawrenceville, Georgia. Died 29 January 1931 in Lawrenceville, Georgia. Buried in Shadowlawn Cemetery, Lawrenceville, Georgia. LH, NLH, SR, NPS, OS, CSR

Strickland, Charlton H. Enlisted at Lawrenceville, Georgia (Gwinnett County), 16 July 1861. Private, Company I (Hutchins Guards), 16th Georgia Infantry Regiment. Promoted to 1st sergeant. Appointed orderly to the regimental commander November 1861. Appointed 2nd lieutenant, date of rank 5 June 1863. Transferred to Company C, 3rd Battalion Sharpshooters 8 June 1863. Promoted to 1st lieutenant. Promoted to Captain 24 November 1864. Inspection report dated 28 February 1865 shows him absent without leave. No later record. HGC, NLH, SR, NPS, OS, CSR

Ware, Samuel H. Enlisted at Augusta, Georgia (Richmond County), 15 May 1862. 1st Lieutenant, Company D (Davis Invincibles), 18th Georgia Infantry Regiment. Transferred to Company C, 3rd Battalion Sharpshooters. Date of rank 8 June 1863. Resigned 4 March 1864. Dropped from rolls 24 November 1864. HGC, SR, NPS, OS, CSR

Enlisted Men:

Adair, William M. Enlisted at Lawrenceville, Georgia (Gwinnett County), 16 July 1861. Private, Company I (Hutchins Guards), 16th Georgia Infantry Regiment. Transferred to Company C, 3rd Battalion Sharpshooters 8 June 1863. Killed at Gettysburg 4 July 1863. HGC, NLH, SR, NPS, CSR.

Allen, Benjamin F. Enlisted at Cleveland, Georgia (White County), 24 August 1861. Private, Company C (White County Marksmen), 16th Georgia Infantry Regiment. Transferred to Company B, 3rd Battalion Sharpshooters 8 June 1863. Promoted from the ranks to 2nd sergeant 14 June 1863. Captured at Sailor's Creek 6 April 1865. Imprisoned at Point Lookout; released 22 June 1865. Born 1842 in White County, Georgia. LH, SR, NPS, CSR

Allen, Levi Enlisted at Cleveland, Georgia (White County), 24 August 1861. Private, Company C (White County Marksmen), 16th Georgia Infantry Regiment. Transferred to Company B, 3rd Battalion Sharpshooters 9 July 1864. Surrendered at Appomattox 9 April 1865. SHSP, SR, NPS, CSR

Arwood, J. B. Private, Company C, 3rd Battalion Sharpshooters. Admitted to Jackson Hospital, Richmond, Virginia 9 October 1864. Returned to duty 13 October 1864. No later record. SR, NPS, CSR

Barrett, J. M. Enlisted at Augusta, Georgia (Richmond County), 22 February 1864. Private, Company C, 3rd Battalion Sharpshooters. Discharged for being a minor June 1864. SR, NPS

Beard, James Robinson Enlisted at Center Hill, Georgia (Jackson County), 17 July 1861. 2nd Corporal, Company B (Center Hill Guards), 16th Georgia Infantry Regiment. Transferred to Company C, 3rd Battalion Sharpshooters 8 June 1863. Captured at High Bridge, Virginia (Sailor's Creek) 6 April 1865. Imprisoned at Point Lookout; released 24 June 1865. Oath shows him to be five feet eight inches tall, with fair complexion, light brown hair and gray eyes. Born 8 September 1815; died 25 May 1900. Buried in Hoschton City Cemetery, Hoschton, Georgia. Reverend. LH, SR, NPS, TMWG,

Black, James W. Enlisted at Yorktown, Virginia 3 February 1862. Private, Company D (Danielsville Guards), 16th Georgia Infantry Regiment. Admitted to Chimborazo Hospital #2, Richmond 24 March 1862. Returned to duty 6 April 1862. Transferred to Company C, 3rd Battalion Sharpshooters 8 June 1863. Captured at High Bridge, Virginia (Sailor's Creek) 6 April 1865. Imprisoned at Point Lookout; released 9 June 1865. LH, SR, NPS, CSR

Braziel, James Harrison Enlisted at Lawrenceville, Georgia (Gwinnett County), 16 July 1861. Private, Company I (Hutchins Guards), 16th Georgia Infantry Regiment. Transferred to Company C, 3rd Battalion Sharpshooters 8 June 1863. Wounded, date and location not recorded. Captured at Farmville, Virginia (Sailor's Creek) 6 April 1865. Imprisoned at Point Lookout; released 24 June 1865. Oath of Allegiance indicates he was five feet eleven inches tall, with light complexion, brown hair and hazel eyes. Born 18 June 1840, died 28 January 1902. Buried in Old Suwanee Baptist Church Cemetery, Buford, Georgia. UDC, NLH, SR, NPS, CSR

Bullock, James H. Enlisted at Athens, Georgia (Clarke County), 11 July 1861. Private. Transferred to Company C, 3rd Battalion Sharpshooters 8 June 1863. On furlough from 5 January 1864 until 9 February 1864. Captured at Front Royal 16 August 1864. Committed to Old Capitol Prison, Washington, D.C. 21 August 1864. Transferred to Elmira 28 August 1864; released 7 July 1865. Oath of Allegiance indicates he was five feet ten inches tall, with florid complexion, Dark hair and hazel eyes. Born in Madison County 19 October 1838. Buried in the Bullock Cemetery, Madison County, Georgia. LH, UDC, SR, NPS, CSR

Burson, Joseph Green Enlisted at Goldsboro, North Carolina 1 April 1862. Private, Company B (Center Hill Guards), 16th Georgia Infantry Regiment. Admitted to General Hospital, Camp Winder, Richmond 7 May 1862. Returned to duty 20 May 1862. Admitted to Chimborazo Hospital #2, Richmond 5 June 1863. Transferred to Company C, 3rd Battalion Sharpshooters 15 July 1863. Roll for August 1863 shows him absent without leave. No later record. Born 28 August 1837 in Georgia; Died 1 March 1911 in Barrow County, Georgia. LH, SR, NPS, CSR

Butler, Henry H. Enlisted at Center Hill, Georgia (Jackson County), 17 July 1861. Private, Company B (Center Hill Guards), 16th Georgia Infantry Regiment. Captured at South Mountain, Maryland 15 September 1862 (Crampton's Gap). Imprisoned at Fort Delaware. Released for exchange 2 October 1862. Declared exchanged at Aiken's Landing, Virginia 10 November 1862. Transferred to Company C, 3rd Battalion Sharpshooters with the rank of 3rd Sergeant. Wounded at Front Royal 16 August 1864. Roll dated 29 January 1865 shows him absent, wounded. No later record. SR, NPS, CSR

Carter, John Enlisted 17 March 1864. Private, Company C, 3rd Battalion Sharpshooters. Wounded at the Wilderness 6 May 1864. No later record. SR, NPS, CSR

Chandler, Dudley Cromer Enlisted at Athens, Georgia (Clarke County), 11 July 1861. Private, Company A (Madison County Greys), 16th Georgia Infantry Regiment. Admitted to General Hospital, Petersburg, Virginia for the treatment of debilitas 14 April 1862. Returned to duty 15 May 1862. Admitted to Chimborazo Hospital #5, Richmond for the treatment of dysentery 20 August 1862. Returned to duty 29 September 1862. Admitted to CSA Hospital, Charlottesville, Virginia 19 January 1863 for treatment of rheumatism. Returned to duty 3 February 1863. Transferred to Company C, 3rd Battalion Sharpshooters 8 June 1863. Captured at Farmville, Virginia (Sailor's Creek) 6 April 1865. Imprisoned at Point Lookout; released 26 June 1865. Oath of Allegiance indicates he was five feet eleven inches tall, with light complexion, dark hair and dark gray eyes. Born in 1840. LH, SR, NPS, CSR

Clark, John T. Enlisted at Lawrenceville, Georgia (Gwinnett County), 16 July 1861. Private, Company I (Hutchins Guards), 16th Georgia Infantry Regiment. Transferred to Company C, 3rd Battalion Sharpshooters 1 May 1863. Captured at Gettysburg. Imprisoned at Fort Delaware. Took Oath of Allegiance to the U.S. 5 September 1863. Turned over to the commanding officer of the 3rd Maryland Cavalry. No later record. Born 1836 in Georgia. SGC, SR, GCF, NPS, CSR

Collins, John O. Enlisted 10 August 1861. Private, Company D (Danielsville Guards), 16th Georgia Infantry Regiment. Transferred to Company C, 3rd Battalion Sharpshooters with the rank of 1st corporal. Wounded at Cedar Creek 19 October 1864. Admitted to General Hospital #9, Richmond 20 November 1864. Granted sixty-day furlough 21 November 1864. No later record. HGC, SR, NPS, CSR

Cone, Seaborn A. Enlisted at Center Hill, Georgia (Jackson County), 17 July 1861. Private, Company B (Center Hill Guards), 16th Georgia Infantry Regiment. Wounded in the side and captured at Crampton's Gap 14 September 1862. Paroled at Burkittsville, Maryland 13 October 1862. Transferred to Company C, 3rd Battalion Sharpshooters 8 June 1863. Captured at High Bridge, Virginia (Sailor's Creek) 6 April 1865. Imprisoned at Point Lookout; released 26 June 1865. Oath of Allegiance indicates he was five feet ten inches tall, with light complexion, light brown hair and hazel eyes. LH, SR, NPS, CSR

Cosby, William Phillip Enlisted in the Center Hill Guards (Jackson County) 17 July 1861. Private, Company B, 16th Georgia Infantry Regiment. Captured at Crampton's Gap 14 September 1862. Imprisoned at Fort Delaware; released for exchange 2 October 1862; received at Aiken's Landing 2 November 1862. Transferred to Company C, 3rd Battalion Sharpshooters 8 June 1863 with the rank of 3rd corporal. Wounded in the right leg at Spotsylvania 10 May 1864. Admitted to Jackson Hospital, Richmond 15 May 1864. Furloughed for sixty days on 28 May 1864. No later record. Born 5 July 1842. Died 20 March 1910. Buried in Appalachee Baptist Church Cemetery, Gwinnett County, Georgia. LH, UDC, SR, NPS, CSR

Davidson, James A. Enlisted in Habersham County 24 July 1861. Private, Company E (Cobb Infantry), 16th Georgia Infantry Regiment. Captured at Crampton's Gap 14 September 1862. Imprisoned at Fort Delaware. Received for exchange at Aiken's Landing 10 November 1862. Transferred to Company C, 3rd Battalion Sharpshooters June 8, 1863. Killed in action at Hagerstown, Maryland 11 July 1863. HGC, SR, NPS, CSR, HCH

Davis, General Whitner Enlisted at Lawrenceville, Georgia (Gwinnett County), 16 July 1861. Private, Company I (Hutchins Guards), 16th Georgia Infantry Regiment. Transferred to Company C, 3rd Battalion Sharpshooters 1 May 1863. Wounded at Chancellorsville 3 May 1863. Admitted to General Hospital #1, Richmond. Furloughed for thirty days 30 June 1863. Roll dated August 1864, last on file, states he was absent, wounded. No later record. Born 18 March 1837 in Gwinnett County, Georgia; Died 26 September 1894 in Banks County, Georgia. Buried in Davis Cemetery, Banks County, Georgia. LH, NLH, SR, NPS, CSR.

Davis, Samuel Enlisted at Greenville, South Carolina 13 April 1861. Private. Transferred to Company A (Madison County Greys), 16th Georgia Infantry Regiment 1 March 1863. Transferred to Company C, 3rd Battalion Sharpshooters 8 June 1863. Admitted to General Hospital, Charlottesville, Virginia 28 June 1863. Returned to duty 5 August 1863. Wounded at the Wilderness 6 May 1864. Admitted to CSA General

Hospital #11, Charlotte, North Carolina 15 January, 1865. Returned to duty 12 April 1865. No later record. LH, SR, NPS, CSR

Doster, William Z. A. Enlisted at Center Hill Georgia (Jackson County), 17 July 1861. Private, Company B (Center Hill Guards), 16th Georgia Infantry Regiment. Captured at Frederick, Maryland 13 July 1862. Imprisoned at Fort Delaware; released for exchange 2 October 1862; received at Aiken's Landing 10 November 1862. Transferred to 3rd Battalion Sharpshooters 8 June 1863; served in Company C and Company D. Promoted to sergeant. Detailed as a shoemaker January and February 1864. Captured at Farmville, Virginia (Sailor's Creek) 6 April 1865. Imprisoned at Point Lookout; released 26 June 1865. Oath of Allegiance indicates he was five feet eight inches tall, with fair complexion, brown hair and blue eyes. LH, SR, NPS, CSR

Dyer, Samuel Z. Enlisted at Lawrenceville, Georgia (Gwinnett County), 16 July 1861. Private, Company I (Hutchins Guards), 16th Georgia Infantry Regiment. Transferred to Company C, 3rd Battalion Sharpshooters 8 June 1863 with the rank of 5th sergeant. Captured at Farmville, Virginia (Sailor's Creek) 6 April 1865. Imprisoned at Point Lookout; released 26 June 1865. Born 1836 in Gwinnett County, Georgia. Oath of Allegiance indicates he was five feet eleven inches tall, with fair complexion, sandy hair and hazel eyes. LH, NLH, SR, NPS, CSR

Farrill, Andrew J. Enlisted at Lawrenceville, Georgia (Gwinnett County), 16 July, 1861. 2nd Sergeant, Company C, 3rd Battalion Sharpshooters. Detailed as Commissary Sergeant August 1864. Admitted to Jackson Hospital, Richmond for the treatment of pneumonia 4 January 1865. Returned to duty 20 January 1865. Surrendered at Appomattox 19 April 1865. HGC, SHSP, SR, NPS, CSR

Ferguson, James S. Enlisted at Center Hill, Georgia (Jackson County), 17 July 1861. Private, Company B (Center Hill Guards), 16th Georgia Infantry Regiment. Transferred to Company C, 3rd Battalion Sharpshooters 1 May 1864. Wounded at the Wilderness 6 May 1864. Admitted to CSA Hospital, Charlottesville, Virginia 12 May 1864. Furloughed for sixty days 24 May 1864. On wounded furlough 26 February 1865. No later record. LH, SR, NPS, CSR

Gholston, Willis W. Enlisted at Yorktown, Virginia 1 February 1862. Private, Company A (Madison County Greys), 16th Georgia Infantry Regiment. Transferred to Company C, 3rd Battalion Sharpshooters 8 June 1863. Wounded in the head May 1864. Admitted to Jackson Hospital, Richmond 15 May 1864. Returned to duty July 1864. Wounded and captured at Front Royal 16 August 1864. Committed to Old Capitol Prison, Washington, D.C. 21 August 1864. Transferred to Elmira 28 August 1864; released 16 June 1865. Oath of Allegiance indicates he was six feet tall, with florid complexion, dark hair and blue eyes. LH, SR, NPS, CSR

Grayham, Isaiah Gordon Enlisted at Athens, Georgia (Clarke County), 11 July 1861. Private, Company A (Madison County Greys), 16th Georgia Infantry Regiment. Transferred to 3rd Battalion Sharpshooters 8 June 1863; served in Company C and D. Wounded and captured at Front Royal 16 August 1864. Committed to Old Capitol

Prison 21 August 1864. Transferred to Elmira 28 August 1864; released 16 June 1865. Oath of Allegiance indicates he was five feet eleven inches tall, with fair complexion, light hair and blue eyes. Born 10 May 1839. Died 8 April 1917. Buried in Brown Cemetery, Madison County, Georgia. LH, UDC, SR, NPS, CSR

Grayham, John H. Enlisted at Athens, Georgia (Clarke County), 11 July 1861. Private. Transferred to Company C, 3rd Battalion Sharpshooters 8 June 1863. Captured at Front Royal 16 August 1864. Committed to Old Capitol Prison 21 August 1864. Transferred to Elmira 28 August 1864; released 16 June 1865. Oath of Allegiance indicates he was five feet seven inches tall, with fair complexion, dark hair and blue eyes. HGC, SR, NPS, CSR

Grayham, William D. Enlisted at Athens, Georgia (Clarke County), 10 August 1861. Private, Company D (Danielsville Guards), 16th Georgia Infantry Regiment. Transferred to Company C, 3rd Battalion Sharpshooters 8 June 1863. Roll dated 29 January 1865 indicates he was present. No later record. Born in 1844; Died in 1879. HGC, SR, NPS, CSR

Gunnells, A. J. Enlisted in Virginia, date not recorded. Private, Company C, 3rd Battalion Sharpshooters. Captured at Front Royal 16 August 1864. Committed to Old Capitol Prison, Washington, D. C. 21 August 1864. Transferred to Elmira 28 August 1864. Transferred for exchange 11 October 1864. Received for exchange at Venus Point, Savannah River 15 November 1864. No later record. SR, NPS, CSR

Herring, Elisha Enlisted at Athens, Georgia (Clarke County), 11 July 1861. Private, Company A (Madison County Greys), 16th Georgia Infantry Regiment. Wounded in the hand near Richmond 1 July 1862. Admitted to General Hospital, Howard's Grove, Richmond 4 July 1862. Furloughed 8 July 1862. Admitted to General Hospital #18, Richmond 2 August 1862. Furloughed 2 September 1862. Transferred to Company C, 3rd Battalion Sharpshooters 8 June 1863. Captured at High Bridge, Virginia (Sailor's Creek) 9 April 1865. Imprisoned at Point Lookout; released 28 June 1865. Oath of Allegiance indicates he was five feet nine inches tall, with light complexion, brown hair and gray eyes. Born 1840; Died 1916. LH, SR, NPS, CSR

Huff, T. R. Enlisted at Chattanooga, Tennessee 30 October 1863. Private, Company C, 3rd Battalion Sharpshooters. Wounded at Knoxville, Tennessee 27 November 1863. Captured 5 December 1863 and admitted to Middlebrook Hospital (U.S.). Died of gangrene from leg amputation while in hospital 10 December 1863. Born 1846 in Gwinnett County, Georgia. HGC, SR, NPS, CSR

Hutchins, Peyton Randolph Enlisted at Waller's Tavern, Virginia 1 September 1863. Private, Company C, 3rd Battalion Sharpshooters. Wounded in the mouth, date and location not recorded. Admitted to Jackson Hospital, Richmond 10 September 1864. Furloughed for thirty days 16 September 1864. Returned to duty. Surrendered at Appomattox 9 April 1865. Younger brother of Nathan L. Hutchins Jr. Born 14 July 1845 in Lawrenceville, Georgia. HGC, NLH, SHSP, SR, NPS, CSR

Johnston, Jonathan L. Enlisted at Calhoun, Georgia (Gordon County), 12 July 1862. Private. Transferred to Company C, 3rd Battalion Sharpshooters. Captured at High Bridge, Virginia (Sailor's Creek) 6 April 1865. Imprisoned at Point Lookout; released 28 June 1865. Oath of Allegiance indicates he was six feet tall, with light complexion, brown hair and hazel eyes. SR, NPS, CSR

Kirk, James W. Enlisted at Athens, Georgia, 11 July 1861. Private, Company A (Madison County Greys), 16th Georgia Infantry Regiment. Teamster. Transferred to Company C, 3rd Battalion Sharpshooters 8 June 1863. Promoted to corporal. Surrendered at Appomattox 9 April 1865. Brother of Samuel King. Born in 1842. Buried in the Kirk Cemetery, Madison County, Georgia. LH, UDC, SR, NPS, CSR

Maltbie, Elisha W. Enlisted in Company I (Hutchins Guards), 16th Georgia Infantry Regiment. Private. Transferred to Company C, 3rd Battalion Sharpshooters 8 June 1863. No later record. NLH (No service record in the 3rd Battalion Sharpshooters)

Martin, William A. Enlisted at Athens, Georgia (Clarke County), 11 July 1862. Private, Company A (Madison County Greys), 16th Georgia Infantry Regiment. Transferred to Company C, 3rd Battalion Sharpshooters 8 June 1863. Captured at Front Royal 16 August 1864. Committed to Old Capitol Prison, Washington, D. C., 21 August 1864. Transferred to Elmira 28 August 1864; released 21 June 1865. Oath of Allegiance indicates he was five feet eleven inches tall, with florid complexion, dark hair and hazel eyes. LH, SR, NPS, CSR

McMillan, Asa Enlisted at Lawrenceville, Georgia (Gwinnett County), 16 July 1861. Private, Company I (Hutchins Guards), 16th Georgia Infantry Regiment. Admitted to Seminary Hospital, Williamsburg, Virginia for treatment of bronchitis 5 March 1862. Returned to duty 17 March 1862. Captured at Crampton's Gap 14 September 1862. Imprisoned at Fort Delaware; sent for exchange to Aiken's Landing 2 October 1862. Returned to regiment. Transferred to Company C, 3rd Battalion Sharpshooters 8 June 1863. Detailed as shoemaker. Captured at High Bridge, Virginia (Sailor's Creek) 6 April 1865. Imprisoned at Point Lookout; released 29 June 1865. Oath of Allegiance indicates he was six feet two inches tall, with light complexion, brown hair and gray eyes. Born 18 June 1829. Died 28 February 1890. Buried in the McMillan Family Cemetery, Gwinnett County, Georgia. LH, UDC, NLH, SR, NPS, CSR

McWhirter, Andrew J. Enlisted at Richmond, Virginia 10 August 1861. Corporal, Company D (Danielsville Guards), 16th Georgia Infantry Regiment. Transferred to Company C, 3rd Battalion Sharpshooters. Promoted to corporal. Surrendered at Appomattox 9 April 1865. HGC, SHSP, SR, NPS, CSR

Moon, Robert M. Enlisted at Center Hill, Georgia (Jackson County), 17 July 1861. Private, Company B (Center Hill Guards), 16th Georgia Infantry Regiment. Transferred to Company C, 3rd Battalion Sharpshooters 8 June 1863. Captured at Front Royal 16 August 1864. Committed to Old Capitol Prison, Washington, D. C., 21 August 1864. Transferred to Elmira 28 August 1864; released for exchange 11 October 1864. Exchanged 29 October 1864. Received at Venus Point, Savannah River 15

November 1864. No later record. Born 4 August 1842. Died 13 November 1886. Buried in the Winder Chapel Christian Church Cemetery, Winder, Georgia. LH, UDC, SR, NPS, CSR

Morgan, George N. Enlisted at Lawrenceville, Georgia (Gwinnett County), 16 July 1861. Private, Company I (Hutchins Guards), 16th Georgia Infantry Regiment. Transferred to Company C, 3rd Battalion Sharpshooters. Detailed to Jackson Hospital, Richmond 25 May 1864 as a nurse. Furloughed for thirty days 4 September 1864. On detached duty to Jackson Hospital as ward master 26 November 1864. Furloughed for forty days 1 February 1865. No later record. HGC, SR, NPS, CSR

Morris, Dilmus Enlisted at Yorktown, Virginia 17 February 1862. Private, Company B (Center Hill Guards), 16th Georgia Infantry Regiment. Admitted to Chimborazo Hospital #2, Richmond for treatment of debility 7 June 1862. Returned to duty from hospital 15 June 1862. Admitted to General Hospital, Camp Winder, Richmond for treatment of chronic diarrhea 4 September 1862. Furloughed for twenty days 25 October 1862. Returned to duty. Transferred to Company C, 3rd Battalion Sharpshooters 8 June 1863. Captured at Front Royal 16 August 1864. Committed to Old Capitol Prison, Washington, D. C. 21 August 1864. Transferred to Elmira 28 August 1864; released 11 July 1865. Oath of Allegiance indicates that he was five feet seven inches tall, with Fair complexion, dark hair and gray eyes. LH, SR, NPS, CSR

Morris, Walter C. Enlisted at Center Hill, Georgia (Jackson County), 17 July 1861. Private, Company C, 3rd Battalion Sharpshooters. Captured at Front Royal 16 August 1864. Committed to Old Capitol Prison, Washington, D. C. 21 August 1864. Transferred to Elmira 28 August 1864. Died of variola in prison 15 February 1865. Buried in Woodlawn National Cemetery, Elmira, New York; grave number 2173. ST, IE, SR, NPS, CSR

Nelms, Thomas P. Enlisted at Lawrenceville, Georgia (Gwinnett County), 16 July 1861. Private, Company I (Hutchins Guards), 16th Georgia Infantry Regiment. Transferred to Company C, 3rd Battalion Sharpshooters 8 June 1863 with the rank of 1st sergeant. Wounded at the Wilderness 6 May 1864. Absent, wounded at the end of the war. LH, NLH, SR, NPS, CSR

Owens, William B. Enlisted in Company B, 16th Georgia Infantry Regiment. Private. Transferred to Company C, 3rd Battalion Sharpshooters 8 June 1861. Wounded in the leg at the Wilderness 6 May 1864. Admitted to the Episcopal Church Hospital, Williamsburg, Virginia 12 June 1864. No later record. HGC, SR, NPS, CSR

Phillips, W. F. Enlisted at Greenville, Tennessee 17 March 1864. Private, Company C, 3rd Battalion Sharpshooters. Wounded at the Wilderness 6 May 1864. Captured at Front Royal 16 August 1864. Committed to Old Capitol Prison, Washington, D. C. 21 August 1864. Transferred to Elmira 28 August 1864. Released for exchange 11 October 1864. Exchanged 29 October 1864. No later record. HGC, SR, NPS, CSR

Porterfield, Russell J. Enlisted at Danielsville, Georgia (Madison County), 1 August 1861. 4th Corporal, Company D (Danielsville Guards), 16th Georgia Infantry Regiment. Admitted to Chimborazo Hospital #2, Richmond for treatment of chronic rheumatism 24 April 1862. Returned to duty 7 May 1862. Transferred to Company C, 3rd Battalion Sharpshooters 8 June 1863 with the rank of private. Died 1 April 1864; cause and location not recorded. HGC, SR, NPS, CSR

Scott, T. J. Enlisted for the war at Danielsville, Georgia (Madison County), 5 August 1861. Private, Company D, 16th Georgia Infantry Regiment. Promoted to 3rd Corporal. Detailed as nurse by Regimental Surgeon Eldridge 22 July 1862. Transferred to Company C, 3rd Battalion Sharpshooters. Promoted to Hospital Steward in 1864. Surrendered at Appomattox 9 April 1865. SHSP, NPS, CSR, SR

Self, William Enlisted at Richmond, Virginia 15 August 1861. Private, Company I, 16th Georgia Infantry Regiment. Wounded in the leg at Fredericksburg 12 November 1862. Admitted to CSA Hospital, Farmville, Virginia 21 November 1862. Returned to duty 17 February 1863. Transferred to Company C, 3rd Battalion Sharpshooters. Wounded in the left arm at Cedar Creek 17 October 1864. Admitted to CSA Hospital, Charlottesville, Virginia 24 October 1864. No later record. HGC, NPS, CSR, SR

Slaton, Wade H. Enlisted at Center Hill, Georgia (Jackson County), 17 July 1861. Private, Company B (Center Hill Guards), 16th Georgia Infantry Regiment. Wounded at Crampton's Gap 14 September 1862. Admitted to Institute Hospital, Richmond 13 October 1862. Furloughed for thirty days to Athens, Georgia, 18 October 1862. Returned to duty. Transferred to Company C, 3rd Battalion Sharpshooters 8 June 1863. Admitted to Jackson Hospital, Richmond for treatment of old leg wound 18 September 1864. Furloughed for sixty days 2 November 1864. On wounded furlough at the end of the war. Born 1840 in Jackson County, Georgia. Hospital Register dated 13 October 1862 states he was 17 years of age. LH, NPS, CSR, SR

Smith, Pearson C. Enlisted at Augusta, Georgia (Richmond County), 15 May 1862. Private, Company D (Danielsville Guards), 16th Georgia Infantry Regiment. Admitted to Chimborazo Hospital #4, Richmond 6 July 1862. Returned to duty 19 July 1862. Wounded in the side at Fredericksburg 13 December 1862. Transferred to Company C, 3rd Battalion Sharpshooters 8 June 1863. Surrendered at Appomattox 9 April 1865. HGC, SHSP, NPS, CSR, SR

Smith, Sanford Enlisted at Center Hill, Georgia (Jackson County), 17 July 1861. Private, Company B (Center Hill Guards), 16th Georgia Infantry Regiment. Captured at Crampton's Gap 14 September 1862. Imprisoned at Fort Delaware; released for exchange 2 October 1862; received at Aiken's Landing 10 October 1862. Transferred to Company C, 3rd Battalion Sharpshooters 8 June 1863. Wounded in 1863. Admitted to Camp Winder Hospital 14 July 1863. Furloughed for thirty days 30 July 1863. Deserted at Petersburg 17 July 1864. No later record. LH, NPS, CSR, SR

Spence, William D. Enlisted at Richmond, Virginia 13 August 1861. Private, Company B (Center Hill Guards), 16th Georgia Infantry Regiment. Admitted to

General Hospital #18, Richmond for treatment of dysentery 27 August 1862. Transferred 30 August 1862. Returned to duty. Transferred to Company C, 3rd Battalion Sharpshooters 8 June 1863. Detailed as a teamster from 24 October 1863 until 31 December 1863. Killed in action at Front Royal 16 August 1864. LH, NPS, CSR, SR

Stephens, James E. Enlisted at Richmond, Virginia 10 August 1861. Private, Company D (Danielsville Guards), 16th Georgia Infantry Regiment. Transferred to Company C, 3rd Battalion Sharpshooters. Wounded in the left hand, date and location not recorded. Admitted to Jackson Hospital 28 May 1864. Furloughed for sixty days 4 June 1864. Returned to duty. Captured at Front Royal 16 August 1864. Committed to Old Capitol Prison, Washington, D. C. 21 August 1864. Transferred to Elmira 28 August 1864. Died in prison of chronic diarrhea 14 March 1865. Buried in Woodlawn National Cemetery, Elmira, New York, grave number 2434. ST, IE, NPS, CSR, SR

Vanderford, Richard A. Enlisted at Center Hill, Georgia (Jackson County), 17 July 1861. 2nd Sergeant, Company B (Center Hill Guards), 16th Georgia Infantry Regiment. Wounded in the arm at Captured at Crampton's Gap 14 September 1862. Imprisoned at Fort Delaware. Released for exchange 2 October 1862. Declared exchanged at Aikens Landing 10 November 1862. Transferred to Company C, 3rd Battalion Sharpshooters 8 June 1863. Captured at High Bridge, Virginia (Sailor's Creek) 6 April 1865. Imprisoned at Point Lookout; released 21 June 1865. Oath of Allegiance indicates he was five feet eight inches tall, with dark complexion, brown hair and hazel eyes. LH, NPS, CSR, SR

Watson, James S. Enlisted at Fredericksburg, Virginia 20 February 1863. Private, Company C, 3rd Battalion Sharpshooters. Deserted 4 January 1864. No later record. HGC, NPS, CSR, SR

Witcher, William H. Enlisted at Yorktown, Virginia 1 May 1862. Private, Company A (Madison County Greys), 16th Georgia Infantry Regiment. Captured at Crampton's Gap 14 September 1862; paroled. Returned to regiment. Transferred to Company C, 3rd Battalion Sharpshooters. Surrendered at Appomattox 9 April 1865. HGC, SHSP, NPS, CSR, SR

Sharpshooter Company D

Company Officers:

Almond, James M Enlisted at Madison, Georgia (Morgan County), 29 July 1861. Private, Company G (Panola Guards), Cobb's Legion. Transferred to Company D, 3rd Battalion Sharpshooters with the rank of 2nd lieutenant. Captured at Front Royal, Virginia 16 August 1864. Received at Elmira from Old Capitol Prison 29 August 1864; died in prison of chronic diarrhea 18 May 1865. Buried in Woodlawn Cemetery, Elmira, New York; grave number 2952. SR, BL

Bunt, Delona Enlisted 1 August 1861 at Decatur, Georgia (Dekalb County). Private, Company C (Stephens Rifles), Cobb's Legion Infantry Battalion. Transferred to

Company D 3rd Battalion Sharpshooters. Promoted to 1st Lieutenant 5 June 1863. Captured at Front Royal 16 August 1864. Committed to Old Capitol Prison 21 August, 1864. Transferred to Fort Delaware August 27, 1864. His signature in Major W. E. Simmons' diary shows that he was imprisoned at Fort Delaware. Released 17 June 1865. Born in 1839. SR, NPS, RO, OS, CSR

Cole, Young A. Enlisted at Bowdon, Georgia (Carroll County), 30 July 1861. Sergeant, Company B (Bowdon Volunteers), Cobb's Legion Infantry Battalion. Captured at Crampton's Gap 14 September 1862. Admitted to Chimborazo Hospital #4, Richmond 4 May 1863. Returned to duty 2 June 1863. Admitted to Chimborazo Hospital #2 for treatment of erysipelas 7 June 1863. Transferred to Company D, 3rd Battalion Sharpshooters with the rank of 2nd Lieutenant 8 June 1863. Furloughed for 30 days 1 August 1863. Wounded in left foot 21 June 1864. Sent to General Hospital #4, Richmond 22 June 1864. Sent to General Hospital 6 July 1864 for amputation of toe. Admitted to General Hospital #4, Richmond 27 October 1864; furloughed 15 November 1864. Admitted to Stuart Hospital, Richmond 26 November 1864. Returned to duty 6 December 1864. Captured at Sailors Creek 6 April 1865. Imprisoned at Johnson's Island; released 18 June 1865. Oath of Allegiance indicates he was five feet nine inches tall, with florid complexion, light hair and blue eyes. Born in 1836. SR, NPS, RO, OS, CSR

Enlisted Men:

Baggett, William M. Enlisted at Decatur, Georgia (Dekalb County), 1 August 1861. Private, Company C (Stephens Rifles), Cobb's Legion Infantry Battalion. Admitted to Chimborazo Hospital #2, Richmond for Jaundice 21 February 1863. Admitted to Danville Hospital 14 March 1863 for Rheumatism. Returned to duty 18 March 1863. Transferred to Company D, 3rd Battalion Sharpshooters. Captured at Mine Run 10 May 1864. Imprisoned at Fort Delaware; received 21 May 1864. Exchanged 7 March 1865. Born *ca.* 1838. No later record. SR, NPS, RO, CSR

Ball, Isaac C. Enlisted at Madison, Georgia (Morgan County), 16 February 1863. Private, Company D, 3rd Battalion Sharpshooters. Returned to duty 7 February 1864. Admitted to Jackson Hospital, Richmond 30 May 1864 for treatment of acute diarrhea. Captured at Farmville, Virginia (Sailor's Creek) 6 April 1865. Imprisoned at Point Lookout. Released 7 June 1865. SR, NPS, CSR

Beauchamp, Jasper C. Enlisted at Decatur, Georgia (Dekalb County), 1 August 1861. Private, Company C (Stephens Rifles), Cobb's Legion Infantry Battalion. Detailed as Wagoner (Teamster) November 1861. Transferred to Company D, 3rd Battalion Sharpshooters. Captured about 7 December 1863. Captured at Front Royal 16 August 1864. Admitted to Old Capitol Prison, Washington D. C. 21 August 1864. Transferred to Elmira 28 August 1864; released 23 June 1865. Oath of Allegiance shows him to be six feet one inch tall, with florid complexion, dark hair and hazel eyes. SR, NPS, CSR

Beauchamp, Joseph X. Enlisted at Jonesboro, Georgia (Clayton County), 1 June 1863. Private Assigned to Company D, 3rd Battalion Sharpshooters. Appointed 2nd corporal 15 June 1863. Promoted to 5th sergeant. Wounded at Knoxville in right elbow

19 November 1863. Retired (medical disability) 10 February 1865. Certificate of Discharge shows him to be six feet tall, with fair complexion, light hair and blue eyes. SR, NPS, CSR

Berry, William W. Enlisted at Decatur, Georgia (Dekalb County), 1 August 1864. Private, Company C (Stephens Rifles (Dekalb County), Cobb's Legion Infantry Battalion. Teamster. Admitted to General Hospital, Charlottesville, Virginia 6 November 1862. Transferred to Company D, 3rd Battalion Sharpshooters. Killed at Cold Harbor 1 June 1864. Born in 1840. SR, NPS, CSR

Boss, Elijah W. Enlisted at Decatur, Georgia (Dekalb County), 10 September 1862. Private, Company A (Lamar Infantry), Cobb's Legion Infantry Battalion. Transferred to Company D, 3rd Battalion Sharpshooters 8 June 1863. Wounded in 1863, date and location not recorded. Admitted to Jackson Hospital, Richmond 6 October 1864. Returned to duty 12 October 1864. Surrendered at Appomattox 9 April 1865. LH, SR, NPS, RO

Brewer, Ethan M. Enlisted in Newton County 1 August 1861. Private, Company A (Lamar Infantry) Cobb's Legion Infantry Battalion. Transferred to Company D, 3rd Battalion Sharpshooters. Deserted 22 September 1863. Captured and returned to command 25 February 1864. Court Martial 5 April 1864; charged with desertion; sentenced to hard labor. Admitted to Hospital #13, Richmond for treatment of dyspepsia 7 July 1864. Sent to Castle Thunder Prison (CSA) 21 July 1864. No later record. CM, SR, NPS, CSR

Brown, Rufus D. Enlisted at Madison, Georgia (Morgan County), 29 July 1861. Private, Company D, 3rd Battalion Sharpshooters. Captured at Front Royal 16 August 1864. Committed to Old Capitol Prison, Washington, D. C. 21 August 1864. Transferred to Elmira 28 August 1864; released 7 July 1865. Oath of Allegiance indicates he was six feet tall, with fair complexion, light hair and blue eyes. SR, NPS, CSR, BL

Cheek, Thomas S. Enlisted at Covington, Georgia (Newton County), 1 August 1861. Private, Company A (Lamar Infantry), Cobb's Legion Infantry Battalion. Transferred to Company D, 3rd Battalion Sharpshooters 1 May 1863. Detailed to conduct Union prisoners to Richmond 10 December 1863. Wounded in the neck, date and location not recorded. Admitted to Jackson Hospital in Richmond 15 May 1864. Transferred to CSA General Hospital, Danville, Virginia 22 May 1864; returned to duty 2 July 1864. Captured at Front Royal 16 August 1864. Committed to Old Capitol Prison 21 August 1864. Transferred to Elmira 28 August 1864; paroled and released for exchange 11 October 1864. Exchanged at Point Lookout 29 October 1864. Died at sea 9 November 1864 *en route* to Venus Point, Savannah River. SR, NPS, CSR

Chewning, John A. Enlisted at Decatur, Georgia (Dekalb County), 12 February 1862. Private, Company C (Stephens Rifles), Cobb's Legion Infantry Battalion. Captured at Crampton's Gap 14 September 1862. Imprisoned at Fort Delaware. Released for exchange 2 October 1862. Exchanged 10 November 1862 at Aiken's Landing. Appointed 5th Sergeant 1 December 1862. Transferred to Company D 3rd

Battalion Sharpshooters. Appointed 1st Sergeant 15 June 1863. Sent to hospital 6 November 1863. Returned to duty 29 November 1863. Captured at Front Royal 16 August 1864. Committed to Old Capitol Prison, Washington, D. C. 21 August 1864. Transferred to Elmira 28 August 1864; released 7 July 1865. Oath of Allegiance indicates he was six feet tall, with florid complexion, light hair and hazel eyes. SR, NPS, CSR

Cook, John H. Enlisted at Covington, Georgia (Newton County), 1 May 1862. Private, Company A (Lamar Rifles), Cobb's Legion Infantry Battalion. Transferred to Company D, 3rd Battalion Sharpshooters. Killed in action on 10 or 11 May 1864; location not recorded. SR, NPS, CSR

Crockett, Andrew J. Enlisted at Decatur, Georgia (Dekalb County), 1 August 1861. Private, Company C (Stephens Rifles), Cobb's Legion Infantry Battalion. Admitted to Winder Hospital, Richmond 25 September 1862. Furloughed thirty days 7 November 1862. Transferred to Company D, 3rd Battalion Sharpshooters. Name appears on a receipt roll for Liberty Hospital 19 April 1864. No later record. Born *ca.* 1836. SR, CSR

Davis, Miles A. Enlisted at Decatur, Georgia (Dekalb County), 1 August 1861. Private, Company C (Stephens Rifles), Cobb's Legion Infantry Battalion. Promoted to 2nd Corporal 1861. Promoted to 3rd Sergeant 1862. Admitted to Chimborazo Hospital #2 for the treatment of pneumonia 25 January 1863. Returned to duty 30 March 1863. Admitted to Chimborazo Hospital #2, Richmond June 5, 1863. Admitted to Jackson Hospital for the treatment of rheumatism 5 August 1863. Returned to duty 21 August 1863. Transferred to Company D, 3rd Battalion Sharpshooters 1 January 1864. Admitted to Jackson Hospital, Richmond 29 July 1864 for treatment of chronic diarrhea. Furloughed for thirty days on 25 August 1864. Admitted to Jackson Hospital for treatment of chronic diarrhea 15 September 1864. Returned to duty 30 September 1864. Promoted to sergeant. Captured at Farmville, Virginia (Sailor's Creek) 6 April 1865. Imprisoned at Point Lookout. Died in prison of chronic dysentery 13 June 1865. Buried in the Confederate Cemetery, Point Lookout, Maryland, grave number 2121. ST, IE, SR, NPS, CSR

Day, Jesse C. Enlisted at Covington, Georgia (Newton County), 1 August 1861. Private, Company A (Lamar Infantry), Cobb's Legion Infantry Battalion. Transferred to Company D, 3rd Battalion Sharpshooters. Transferred back to Cobb's Legion Infantry Battalion 22 June 1864. Captured at Farmville, Virginia (Sailor's Creek) 6 April 1865. Imprisoned at Newport News 14 April 1865; released 25 June 1865. Oath indicates he was five feet eleven inches tall, with fair complexion, dark hair and blue eyes. SR, NPS, RO, CSR

Delay, Hiram R. Enlisted at Decatur, Georgia (Dekalb County), 1 August 1861. Private, Company C (Stephens Rifles, Cobb's Legion Infantry Battalion. Admitted to Camp Winder Hospital, Richmond. Returned to duty 30 October 1862. Transferred to Company D, 3rd Battalion Sharpshooters 8 June 1863. Captured 1 July 1863. No later record. SR, NPS, CSR

Doster, William Z. A. Enlisted at Center Hill, Georgia (Jackson County), 17 July 1861. Private, Company B (Center Hill Guards), 16th Georgia Infantry Regiment. Captured at Frederick, Maryland, 13 July 1862. Imprisoned at Fort Delaware; released for exchange 2 October 1862; received at Aiken's Landing 10 November 1862. Transferred to 3rd Battalion Sharpshooters 8 June 1863; served in Company C and Company D. Promoted to sergeant. Detailed as a shoemaker January and February 1864. Captured at Farmville, Virginia (Sailor's Creek) 6 April 1865. Imprisoned at Point Lookout; released 26 June 1865. Oath of Allegiance indicates he was five feet eight inches tall, with fair complexion, brown hair and blue eyes. LH, SR, NPS, CSR

Dougherty, Charles L. Enlisted at Decatur, Georgia (Dekalb County), 15 May 1862. Private, Company D, 3rd Battalion Sharpshooters. Captured at Front Royal, 16 August 1864. Committed to Old Capitol Prison, Washington, D. C. 21 August 1864. Transferred to Elmira 28 August 1864. Died in prison of variola 31 January 1865. Buried at Woodlawn Cemetery, Elmira, New York, grave number 1780. ST, IE, SR, NPS, CSR

Echols, Joseph D. Enlisted at Decatur, Georgia (Dekalb County), 1 August 1861. Private, Company C (Stephens Rifles), Cobb's Legion Infantry Battalion. Captured at Sharpsburg 17 September 1862. Paroled, date and location not recorded. Transferred to Company D, 3rd Battalion Sharpshooters. Wounded in left leg. Admitted to Chimborazo Hospital #4, Richmond 20 July 1863. Furloughed for thirty-five days 8 August 1863. Admitted to Jackson Hospital, Richmond 25 May 1864. Returned to duty 3 August 1864. Admitted to Jackson Hospital for treatment of old wound 11 August 1864. Furloughed for thirty days 11 September 1864. No later record. SR, NPS, CSR

Friddell, Joseph L. Enlisted at Decatur, Georgia (Dekalb County), 1 August 1861. Private, Company C (Stephens Rifles), Cobb's Legion Infantry Battalion. Wounded at Crampton's Gap 14 September 1862. Treated for severe shoulder and leg wound in the USA Field Hospital, Burkittsville, Maryland. Captured at Sharpsburg 28 September 1862. Imprisoned at Fort McHenry; paroled 11 October 1862 and sent to Fort Monroe for exchange. Returned to regiment. Transferred to Company D, 3rd Battalion Sharpshooters 8 June 1863. Promoted to corporal November 1863. Captured near Petersburg 21 June 1864. Imprisoned at Point Lookout; exchanged 1 November 1864. No later record. SR, RO, CSR

Galbreth, Thomas S. Enlisted at Fredericksburg, Virginia 28 March 1863. Private, Cobb's Legion Infantry Battalion. Transferred to Company D, 3rd Battalion Sharpshooters. Deserted 2 May 1863. Took Oath of Allegiance to the U.S. at Chattanooga, TN 8 March 1864. No later record. Oath indicates he was five feet ten inches tall, with dark complexion, dark hair and blue eyes. SR, NPS, CSR

Garner, John G. Enlisted at Bowdon, Georgia (Carroll County), 1 August 1862. Private, Company B (Bowdon Volunteers), Cobb's Legion Infantry Battalion. Detailed as a hospital nurse. Admitted to Chimborazo Hospital #3, Richmond for treatment of diarrhea 1 November 1862. Transferred to CSA General Hospital, Danville, Virginia 2 November 1862. Returned to duty 17 January 1863. Transferred to Company D, 3rd Battalion Sharpshooters 15 June 1863 with the rank of corporal. Captured in

Winchester, Virginia 21 June 1864. Admitted to U.S. Hospital, Winchester, Virginia. Returned to duty 27 January 1864. No later record. RO, CSR, SR

Grayham, Isaiah Gordon Enlisted at Athens, Georgia (Clarke County), 11 July 1861. Private, Company A (Madison County Greys), 16th Georgia Infantry Regiment. Transferred to 3rd Battalion Sharpshooters 8 June 1863; served in Company C and D. Wounded and captured at Front Royal 16 August 1864. Committed to Old Capitol Prison 21 August 1864. Transferred to Elmira 28 August 1864; released 16 June 1865. Oath of Allegiance indicates he was five feet eleven inches tall, with fair complexion, light hair and blue eyes. Born 10 May 1839. Died 8 April 1917. Buried in Brown Cemetery, Madison County, Georgia. LH, UDC, SR, NPS, CSR

Guess, Henry W. Enlisted at Decatur, Georgia (Dekalb County), 1 August 1861. Private, Company C (Stephens Rifles), Cobb's Legion Infantry Battalion. Transferred to Company D, 3rd Battalion Sharpshooters. Admitted to hospital. Returned to duty 30 January 1864. Captured at Front Royal 16 August 1864. Committed to Old Capitol Prison, Washington, D. C. 21 August 1864. Transferred to Elmira 28 August 1864; released 7 July 1865. Oath of Allegiance indicates he was five feet ten inches tall, with florid complexion, dark hair and hazel eyes. SR, NPS, CSR

Hays, Jasper P. Enlisted at Carrollton, Georgia (Carroll County), 1 August 1861. Private, Company F (Carroll Boys), Cobb's Legion Infantry Battalion. Admitted to General Hospital #12, Richmond 28 September 1862. Returned to duty. Admitted to Camp Winder Hospital #4, Richmond 21 October 1862. Returned to duty 11 November 1862. Transferred to Company D, 3rd Battalion Sharpshooters. Appointed 4th Sergeant 15 June 1863. Detached for light duty at the headquarters of the Army of Northern Virginia 4 September 1863. No later record. Born *ca.* 1832. SR, NPS, RO, CSR

Henderson, Newton Enlisted at Decatur, Georgia (Dekalb County 1 August 1861. Private, Company C (Stephens Rifles), Cobb's Legion Infantry Battalion. Teamster February 1862. Transferred to Company D, 3rd Battalion Sharpshooters 1 May 1863. Wounded in the left hand at Chancellorsville. Admitted to Chimborazo Hospital #4, Richmond 6 May 1863. Transferred to Chimborazo Hospital #2, 9 May 1863. Transferred to the 36th Georgia Infantry Regiment 11 November 1863. SR, NPS, CSR

Henderson, Samuel J. Enlisted at Covington, Georgia (Newton County), 1 May 1862. Private, Company A, Cobb's Legion Infantry Battalion. Transferred to Company D, 3rd Battalion Sharpshooters. Retired to Invalid Corps 26 July 1864. SR, NPS, RO

Hogan, William J. Enlisted at Madison, Georgia (Morgan County), 29 July 1861. 4th Corporal, Company G, Cobb's Legion Infantry Battalion. Demoted to private November 1862. Transferred to Company D, 3rd Battalion Sharpshooters. Appointed 5th sergeant from ranks 15 June 1863. Returned to duty 19 January 1864. Final roll dated 30 January 1865 shows him "missing since 19 October 1864." No later record. Born *ca.* 1840. SR, NPS, CSR, BL

Huff, Burrell H. Enlisted at Carrollton, Georgia (Carroll County), 20 March 1862. Private, Company F (Carroll Boys), Cobb's Legion Infantry Battalion. Transferred to Company D, 3rd Battalion Sharpshooters. Transferred to Cobb's Legion 1 November 1863. Captured at Farmville, Virginia (Sailor's Creek) 6 April 1865. Imprisoned at Newport News; released 25 June 1865. Oath of Allegiance indicates he was five feet ten inches tall, with dark complexion, black hair, and hazel eyes. SR, NPS, CSR

Jett, John T. Enlisted for the war at Decatur, Georgia (Dekalb County), 1 August 1861. Private, Company C (Stephens Rifles), Cobb's Legion Infantry Battalion. Promoted to Corporal. Admitted to Hospital, Richmond 24 November 1862. Returned to duty 26 November 1862. Transferred to Company D, 3rd Battalion Sharpshooters. Appointed 2nd Sergeant 15 June 1863. Wounded at Chattanooga, September 1863. Died from wounds 27 September 1863. Born *ca.* 1837. SR, NPS, CSR

Johnson, John J. Enlisted for the war at Camp McDonald (Cobb County) 1 June 1861. Private. Transferred to Company D, 3rd Battalion Sharpshooters. Wounded, date and location not recorded. On detached duty from September 1863 through February 1864, and from May through June 1864. Detached for light duty February 1865. Surrendered at Appomattox 9 April 1865. SR, NPS, CSR

Jones, Charles H. Enlisted at Richmond, Virginia August or September 1861. Private, Company A (Lamar Infantry), Cobb's Legion Infantry Battalion. Transferred to Company D, 3rd Battalion Sharpshooters. Captured at Front Royal 16 August 1864. Committed to Old Capitol Prison, Washington, D. C. 21 August 1864. Transferred to Elmira 28 August 1864; released 19 May 1865. Oath of Allegiance indicates he was five feet nine inches tall, with dark complexion, black hair and black eyes. Requested Permission to take the Oath of Allegiance 30 November 1864, stating that he was from Maine and had volunteered for Confederate service on 12 July 1862 to avoid conscription. SR, NPS, RO, CSR

King, John W. Enlisted at Bowdon, Georgia (Carroll County), 30 July 1861. 1st Sergeant, Company B (Bowdon Volunteers), Cobb's Legion Infantry Battalion. Transferred to Company D, 3rd Battalion Sharpshooters 1 May 1863. Promoted to Captain, date of rank 5 June 1863. Captured at Front Royal 16 August 1864. Committed of Old Capitol Prison, Washington, D. C. 21 August 1864. Transferred to Fort Delaware 27 August 1864; released 17 June 1865. Oath of Allegiance indicates he was five feet nine inches tall, with fair complexion, dark hair and blue eyes. Born 30 June 1837. NLH, HB, SR, NPS, RO, OS, CRS

Langford, Joseph S. Enlisted at Decatur, Georgia (Dekalb County), 5 September 1861. Private, Company C (Stephens Rifles), Cobb's Legion Infantry Battalion. Transferred to Company D, 3rd Battalion Sharpshooters. Captured at High Bridge, Virginia (Sailor's Creek) 6 April 1865. Imprisoned at Point Lookout; released 28 June 1865. Oath of Allegiance indicates he was five feet eight inches tall, with dark complexion, black hair and black eyes. SR, NPS, CSR

McCullough, William H. Enlisted at Covington, Georgia (Newton County), September 10, 1861. Private, Company A (Lamar Infantry), Cobb's Legion Infantry Battalion. Transferred to Company D, 3rd Battalion Sharpshooters. Captured at Gettysburg July 1, 1863. No later record. SR, NPS, CSR

McWright, James S. Enlisted at Bowdon, Georgia (Carroll County), 30 July 1861. Private, Company B (Bowdon Volunteers), Cobb's Legion Infantry Battalion. Transferred to Company D, 3rd Battalion Sharpshooters. Wounded in left leg, date not recorded. Admitted to Jackson Hospital, Richmond 29 July 1864. Furloughed for thirty days 3 August 1864. Returned to duty. Admitted to Jackson Hospital, Richmond for treatment of shell wound 6 October 1864. Returned to duty 12 October 1864. No later record. SR, NPS, RO, CSR

Middlebrooks, John B. Enlisted at Covington, Georgia (Newton County), 1 August 1861. Sergeant, Company A (Lamar Infantry), Cobb's Legion Infantry Battalion. Transferred to Company D, 3rd Battalion Sharpshooters 8 June 1863. Promoted to 3rd sergeant from ranks 15 June 1863. Wounded in right elbow. Admitted to Jackson Hospital, Richmond 15 May 1864. Transferred to CSA Hospital, Danville, Virginia 23 May 1864. Furloughed 26 May 1864. Returned to duty. Captured at Front Royal 16 August 1864. Committed to Old Capitol Prison, Washington, D. C. 21 August 1864. Transferred to Elmira 28 August 1864; released 19 May 1865. Oath of Allegiance indicates he was six feet tall, with dark complexion, dark hair and blue eyes. Born *ca.* 1838. SR, NPS, RO, OS, CSR

Minton, William H. Enlisted at Yorktown, Virginia, 16 November 1861. Private, Company G (Panola Guards), Cobb's Legion Infantry Battalion. Captured at Crampton's Gap 14 September 1862. Imprisoned at Fort Delaware. Released for exchange at Aiken's Landing Virginia 2 October 1862. Transferred to Company D, 3rd Battalion Sharpshooters. Wounded, location not recorded. Admitted to Chimborazo Hospital #2, 16 July 1863. Transferred to Jackson Hospital, Richmond 7 August 1863. Furloughed for thirty days 17 October 1863. Returned to duty. Captured at the Wilderness 6 May 1864. No later record. SR, NPS, CSR

Moss, Wiley J. Enlisted at Savannah, Georgia (Chatham County), 19 April 1862. Private. Transferred to Company D, 3rd Battalion Sharpshooters. Captured at Front Royal 16 August 1864. Committed to Old Capitol Prison, Washington, D.C., 21 August 1864. Transferred to Elmira 28 August 1864. Died in prison of chronic diarrhea 4 December 1864. Buried in Woodlawn National Cemetery, Elmira, New York; grave number 881. ST, IE, SR, NPS, CSR

Mott, James B. Enlisted at Fredericksburg, Virginia 22 April 1861. Private, Company D, 3rd Battalion Sharpshooters. Surrendered at Appomattox 9 April 1865. SHSP, SR, NPS, CSR

New, John H. Enlisted for the War at Decatur, Georgia (Dekalb County), 10 May 1862. Private, Company C (Stephens Rifles), Cobb's Legion Infantry Battalion. Transferred to Company D, 3rd Battalion Sharpshooters 8 June 1863. Admitted to CSA

Hospital Charlottesville, Virginia for treatment of pneumonia 27 July 1863. Returned to duty 15 August 1863. Admitted to Jackson Hospital, Richmond 17 June 1864 for treatment of dysentery. Returned to duty 22 June 1864. Admitted to Jackson Hospital, Richmond for treatment of hemorrhoids 24 July 1864. Returned to duty 3 August 1864. Present on muster roll for August 1864, last on file. No later record. NPS, CSR, SR

Newton, William W. Enlisted at Bowdon, Georgia (Carroll County), 30 July 1861. Private, Company B (Bowdon Volunteers), Cobb's Legion Infantry Battalion. Transferred to Company D, 3rd Battalion Sharpshooters 8 June 1863 with the rank of corporal. Surrendered at Appomattox 9 April 1865. SHSP, SR, NPS, CSR

Oglesby, Thomas L. Enlisted at Covington, Georgia (Newton County), 19 September 1861. Private, Company A (Lamar Infantry), Cobb's Legion Infantry Battalion. Captured at Crampton's Gap 14 September 1862. Imprisoned at Fort Delaware. Released for exchange 2 October 1862. Exchanged at Aiken's Landing, Virginia before 10 November 1862. Transferred to Company D, 3rd Battalion Sharpshooters 8 June 1863. Appointed corporal from the ranks 10 June 1863. Captured at Front Royal 16 August 1864. Committed to Old Capitol Prison, Washington, D. C. 21 August 1864. Transferred to Elmira 28 August 1864: released 16 June 1865. No later record. Oath of Allegiance indicates he was five feet nine inches tall, with dark complexion, dark hair and hazel eyes. SR, NPS, RO, CSR

Pierce, Andrew J. Enlisted at Decatur, Georgia (Dekalb County), 1 August 1861. Private, Company C (Stephens Rifles), Cobb's Legion Infantry Battalion. Transferred to Company D, 3rd Battalion Sharpshooters 8 June 1863. Roll dated December 1864 shows him present. No later record. Born *ca.* 1840. SR, NPS, CSR

Pierce, George W. Enlisted at Decatur, Georgia (Dekalb County), 29 July 1862. Private, Company C (Stephens Rifles), Cobb's Legion Infantry Battalion. Transferred to Company D, 3rd Battalion Sharpshooters 8 June 1863. Roll dated December 1864 shows him absent, sick. No later record. SR, NPS, CSR

Poole, William Enlisted at Covington, Georgia (Newton County), 1 August 1861. Private. Transferred to Company D, 3rd Battalion Sharpshooters 8 June 1863. Transferred to the 53rd Georgia Infantry Regiment 16 August 1863. SR, NPS, CSR

Sheppard, Andrew J. (Shepherd) Enlisted at Decatur, Georgia (Dekalb County), 1 August 1861. Private Company C (Stephens Rifles), Cobb's Legion Infantry Battalion. Transferred to Company D, 3rd Battalion Sharpshooters 8 June 1863. Absent without leave from 28 January 1864 until 25 February 1864. Court Martial sentenced him to stoppage of one month's pay. Admitted to Camp Winder Hospital, Richmond May 1864. Died 10 June 1864. NPS, CSR, SR

Short, Wesley Enlisted at Madison, Georgia (Morgan County), 10 May 1862. Private, Company G, Cobb's Legion Infantry Battalion. Transferred to Company D, 3rd Battalion Sharpshooters. Died 19 January 1864. SR, CSR

Smith, William H. Enlisted at Decatur, Georgia (Dekalb County), 12 November 1862. Private, Company C (Stephens Rifles), Cobb's Legion Infantry Battalion. Transferred to Company D, 3rd Battalion Sharpshooters 8 June 1863. Admitted to CSA Hospital, Charlottesville, Virginia 25 August 1864. Transferred to Camp Winder Hospital, Richmond 13 September 1863. Returned to duty 16 September 1863. Roll dated June 1864 shows him on duty at the military prison, Atlanta, Georgia. CSR, SR

Starnes, Peyton P. Enlisted in Carroll County, Georgia, 15 August 1861. Private, Company F (Carroll Boys), Cobb's Legion Infantry Battalion. Transferred to Company D, 3rd Battalion Sharpshooters. Deserted 13 May 1862. Apprehended or returned to regiment on his own free will. Court Martial 18 April 1863, charge and punishment not recorded. Wounded in the left hand at Chancellorsville 3 May 1863. Admitted to Chimborazo Hospital #4 Richmond 6 May 1863. Transferred to Chimborazo Hospital #2, Richmond 9 May 1863. Roll dated August 1864 states he was absent, sick. No later record. Born, *ca.* 1843. NPS, CSR, SR

Wheeler, Lawrence L. Enlisted at Covington, Georgia (Newton County), 1 September 1861. Private, Company A (Lamar Infantry), Cobb's Legion Infantry Battalion. Transferred to Company D, 3rd Battalion Sharpshooters 8 June 1863. Deserted 1 August 1863. Returned to regiment and placed under guard. Deserted May 1864. No later record. NPS, RO, CSR, SR

Wittick, Lucious ("Luke") L. Enlisted at Augusta, Georgia (Richmond County), 2 May 1861. Re-enlisted at Madison, Georgia (Morgan County), 15 May 1862. Private, Company G (Panola Guards), Cobb's Legion Infantry Battalion. Transferred to Company D, 3rd Battalion Sharpshooters 8 June 1863. Declined. Returned to regiment. Wounded in the left hand May 1864, location not recorded. Roll for August 1864, last on file, indicates he was detailed to the quartermaster's department in Madison, Georgia, for enrolling duty. No later record. SR, NPS, CSR, BL

Wood, William C. Enlisted at Decatur, Georgia (Dekalb County), 12 July 1862. Private, Company C (Stephens Rifles), Cobb's Legion Infantry Battalion. Transferred to Company D, 3rd Battalion Sharpshooters. Wounded, date and location not recorded. Roll dated 31 August 1864, last on file, shows him absent, sick. No later record. NPS, CSR, SR

Yarbray, John O. Enlisted at Covington, Georgia (Newton County), 11 June 1861. Private, Company B (Newton Rifles), 18th Georgia Infantry Regiment. Transferred to Company D, 3rd Battalion Sharpshooters 16 August 1863. Admitted to hospital, name and date not recorded. Returned to duty 9 March 1864. Wounded in right thigh, date and location not recorded. Admitted to Jackson Hospital, Richmond, May 1864. Roll for August 1864, last on file, shows he was absent, sick. No later record. SR, NPS, CSR

Young, Elijah D. Enlisted at Madison, Georgia (Morgan County), 15 May 1862. Private, Company G (Panola Guards), Cobb's Legion Infantry Battalion. Transferred to Company D, 3rd Battalion Sharpshooters. Roll dated 1 January 1864 states he was in hospital since 1 October 1863. Returned to duty 2 April 1864. Admitted to Jackson

Hospital 6 October 1864. Returned to duty 12 October 1864. Admitted to Jackson Hospital, Richmond for treatment of chronic diarrhea 24 December 1864; returned to duty 26 February 1865. Surrendered at Appomattox 9 April 1865. SHSP, SR, NPS, CSR

Young, James H. Enlisted at Madison, Georgia (Morgan County), 15 May 1862. Private, Company G (Panola Guards), Cobb's Legion Infantry Battalion. Transferred to Company D, 3rd Battalion Sharpshooters. Captured at High Bridge, Virginia (Sailor's Creek) 6 April 1865. Imprisoned at Point Lookout; released 8 June 1865. NPS, CSR, SR

Young, Moses W. Enlisted at Madison, Georgia (Morgan County), 24 March 1864. Private, Company D, 3rd Battalion Sharpshooters. Captured 1865, location not recorded. Name appears on a list of parolees at Newton, North Carolina 19 April 1865. NPS, CSR, SR

Sharpshooter Company E

Company Officers:

Ardis, Payson L. Enlisted at Charleston, South Carolina 9 May 1861. Private, Company I (Palmetto Guards), 2nd South Carolina Infantry Regiment. Transferred to Company L (Blackwell Volunteers), Phillips Legion Infantry Battalion 8 August 1862. Transferred to Company E, 3rd Battalion Sharpshooters 5 June 1863 with the rank of 1st lieutenant. Captured at Front Royal 16 August 1864. Sent to Old Capitol Prison 21 August 1864. Imprisoned at Fort Delaware 27 August 1864; released 17 June 1865. Oath indicates that he was five feet eleven inches tall, with dark hair, dark complexion and blue eyes. Born in 1841. Son of David and E. C. Ardis. PL, GSS, SR, NPS, OS, CSR

Martin, John F. Enlisted at Lawrenceville, Georgia (Gwinnett County), 16 July 1861. 2nd Lieutenant, Company H (Flint Hill Grays), 16th Georgia Infantry Regiment. Transferred to Company E, 3rd Battalion Sharpshooters. Promoted to Captain, date of rank 5 June 1863. Captured at Front Royal 16 August 1864. Committed to Old Capitol Prison, Washington, D. C. 21 August 1864. Transferred to Fort Delaware 27 August 1865; released 17 June 1865. Oath of Allegiance indicates he was five feet ten inches tall, with fair complexion, black hair and gray eyes. HGC, NLH, SR, NPS, OS, CSR

Enlisted Men:

Archer, John M. Enlisted at Jefferson, Georgia (Jackson County), 20 July 1861. Private, Company G (Jackson Rifles), 16th Georgia Infantry Regiment. Captured at Crampton's Gap, Maryland 14 September 1862; received for exchange at Aiken's Landing, Virginia 10 November 1862. Transferred to Company E, 3rd Battalion Sharpshooters 8 June 1863. Captured at Front Royal 16 August 1864. Imprisoned at Elmira; released 14 June 1865. LH, SR, NPS, CSR

Arrowood, Isham D. Enlisted in Rabun County, Georgia, 24 August 1861. Private, Company E (Rabun Gap Riflemen), 24th Georgia Infantry Regiment. Admitted to General Hospital, Howard's Grove, Richmond 4 March 1863. Returned to duty 31 March 1863. Transferred to Company E, 3rd Battalion Sharpshooters 8 June 1863. Wounded in the arm at Petersburg 10 June 1864. Admitted to Camp Winder Hospital, Richmond. Admitted to Jackson Hospital, Richmond, 10 October 1864. Discharged from service due to disability. Born in 1825. LH, SR, NPS, CSR, FP

Barrett, Milton Enlisted at Camp McDonald (Cobb County) 13 June 1861. Private, Company A (Acworth Infantry), 18th Georgia Infantry Regiment. Transferred to Company E, 3rd Battalion Sharpshooters 8 June 1863 with the rank of corporal. Captured at Front Royal 16 August 1864. Imprisoned at Old Capitol Prison Washington, D. C. 21 August 1864. Transferred to Elmira 28 August 1864; died of Variola while in prison 12 February 1865. Buried at Woodlawn Cemetery, Elmira, New York; grave number 2031. ST, SR, NPS, CSR

Beck, Jasper Newton Jr. Enlisted in Rabun County, Georgia, 24 August 1861. Private, Company E (Rabun Gap Riflemen), 24th Georgia Infantry Regiment. Transferred to Company E, 3rd Battalion Sharpshooters 8 June 1863. Killed in action at Gettysburg 3 July 1863. LH, SR, NPS, CSR

Benson, Oscar Enlisted in Gwinnett County, Georgia, 11 August 1861. Private, Company H (Flint Hill Grays), 16th Georgia Infantry Regiment. Transferred to Company E, 3rd Battalion Sharpshooters 8 June 1863 with the rank of 2nd sergeant. Wounded in 1863, date and location not recorded. Captured at Front Royal 16 August 1864. Committed to Old Capitol Prison, Washington, D. C. 21 August 1864. Transferred to Elmira 28 August 1864; released for exchange 14 March 1865; received at Boulware & Cox's Wharves 21 March 1865. No later record. LH, HGC, SR, NPS, CSR

Brewer, James P. Enlisted at Greensboro, Georgia (Greene County), 16 May 1862. Private, Company A (Greene Rifles) Phillips Legion Infantry Battalion. Transferred to Company E, 3rd Battalion Sharpshooters 1 May 1863. No later record. 1906 Roster Commission Roll shows that he transferred to Company E in May 1863, but no record exists for a James P. Brewer in this unit, only James P. "Brue." PL, SR, NPS, CSR

Burnett, Samuel P. Enlisted in Gwinnett County, Georgia, 24 August 1861. Private, Company F (Gwinnett Independent Blues), 24th Georgia Infantry Regiment. Admitted to General Hospital #21, Richmond for treatment of debility 8 May 1863. Returned to duty 14 May 1863. Transferred to Company E, 3rd Battalion Sharpshooters 8 June 1863. Captured at Front Royal 16 August 1864. Committed to Old Capitol Prison, Washington, D. C. 21 August 1864. Transferred to Elmira 28 August 1864; released 7 July 1865. Oath of Allegiance indicates he was six feet three inches tall, with fair skin, dark hair and blue eyes. LH, SR, NPS, CSR

Cotton, James S. Enlisted in Company E, 3rd Battalion Sharpshooters 2 April 1864. Private. Captured at Front Royal 16 August 1864. Imprisoned at Elmira; released 15 May 1865. Oath of Allegiance indicates he was five feet six inches tall, with fair complexion, light hair and blue eyes. SR, NPS, CSR

Crawford, James Talbot Enlisted at Fredericksburg, Virginia 25 November 1862. Private, Company A, Phillips Legion Infantry Battalion. Transferred to Company E, 3rd Battalion Sharpshooters 1 May 1863. Wounded at Cold Harbor 1 June 1864. Admitted to Confederate Hospital, Petersburg, Virginia 3 June 1864. Furloughed 17 June 1864. Deserted and took Oath of Office to the U.S. 1 March 1865. Sent to Nashville, Tennessee. Born 18 May 1833 in Greene County, Georgia. Died 29 November 1919 in Suwanee County Florida. Brother of Lucious A. Crawford of Phillips Legion Infantry Battalion. PL, SR, NPS, CSR

Dodd, Albert M. Enlisted in White County, Georgia, 24 August 1861. Private, Company C (White County Marksmen), 24th Georgia Infantry Regiment. Transferred to Company E, 3rd Battalion Sharpshooters 8 June 1863. Deserted, date and location not recorded. Returned to duty 7 November 1864. Placed in confinement. Captured at Farmville, Virginia (Sailor's Creek) 6 April 1865. Imprisoned at Point Lookout; released 26 June 1865. Oath of Allegiance indicates he was six feet tall, with dark complexion and blue eyes. LH, SR, NPS, CSR

Durham, William P. Enlisted at Acworth, Georgia (Cobb County), 17 February 1862. Private, Company A (Acworth Infantry), 18th Georgia Infantry Regiment. Admitted to General Hospital, Farmville, Virginia for treatment of rheumatism 14 November 1862. Returned to duty 3 December 1862. Transferred to Company E, 3rd Battalion Sharpshooters 1 August 1863. Transferred back to Company A, 18th Georgia Infantry Regiment in August 1863. Captured at Cedar Creek 19 October 1864. Imprisoned at Point Lookout; died from scurvy in prison 12 May 1865. LH, SR, NPS, CSR

Fields, Benjamin F. Enlisted at Suffolk, Virginia 6 March 1862. Private, Company G (Jackson Rifles), 16th Georgia Infantry Regiment. Transferred to Company E, 3rd Battalion Sharpshooters 8 June 1863. Admitted to Jackson Hospital, Richmond for treatment of gastritis 21 July 1864. Returned to duty 19 September 1864. Captured at Farmville, Virginia (Sailor's Creek) 6 April 1865. Imprisoned at Point Lookout; released 27 June 1865. Oath of Allegiance indicates he was six feet two inches tall, with fair complexion, brown hair and blue eyes. LH, SR, NPS, CSR

Fields, Thomas J. Enlisted at Jefferson, Georgia (Jackson County), 20 July 1861. 1st Corporal, Company G (Jackson Rifles), 16th Georgia Infantry Regiment. Transferred to Company E, 3rd Battalion Sharpshooters with the rank of 1st corporal. Captured at Front Royal 16 August 1864. Committed to Old Capitol Prison, Washington D. C. 21 August 1865. Transferred to Elmira 28 August 1865; released 16 June 1865. Oath of Allegiance indicates he was five feet eleven inches tall, with florid complexion, auburn hair and hazel eyes. Born 9 November 1840. Died 8 August 1913. Buried in Mizpah Presbyterian Church Cemetery, Jefferson, Georgia. UDC, CSR, SR, TMWG, NPS, LH

Floyd, William Enlisted at Suffolk, Virginia 28 February 1862. Private, in Company F (Gwinnett Independent Blues), 24th Georgia Infantry Regiment. Admitted to Chimborazo Hospital #2, Richmond for treatment of rheumatism 26 March 1863. Transferred to Company E, 3rd Battalion Sharpshooters 8 June 1863. Admitted to

Jackson Hospital, Richmond 3 July 1864. Returned to duty 19 August 1864. Captured at High Bridge, Virginia (Sailor's Creek) 6 April 1865. Imprisoned at Point Lookout; released 27 June 1865. Oath of Allegiance indicates he was five feet nine inches tall, with dark complexion, black hair and hazel eyes. Born in 1845. Pension application states that he was born in 1843. Died in 1936. Buried in the Stone Pile Baptist Church Cemetery, Clarkesville, Georgia. UDC, SR

Frankham, Joseph B. B. Enlisted at Suffolk, Virginia 4 March 1862. Private. Private. Transferred to Company E, 3rd Battalion Sharpshooters. Admitted to Jackson Hospital for the treatment of rheumatism 14 June 1864. Returned to duty 3 August 1864. Admitted to Jackson Hospital, Richmond for treatment of chronic diarrhea 9 August 1864. Furloughed for thirty days 14 August 1864. Captured at High Bridge, Virginia (Sailor's Creek) 6 April 1865. Imprisoned at Point Lookout; released 27 June 1865. Oath of Allegiance indicates he was five feet seven inches tall, with light complexion, brown hair and gray eyes. SR, NPS, CSR

Gailey, Simeon D. Enlisted at Suffolk, Virginia 28 February 1862. Private, Company E, 3rd Battalion Sharpshooters. Captured at Gettysburg 2 July 1863. Service record remarks: "Taken prisoner in Pennsylvania in the hands of the abolitionists." Treated at DeCamp's General Hospital, David's Island, New York Harbor; released for parole 22 October 1863. Returned to duty. Admitted to Camp Winder Hospital 29 October 1863 for treatment of pneumonia. Furloughed for thirty days 4 November 1863. Surrendered and paroled at Augusta, Georgia, 18 May 1865. SR, NPS

Ginn, Jesse G. Enlisted at Jefferson, Georgia (Jackson County), 20 July 1861. Private, Company G (Jackson Rifles), 16th Georgia Infantry Regiment. Transferred to Company E, 3rd Battalion Sharpshooters with the rank of 1st sergeant. Killed at Gettysburg, 3 July 1863. SR, NPS, CSR

Goodwin, John Solomon Enlisted at Acworth, Georgia (Cobb County), 24 February 1862. Private, Company A (Acworth Infantry), 18th Georgia Infantry Regiment. Transferred to Company E, 3rd Battalion Sharpshooters 8 June 1863. Wounded at Spotsylvania 12 May 1864. Furloughed for sixty days. Captured in Covington, Georgia, 23 July 1864. Imprisoned at Camp Chase; released for exchange and transferred to City Point, Virginia 4 March 1865. No later record. Born in 1844. Died in 1925. Buried at Midway Church Cemetery, Fulton County, Georgia. LH, UDC, SR, NPS, CSR

Hainey, William J. Enlisted at Jefferson, Georgia (Jackson County), 20 July 1861. Private, Company G (Jackson Rifles), 16th Georgia Infantry Regiment. Captured at Frederick City, Maryland 12 September 1862. Imprisoned at Fort Delaware; paroled 30 September 1862. Sent for exchange 2 October 1862. Exchanged at Aiken's Landing, date not recorded. Admitted to Camp Winder Hospital #5, Richmond 9 October 1862. Furloughed for thirty days 17 October 1862. Returned to duty. Transferred to Company E, 3rd Battalion Sharpshooters 8 June 1863. Promoted to 3rd sergeant 4 July 1863. Wounded at Knoxville 17 November 1863. Returned home on wounded furlough. Roll for August 1864 shows him on expired furlough. Disabled. LH, SR, NPS, CSR

Hall, John Enlisted in Company A, Phillips Legion Infantry Battalion. Transferred to Company E, 3rd Battalion Sharpshooters. Promoted to sergeant. Captured at Front Royal 16 August 1864. Committed to Old Capitol Prison, Washington, D. C. 21 August 1864. Transferred to Elmira 28 August 1864. No later record. SR, NPS, CSR

Harper, Daniel B. Enlisted at Camp McDonald (Cobb County) 13 June 1861. 2nd Corporal, Company A (Acworth Infantry), 18th Georgia Infantry Regiment. Transferred to Company E, 3rd Battalion Sharpshooters 8 June 1863. Roll for September 1863 indicates that he "returned to the 18th Georgia Infantry Regiment." Promoted to 3rd Sergeant. Received as a deserter by U.S. forces 10 February 1865. Took Oath of Allegiance to the U.S. Government at City Point, Virginia 12 February 1865. Sent to Washington D. C. 15 February 1865. Transportation furnished to Nashville, Tennessee. Oath of Allegiance indicates he was five feet ten inches tall, with dark complexion, brown hair and blue eyes. SR

Hull, George S. Enlisted at Camp McDonald (Cobb County) 13 June 1861. Private, Company A (Acworth Infantry), 18th Georgia Infantry Regiment. Admitted to General Hospital #20, Richmond 17 November 1862. Returned to duty 27 November 1862. Admitted to Chimborazo Hospital #2, Richmond for the treatment of rheumatism 25 March 1863. Returned to duty 1 April 1863. Transferred to Company E, 3rd Battalion Sharpshooters 8 June 1863. Admitted to Chimborazo Hospital #2, Richmond. Deserted and took the Oath of Allegiance to the U.S. Government in Washington D. C. 15 February 1865. Furnished transportation to Nashville, Tennessee. Oath of Allegiance indicates he was five feet nine inches tall, with light complexion, light hair and gray eyes. Born *ca.* 1843 in Georgia. LH, SR, NPS

Little, Francis M. Enlisted in Hall County, Georgia, 24 August 1861. Private, Company I (Glade Guards), 24th Georgia Infantry Regiment. Transferred to Company E, 3rd Battalion Sharpshooters 8 June 1863. Captured at Spotsylvania 22 May 1864. Imprisoned at Point Lookout; released for exchange 14 March 1865; received at Aiken's Landing 16 March 1865. No later record. LH, NPS, CSR (Service record missing for 3rd Battalion Sharpshooters)

Lowry, Samuel B. Enlisted 24 August 1861. Private, Company I (Glade Guards Volunteer Rifles), 24th Georgia Infantry Regiment. Transferred to Company E, 3rd Battalion Sharpshooters. Wounded and captured at Gettysburg 3 July 1863; paroled 1 August 1863. Amputee (leg). At home, end of war. LH, NPS, CSR (No service record for 3rd Battalion Sharpshooters)

Martin, Absalem Enlisted in Hall County, Georgia, 24 August, 1861. Private, Company I (Glade Guards Volunteer Rifles), 24th Georgia Infantry Regiment. Admitted to Chimborazo Hospital #2, Richmond 21 December 1862. Transferred to CSA Hospital, Danville, Virginia 1 January 1863 for treatment of rheumatism. Returned to duty 17 January 1863. Transferred to Company E, 3rd Battalion Sharpshooters 8 June 1863. Admitted to Jackson Hospital, Richmond 7 August 1864. Returned to duty 13 September 1864. Captured at Richmond 3 April 1865. Imprisoned at Newport News;

released 15 June 1865. Oath of Allegiance indicates he was five feet six inches tall, with light complexion, black hair and blue eyes. LH, SR, NPS, CSR

Martin, Elijah Enlisted in Hall County, Georgia, 24 August 1861. Private, Company I (Glade Guards Volunteer Rifles, 24th Georgia Infantry Regiment. Transferred to Company E, 3rd Battalion Sharpshooters 8 June 1863. Roll for August 1864 shows him absent without leave. No later record. LH, SR, NPS, CSR

Myes, Jeremiah (Mize) Enlisted in Hart County, Georgia, 24 August 1861. Private, Company B (Hart Volunteers), 24th Georgia Infantry Regiment. Admitted to CSA Hospital, Farmville, Virginia for treatment of debility 13 November 1862. Returned to duty 2 December 1862. Transferred to Company E, 3rd Battalion Sharpshooters. Captured at Cedar Creek. Imprisoned at Point Lookout; released 29 June 1865. Oath of Allegiance indicates he was five feet eight inches tall, with light complexion, brown hair and blue eyes. SR, NPS, CSR

Nash, Andrew M. (Andrew E.) Enlisted in Gwinnett County, Georgia, 11 August 1861. Private, Company H, 16th Georgia Infantry Regiment. Wounded in the hand at Fredericksburg 13 December 1861. Transferred to Company E, 3rd Battalion Sharpshooters. Deserted 1 August 1863 at Culpeper Court House. Apprehended and delivered to CSA authorities 29 February 1864. Deserted 6 April 1864. Court Martialed and sentenced to a firing squad 3 July 1864. No later record. NPS, CSR, SR

Owens, George S. Enlisted at Camp McDonald (Cobb County) 13 June 1861. Private, Company A (Acworth Infantry), 18th Georgia Infantry Regiment. Transferred to Company E, 3rd Battalion Sharpshooters 8 June 1863. Returned to the 18th Georgia Infantry Regiment October 1863. Wounded at Knoxville 29 November 1863. Retired to the Invalid Corps 26 August 1864 (wounds). Died 4 May 1924 in Marietta, Georgia. LH, SR, NPS, CSR

Porter, William Anthony Enlisted at Camp McDonald (Cobb County) 26 June 1861. Private, Company A (Greene Rifles) Phillips Legion Infantry Battalion. Transferred to Company E, 3rd Battalion Sharpshooters 1 May 1863. Appointed 2nd Sergeant, date of rank 1 June 1863. Promoted to 1st Sergeant 4 July 1863. Captured at High Bridge, Virginia (Sailor's Creek) 6 April 1865. Imprisoned at Point Lookout; released 17 June 1865. Oath of Allegiance indicates he was five feet eight inches tall, with fair complexion, brown hair and hazel eyes. Born in 1840. Younger brother of Horatio W. Porter of Company A, Cobb's Legion Infantry Battalion. Buried in Penfield Cemetery, Greene County, Georgia. PL, SR, NPS, CSR

Pruett, Joshua A. Enlisted at Suffolk, Virginia 28 March 1862. Private, Company G (Hall Volunteers), 24th Georgia Infantry Regiment. Transferred to Company E, 3rd Battalion Sharpshooters 8 June 1863. Captured at Front Royal 16 August 1864. Committed to Old Capitol Prison, Washington, D. C. 21 August 1864. Transferred to Elmira 28 August 1864. Released 7 July 1865. Oath of Allegiance indicates he was five feet five inches tall, with florid complexion, auburn hair and blue eyes. Born in Georgia in 1840. LH, SR, NPS, CSR

Shaw, Alexander E. Enlisted at Greensboro, North Carolina 22 April 1864. Private, Company E, 3rd Battalion Sharpshooters. Captured at Front Royal 16 August 1864. Committed to Old Capitol Prison, Washington, D. C. 21 August 1864. Transferred to Elmira 28 August 1864. Died in prison of chronic diarrhea 8 May 1865. Buried in Woodlawn National Cemetery, Elmira, New York; grave number 2777. ST, IE, NPS, CSR, SR

Shelton, John E. Enlisted at Camp McDonald (Cobb County) 16 June 1861. 3rd Corporal, Company A (Acworth Infantry), 18th Georgia Infantry Regiment. Transferred to Company E, 3rd Battalion Sharpshooters. Appointed 2nd Lieutenant, date of rank 5 June 1863. Captured at Front Royal 16 August 1864. Committed to Old Capitol Prison, Washington, D. C., 21 August 1864. Transferred to Fort Delaware 27 August 1864; released 17 June 1865. Oath of Allegiance indicates he was five feet eleven inches tall, with ruddy complexion, light hair and blue eyes. SR, NPS, OS, CSR

Smith, George A. Enlisted at Camp McDonald (Cobb County) 26 June 1862. Private, Company A (Acworth Infantry), 18th Georgia Infantry Regiment. Transferred to Company E, 3rd Battalion Sharpshooters 8 June 1863. Captured at Front Royal 16 August 1864. Committed to Old Capitol Prison, Washington, D. C. 21 August 1864. Transferred to Elmira 28 August 1864. Released for exchange on 9 February 1865; received at Boulware & Cox's Wharves 21 February 1865. Paroled at Greensboro, North Carolina 12 May 1865. Born in North Carolina 15 November 1842. Buried in the Midway Methodist Church Cemetery, Barrow County, Georgia. LH, UDC, NPS, CSR, SR

Snead, James N. Enlisted at Lawrenceville, Georgia (Gwinnett County), 16 July 1861. Private, Company I (Hutchins Guards), 16th Georgia Infantry Regiment. Transferred to Company E, 3rd Battalion Sharpshooters 8 June 1863. Captured at Front Royal 16 August 1864. Committed to Old Capitol Prison, Washington, D. C. 21 August 1864. Transferred to Elmira 38 August 1864. Died in prison of Variola 22 February 1865. Buried in Woodlawn National Cemetery, Elmira, New York, grave number 2236. SR

Snead, John C. Enlisted at Lawrenceville, Georgia (Gwinnett County), 16 July 1861. Private, Company I (Hutchins Guards), 16th Georgia Infantry Regiment. Transferred to Company E, 3rd Battalion Sharpshooters 8 June 1863. Wounded at the Wilderness 6 May 1864. Captured at Farmville, Virginia (Sailor's Creek) 6 April 1865. Imprisoned at Point Lookout; released 19 June 1865. Oath of Allegiance indicates he was five feet ten inches tall, with light complexion, brown hair and hazel eyes. NPS, CSR, SR

Veal, James M. Enlisted in Hall County, Georgia, 24 August 1861. Private, Company I (Glade Guards Volunteer Rifles), 24th Georgia Infantry Regiment. Transferred to Company E, 3rd Battalion Sharpshooters 8 June 1863. Captured at High Bridge, Virginia (Sailor's Creek) 6 April 1865. Imprisoned at Point Lookout; released 21 June 1865. Oath of Allegiance indicates he was five feet seven inches tall, with dark complexion, black hair and gray eyes. LH, NPS, CSR, SR

Wagnon, George H. Enlisted at Greensboro, Georgia (Greene County), 1 March 1862. Private, Company A (Greene Rifles), Phillips Legion Infantry Battalion. Transferred to Company E, 3rd Battalion Sharpshooters 1 May 1863. Appointed 2nd corporal 1 June 1863. Captured at Front Royal 16 August 1864. Committed to Old Capitol Prison, Washington, D. C. 21 August 1864. Transferred to Elmira 28 August 1864; released 7 July 1865. Oath of Allegiance indicates he was five feet eight inches tall, with florid complexion, dark hair and blue eyes. Brother of Pitman Monroe Wagnon. PL, NPS, CSR, SR

Wagnon, James D. Enlisted at Greensboro, Georgia (Greene County), 1 July 1863. Private, Company A (Greene Rifles), Phillips Legion Infantry Battalion. Transferred to Company E, 3rd Battalion Sharpshooters. Captured at Front Royal 16 August 1864. Committed to Old Capitol Prison, Washington D. C. 21 August 1864. Transferred to Elmira 28 August 1864; exchanged 2 March 1865. PL, NPS, CSR, SR

Wagnon, Pitman Monroe Enlisted at Camp McDonald (Cobb County) 26 June 1861. Private, Company A (Greene Rifles), Phillips Legion Infantry Battalion. Transferred to Company E, 3rd Battalion Sharpshooters 1 May 1863. Wounded at Knoxville 29 November 1863. Absent without leave at the end of the war. Brother of George H. Wagnon. Born in 1840. Died in 1918. PL, CSR, SR

Wall, John Enlisted in Rabun County, Georgia, 24 August 1861. Private, Company E (Rabun Gap Riflemen), 24th Georgia Infantry Regiment. Appointed 4th sergeant 1 June 1863. Transferred to Company E, 3rd Battalion Sharpshooters 8 June 1863. Captured at Front Royal 16 August 1864. Imprisoned at Elmira; released 29 May 1865. Oath of Allegiance indicates he was five feet eight inches tall, with fair complexion, light hair and blue eyes. LH, NPS, CSR, SR

Wall, John Beck LaFayette Enlisted in Rabun County, Georgia, 24 August 1861. Private, Company E (Rabun Gap Riflemen), 24th Georgia Infantry Regiment. Captured at Crampton's Gap 14 September 1862. Imprisoned at Fort Delaware; delivered for exchange at Aiken's Landing 6 October 1863. Returned to regiment. Transferred to Company E, 3rd Battalion Sharpshooters 8 June 1863. Pension records show that he was on detail in Virginia to procure rations at the end of the war. Captured and paroled in Athens, Georgia, 8 May 1865. Born 1 January 1844. Died 26 May 1929 in Atlanta, Georgia. Buried in Crestlawn Cemetery, Atlanta, Georgia. LH, NPS, CSR, SR

Wall, Littleton M. Enlisted in Rabun County, Georgia, 24 August 1861. Private, Company E (Rabun Gap Riflemen), 24th Georgia Infantry Regiment. Wounded at Chancellorsville 6 May 1863. Transferred to Company E, 3rd Battalion Sharpshooters 8 June 1863. Detailed as nurse at Jackson Hospital, Richmond 24 June 1864. Returned to duty 6 July 1864. Sent to the Invalid Corps 2 September 1864. Retired by Medical Examining Board 10 September 1864. LH, NPS, CSR, SR

Wall, Martin Enlisted in Rabun County, Georgia, 24 August 1861. Private, Company E (Rabun Gap Riflemen), 24th Georgia Infantry Regiment. Transferred to

Company E, 3rd Battalion Sharpshooters 8 June 1863. Killed in action at Spotsylvania Court House 10 May 1864. LH, NPS, CSR, SR

Wall, Nace L. Enlisted at Suffolk, Virginia 14 March 1862. Private, Company E (Rabun Gap Riflemen), 24th Georgia Infantry Regiment. Transferred to Company E, 3rd Battalion Sharpshooters 8 June 1863. Roll for 31 August 1864 shows him present. No later record. LH, NPS, CSR, SR

Walraven, Elijah Enlisted at Acworth, Georgia (Cobb County), 21 February 1862. Private, Company A (Acworth Infantry), 18th Georgia Infantry Regiment. Transferred to Company E, 3rd Battalion Sharpshooters 8 June 1863. Wounded in the face (artillery shell) at Spotsylvania 12 May 1864. Admitted to Jackson Hospital, Richmond 15 May 1864. Furloughed for sixty days 23 May 1864. Returned to regiment. Captured at Front Royal 16 August 1864. Committed to Old Capitol Prison, Washington, D. C. 21 August 1864. Transferred to Elmira 28 August 1864; released 7 July 1865. Oath of Allegiance indicates he was five feet eleven inches tall, with sallow complexion, dark hair and blue eyes. NPS, CSR, SR

Westmoreland, James J. Enlisted in Hall County, Georgia, 8 August 1861. Private, Company G (Hall Volunteers), 24th Georgia Infantry Regiment. Admitted to CSA Hospital, Charlottesville, Virginia for treatment of debilitas 10 February 1863. Returned to duty 17 February 1863. Transferred to Company E, 3rd Battalion Sharpshooters 8 June 1863. Admitted to CSA General Hospital, Charlottesville, Virginia. Returned to duty. Captured at Front Royal 16 August 1864. Committed to Old Capitol Prison, Washington, D. C. 21 August 1864. Transferred to Elmira 28 August 1864; released 21 June 1865. Oath of Allegiance indicates he was five feet six inches tall, with fair complexion, auburn hair and blue eyes. Born 22 April 1843. Died 27 March 1912. Buried in Nacoochee Methodist Church Cemetery, Sautee, Georgia. LH, UDC, NPS, CSR, SR

Wilson, John G. Enlisted at Suffolk, Virginia 4 March 1862. Private, Company G (Hall Volunteers), 24th Georgia Infantry Regiment. Transferred to Company E, 3rd Battalion Sharpshooters 8 June 1863 with the rank of 4th corporal. Captured at Front Royal 16 August 1864. Committed to Old Capitol Prison, Washington, D. C. 21 August 1864. Transferred to Elmira 28 August 1864; released 29 May 1865. Oath of Allegiance indicates he was five feet ten inches tall, with florid complexion, auburn hair and blue eyes. LH, NPS, CSR, SR

Winters, Marion Enlisted in Hall County, Georgia, 24 August 1861. Private, Company I (Glade Guards Volunteer Rifles), 24th Georgia Infantry Regiment. Wounded in the thigh at Crampton's Gap 14 September 1862. Treated at U.S. Field Hospital, Burkittsville, Maryland. Paroled and returned to regiment. Transferred to Company E, 3rd Battalion Sharpshooters 8 June 1863. Captured at High Bridge, Virginia (Sailor's Creek) 6 April 1865. Imprisoned at Point Lookout; released 22 June 1865. Oath of Allegiance indicates he was five feet five inches tall, with dark complexion, black hair and hazel eyes. LH, NPS, CSR, SR

Wood, James R. Enlisted at Suffolk, Virginia 1 March 1862. Private, Company G (Jackson Volunteers), 16th Georgia Infantry Regiment. Transferred to Company E, 3rd Battalion Sharpshooters 8 June 1863. Wounded at Chancellorsville 3 May 1863. At home, wounded at the end of the war. Buried in the Galilee Christian Church Cemetery, Arcade, Georgia. LH, UDC, NPS, TMWG, CSR, SR

Wright, Lorenzo Dow Enlisted at Camp Prichard, South Carolina 15 May 1862. Private, Company A (Greene Rifles), Phillips Legion Infantry Battalion. Wounded at Sharpsburg 17 September 1862. Transferred to Company E, 3rd Battalion Sharpshooters 1 May 1863. Bugler. Surrendered at Appomattox 9 April 1865. Born in 1846. Died 4 January 1922 in Ellis County Texas. PL, NPS, CSR, SR

Young, W. E. Private, Company E, 3rd Battalion Sharpshooters. Roll for December 1863, last on file, indicates he was absent, furloughed. No later record. SR

Sharpshooter Company F

Company Officers:

Barrett, Joseph W. Enlisted in Cobb County, Georgia, 14 June 1861. Private, Company D (Polk County Rifles), Phillips Legion Infantry Battalion. Wounded at Chancellorsville 6 May 1863. Transferred to Company F, 3rd Battalion Sharpshooters 1 May 1863 with the rank of 2nd lieutenant. Admitted to Jackson Hospital, Richmond 6 June 1864. Returned to duty 17 October 1864. Retired from service and transferred to the Invalid Corps 11 January, 1865. Brother of Arthur J. Barrett. Born in 1840. PL, SR, NPS, OS, CSR

Gober, Newton Napoleon Enlisted in Company L, Phillips Legion Infantry Battalion 15 March 1862. Elected 1st lieutenant. Transferred to Company F, 3rd Battalion Sharpshooters 1 May 1863. Detailed to return home as a recruiting officer 4 February 1863. Promoted to Captain with the date of appointment 5 August 1863; date of rank 5 June 1863; and the date of confirmation 17 February 1864. Captured at Harper's Farm (Sailor's Creek) 6 April 1865. Committed to Old Capitol Prison, Washington D. C. 14 April 1865. Transferred to Johnson's Island 17 April 1865; released 18 June 1865. Oath of allegiance indicates he was five feet eleven inches tall, with fair complexion, dark hair and blue eyes. Buried in the Confederate Cemetery, Marietta, Georgia. UDC, GSS, NLH, PL, SR, NPS, OS, CSR

Montgomery, William Rhadamanthus Enlisted at Marietta, Georgia (Cobb County), 9 May 1861. 1st Sergeant, Company L (Blackwell Volunteers), Phillips Legion Infantry Regiment, 1 April 1862. Transferred to Company F, 3rd Battalion Sharpshooters 1 May 1863. Promoted to 1st lieutenant, date of rank 5 June 1863. Admitted to Receiving Hospital, Gordonsville, Virginia 8 August 1864. Transferred to Richmond 13 August 1864. Admitted to General Hospital #4, Richmond 14 August 1864. Returned to duty 19 August 1864. Inspection report dated 28 February 1865 states he was absent with leave. On furlough *en route* to the theater of war at the end of the war. PL, GSS, SR, NPS, OS, CSR

Enlisted Men:

Bard, Henry H. Enlisted at Camp McDonald (Cobb County) 11 June 1861. Private, Company B (Dalton Guards), Phillips Legion Infantry Battalion. Quartermaster's Clerk. Transferred to Company F, 3rd Battalion Sharpshooters 1 May 1863. Died in 1864, date, location, and cause not recorded. Born in Pennsylvania in 1843. PL, SR, NPS, CSR

Barrett, Arthur J. Enlisted on 14 May 1862. Private, Company D (Polk Rifles), Phillips Legion Infantry Battalion. Admitted to Chimborazo Hospital #2, Richmond 29 March 1863; furloughed 24 April 1863. Transferred to Company F, 3rd Battalion Sharpshooters 1 May 1863 with the rank of corporal. Captured at Strasburg, Maryland 23 October 1864. Imprisoned at Point Lookout, Maryland; released for exchange 17 March 1865. Brother of Joseph W. Barrett. Born 10 June 1844 in Georgia; died 17 October 1906. Buried Blackwood Springs Baptist Church Cemetery, Calhoun, Georgia. PL, SR, NPS, CSR

Barrett, John R. Enlisted on 11 June 1861. Private, Company C, Phillips Legion Infantry Battalion. Teamster. Transferred to Company F, 3rd Battalion Sharpshooters. Admitted to Jackson Hospital, Richmond 8 August 1864. Roll for 31 August 1864 indicates he was absent without leave. No later record. Born *ca.* 1841. SR, NPS

Bellah, John H. Enlisted at Camp McDonald (Cobb County) 25 June 1861. Private, Company C (Habersham Volunteers), Phillips Legion Infantry Battalion. Admitted to Chimborazo Hospital #1, Richmond 6 September 1862. Returned to duty 28 September 1862. Admitted to Chimborazo Hospital #1, Richmond 26 November 1862. Returned to duty 8 December 1862. Wounded at Fredericksburg 13 December 1862. Transferred to Company F, 3rd Battalion Sharpshooters 1 May 1863. Declined and remained with Company C in Phillips Legion infantry Battalion. Wounded at Chancellorsville May 1863. Promoted to sergeant in 1864. Killed in action at Cedar Creek 19 October 1864. Born in Georgia, 19 March 1841. Brother of Richard and Robert Bellah of Phillips Legion Infantry Battalion. PL, SR, NPS, CSR

Brooks, John A. Enlisted in Georgia 14 May 1862. Private, Company D (Polk Rifles), Phillips Legion Infantry Battalion. 1906 Roster Commission Roll states that he was wounded at South Mountain (Crampton's Gap) 14 September 1862. Transferred to Company F, 3rd Battalion Sharpshooters 1 May 1863. Wounded at the Wilderness 6 May 1864. No later record. PL, SR, NPS, CSR

Burton, William Crow R. Enlisted at Marietta, Georgia (Cobb County), 15 March 1862. Private, Company L, (Blackwell Volunteers) Phillips Legion Infantry Battalion. Transferred to Company F, 3rd Battalion Sharpshooters 1 May 1863. Detailed as teamster. Captured at High Bridge, Virginia (Sailor's Creek) 6 April 1865. Imprisoned at Point Lookout; released 24 June 1865. Oath of Allegiance indicates he was five feet ten inches tall, with light complexion, light brown hair and gray eyes. Born 1840 in South Carolina. Died 4 February 1922 in Cullman County Alabama. Buried City Cemetery, Cullman, Alabama. PL, SR, NPS, CSR

Calahan, John S. Enlisted on 11 July 1861. Private, Company B (Dalton Guards), Phillips Legion Infantry Battalion. Drummer. Transferred to Company F, 3rd Battalion Sharpshooters. AWOL from 13 November 1863. Deserted, date and location not recorded. Took Oath of Allegiance to the U.S. Government on 1 March 1864 in Chattanooga, TN. No later record. Oath of Allegiance indicates he was five feet five inches tall, with dark complexion, dark hair and blue eyes. PL, SR, NPS, CSR

Carter, James A. Enlisted on 11 June 1861. Private, Company C (Habersham Volunteers), Phillips Legion Infantry Battalion. Transferred to Company F, 3rd Battalion Sharpshooters 1 May 1863. Captured at Gettysburg 3 July 1863. Imprisoned at Fort Delaware; released 16 June 1865. Son of W. M. Carter Sr. and brother of James Carter, both of Phillips Legion Infantry Battalion. Died 1892. SR, NPS, CSR

Cheek, James H. Enlisted at Marietta, Georgia (Cobb County), 15 March 1862. Private, Company L (Blackwell Volunteers), Phillips Legion Infantry Battalion. Admitted to CSA General Hospital, Charlottesville, Virginia 6 November 1862. Returned to duty 14 December 1862. Transferred to Company F, 3rd Battalion Sharpshooters 1 May 1863. Promoted to 3rd corporal. Wounded in the right leg at the Wilderness 6 May 1864. Promoted to 5th Sergeant. Admitted to Jackson Hospital, Richmond 15 May 1864. No later record. PL, SR, NPS, CSR

Cleavland, Henry C. Enlisted at Marietta, Georgia (Cobb County), 28 April 1861. Private, Company M (Denmead Volunteers), Phillips Legion Infantry Battalion. Admitted to Chimborazo Hospital #2, Richmond 17 January 1863. Returned to duty 24 January 1863. Transferred to Company F, 3rd Battalion Sharpshooters 1 May 1863. Captured at Front Royal 16 August 1864. Imprisoned at Elmira; released for exchange 2 March 1865. Admitted to Jackson Hospital, Richmond 7 March 1865; released 8 March 1865. Furloughed for thirty days. No later record. Born in 1844. PL, SR, NPS, CSR

Dawson, J. W. Enlisted in Tennessee 20 March 1864. Private, Company F, 3rd Battalion Sharpshooters. Wounded at the Wilderness 6 May 1864. Deserted October 1864. Took Oath of Allegiance to the U.S. on 31 October 1864 in New Creek, West Virginia. Oath indicates he was six feet tall, with light complexion, light hair and blue eyes. No later record. Born *ca.* 1835. SR, NPS, CSR

Devenport, Josiah Enlisted in Georgia 29 May 1862. Private, Company F (Davis Guards), Phillips Legion Infantry Battalion. Transferred to Company F, 3rd Battalion Sharpshooters. Admitted to Jackson Hospital, Richmond for treatment of chronic diarrhea 16 June 1864. Transferred to Camp Winder Hospital, Richmond 28 June 1864. Died in hospital of chronic diarrhea 3 November 1864. Born *ca.* 1829. SR, NPS, CSR

Earp, George Perryman Enlisted at Marietta, Georgia (Cobb County), 6 May 1862. Private, Company O (Marietta Guards), Phillips Legion Infantry Battalion. Admitted to Chimborazo Hospital #2, Richmond for treatment of rheumatism 9 November 1862. Returned to duty 15 December 1862. Transferred to Company F, 3rd Battalion Sharpshooters 1 May 1863. Returned to Company O, Phillips Georgia Legion.

Surrendered at Appomattox 9 April 1865. Pension application indicated that he was born in North Carolina in 1827 and died 10 December 1910. PL, SR, NPS, CSR

Edwards, Adonza B. Enlisted at Camp McDonald (Cobb County) 11 June 1861. Private, Company B (Dalton Guards), Phillips Legion Infantry Battalion. Transferred to Company F, 3rd Battalion Sharpshooters 1 May 1863 with the rank of corporal. Promoted to sergeant July 1864. Captured at Front Royal 16 August 1864. Committed to Old Capitol Prison, Washington, D. C., 20 August 1864. Transferred to Elmira 28 August 1864; released 21 June 1865. Oath of Allegiance indicates that he was five feet nine inches tall, with dark complexion, dark hair and hazel eyes. Brother of James F. Edwards of Phillips Legion Infantry Battalion. PL, SR, NPS, CSR

Elliott, James W. Enlisted at Camp McDonald (Cobb County) 11 June 1861. Private, Company C (Habersham Volunteers), Phillips Legion Infantry Battalion. Transferred to Company F, 3rd Battalion Sharpshooters 1 May 1863 with the rank of corporal. Wounded May 1864. Admitted to Jackson Hospital, Richmond. Returned to duty. Captured at Front Royal 16 August 1864. Committed to Old Capitol Prison, Washington, D. C. 20 August 1864. Transferred to Elmira 28 August 1864. Died in prison of Typhoid Fever 4 September 1864. Born in 1839. ST, PL, SR, NPS, CSR

England, Joseph Curtis Enlisted at Camp McDonald (Cobb County) June 1861. Private, Company B (Dalton Guards), Phillips Legion Infantry Battalion. Promoted to Corporal June 1862. Captured at Boonsboro, Maryland (Fox's Gap) 15 September 1862. Imprisoned at Fort Delaware. Released for exchange 10 October 1862. Exchanged 2 November 1862. Admitted to General Hospital #19, Richmond 28 December 1862. Transferred to Camp Winder Hospital, Richmond 21 January 1863. Returned to duty 27 January 1863. Transferred to Company F, 3rd Battalion Sharpshooters 1 May 1863. Admitted to General Hospital #16, Richmond for treatment of typhoid fever. Furloughed for thirty days on 4 July 1863. Promoted to sergeant. Wounded in the left arm at Spotsylvania 12 May 1864. Admitted to Jackson Hospital, Richmond 15 May 1864. Transferred to CSA Hospital #11 Charlotte, North Carolina 3 June 1864. Returned to duty 23 August 1864. Captured at High Bridge (Sailor's Creek) 6 April 1865. Imprisoned at Point Lookout; released 11 June 1865. Oath of Allegiance indicates he was five feet nine inches tall, with light complexion, dark brown hair and hazel eyes. Born in Burke County North Carolina 28 October 1835. Died 21 January 1922. Buried in Swamp Creek Baptist Church Cemetery, Whitfield County, Georgia. PL, SR, NPS, CSR

Fincher, Henry J. Enlisted on 14 May 1862. Private, Company D (Polk Rifles), Phillips Legion Infantry Battalion. Admitted to Chimborazo Hospital #2, Richmond for treatment of rheumatism 22 November 1862. Returned to duty 16 December 1862. Transferred to Company F, 3rd Battalion Sharpshooters 1 May 1863. Wounded at Chancellorsville 3 May 1863. Admitted to Camp Winder 9 May 1863. Hand amputated. Permanently disabled. Sent home in 1863. PL, SR, NPS, CSR

Green, Joseph B. Enlisted in Cobb County, Georgia, 14 June 1861. Private, Company D (Polk Rifles), Phillips Legion Infantry Battalion. Transferred to Company

F, 3rd Battalion Sharpshooters 1 May 1863. Admitted to Marietta, Georgia Hospital. Roll dated 30 January 1865 indicates he was absent, sick. No later record. Born 1841 in South Carolina. Died in 1904. Brother of James R. Green of Phillips Legion Infantry Battalion. PL, SR, NPS, CSR

Griffin, Thomas W. Enlisted at Camp McDonald (Cobb County) 11 June 1861. Private, Company B (Dalton Guards), Phillips Legion Infantry Battalion. Detailed to Union Hotel Hospital, Winchester, Virginia as a nurse 13 September 1862. Transferred to Company F, 3rd Battalion Sharpshooters 1 May 1863. Wounded at Chancellorsville 6 May 1863. Admitted to the Lynchburg, Virginia Hospital. Admitted to CSA General Hospital, Farmville, Virginia 15 July 1863. Returned to duty 29 July 1863. Discharged due to wound in 1864. PL, SR, NPS, CSR

Hardy, Thomas J. Enlisted at Camp Pritchard, South Carolina 6 May 1862. Private, Company O (Marietta Guards), Phillips Legion Infantry Battalion. Transferred to Company F, 3rd Sharpshooter Battalion 1 May 1863 with the rank of 3rd corporal. Demoted to private. Captured at Front Royal 16 August 1864. Committed to Old Capitol Prison, Washington, D. C. 21 August 1864. Transferred to Elmira 28 August 1864; released 16 June 1865. Oath of Allegiance indicates he was five feet ten inches tall, with florid complexion, light hair and blue eyes. PL, SR, NPS, CSR

Heaton, Zachariah P. Enlisted in Cobb County, Georgia, 11 June 1861. Private, Company C (Habersham Volunteers), Phillips Legion Infantry Battalion. Admitted to General Hospital #18, Richmond 15 October 1862. Returned to duty 13 November 1862. Wounded at Fredericksburg 13 December 1862. Treated at Winder Hospital, Richmond. Returned to duty 23 January 1863. Transferred to Company F, 3rd Battalion Sharpshooters 1 May 1863. Deserted at Caledonia, Pennsylvania 30 June 1863. Captured at Gettysburg 5 July 1863. Imprisoned at Fort Delaware. Took Oath of Office to the U.S. Government on 1 September 1863. Turned over to Company D, 3rd Maryland Cavalry (U.S.) 5 September 1863. Deserted from U.S. unit on 24 December 1863 from steamer leaving Baltimore. U.S. enlistment shows him to be six feet tall, with brown hair and blue eyes. Brother of Pink Heaton. Born *ca.* 1843. PL, SR, NPS, CSR

Henderson, John M. Enlisted on 20 September 1862. Private, Company O (Marietta Guards), Phillips Legion Infantry Battalion. Transferred to Company F, 3rd Battalion Sharpshooters 1 May 1863. Wounded in the shoulder at Spotsylvania 12 May 1864. Admitted to Jackson Hospital, Richmond 15 May 1864. Transferred to CSA Hospital, Danville, Virginia 20 May 1864. Furloughed 23 May 1864. Captured in Cobb County, Georgia, 1 August 1864; took Oath of Allegiance to the U.S. Government and sent north of the Ohio River 27 August 1864. Oath of Allegiance indicates he was five feet eight inches tall, with dark complexion, black hair and brown eyes. Born in 1841. PL, SR, NPS, CSR

Herring, E. R. Enlisted at Marietta, Georgia (Cobb County), 28 April 1862. Private, Company M (Denmead Volunteers), Phillips Legion Infantry Battalion. Admitted to General Hospital #13, Richmond 12 August 1862. Returned to duty 19

August 1862. Transferred to Company F, 3rd Battalion Sharpshooters 1 May 1863. Last shown on roll for August 1863. No later record. PL, SR, NPS, CSR

Howard, John J. Enlisted at Camp McDonald (Cobb County), 11 June 1861. Corporal, Company C (Habersham Volunteers), Phillips Legion Infantry Battalion. Transferred to Company F, 3rd Battalion Sharpshooters 1 May 1863. Deserted at Gettysburg 3 July 1863. Captured 5 July 1863. Imprisoned at Point Lookout. Took Oath of Office to the U.S. Government and joined the 3rd Maryland Cavalry (U.S.). Served with the 3rd Maryland until September 1865. PL, SR, NPS, CSR

Howell, James Franklin Enlisted at Camp McDonald (Cobb County) 13 July 1861. Private, Company B (Dalton Guards), Phillips Legion Infantry Battalion. Transferred to Company F, 3rd Battalion Sharpshooters 1 May 1863 with the rank of corporal. Captured at Fairfield, Pennsylvania 6 July 1863. Imprisoned at Point Lookout; released 18 February 1865 for exchange. No later record. PL, SR, NPS, CSR

Howze, Darius N. Enlisted at Camp Prichard, South Carolina 6 May 1862. Private, Company O (Marietta Guards), Phillips Legion Infantry Battalion. Admitted to Chimborazo Hospital, Richmond for treatment of chronic diarrhea 9 November 1862. Returned to duty 1 December 1862. Transferred to Company F, 3rd Battalion Sharpshooters 1 May 1863. Last shown on roll for January 1865 on furlough. No later record. PL, SR, NPS, CSR

Hughes, John J. Enlisted in Cobb County, Georgia, 8 August 1861. Private, Company C (Habersham Volunteers), Phillips Legion Infantry Battalion. Transferred to Company F, 3rd Battalion Sharpshooters 1 May 1863. Captured at Knoxville 29 November 1863. Sent to Camp Chase 15 December 1863; paroled. 19 January 1864 roll shows him absent, sick in hospital. Returned to duty. Captured at Front Royal 16 August 1864. Committed to Old Capitol Prison, Washington, D. C. 21 August 1864. Transferred to Elmira 28 August 1864; released for exchange 29 October 1864. Returned to duty. Admitted to Jackson Hospital, Richmond 17 January 1865. Returned to duty 13 February 1865. Captured at Sailor's Creek 6 April 1865. Imprisoned at Point Lookout; released 28 June 1865. Oath of Allegiance indicates he was five feet eight inches tall, with fair complexion, dark hair and dark eyes. PL, SR, NPS, CSR

King, Jonathan F. Enlisted at Camp McDonald (Cobb County) 14 June 1861. Private, Company D (Polk Rifles), Phillips Legion Infantry Battalion. Admitted to Camp Winder Hospital, Richmond 12 November 1862. Returned to duty 4 December 1862. Transferred to Company F, 3rd Battalion Sharpshooters 1 May 1863. Wounded at Chancellorsville. Joined the 6th Georgia Cavalry Regiment later in the war. PL, SR, NPS, CSR

Kistleburg, William Howard Enlisted on 11 June 1861. Private, Company C, Phillips Legion Infantry Battalion. Transferred to Company F, 3rd Battalion Sharpshooters 1 May 1863. Captured at High Bridge (Sailor's Creek) 6 April 1865. Imprisoned at Point Lookout; released 19 June 1865. Oath of Allegiance indicates he was five feet ten inches tall, with dark complexion, brown hair and gray eyes. Brother of James Kistleburg of Phillips Legion. Born in Georgia in 1842. PL, SR, NPS, CSR

Maloy, John A. Enlisted on 8 May 1862. Private, Company B (Whitfield Guards), Phillips Legion Infantry Battalion. Transferred to Company F, 3rd Battalion Sharpshooters 1 May 1863. Captured at Front Royal, 16 August 1864. Committed to Old Capitol Prison, Washington, D. C. 21 August 1864. Transferred to Elmira 28 August 1864. Took Oath of Allegiance to the U.S. Government on 1 November 1864 and sent to Indiana. PL, SR, NPS, CSR

Manning, John W. Transferred from the 3rd Arkansas Infantry Regiment 1 October 1862. Private, Company C (Habersham Volunteers), Phillips Legion Infantry Battalion. Admitted to Institute Hospital, Richmond for treatment of scarlet fever 24 September 1862. Furloughed 28 October 1862. Returned to duty. Transferred to Company F, 3rd Battalion Sharpshooters 1 May 1863 with the rank of 2nd Sergeant. Wounded and captured at Gettysburg 2 July 1863. Sent to DeCamp General hospital, David's Island, New York July 1863. Paroled 1 September 1863. Admitted to Confederate Hospital, Petersburg, Virginia 15 September 1863. Furloughed 24 September 1863. Transferred to the Invalid Corps 12 July 1864. No later record. Born 1830 in Georgia. PL, SR, NPS, CSR

Mills, William H. Enlisted in Cobb County, Georgia, 11 June 1861. Private, Company C (Habersham Volunteers), Phillips Legion Infantry Battalion. Wounded in the hand at 2nd Manassas 30 August 1862. Admitted to Chimborazo Hospital #2, Richmond 5 September 1862. Returned to duty 2 October 1862. Transferred to Company F, 3rd Battalion Sharpshooters 1 May 1863 with the rank of 4th Sergeant. Admitted to Hospital. Roll dated 30 January 1865 states he was absent without leave. No later record. Born in 1835. PL, SR, NPS, CSR

Moore, Jesse H. Enlisted at Marietta, Georgia (Cobb County), 28 April 1862. Private, Company M (Denmead Volunteers), Phillips Legion Infantry Battalion. Admitted to the Institute Hospital, Richmond for treatment of chronic diarrhea 28 October 1862. Returned to duty 30 December 1862. Transferred to Company F, 3rd Battalion Sharpshooters 1 May 1863. Captured at Farmville, Virginia (Sailor's Creek) 6 April 1865. Imprisoned at Point Lookout; released 29 June 1865. Oath of Allegiance indicates he was five feet eleven inches tall, with dark complexion, black hair and hazel eyes. Born *ca.* 1836. PL, SR, NPS, CSR

Owens, David Enlisted in Whitfield County, Georgia, 11 June 1861. Private, Company B (Dalton Guards), Phillips Legion Infantry Battalion. Transferred to Company F, 3rd Battalion Sharpshooters 1 May 1863. Deserted 14 December 1863. Took Oath of Allegiance to the U.S. Government 5 January 1864 and sent north of the Ohio River. Oath of Allegiance indicates he was five feet five inches tall, with dark complexion, black hair and hazel eyes. PL, SR, NPS, CSR

Pace, John C. Enlisted at Marietta, Georgia (Cobb County), 6 May 1862. Private, Company F, Phillips Legion Infantry Battalion. Transferred to Company F, 3rd

Battalion Sharpshooters 8 June 1863. Service record indicates he returned to his infantry battalion; date not recorded. SR, NPS, CSR

Rich, J. Newton Enlisted in Cobb County, Georgia, 25 June 1861. Private, Company C (Habersham Volunteers), Phillips Legion Infantry Battalion. Wounded at Fredericksburg 13 December 1862. Transferred to Company F, 3rd Battalion Sharpshooters 1 May 1863. Wounded in the right knee at Chancellorsville 3 May 1863. Discharged due to permanent disability; date not recorded. Born 31 October 1832. PL, SR, NPS, CSR

Richardson, David Enlisted at Camp Pritchard, South Carolina May 26, 1862. Private, Company B (Dalton Guards), Phillips Legion Infantry Battalion. Transferred to Company F, 3rd Battalion Sharpshooters June 8, 1863. Killed in action at Chattanooga September 22, 1863. PL, SR, NPS, CSR

Ruede, William E. Enlisted at Marietta, Georgia (Cobb County), 7 April 1862. 4th Corporal, Company L (Blackwell Volunteers), Phillips Legion Infantry Battalion. Selected to transfer to Company F, 3rd Battalion Sharpshooters 1 May 1863. Killed in action at Chancellorsville 6 May 1863. PL, GSS, SR

Shoemaker, Thomas J. Enlisted at Camp McDonald (Cobb County) 11 June 1861. Private, Company B (Dalton Guards), Phillips Legion Infantry Battalion. Transferred to Company F, 3rd Battalion Sharpshooters 1 May 1863. Wounded at Chancellorsville 3 May 1863. Admitted to Chimborazo Hospital #4, Richmond 6 May 1863. Returned to duty 31 July 1863. Roll dated 4 December 1864 states that he was detailed at corps headquarters. Deserted at Petersburg 22 March 1865. Took Oath of Allegiance to the U.S. 27 March 1865. Furnished transportation to Knoxville, Tennessee 30 March 1865. PL, NPS, CSR

Shular, A. J. Enlisted in Cobb County, Georgia, 8 August 1861. Private, Company D (Polk Rifles), Phillips Legion Infantry Battalion. Admitted to General Hospital #13, Richmond 12 August 1862. Returned to duty 30 August 1862. Admitted to Camp Winder Hospital, Richmond, date not recorded. Returned to duty 23 October 1862. Transferred to Company F, 3rd Battalion Sharpshooters 1 May 1863. Wounded at Chancellorsville 6 May 1863. Service record states that he served in the 3rd and 6th Georgia Cavalry in 1864, but this is not corroborated by his pension application. No later record. Born *ca.* 1843. PL, NPS, CSR, SR

Stephens, Joshua P. Enlisted on 1 June 1861 in Atlanta, Georgia. Private, Company H, 7th Georgia Infantry Regiment. Wounded in the thigh at First Manassas 21 July 1861. Admitted to Orange Hospital, Orange Court House, Virginia 23 July 1861. Furloughed for thirty days 14 August 1861. Returned to duty 28 October 1861. Promoted to 1st corporal 15 July 1862. Transferred to Company L (Blackwell Volunteers), Phillips Legion Infantry Battalion 8 June 1863. Transferred to Company F, 3rd Battalion Sharpshooters. Reduced in rank to private. Captured at Gettysburg 3 July 1863. Imprisoned at Fort Delaware; released 15 June 1865. Oath of Allegiance indicates he was five feet five inches tall, with dark complexion, dark hair and dark eyes. NPS, CSR, SR

Steward, John M. Enlisted in Company D, Phillips Legion Infantry Battalion 14 May 1862. Private. Transferred to Company F, 3rd Battalion Sharpshooters 1 May 1863. Roll for August 1864 dated 30 January 1865 states that he deserted on 5 July 1864. Captured at Bulls Gap (Greene County), Tennessee 5 September 1864. Sent to Chattanooga, Tennessee 13 September 1864. Imprisoned in Nashville, Tennessee and sent to U.S. Prison, Louisville Kentucky. Discharged and transferred to Camp Douglas 29 October 1864; released 12 May 1865. Oath of Allegiance indicates he was five feet eight inches tall, with fair complexion, light hair and blue eyes. Born 3 August 1838. Died 18 December 1896. Buried in Greenwood Cemetery, Cedartown, Georgia. PL, NPS, CSR, SR

Stewart, Levi A. Enlisted at Marietta, Georgia (Cobb County), 1 May 1864. Private, Company F, 3rd Battalion Sharpshooters. Admitted to Jackson Hospital, Richmond for treatment of scabies 28 November 1864. Returned to duty 1 January 1865. Captured at Sailor's Creek 6 April 1865. Imprisoned at Point Lookout; released 30 June 1865. Oath of Allegiance indicates he was five feet ten inches tall, with light complexion, dark hair and hazel eyes. PL, NPS, CSR, SR

Stewart, Noah H. Enlisted at Marietta, Georgia (Cobb County), 28 April 1862. Private, Company M (Denmead Volunteers), Phillips Legion Infantry Battalion. Transferred to Company F, 3rd Battalion Sharpshooters 1 May 1863. Killed in action at Knoxville 24 November 1863. PL, NPS, CSR, SR

Stewart, Tapley H. Enlisted in South Carolina 25 June 1862. Private, Company A (Greene Rifles), Phillips Legion Infantry Battalion. Transferred to Company F, 3rd Battalion Sharpshooters 1 May 1863. Promoted to corporal in 1864. Captured at Front Royal 16 August 1864. Committed to Old Capitol Prison, Washington, D. C. 21 August 1864. Transferred to Elmira 28 August 1864; released for exchange 14 March 1865. Received at Boulware & Cox's Wharves 17 March 1865. Born 25 August 1844. Died 26 December 1920. PL, NPS, CSR, SR

Stone, Thomas Jefferson Enlisted at Camp McDonald (Cobb County) 11 June 1861. Private, Company D (Polk Rifles), Phillips Legion Infantry Battalion. Transferred to Company F, 3rd Battalion Sharpshooters 1 May 1863 with the rank of 3rd Sergeant. Admitted to hospital in Rome Georgia. Died in the hospital of typhoid pneumonia 1 December 1863. Born 1836 in South Carolina. PL, NPS, CSR, SR

Taylor, Zachary F. Enlisted 1 March 1862. Private, Company C (Habersham Volunteers), Phillips Legion Infantry Battalion. Private. Transferred to Company F, 3rd Battalion Sharpshooters 1 May 1863. Captured at Front Royal 16 August 1864. Committed to Old Capitol Prison, Washington, D. C. 21 August 1864. Transferred to Elmira. Released for exchange 10 March 1865. Born 14 February 1840 in Cobb County, Georgia. Died 7 September 1911 in Dade County, Georgia. Buried in Whitt Sitton Cemetery, Dade County, Georgia. PL, NPS, CSR, SR

Vaughn, William P. Enlisted at Camp McDonald (Cobb County) 4 August 1861. Private, Company D (Polk Rifles), Phillips Legion Infantry Battalion. Roll for January and February 1863 states he was under arrest for being absent without leave. Transferred to Company F, 3rd Battalion Sharpshooters 1 May 1863. Wounded 8 September 1863, location not recorded. Admitted to Camp Winder Hospital, Richmond 1 September 1863. Furloughed for thirty days 11 September 1863. Deserted 15 November 1863. Imprisoned at U.S. Prison, Louisville, Kentucky. Took the Oath of Allegiance to the U.S. Government 23 December 1863, and sent north of the Ohio River. Attempted to enlist in the Union army, but was rejected. Oath of Allegiance indicates he was five feet eight inches tall, with dark complexion, light hair and hazel eyes. Born in 1839. PL, CSR, SR

Vawter, Rawley A. Enlisted at Richmond, Virginia 26 March 1862. Private, Company M (Denmead Volunteers), Phillips Legion Infantry Battalion. Transferred to Company F, 3rd Battalion Sharpshooters 1 May 1863. Deserted 14 December 1863 in Tennessee. Imprisoned at U.S. Military Prison, Louisville, Kentucky. Took the Oath of Allegiance to the U.S. Government 10 January 1864 and sent north of the Ohio River. Oath of Allegiance indicates he was five feet eight inches tall, with fair complexion, light hair and black eyes. PL, NPS, CSR, SR

Waters, Thomas Willoughby Enlisted at Marietta, Georgia (Cobb County), 21 July 1861. Private, Company D (Polk Rifles), Phillips Legion Infantry Battalion. Wounded at Sharpsburg 17 September 1862. Transferred to Company F, 3rd Battalion Sharpshooters 1 May 1863 with the rank of 1st Sergeant. Captured at Front Royal 16 August 1864. Committed to Old Capitol Prison 21 August 1864. Transferred to Elmira 28 August 1864. Died in prison of pneumonia 17 April 1865. Buried in Woodlawn National Cemetery, Elmira, New York, grave number 1364. PL, IE, NPS, CSR, SR

Watts, J. R. Enlisted at Lynchburg, Virginia 16 August 1861. Private, Company B (Dalton Guards), Phillips Legion Infantry Battalion. Transferred to Company F, 3rd Battalion Sharpshooters 8 June 1863. Captured at Gettysburg 3 July 1863. Sent to U.S. General Hospital, Gettysburg 25 July 1863. Sent to West Hospital (U.S.), Baltimore, Maryland 26 July 1863. Transferred to Point Lookout 20 August 1863. Escaped from prison 2 May 1864. Returned to regiment. Captured at Front Royal August 16, 1864. Committed to Old Capitol Prison, Washington, D. C. 21 August 1864. Transferred to Elmira 28 August 1864; released 11 July 1865. Oath of Allegiance indicates he was six feet tall, with florid complexion, dark hair and hazel eyes. SR

Whitehead, Simeon Enlisted at Marietta, Georgia (Cobb County), 28 April 1862. Private, Company M, (Denmead Volunteers) Phillips Legion Infantry Battalion. Transferred to Company F, 3rd Battalion Sharpshooters 1 May 1863. Admitted to Confederate Hospital, Petersburg, Virginia 15 September 1863. Returned to duty 19 September 1863. Present on January 1865 roll. No later record. Buried in an unmarked grave in Oak Hill Cemetery, Cartersville, Georgia. PL, NPS, CSR, SR

Wimpie, Robert F. Enlisted on 1 March 1862. Private, Company D (Polk Rifles), Phillips Legion Infantry Battalion. Wounded at Fredericksburg 13 December 1862. Transferred to Company F, 3rd Battalion Sharpshooters 1 May 1863. Captured at Gettysburg 3 July 1863. Imprisoned at Fort Delaware; received 12 July 1863. Took Oath of Allegiance to the U.S. Government 1 August 1863 and joined a U.S. artillery unit. No later record. PL, NPS, CSR, SR

Wood, Robert M. Enlisted at Marietta, Georgia (Cobb County), 28 April 1862. Private, Company M (Denmead Volunteers), Phillips Legion Infantry Battalion. Admitted to Camp Winder General Hospital for treatment of debilitas 28 October 1862. Returned to duty 10 November 1862. Promoted to corporal. Transferred to Company F, 3rd Battalion Sharpshooters 8 June 1863. Promoted to sergeant. Wounded (shell) at Spotsylvania 12 May 1864. Admitted to Jackson Hospital, Richmond 18 May 1864. Returned to duty. Captured at Front Royal 16 August 1864. Sent to Old Capitol Prison 21 August 1864. Imprisoned at Elmira 28 August 1864. Sent to U.S. General Hospital 13 July 1865; released 19 July 1865. Oath of Allegiance shows him to be five feet seven inches tall, with fair complexion, dark hair and blue eyes. PL, NPS, CSR, SR

Declined Appointment to 3rd Battalion Sharpshooters

Anderson, William D. Enlisted at Richmond, Virginia 22 May 1861. Private, Company M (Denmead Volunteers), Phillips Legion Infantry Battalion. Elected 2nd Lieutenant 26 February 1863. Transferred to Company F, 3rd Battalion Sharpshooters with the rank of Captain 8 June 1863. Declined appointment and promotion 9 June 1863. Returned to regiment. Wounded. Admitted to Howards Grove General Hospital, Richmond. Retired 20 January 1865. Assigned to the Invalid Corps in Georgia under Major General Howell Cobb 27 January 1865. No later record. GSS, SR, NPS, CSR

Bellah, Richard Watson Enlisted on 1 March 1862; private. Assigned to Company C, Phillips Legion Infantry Battalion. Transferred to Company F, 3rd Battalion Sharpshooters 1 May 1863. Declined and remained with Company C in Phillips Legion infantry Battalion. Captured at Sailors Creek 6 April 1865. Imprisoned at Point Lookout; released 24 June 1865. Oath of Allegiance indicates that he was five feet five inches tall, with fair complexion, brown hair and blue eyes. Born in Georgia November 29, 1843. Grave marker indicates he died 8 January 1935. Brother of John and Robert Bellah of Phillips Legion Infantry Battalion. SR, NPS, CSR

Fuller, Peyton W. Enlisted in Cobb County, Georgia, 11 June 1861. Private, Company C (Habersham Volunteers), Phillips Legion Infantry Battalion. Promoted to corporal, color guard. Promoted to Color Sergeant. Transferred to Company F, 3rd Battalion Sharpshooters. Elected 2nd lieutenant; declined. Killed in action at Chancellorsville 2 May 1863. PL, SR, NPS, OS, CSR

Nichols, Joseph G. Enlisted in Towns County, Georgia, 24 August 1861. Private, Company D (Hiawassee Volunteers), 24th Georgia. Elected 2nd Lieutenant 8 August 1862. Transferred to Company E, 3rd Battalion Sharpshooters. Wounded at

Chancellorsville 3 May 1863. Appointed 2nd Lieutenant, date of rank 5 June 1863. Declined appointment. No later record. LH, SR, NPS OS, CSR

Ross, Frederick E. Enlisted at Bowdon, Georgia (Carroll County), 30 July 1862. 2nd Lieutenant, Company B (Bowdon Volunteers), Cobb's Legion Infantry Battalion. Promoted to 1st Lieutenant 16 April 1862. Transferred to Company D, 3rd Battalion Sharpshooters. Promoted to captain, date of rank 5 June 1863. Declined. Roster dated January 1865 states he was killed 3 May 1863. SR, NPS, RO, OS, CSR

Smith, Henry H. Enlisted in the Hiwassee Volunteers (Towns County) 24 August 1861. 2nd Lieutenant, Company D (Hiwassee Volunteers), 24th Georgia Infantry Regiment. Promoted to Captain. Wounded in the arm at Malvern Hill 1 July 1862. Transferred to the 3rd Battalion Sharpshooters 8 June 1863. Promoted to major, date of rank 10 June 1863. Declined appointment. Killed in action at the Wilderness 6 May 1864. NLH, SR, NPS, OS, CSR

Windsor, James M. Enlisted for three years at Camp McDonald (Cobb County) 13 June 1861. Private, Company H, 18th Georgia Infantry Regiment. Promoted to 4th Sergeant August 1862. Wounded at Sharpsburg 17 September 1862. Transferred to Company A, 3rd Battalion Sharpshooters 17 June 1863 and promoted to 1st Lieutenant to take rank 5 June 1863; declined. Returned to regiment. Captured near Cartersville, Georgia, 28 September 1864. Received at U.S. Military Prison, Louisville. Transferred to Camp Chase 22 October 1864. Died of smallpox in prison 14 December 1864. Buried in Camp Chase Cemetery 0.3 mi. south of the prison, grave number 553. SR, NPS, OS, CSR

Wittick, Lucious ("Luke") L. Enlisted at Augusta, Georgia (Richmond County), 2 May 1861. Re-enlisted at Madison, Georgia (Morgan County), 15 May 1862. Private, Company G (Panola Guards), Cobb's Legion Infantry Battalion. Transferred to Company D, 3rd Battalion Sharpshooters 8 June 1863. Declined. Returned to regiment. Wounded in the left hand May 1864, location not recorded. Roll for August 1864, last on file, indicates he was detailed to the quartermaster's department in Madison, Georgia for enrolling duty. No later record. SR, NPS, CSR

Wright, James O. Enlisted at Camp McDonald (Cobb County) 26 June 1861. Private, Company A (Greene Rifles), Phillips Legion Infantry Battalion. Selected for transfer to Company A, 3rd Battalion Sharpshooters. According to his service records, he declined and returned to Company A, Phillips Legion Infantry Battalion. Captured at Front Royal 16 August 1864. Imprisoned at Elmira; released 21 June 1865. Oath of Allegiance indicates he was six feet one inch tall, with florid complexion, gray hair and black eyes. Born *ca.* 1842. SR, NPS, CSR

No Service Record Entries for 3rd Battalion Sharpshooters

The following men were <u>not</u> identified as being in the 3rd Battalion Sharpshooters by their service records, but were listed as being in the 3rd Battalion by one or more other reference sources. It is possible that one or more were selected for the sharpshooter battalion but declined their appointment.

Jackson, Jesse M. Enlisted in Company O, Phillips Legion Infantry Battalion. Private. Transferred to Company B, 3rd Battalion Sharpshooters. No later record. SR, NPS, CSR

Jackson, Martin V. Enlisted in Company C, 16th Georgia, 1 May 1864. Private. Musician. Transferred to Company B 3rd Battalion Sharpshooters with the rank of captain. Captured at Sailor's Creek 6 April 1865. Imprisoned at Johnson's Island; released 18 June 1865. Buried at Carroll's United Methodist Church Cemetery, Franklin County, Georgia. LH, UDC, HHC, SR, TMWG, CSR

Johnson, J. H. Private, Company D, 3rd Battalion Sharpshooters. Surrendered at Appomattox 9 April 1865. SHSP, SR

Waters, Jesse R. Enlisted in the Dalton Guards (Whitfield County)11 June 1861. Private, Company B, Phillips Legion Infantry Battalion. Transferred to Company F, 3rd Battalion Sharpshooters 1 May 1863. Captured at Gettysburg 2 July 1863. Imprisoned at Point Lookout; escaped from prison 2 May 1864. At Petersburg Hospital 12 June 1864. Sent to Raleigh, North Carolina 14 June 1864. No later record. PL, NPS, CSR

York, M. V. Enlisted on 1 December 1861. Private, Company G (Hall Volunteers), 24th Georgia Infantry Regiment. Transferred to Company E, 3rd Battalion Sharpshooters 8 June 8, 1863. Captured at Gettysburg 2 July 1863. Exchanged in 1863. Discharged from military service on 1 October 1863. LH

Bibliography

1. Primary Sources

Byrd, Daniel Madison Jr. *Them Brave Georgians.* Unpublished manuscript, c. 1960.
Author's note: Madison Byrd's unpublished manuscript cites originals or copies of the
following documents from William E. Simmons: the autograph book kept at Fort
Delaware Prison; the memorandum prepared by Simmons for Clark Howell
covering the high points of his life; miscellaneous papers such as official
appointment as a presidential elector, admission to practice in Federal District
Court, etc.; all manuscripts in National and State Archives containing his name or
reporting specifically on the activities of the 16th Georgia Infantry Regiment or 3rd
Battalion Georgia Sharpshooters. There is a copy of *Them Brave Georgians* at the
Gwinnett Historical Society archives in Lawrenceville, Georgia, and at the Fort
Delaware Society archives in Delaware City, Delaware.

Buck, Marcus B. Diary. Confederate Museum, Front Royal, VA.
Blackmore, Letitia. Diary. Confederate Museum, Front Royal, VA.
Cobb, Howell. Papers. Hargrett Rare Book & Manuscript Library. University of
Georgia, Athens.
Cobb, T. R. R. Papers. Hargrett Rare Book & Manuscript Library. University of
Georgia, Athens.
*Compiled Service Records of Confederate Soldiers Who Served in Organizations from the State
of Georgia.* Microcopy 266, RG 109, National Archives and Records
Administration, Washington, DC.
"Collection of Confederate Letters." Drawer 186, box 31, Georgia Department of
Archives & History, Morrow, GA.
Confederate Diaries, Volume 6. Georgia Department of Archives and History, Morrow,
GA.
Eckardt, Charles. Diary. Confederate Museum, Front Royal, VA.
Heidler, Florence Hodgson. Letters. Hargrett Rare Book & Manuscript Library.
University of Georgia, Athens.
Hutchins, Nathan L. Jr. Letters.
———. Roster of Hutchins Guards. Hutchins Family Genealogy File. Gwinnett
Historical Society Archives, Lawrenceville, GA.
Jordan, Allen C. Family papers. Hargrett Rare Book & Manuscript Library. University of
Georgia, Athens.
Longstreet Papers. Southern Historical Collection. University of North Carolina, Chapel
Hill.
MacKay-Stiles Collection. Correspondence of Captain Benjamin Edward Stiles. MS
#470. Southern Historical Collection. University of North Carolina, Chapel Hill.
Mobley, Jim. Letters. Emory University Archives, Atlanta, GA.
Reese, A. J. Letters. Georgia Department of Archives and History, Morrow, GA.
Reynolds, James A. Diary. Richmond National Battlefield Park, VA. Photocopy.
Richardson, Sue. Diary. Confederate Museum, Front Royal, VA.

Simmons, William E. Biographical sketch. Georgia Department of Archives and History, Morrow, GA.
————. Diary. Georgia Department of Archives and History, Morrow, GA.
————. Genealogy File. Gwinnett Historical Society, Lawrenceville, GA.
UDC Bound Transcripts, Volumes 6 and 9. Georgia Department of Archives and History, Morrow, GA.

2. Newspapers
Atlanta Constitution
Atlanta Journal
Augusta Weekly Chronicle & Sentinel
Charleston Mercury
Gwinnett Daily News (Lawrenceville, GA)
Richmond Dispatch
Southern Banner (Athens, GA)
Southern Confederacy (Atlanta, GA)
Southern Watchman (Athens, GA)
Tulsa World

3. Official Publications
Candler, Allen D. *The Confederate Records of the State of Georgia.* 6 volumes. Atlanta: C. P. Byrd, State Printer, 1909–1911.
Compiled service records of Confederate soldiers from organizations in the State of Georgia. Georgia Department of Archives and History, Morrow GA.
U.S. War Department. *The War of the Rebellion: A Compilation of the Official Records of the Union and Confederate Armies.* 70 volumes. Washington, DC: U.S. Printing Office, 1880–1901.

4. Other Printed Materials
Hallowed Banners: Historic Flags in the Georgia Capitol Collection. Atlanta: Office of the Secretary of State, 2005.
Confederate Prisoners of War at Fort Delaware. Pamphlet. Fort Delaware Historical Society, Delaware City, DE. No date.
Heidler, David S. and Jeanne T., editors. *Encyclopedia of the American Civil War: A Political, Social, and Military History.* 2 vols. Santa Barbara, CA: ABC-CLIO, Inc., 2000.
Henderson, Lillian. *Roster of the Confederate Soldiers of Georgia, 1861–1865.* 5 vols. Hapeville, GA: Longino & Porter, Inc., n.d.
Keen, Nancy Travis. *Confederate Prison,ers of War at Fort Delaware.* Pamphlet. Fort Delaware Historical Society, Delaware City DE.
Orr, Timothy J. "'Sharpshooters Made a Grand Record This Day': Combat on the Skirmish Line at Gettysburg on July 3," in *The Third Day: The Fate of a Nation, July 3, 1863.* Gettysburg: Gettysburg National Military Park, 2010.
Southern Historical Society Papers. 1876–1944. 52 vols. Richmond, VA.

5. Books

Alexander, E. Porter. *Fighting for the Confederacy: Personal Recollections of General E. Porter Alexander*. Edited by Gary Gallagher. Chapel Hill: University of North Carolina Press, 1989.

———. *Military Memoirs of a Confederate*. 1907. Reprint, Dayton, OH: Press of Morningside Bookshop, 1977.

Allan, William. *The Army of Northern Virginia in 1862*. Cambridge MA: Houghton, Mifflin & Company, 1892.

Avery, F. W. *History of Georgia*. New York: Brown and Derby, 1881.

Axelrod, Alan. *Chronicle of the Indian Wars*. New York: Konecky & Konecky, 1993.

Battles and Leaders of the Civil War. 4 vols. Reprint, Seacaucus, NJ: Castle Books, 1956.

Benson, Berry. *Berry Benson's Civil War Book: Memoirs of a Confederate Scout and Sharpshooter*. Edited by Susan Williams Benson. 1962. Reprint, Athens: University of Georgia Press, 1992.

Black, Robert C., III. *The Railroads of the Confederacy*. Chapel Hill: University of North Carolina Press, 1952.

von Borcke, Heros, *Memoirs of the Confederate War*. vols. 1, 2. 1866. Reprint, Dayton OH: Morningside House, 1985.

Bowman, John S., editor. *The Civil War Almanac*. New York: Barnes & Noble Books, 2005.

Brack, Elliott E. *Gwinnett: A Little Above Atlanta*. Norcross, GA: Brack Group, 2008.

Bradford, Ned, editor. *Battles and Leaders of the Civil War*. New York: Grammercy Books, 2001.

Brent, Joseph L. *Memoirs of the War Between the States*. New Orleans, LA: Fontana Printing Co., 1940.

Brown, Kent Masterson. *Retreat From Gettysburg: Lee, Logistics, & the Pennsylvania Campaign*. Chapel Hill: University of North Carolina Press, 2005.

Brown, Russell K. *Our Connection with Savannah: A History of the 1st Battalion Georgia Sharpshooters*. Macon: Mercer University Press, 2004.

Bryan, T. Conn. *Confederate Georgia*. 3rd ed. Athens: University of Georgia Press, 1964.

Bunch, Jack A. *Roster of the Courts-Martial in the Confederate States Armies*. Shippensburg, PA: White Mane Books, 2001.

Cannan, John. *Bloody Angle: Hancock's Assault on the Mule Shoe Salient May 12, 1864*. Battleground America Guides. South Yorkshire, England: Leo Cooper, n.d.

Carman, Ezra A. *The Maryland Campaign of September 1862*. Vol. 1, *South Mountain*. Edited by Thomas G. Clemens. El Dorado Hills, CA: Savas Beatie, 2010.

Cashin, Edward J. *A Confederate Legend: Berry Benson in War and Peace*. Macon: Mercer University Press, 2008.

Clemmer, Greg S. *Valor in Gray: Recipients of the Confederate Medal of Honor*. Staunton, VA: Hearthside Publishing Co., 1998.

Coffman, Richard M. and Kurt D. Graham. *To Honor These Men: A History of the Phillips Georgia Legion Infantry Battalion*. Macon: Mercer University Press, 2007.

Coleman, Kenneth, editor. *A History of Georgia*. 2nd ed. Athens: University of Georgia Press, 1991.

Cook, James F. *Governors of Georgia 1754–2004*. 3rd ed. Macon: Mercer University Press, 2005.

Coulter, E. Merton. *Lost Generation: The Life and Death of James Barrow, C.S.A.* Confederate Centennial Studies, No. 1. Tuscaloosa, AL: Confederate Publishing Company, Inc., 1956.

Cowley, Robert. *With My Face to the Enemy: Perspectives on the Civil War.* New York: G. P. Putnam's Sons, 2001.

Current, Richard N., editor. *Encyclopedia of the Confederacy.* 4 vols. New York: Simon & Schuster, 1993.

Davis, Burke. *Jeb Stuart: The Last Cavalier.* New York: Fairfax Press, 1988.

Davis, Robert S. Jr. *The Georgia Black Book.* Vol. 1. Easley, SC: Southern Historical Press, Inc., 1982.

Debo, Angie. *Tulsa.* Norman: University of Oklahoma Press, 1943.

Dickert, D. Augustus. *History of Kershaw's Brigade.* 1899. Reprint, Wilmington, NC: Broadfoot Publishing Company, 1990.

Dunlop, W. S. *Lee's Sharpshooters or the Forefront of Battle: A Story of Southern Valor That Never Has Been Told Before.* 1899. Reprint, Dayton, OH: Morningside House, Inc., 1988.

Dunn, Nina Lane. *Tulsa's Magic Roots.* Tulsa: NLD Corporation, 1979.

Dyer, Thomas G. *The University of Georgia: A Bicentennial History 1785–1985.* Athens: University of Georgia Press, 1985.

Evans, Clement A., editor. *Confederate Military History: A Library of Confederate States History...Written by Distinguished Men of the South.* 17 vols. 1899. Reprint (extended ed.), Wilmington, NC: Broadfoot Publishing Co., 1987.

Fetzer, Dale and Bruce Mowday. *Unlikely Allies: Fort Delaware's Prison Community in the Civil War.* Mechanicsburg, PA: Stackpole Books, 2000.

Flanigan, James C. *History of Gwinnett County, Georgia.* Vol. 1. 1943. Reprint, Gwinnett Historical Society, 1995.

———. *History of Gwinnett County, Georgia.* Vol. 2. 1959. Reprint, Gwinnett Historical Society, 1999.

Folsom, James Madison. *Heroes and Martyrs of Georgia: Georgia's Record in the Revolution of 1861.* 1864. Reprinted as vol. 4 of *The Army of Northern Virginia.* Baltimore, MD: Butternut & Blue, 1995.

Foreman, Grant. *Indian Removal.* Vol. 2 in The Civilization of the American Indian Series. Norman: University of Oklahoma Press, 1989.

Franks, Kenny A., editor. *The Oklahoma Petroleum Industry.* Norman: University of Oklahoma Press, 1980.

———, Paul F. Lambert, and Carl N. Tyson. *Early Oklahoma Oil: A Photographic History, 1859–1936.* The Montague History of Oil Series, no. 2. College Station: Texas A&M University Press, 1981.

Freeman, Douglas Southall. *Lee's Lieutenants.* 3 vols. New York: Charles Scribner's Sons, 1942.

Freemantle, Sir Arthur James Lyon. *Three Months in the Southern States: The Diary of an English Soldier.* 1863. Reprint, Marshall, VA: Greenhouse Publishing Co., n.d.

Furgurson, Ernest B. *Not War but Murder: Cold Harbor 1864.* New York: Vintage Books, 2000.

Gallagher, Gary W., editor. *Chancellorsville: The Battle and Its Aftermath.* Chapel Hill: University of North Carolina Press, 1996.

Gallman, J. Matthew, editor. *The Civil War Chronicle.* New York: Gramercy Books, 2000.

Glatthaar, Joseph T. *General Lee's Army: From Victory to Collapse.* New York: Free Press, 2008.

Goble, Danny. *Tulsa! Biography of the American City.* Tulsa, OK: Council Oak Books, 1997.

Gottfried, Bradley M. *Brigades of Gettysburg.* Cambridge, MA: Da Capo Press, 2002.

———. *The Maps of Gettysburg: An Atlas of the Gettysburg Campaign, June 3 –July 13, 1863.* New York: Savas Beatie, 2007.

Griffin, Louis Turner and John Erwin Talmadge. *Georgia Journalism 1763–1950.* Decatur, GA: University of Georgia Press, 1951.

Handy, Reverend Isaac W. K. *Imprisoned for Conscience Sake: Fifteen Months at Fort Delaware, A Private Journal.* 1874. Reprint, Harrisonburg, VA: Sprinkle Publications, 2007.

Heider, David S. and Janet T., editors. *Encyclopedia of the American Civil War.* Vols. 1–5. Santa Barbara, CA: ABC-CLIO, Inc., 2000.

Howard, McHenry. *Recollections of a Maryland Confederate Soldier and Staff Officer Under Johnston, Jackson and Lee.* 1914. Reprint, Dayton, OH: Morningside Bookshop, 1975.

Jaynes, Gregory. *The Killing Ground: Wilderness to Cold Harbor.* Alexandria, VA: Time-Life Books, 1986.

Joslyn, Mauriel P. *Immortal Captives: The Story of 600 Confederate Officers and the United Prisoner Prisoner of War Policy.* Gretna, LA: Pelican Publishing Company, Inc., 2008.

Katcher, Philip. *Sharpshooters of the American Civil War.* Osceola, WI: MBI Publishing, 2002.

Kaufhold, Sidney, editor. *The Hart of Georgia: A History of Hart County, Georgia.* Savannah River Valley Genealogical Society. Alpharetta, GA: W. H. Wolfe Associates, 1992.

Kemm, James O. *Tulsa: Oil Capital of the World.* Images of America. Charleston, SC: Arcadia Publishing, 2004.

Kerlin, Robert H. *Confederate Generals of Georgia and Their Burial Sites.* Fayetteville, GA: Americana Historical Books, 1994.

Kidd, James H. *Personal Recollections of a Cavalryman with Custer's Michigan Cavalry Brigade in the Civil War.* 1908. Reprint, Iona, MI: Sentinel Printing Co., 1997.

Kirwin, A. D., editor. *Johnny Green of the Orphan Brigade: The Journal of a Confederate Soldier.* Lexington: University of Kentucky Press, 1956.

Knight, Lucian Lamar. *Georgia's Bi-Centennial Memoirs and Memories.* 4 vols. Published by the author, 1931.

Krick, Robert K. *Civil War Weather in Virginia.* Tuscaloosa: University of Alabama Press, 2007.

———. *Lee's Colonels: A Biographical Register of the Field Officers of the Army of Northern Virginia.* Dayton, OH: Morningside House, Inc., 1992.

Lane, Mills, editor. *"Dear Mother: Don't grieve about me. If I get killed, I'll only be dead." Letters from Georgia Soldiers in the Civil War.* Savannah, GA: Beehive Press, 1977.

Lemon, James Lile. *Feed Them the Steel! Being the Wartime Recollections of Captain James Lile Lemon Company A, 18th Georgia Infantry C.S.A.* Mark H. Lemon, 2013.

Long, Mary Frazier. *About Lawrenceville.* Madison, GA: Southern Lion Books, 2008.

Longacre, Edward G. *Custer and His Wolverines: The Michigan Cavalry Brigade 1861–1865.* Conshohocken, PA: Combined Publishing, 1997.

Longstreet, James. *From Manassas to Appomattox: Memoirs of the Civil War in America.* 1896. Reprint, New York: Barnes & Noble, Inc., 2004.

MacDonald, John. *Historical Atlas of the Civil War.* New York: Chartwell Books, Inc., 2010.

Marvel, William. *Lee's Last Retreat: The Flight to Appomattox.* Chapel Hill: University of North Carolina Press, 2002.

McCabe, Alice S., editor. *Gwinnett County, Georgia, Families 1818–1968.* Gwinnett Historical Society, Inc., 1988.

McCarthy, Carlton. *Detailed Minutae of Soldier Life in the Army of Northern Virginia 1861–1865.* 1882. Reprint, Richmond, VA: B. F. Johnson Publishing Company, 1899.

McCash, William B. *Thomas R. R. Cobb: The Making of a Southern Nationalist.* Macon: Mercer University Press, 2004.

McClendon, W. A. *Recollections of War Times: By an Old Veteran while under Stonewall Jackson and Lieutenant General James Longstreet.* 1909. Reprint. Edited by Gary Gallagher and Robert K. Krick. Tuscaloosa: University of Alabama Press, 2010.

Miers, Earl Schenck. *The Last Campaign: Grant Saves the Union.* Philadelphia: J. B. Lippincott, 1972.

Montgomery, George F. Jr. *Georgia Sharpshooter: The Civil War Diary and Letters of William Rhadamanthus Montgomery.* Macon: Mercer University Press, 1997.

Montgomery, Horace. *Howell Cobb's Confederate Career.* Confederate Centennial Studies, no. 10. Tuscaloosa: Confederate Publishing Company, Inc., 1958.

Morrow, John Anderson. *The Confederate Whitworth Sharpshooters.* [city?] John A. Morrow, 2002. 2nd edition.

Oeffinger, John C., editor. *A Soldier's General: The Civil War Letters of Major General Lafayette McLaws.* Chapel Hill: University of North Carolina Press, 2002.

Osborne, William H. *The History of the Twenty-ninth Regiment of Massachusetts Volunteer Infantry in the War of the Rebellion.* Boston: Albert J. Wright, 1877.

Owen, William Miller. *In Camp and Battle with the Washington Artillery of New Orleans.* 1865. Reprint, Baton Rouge: Louisiana State University Press, 1999.

Petruzzi, J. David and Steven A. Stanley. *The Gettysburg Campaign in Numbers and Losses.* El Dorado Hills, CA: Savas Beatie, 2012.

Phillips, Ulrich B., editor. *The Correspondence of Robert Toombs, Alexander H. Stephens, and Howell Cobb.* 1913. Reprint, New York: DaCapo Press, 1970.

Plaster, Major John L. *Sharpshooting in the Civil War.* Boulder, CO: Paladin Press, 2009.

Power, J. Tracy. *Lee's Miserables: Life in the Army of Northern Virginia from the Wilderness to Appomattox.* Chapel Hill: University of North Carolina Press, 1998.

———. *An Index to Confederate Soldiers in Gwinnett County, Georgia Units during the War Between the States.* Gwinnett Historical Society, 1975.

Priest, John Michael. *Before Antietam: The Battle for South Mountain.* Shippensburg, PA: White Mane Publishing Company, Inc., 1992.

Ray, Fred L. *Shock Troops of the Confederacy: The Sharpshooter Battalions of the Army of Northern Virginia.* Asheville, NC: CFS Press, 2006.

Richards, Cecile Davis. *Wherever You Go: The Life of Jane Heard Clinton Indian Territory Bride.* New York: iUniverse, Inc., 2003.

Roberson, Elizabeth Whitley. *In Care of Yellow River: The Complete Letters of Eli Pinson Landers.* Fort Lauderdale, FL: Venture Press, 1994.

———. *Weep not for me Dear Mother.* Gretna, LA: Pelican Publishing Company, 1998.

Roddy, Ray. *The Georgia Volunteer Infantry 1861–1865.* Kearney, NE: Morris Publishing, 1998.

Ross, Fitzgerald. *Cities and Camps of the Confederate States.* Urbana: University of Illinois Press, 1958.

Sanders, Charles W. *While in the Hands of the Enemy: Military Prisons of the Civil War.* Baton Rouge, LA: Louisiana State University Press, 2005.

Sears, Stephen W. *Landscape Turned Red: The Battle of Antietam.* New Haven, CT: Ticknor & Fields, 1983.

———. *To the Gates of Richmond: The Peninsula Campaign.* New York: First Mariner Books, 2001.

Seymour, Digby Gordon. *Divided Loyalties: Fort Sanders and the Civil War in East Tennessee.* Knoxville, TN: East Tennessee Historical Society, 2002.

Shaver, Lewellyn. *A History of the Sixteenth Alabama Regiment: Gracie's Alabama Brigade.* Montgomery, AL: Barrett and Brown, 1867.

Shively, Julie. *American Civil War Places.* Nashville, TN: Ideals Publications, 1999.

Sifakis, Stewart. *Who Was Who in the Civil War.* New York: Facts on File, Inc., 1988.

Smedlund, William S. *Camp Fires of Georgia's Troops 1861–1865.* William S. Smedlund, 1994.

Smith, Gerald J. *"One of the Most Daring of Men": The Life of Confederate General William Tatum Wofford.* Vol. 16. Journal of Confederacy History Series. Series edited by John McGlone. Murfreesboro, TN: Southern Heritage Press, 1997.

Sorrel, Gilbert Moxley. *Recollections of a Confederate Staff Officer.* Edited by Bell Irwin Wiley. 1959. Reprint, Wilmington, NC: Broadfoot Publishing Company, 1995.

Speer, Lonnie R. *Portals to Hell: Military Prisons of the Civil War.* Lincoln, NE: University of Nebraska Press, 2005.

Stackpole, Edward J. *The Fredericksburg Campaign.* New York: Bonanza Books, 1957.

Stallings, James E. Jr. *Georgia's Confederate Soldiers Who Died as Prisoners of War 1861–1865.* Atlanta, GA: R. H. Taylor Foundation/James E. Stallings Sr., 2008.

Stancil, W. Dorsey, et al. *Vanishing Gwinnett II: Gwinnett County, Georgia—More Scenes of Bygone Days.* Lawrenceville, GA: Gwinnett Historical Society, 2001.

Steere, Edward. *The Wilderness Campaign.* New York: Bonanza Books, 1960.

Stegeman, John. *These Men She Gave: Civil War Diary of Athens, Georgia.* Athens: University of Georgia Press, 1964.

Stevenson, R. Randolph. *The Southern Side, or Andersonville Prison.* 1876. Reprint, New Market, VA: John M. Bracken Publishing, 1995.

Swanberg, W. A. *Sickles the Incredible.* New York: Charles Scribner's Sons, 1956.

Temple, Brian. *The Union Prison at Fort Delaware: A Perfect Hell on Earth.* Jefferson, NC: McFarland & Company Publishers, 2003.

Trudeau, Noah Andre. *Bloody Roads South: The Wilderness to Cold Harbor, May–June 1864.* Boston: Little, Brown and Company, 1989.

Turner, Nat, editor. *A Southern Soldier's Letters Home: The Civil War Letters of Samuel Burney, Army of Northern Virginia.* Macon: Mercer University Press, 2002.

Warner, Ezra J. *Generals in Gray.* Baton Rouge: Louisiana State University Press, 1959.

Watkins, Sam M. *Company Aytch: Or, A Side Show of the Big Show.* Edited by Thomas Inge. 1882. Reprint, New York: Plume Books, 1999.

Wert, Jeffry D. *Custer: The Controversial Life of George Armstrong Custer.* New York: Simon & Schuster, 1996.

———. *From Winchester to Cedar Creek: The Shenandoah Campaign of 1864.* Mechanicsburg, PA: Stackpole Books, 1989.

Wiley, Bell Irwin. *The Common Soldier in the Civil War.* New York: Scribner's, 1975.

Woodhead, Henry, editor. *Echoes of Glory: Illustrated Atlas of the Civil War.* Alexandria, VA: Time-Life Books, 1998.

———. *Echoes of Glory: Arms and Equipment of the Confederacy.* Alexandria, VA: Time-Life Books, 1998.

Woodward, Evan Morrison. *Our Campaigns: The Second Pennsylvania Reserve Volunteers.* Philadelphia: J. E. Porter, 1865.

Worthy, Marvin Nash. *History of Gwinnett County, Georgia, 1818–1893.* Vol. 3. Gwinnett Board of Commissioners, 1994.

6. Articles

"Confederate Necrology. Tribute of Respect. Tuesday Morning, 11th Day of August, 1863." Georgia Historical Quarterly 19/2 (June 1935): 63–64.

Boothe, J. B. "The Siege of Knoxville and its Results." *Confederate Veteran* 22/6 (June 1914): 266–67.

Byrd, Joseph P., III. "From Civil War Battlefields to the Moon." *Tech Topics* 28/1 (Fall 1991): 4B.

Byrd, Joseph P., IV. "The Saga of Charles Clinton." Gwinnett Historical Society. *The Heritage Quarterly* 39/1–4.

Clinton, Fred S. "First Hospitals in Tulsa." Oklahoma Historical Society. *Chronicles of Oklahoma* 22/1 (Spring 1944).

———. "First Oil and Gas Well in Tulsa County." Oklahoma Historical Society. *Chronicles of Oklahoma* 30/3 (Fall 1953): 312–32.

———. "Hyechka Club." Oklahoma Historical Society. *Chronicles of Oklahoma* 21/4 (Winter 1943): 351–52.

———. "James Hugh McBirney (1870–1944)." Oklahoma Historical Society. *Chronicles of Oklahoma* 22/3 (Fall 1944): 1–5.

———. "The Beginning of the Oklahoma State Hospital Association." Oklahoma Historical Society. *Chronicles of Oklahoma* 22/3 (Fall 1944): 339–53.

———. "The Indian Territory Medical Association." Oklahoma Historical Society. *Chronicles of Oklahoma* 26/1 (Spring 1948): 23–55.

Cook, Henry Howe. "The Story of the Six Hundred." *Confederate Veteran* 5/5 (May 1897): 219–20.

Crisp, Charles F. "True to Their Oaths." *Confederate Veteran* 5/3 (March 1897): 119.

Dent, Stephen. "With Cobb's Brigade at Fredericksburg." *Confederate Veteran* 22/11 (November 1914): 500–501.

Ethier, Eric. "The Union's Savage Politician Who Fought with Sarcasm and Wit." *America's Civil War* 21/4 (September 2008): 23.

"Found Treasure—Correspondence with CSA Soldier George McMillan and His Family." Gwinnett Historical Society. *The Heritage Quarterly* (June 1999).

Harris, F. S. "General James J. Archer." *Confederate Veteran* 3/1 (January 1895): 18–19.

Haskins, Benjamin. "James J. Archer." *Confederate Veteran* 2/11 (November 1894): 355.

Ingram, Laura. "Community Leader, Vet Recognized." *Gwinnett Daily News*, 28 April 2002.

Jones, Charles Edgeworth. "Confederate Brigadiers in Congress." *Confederate Veteran* 5/10 (October 1897): 529.

McWhirter, A. "General Wofford's Brigade in the Wilderness." *Atlanta Journal*, 21 September 1901.

Power, J. Tracy. "Simmons Finds Gwinnett Gold." *Gwinnett Daily News*, 13 July 1975.

———. "Why Lawyers Know Bible Better." *Gwinnett Daily News*, 4 December 1977.

Purifoy, John. "The Splendid Valor Shown at Gettysburg, July 2, 1863." *Confederate Veteran* 34/1 (January 1906): 17–19.

Rhea, Gordon C. "Mule Shoe Redemption." *Confederate Veteran* (September–October, 2007): 20–23, 50–51.

Sanders, Christopher Columbus. "Reminiscences of the Battle of Chancellorsville." *Atlanta Journal*, 23 November 1902.

Sears, Stephen W. "Fire on the Mountain: The Battle of South Mountain." *Blue & Gray* (December–January 1986–1987).

Skelton, John E. "A Hartwell Man." *Civil War Times* (July 2008).

Timmons, A. A. "Sixteenth Georgia at Fredericksburg." *Confederate Veteran* 7/12 (December 1899): 546.

Trantham, William D. "The Wonderful Story of Richard R. Kirkland." *Confederate Veteran* 16/3 (1908): 106.

Welsh, Bill. "Firing the Gap." *America's Civil War* 6/16 (January 1994): 39–44.

Wheelan, Joseph. "The Burning." *America's Civil War* 24/5 (November 2012): 41–47.

Wynn, Bob. "Gwinnett's Best Ever? It Could be James P. Simmons?" *Gwinnett Daily News*, 23 November 1986, 3D.

———. "Simmons Fills Local History Books." *Gwinnett Daily News*, 18 February 1984, 2A.

Young, Captain John D. "A Campaign with Sharpshooters," in *The Annals of the War: Written by Leading Participants, North and South*. 1879. Reprint from *Philadelphia Weekly Times* (26 January 1878), Gettsyburg, PA: Civil War Times, 1974. 267.

Index

1st Georgia Sharpshooter Battalion, 82
1st Georgia Infantry Regiment, 61
1st Michigan Cavalry, 157
1st Pennsylvania Rifles, 96
2nd Georgia Sharpshooter Battalion, 82
2nd Louisiana Infantry Regiment, 25, 36
2nd Michigan Infantry Regiment, 114
2nd Pennsylvania Reserve Infantry, 96
2nd South Carolina Infantry Regiment, 59
2nd Virginia Cavalry, 151
2nd Wisconsin Infantry Regiment, 87
3rd Georgia Sharpshooter Battalion: At
    Appomattox, 177; At Chaffin's Bluff,
    147; At Chancellorsville, 68-71, 73; At
    Chattanooga, 105-106, 110, 112; At
    Cold Harbor, 143-144, 146; At Front
    Royal (Guard Hill), 151-156, 175; At
    Gettysburg, 90-92, 94, 96, 99; At
    Petersburg, 147-148; At Spotsylvania,
    137-139, 141-142; At the Wilderness,
    131-134; East Tennessee Campaign,
    105, 113-116, 125-128; Formation
    and Organization, 65, 75-82; In Camp
    and on the march, 83, 102, 105, 113,
    125-129, 131; Raid on the Archer Iron
    Works, 86-89; Retreat from
    Gettysburg, 100-101; Training, 79-81
3rd South Carolina Infantry Regiment, 85
3rd Vermont Infantry Regiment, 27
4th South Carolina Infantry Battalion, 46
4th Vermont Infantry Regiment, 27
5th Alabama Infantry Regiment, 80
5th Georgia Infantry Regiment, 82
5th Michigan Cavalry, 142, 157
6th Maryland Infantry Regiment (US), 144
6th Massachusetts Infantry Regiment, 162
6th Vermont Infantry Regiment, 27
7th Georgia Infantry Regiment, 164
7th Michigan Cavalry, 155
10th Georgia Infantry Regiment, 39
12th Alabama Infantry Regiment, 161
12th Virginia Infantry Regiment, 134
13th Mississippi Infantry Regiment, 116
13th Virginia Infantry Regiment, 167
15th Georgia Infantry Regiment, 176
15th New York Cavalry, 166
15th North Carolina Infantry Regiment, 37,
    39-40, 46, 51
15th South Carolina Infantry Regiment, 53

16th Alabama Infantry Regiment, 120
16th Georgia Infantry Regiment: At
    Appomattox, 177; At Chancellorsville,
    68-73; At Chattanooga, 107; At
    Fredericksburg, 52-57, 61, 63-64; At
    Front Royal (Guard Hill), 155; At
    Gettysburg, 89-90, 93, 99; At Malvern
    Hill, 76; At the North Anna River,
    142; At Petersburg, 147-148; At
    Sharpsburg (Antietam), 44, 46; At
    Spotsylvania, 141; At the Wilderness,
    131-134; East Tennessee Campaign,
    115-120, 122-127; Formation and
    Organization, 18-21, 25; In Camp and
    on the March, 23, 25-29, 31-34, 37,
    39, 47, 76, 83-84, 90, 98, 126-127,
    129, 131; On the Peninsula, 23-29;
    Training, 21-22
17th Mississippi Infantry Regiment, 116
18th Georgia Infantry Regiment, 51, 55, 61-
    63, 66, 70, 85, 90, 93, 131
18th Mississippi Infantry Regiment, 53
19th Indiana Infantry Regiment, 87
24th Georgia Infantry Regiment, 24, 26, 37,
    39-40, 55, 63, 90, 131, 155, 182
24th Michigan Infantry Regiment 87
27th Connecticut Infantry Regiment, 71
29th Massachusetts Infantry Regiment, 117
29th North Carolina Infantry Regiment, 166
38th Georgia Infantry Regiment, 112, 128,
    148
44th Alabama Infantry Regiment, 134
73rd New York Infantry Regiment (2nd Fire
    Zouaves), 95
138th Pennsylvania Infantry Regiment, 144
145th Pennsylvania Infantry Regiment, 71
157th Ohio Militia Guards, 162
Adair, Pvt. William M., 99
Ahl, Capt. G. W., 169
Akers, William, 208
Alexander, Gen. E. Porter, 57, 114, 119,
    130
Allan, H., 8
Ambrose, Charles (Clinton), 179, 186
Ambrose, George Washington, 179, 207
Ambrose, Mary Ann Wood, 179, 207
Anderson, Maj. Charles W., 105
Anderson, Gen. G. T. ("Tige"), 132-133

Anderson, Gen. Richard Heron, 33, 38, 67-
68, 92, 136-137, 139, 141-143, 147,
149-151, 175-176
Anderson, Gen. Robert Houston, 82
Anderson, Lt. William D., 77
Andrews, Col. John W., 54
Archer, Gen. James J., 86-87
Ardis, Lt. Payson L., 58, 165
Armistead, Gen. Lewis, 32-33
Atkinson, Gov. William Yates, 190-192
Atlanta Constitution, 193
Barksdale, Gen. William, 33, 51, 53, 67, 90,
92
Barrett, Lt. Joseph W., 110
Barringer, Gen. Rufus, 166, 170-171, 173
Barrow, Chancellor David C., 192-193, 208
Barrow, Lt. James, 14, 17, 19
Barry, John, 85
Battalion Sharpshooters, 81
Battle of the Crater, 148
Bayard, Sen. Thomas F., 183
Beall, Gen. William N. R., 171
Bean's Station, Skirmish at, 123
Beauregard, Gen. Pierre G. T., 20
Beck, Pvt. Jasper N., 99
Bell, John, 9
Benning, Gen. Henry Lewis, 96
Benson, Sgt. Oscar, 73
Berdan's Sharpshooters, 76
Bermuda (Blockade Runner), 21
Blackford, Capt. Eugene, 79-81
Bland, Dr. J. C. W., 188
Bland, Sue A., 188
Boggs, Chancellor William, 192
von Borcke, Maj. Heros, 42
Boothe, J. B., 122
Boteler's Ford, 44, 47
Bowran, Lt. Julius S., 60
Bowran, Pvt. William H., 60
Boyd, Capt. Robert J., 19
Bracewell, Wiley R., 13, 182
Bragg, Gen. Braxton, 104-106, 108, 121
Brandy Station, Battle of, 84
Brannon, Lt. W. G., 47
Bratton, Gen. John, 137, 142
Breckenridge, Gen. John C., 8-9, 111, 143-
144, 206
Brown, Capt. ___, 108
Brown, Gov. Joseph Emerson, 5, 21, 176,
184
Bryan, Gen. Goode, 17-18, 23, 25, 28, 54,
91, 93, 98, 115, 137, 142
Buchanan, Pres. James, 14

Buck family, 151
Bullock, Gov. Rufus B., 181-182
Bunt, Lt. Delona, 165
Burney, Pvt. Samuel A., 21, 66-67
Burnside, Gen. Ambrose Everett, 51, 60,
113-114, 121
Burroughs, Ellen E., 98
Byrd, Daniel Madison, 13
Byrd, Daniel Madison, Sr., 189-190
Byrd, Daniel Madison, Jr., 189-190, 193-
194
Byrd, Joseph P., 189
Byrd, Georgia Ambrose
Byrd, Phillip May, 10
Cain, Capt. A. B., 165
Cain, E. L., 208
Candler, Scott, 208
Candler, Warren Akin, 191-192
Cash, Rev. W. W., 206
Cedar Creek, Battle of, 165, 175
Centre Hill Guards, 17-18
Chaffin's Bluff, 147
Chancellorsville, Battle of, 67-73, 78, 134,
207
Charleston Mercury, 16-17
Chattanooga, Siege of, 109
Checote, Principal Chief Samuel, 186
Cherokee Indians, 2-3
Chickamauga, Battle of, 59, 104-105, 108
Choctaw Indians, 3
Christian Soldiers Association, 63
Cleveland, Pres. Grover, 191
Clinton, Dr. Fred Severs, 187-189
Clinton, Jane Carroll Heard, 187, 189
Clinton, Lee, 187, 189
Clinton, Louise Atkins, 186-187
Clinton, Paul, 187, 189
Clinton, Susan Merrill, 188
Cobb, Gen. Howell, 13, 17, 19, 21-23, 25,
27, 31, 33,35, 37-41, 43, 45, 48, 50, 98
Cobb Infantry, 16-18
Cobb, Gen. Thomas R. R., 25, 48, 50-55,
57
Cobb's Legion Infantry Battalion, 21, 25,
39-40, 48, 63, 66, 78, 90, 100, 131,
165
Cold Harbor, Battle of, 143-146, 207
Conley, Gov. Benjamin, 182
Constitutional Union Party, 9
Cooke, Gen. John Rogers, 51, 57
Coppen's Zouave Chasseurs, 36
Cox, Maj. Jessie J., 82

Crampton's Gap, Battle of, 38-42, 47, 60, 155
Crawfish Springs Hospital, 108
Crawford, William H. Jr., 98
Crater, Battle of, 148
Creek Indians, 2-3, 186-187
Crumley, Captain M. P., 78, 165
CSS Logan, 23
Cummings, Lt. Thomas W., 117
Custer, Gen. George Armstrong, 153, 157-158
Dandridge, Skirmish at, 126
Danielsville Guards, 17-18, 24, 47
Davant, Maj. Phillip E., 112, 128, 148
Davidson, Pvt. James A., 99
Davis, Pvt. G. W., 73
Davis, Pres. Jefferson, 22, 36, 62, 111, 124, 170, 172, 175
Davis, Col. Joseph, 22
Deep Bottom, Action at, 147-148
Delaware Places and Features: Brandywine Creek, 161, 163; Delaware Bay, 159, 165; Delaware City, 163; New Castle, 159; Pea Patch Island, 159, 171, 173
Democrat Gubernatorial Convention (1859), 8
Democrat National Convention (1860), 8, 99
Democrat State Conventions (1860), 9
Dennis, Surgeon R. B., 176
Dent, Maj. Stephen, 57
DeSaussure, Col. W. D., 53
Devin, Gen. Thomas C., 157
Dickert, Capt. D. Augustus, 115, 123, 130
Doby, Capt. Alfred E., 134
Doster, Pvt. William A., 125
Douglas, Stephen, 8-9, 206
DuBose, Gen. Dudley McIver, 175-176
Duncan, Hugh, 8
Early, Gen. Jubal Anderson, 143-144, 150
East Tennessee & Georgia Railroad, 112
Eckardt, Dr. Charles, 150-151
Eldridge, Dr. Erwin J., 58
Emory College (Oxford, Georgia), 6-7, 18, 192, 206
Enfield Rifles, 21, 80
Evans, Gen. Clement Anselm, 37, 191
Ewell, Gen. Richard S., 84, 138
Fairview Presbyterian Church, 180
Fellows, Capt. John R., 171, 173
Field, Gen. Charles William, 131, 134, 137-138
Finn's Point, NJ (Cemetery), 165

Flinn, Chaplain William, 19
Flint Hill Grays, 15-17, 19, 28, 34-35, 165
Forrest, Gen. Nathan Bedford, 105-106
Fort Delaware Prison, 47, 87, 159-173, 207
Fort McHenry Prison, 87
Fort Sanders (Fort Loudon), 114-121, 124, 136
Franklin, Gen. William B., 39, 42
Franks, Pvt. J. S., 125
Fredericksburg, Battle of, 53-60, 76, 207
Freedman's Bureau, 174
French, Gen. William H., 54
Fuller, Lt. Peyton W., 73
Gardner, S. B., 150
Gassaway, Pvt. S. F., 28
Georgia Normal & Industrial College, 192
Georgia Ordinance of Secession, 10-11
Georgia Places & Features: Atlanta, 16, 103-104, 167, 175; Augusta, 15, 124, 176; Auraria, 3; Banks County, 155; Buford, 2; Camp Lee, 19-22; Cassville, 61, 175; Chattahoochee River, 2; Columbia County, 17; Dahlonega, 3; Dalton, 16, 121; Dekalb County, 178; Elberton, 187; Evans County, 191; Fort Pulaski, 160; Franklin County, 98; Gwinnett County, 1-4, 10, 13, 19, 34, 62, 98, 174, 193; Habersham County, 16-17, 61; Hall County, 10; Hart County, 17; Jackson County, 3, 17; Jefferson County, 14; Lafayette Road, 105; Lawrenceville, 3, 5, 9, 12-13, 15, 29, 111, 174, 179-180, 193, 206; Level Creek Community, 2-3; Madison County, 17; Meriwether County, 183; Milledgeville, 8, 10, 192; Montgomery County, 10; Newton County, 4; Norcross, 5; Pickens County, 188; Polk County, 110; Ringgold, 2, 104, 111; Rossville, 105; Savannah, 21, 82, 160, 166; Stone Mountain, 15; Suwanee, 2; Walton County, 17; Washington, 176; Yellow River Community, 19
Georgia Secession Convention (1850), 5
Georgia Secession Convention (1861), 10, 61
Georgia Secession, 8, 10-11
Georgia State Democrat Convention (1870), 181
Georgia Tech, 208

Gettysburg, Battle of, 86, 88-98, 156, 172-173, 207
Gholston, Ben, 15
Gholston, Maj. James S., 18, 25, 99
Gibbon, Gen. John, 92
Ginn, Sgt. Jessie G., 99
Gober, Lt. E. F., 15
Goggin, Major J. M., 76-77, 118
Gordon, Gen. John B., 140
Gracie, Gen. Archibald, 120
Grant, Gen. Ulysses S., 130, 135-136, 139-140, 143, 146-147, 158
Green, Dr. James Mercer, 24
Green, Marcus, 85
Griffis, Maj. John C., 110
Griffith, General Richard, 31
Guard Hill, Action at, 151-155, 175
Gwinnett, Button, 2
Gwinnett Manual Labor Institute, 61
Gwinnett Manufacturing Company, 5, 174
Gwinnett Volunteers (Hutchins Guards), 12-13, 15-18, 35, 78, 133, 179, 199
Hall, Lyman, 2
Hampton, Gen. Wade, 142
Hancock, Gen. Winfield Scott, 56, 139-140
Handy, Rev. Isaac W. K., 160-161
Haney, Pvt. David Wayne, 35
Harris, Judge Young I., 187
Hartwell Infantry, 17-18
Harvey, William A., 13
Haskell, Lt. Frank A., 92
Haskins, Benjamin, 87
Heard, Col. James Lawrence, 188
Heard, Melissa Harper, 188
Heard, Gov. Stephen, 187-188
Hibbs, Capt. J. W., 167
Hill, Gen. Ambrose Powell, 86, 132, 143-144
Hill, Gen. Daniel Harvey, 33-34, 45-46
Hill, Chancellor Walter Barnard, 192
Hoke, Gen. Robert Frederick, 144
Holmes, Gen. Theophilus H., 25-26
Hood, Gen. John Bell, 51, 62, 89-90, 112
Hooker, Gen. Joseph, 67, 73, 83
Horseshoe Bend, Battle of, 2-3
Hot Springs, Arkansas, 187
Howard, Lt. McHenry, 162
Hudson, Thomas J. P., 10
Huff, Pvt. John, 142
Humphreys, Gen. Benjamin G., 114-115, 137
Hunnicutt, William M., 15
Hutchins, Harriet Harris, 18

Hutchins, Judge Nathan Louis Sr., 4, 8, 13, 61
Hutchins, Lt. Col. Nathan Louis Jr., 8-9, 12, 14, 18, 62, 66, 78-79, 96, 113-114, 125, 131, 146, 148, 176, 199
Independent Volunteers, 155
Irish Brigade, 56
Iron Brigade, 87
Iverson, Gen. Alfred Jr., 18
Jackson, Gen. Thomas J. ("Stonewall"), 37, 44-45, 68, 73, 134
Jackson Rifles (Volunteers), 17-19
Jefferson, Julia, 167
Jenkins, Gen. Micah, 112, 134
Johnson, Gen. Edward, 140
Johnsons Island Prison, 87
Johnston, Gen. Joseph E., 20, 29-30, 168-169
Jones, Capt. John H., 181
Jones, Thomas H., 8
Jordan, Floyd, 155
Kennedy, W. F., 13
Kershaw, Gen. Joseph, 31, 38, 46, 53, 59, 67, 71, 85, 92, 107, 114-115, 121, 123-125, 127-128, 130, 137-138, 142-143, 145-147, 157, 175-177
Kidd, Major James Harvey, 156-157
Kimball, Gen. Nathan, 54
King, Rev. J. L., 180
King, Dr. J. R., 206
King, Capt. John W., 78, 125-126, 205
Kirkland, Sgt. Richard Rowland, 59
Knoxville, Siege of, 113-115
Lamar, Capt. G. B., 92
Lamar, Col. John B., 23, 41-43
Landers, Sgt. Eli Pinson, 16, 19-20, 24, 28, 34, 52, 72, 78, 107
Lane, Joseph, 9
Latimer, F. H., 10
Lawrence, Capt. James, 3
Lawrenceville Academy, 4, 6
Lawrenceville Manufacturing Co., 5, 174
Lawrenceville News, 7-9, 168, 174, 206
Lawrenceville Publishing Co., 190
Lee, Gen. Fitzhugh, 137, 147-149
Lee, Gen. Robert E., 30, 33, 36, 38, 44, 47-48, 51, 56, 60-61, 78-79, 83, 95, 98, 100-101, 129-130, 136, 140-141, 147, 168-169, 175 177
Lemon, Capt. James Lile, 70, 85, 92-93, 107, 117-118
Levy, Capt. S. Yates, 166
Liddell, James M., 15

Lincoln, Pres. Abraham, 9, 135, 169, 206
Lomax, Gen. Lunsford L., 157
Longstreet, Gen. James, 32, 46, 56, 79, 84-85, 89-91, 93, 95, 98-99, 101, 103-106, 112, 115, 118-121, 124-134, 136, 157, 175
Loring, Gen. William Wing, 25
Madison County Greys, 17-18, 25
Magruder, Gen. John Bankhead, 21, 23, 25, 29-30, 32-33, 75
Mahone, Gen. William, 39, 68, 132-133
Maloney, Pvt. Patrick, 87
Malvern Hill, Battle of, 32-35
Malvern Hill, Second Battle of, 37
Manning, Capt. J. H., 151
Manning, J. S., 117
Martin, Capt. John F., 78, 165
Martin, L. R., 208
Maryland Places & Features: Antietam Creek, 45-46; Baltimore, 8-9, 99, 159, 206; Bloody Lane, 45, 56; Boonsborough Road, 45; Brownsville, 38-39; Burkittsville, 39; Conococheague River, 100; Crampton's Gap, 39; Downsville, 100; Dunker Church, 44; Elk Ridge, 38; Frederick, 38; Funkstown, 100, 207; Hagerstown, 98, 100; Hagerstown Road, 45; Middletown, 38; Pleasant Valley, 38, 42; Sandy Hook, 38; Sharpsburg, 44; Sharpsburg Turnpike, 98; South Mountain, 38-39, 206; Williamsport, 84
Matthews, Dr. Johnson, 182
McBirney, James H., 189
McBirney, Vera Clinton, 187, 189
McClellan, Gen. George B., 26-27, 34-35
McClendon, Pvt. William A., 127
McDaniel, Archibald W., 78
McGowan, Gen. Samuel, 140
McGuire, Lewis S., 19
McIntosh, Maj. ___, 39
McKibbon, Col. Joseph C., 108
McLaws, Gen. Lafayette, 25, 33-34, 36, 38-39, 42, 44-45, 48-50, 54, 68-69, 71-72, 76, 78-79, 84-85, 89, 91-92, 96, 99, 103, 106, 112-114, 118, 122-126, 136
McMillan, Capt. Garnett, 78, 126, 182, 205
McMillan Guards, 182
McMillan, Col. Robert, 26, 55, 58
McMullin, Cpl. William, 41
McRae, Capt. John H. D., 18

McRae, Lt. Col. William, 46-47
McWhirter, Cpl. Andrew J., 133
Meade, Gen. George Gordon, 100, 130
Meagher, Gen. Thomas F., 56
Medlock, 1st Sgt. Thomas L. D., 35
Merrill, Maj. Sherman Morton, 188
Merritt, Gen. Wesley, 152, 157
Miller, Sen. H. V. M., 208
Mills, John, 13
Mitchell, John A., 12, 199
Mobile Bay, 166
Montgomery, Alabama, 5, 11, 48
Montgomery, Capt. John N., 18
Montgomery, Sgt. William R., 58, 69, 77, 105, 114, 126
Mosby, Col. John Singleton, 158
Moses, Maj. Raphael J., 90
Mosley, Lt. Milton M., 160
Munford, Col. Thomas, 39-40
New Castle, Delaware, 159
North Carolina Places & Features: Camp Randolph, 25-26; Cape Fear River, 16; Charlotte, 3, 104; Goldsboro, 25-26; Kinston, 16; Montgomery County, 1; New Bern, 25; Weldon, 25; Wilmington, 16, 104
Old Capitol Prison, 158-159, 207
Olustee, Battle of, 14-15
Orphan Brigade (CSA), 110
Orr, Pvt. William M., 179-180, 186
Overland Campaign, 131-146
Page, Gen. Richard L., 166, 173
Page's Virginia Artillery Battery, 25
Paldi, Angelo, 157
Palmer, Col. Oliver H., 56
Panola Guards, 66
Parham, Col. William A., 39-40
Park, Capt. Robert Emory, 161, 166, 168, 183
Patton, Capt. A. H., 65-66, 73
Pendleton, Gen. William, 136
Pennsylvania Places & Features: Archer Iron Works, 86-88; Big Round Top, 90; Black Horse Tavern, 89; Caledonia Iron Works, 86; Cemetery Ridge, 90; Chambersburg, 85; Chambersburg Pike, 87; Devil's Den, 90; Emmitsburg Road, 89-91, 97-98; Gettysburg, 85; Greenwood, 85-86; Little Round Top, 89-90, 93; McPherson's Woods, 86-87; Peach Orchard, 91-92, 95-96; Pitzer Farm, 89; Rose's Woods, 96; Seminary Ridge, 90, 96; South

Mountain, 85, 206; Wheatfield Road, 92-93; Willoughby's Run, 89

Perry, Gen. William F., 68, 134

Petersburg, Siege of, 146-148, 177, 207

Philadelphia Inquirer, 163, 167

Phillips Legion Infantry Battalion, 51, 71, 73, 77, 85, 90, 100, 110, 131, 144

Pickett, Gen. George Edward, 83, 96

Pilgrim, Isaac, 7

Pleasanton, Gen. Alfred, 84

Poe, Maj. Orlando M., 114

Polk, James, 9

Pool, A., 8

Porter, Chaplain R. K., 57-58

Potomac River, 37, 44, 84, 100-101, 150

Prison Benevolent Association, 171-172

Prison Times Newspaper, 167

Rains, Gen. James E., 167

Ramseur, Gen. Stephen Dodson, 142

Ramsey Volunteers, 17, 19

Randolph, Sec. George W., 25

Ransom, Capt. Dunbar R., 157

Ransom, Gen. Robert, 50-51, 122

Reader, Ed, 15

Reader, Capt. Nathaniel, 19

Red Fork, Indian Territory, 187-188

Reed, Pvt. Isaac A., 164

Reese, Lt. A. J., 69

Reynolds, Capt. Abner M., 18

Richardson, Pvt. David, 105

Richardson family, 151

Richmond & York Railroad, 23

Robertson, Gen. Jerome Bonaparte, 51

Robinson, Adam, 13

Rodes Alabama Sharpshooter Battalion, 79-80

Rodes, Gen. Robert E., 45-46, 138, 140

Rogers, Dr. Wallace, 206

Rosecrans, General William S., 104

Ross, Capt. Fitzgerald, 111

Ross, Lt. Frederick E., 66

Rosser, Gen. Thomas L., 137

Ruede, Cpl. William E., 73

Ruff, Lt. Col. Solon Zacharias, 52, 114, 118

Rutherford, Capt. ____, 58

Sailor's Creek, Battle of, 176-177

Sanders, Capt. Charles H., 144-145

Sanders, Col. Christopher Columbus, 45-46

Sanders, Pvt. Thomas, 20

Sanders, Gen. William P., 114

Schoepf, Gen. Albin, 169

Scott, Rep. Dunlap, 183

Semmes, Gen. Paul Jones, 33, 38-39, 67, 71, 98

Seven Days Battles, 31-35, 56

Seven Pines (Fair Oaks), Battle of, 29-30

Severs, Frederick Ballard, 186

Sharpsburg (Antietam), Battle of, 44-47, 207

Sharpshooter Training, 80-81

Shelton, Lt. John E., 165

Sheridan, Gen. Phillip, 137, 150, 154, 158, 165-166

Sherman, Gen. William T., 167-169, 174-175

Sickles, Gen. Daniel Edgar, 90-91, 95

Simmons, Mrs. ____ Trimble, 4

Simmons, Adam Quimby, 1-2

Simmons, Anna Eliza, 29

Simmons, Anna West, 1-2

Simmons, Caswell W., 2

Simmons, Eillene, 29

Simmons, Eliza Terrell, 1, 206

Simmons, Ida, 29

Simmons, Ida Lamar, 4

Simmons, James, 1

Simmons, James (Pickens County), 10

Simmons, James Pinckney, 1, 4-10, 61, 206

Simmons, James Polk, 29

Simmons, Mary Ambrose, 179-180, 186, 188-190, 193-194, 207

Simmons Mine, 3

Simmons, Sarah Elizabeth, 29

Simmons, Sara Quimby, 1

Simmons, Terrell, 208

Simmons, Major William Eleazer: Archer Iron Works Raid, 86-89; At Chancellorsville, 68, 73, 207; At Chattanooga, 105-108, 110-112, 207; At Crampton's Gap, 40-43, 207; At Cold Harbor, 143, 146, 207; At Fredericksburg, 57, 60-61, 64, 66, 207; At Front Royal (Guard Hill), 150-156, 158, 207; At Gettysburg, 90-91, 93-95, 99, 207; At the Gordonsville Camps, 129; At the North Anna River, 142; At Petersburg, 147-149, 207; At Sharpsburg, 45-46, 207; At Spotsylvania, 136-141, 207; At the Wilderness, 131-134, 136, 207; Deployment to Tennessee, 103, 105; East Tennessee Campaign, 113-116, 119, 121-122, 124-125, 127-129, 207; In Fort Delaware Prison, 159-160, 164-167, 170-173, 178, 195, 207; In

Index

Seven Days Battles, 31, 34-35, 207; Law and Political Career, 174, 177,181-185, 190-191, 196-197, 207; Marriage and Family Ties, 111-112, 178-180, 186-190, 195-196; Retreat from Gettysburg, 100-101; Return to Lawrenceville, 174; University Trustee, 191-193, 195, 208; With 3rd Battalion Georgia Sharpshooters, 77-79, 98, 196, 205, 207; With 16th Georgia, 12-13, 15-18, 22, 24, 27, 29, 37, 195-196, 207; Younger Years 1, 6-9

Sisk, Pvt. William, 22,
Skelton, Capt. John Hampton, 18, 28
Slocum, Gen. Henry, 39
Smith, Charles H. ("Bill Arp"), 4
Smith, Gen. Edmund Kirby, 170, 172, 207
Smith, Gov. James M., 183-184
Smith, Gen. Martin Luther, 132, 134
Smith, Surgeon R. M., 19
Smith, Gen. William F. ("Baldy"), 27, 39, 145
Sorrell, Gen. G. Moxley, 132-133, 136
South Carolina Places & Features: Charleston, 15, 99, 160, 206; Hilton Head, 160; Morris Island, 160
Spence, D. W., 8
Spotsylvania, Battle of, 136-142, 207
Stephens, Alexander Hamilton, 98
Stevens, Rep. Thaddeus, 86
Stiles, Col. Benjamin Edward Jr., 18, 176
Strickland, Capt. Charlton H., 133
Southern Commercial Convention (1858), 5
Starke, Gen. William Edwin, 37
Stiles, Capt. B. Edward, 16, 59, 131
Stuart, Gen. James Ewell Brown, 38-39, 42, 46, 84, 142
Taylor, Gen. Richard, 170, 172
Tennessee Places & Features: Bain's Crossroads, 122; Bristol (TN/VA), 127, 129; Camp Lookout, 109; Chattanooga, 2, 15-16, 104-105, 109-111, 119, 121; Chickamauga Creek, 104; French Broad River, 126; Greenville, 127, 148; Holston River, 113, 123; Kingston Pike, 114; Knoxville, 15-16, 112, 119-121, 124; Lenoir's Station, 113; Lookout Mountain, 109; Loudon, 113; Missionary Ridge, 105-106, 109, 111, 121; Morristown, 123, 125; Morristown-Strawberry Plains Road,

126; Murfreesboro, 1; New Market, 125; Philadelphia, 113; Rogersville, 122; Russellville, 123; Rutherford County, 1; Sweetwater, 112; Tennessee River, 113; Tyner's Station, 112; Warren County, 1
Thom, Captain R. T., 166
Thomas, Col. Henry P., 12-13, 18, 25, 98, 117, 119, 131
Thompson, Capt. Augustus C., 18-19
Toombs, Gen. Robert, 176, 184
Torbert, Gen. Alfred, 158
Towns, Gov. George, 61
Troup Artillery, 91, 100
Tulsa, Oklahoma, 186-189
Turner, Sec. R. M. T., 22
Underwood, Pvt. John H., 20
University of Georgia (Franklin College), 14, 48, 61, 98, 190-193, 208
Vance, Gen. Robert R., 166-167
Vance, Gov. Zebulon, 166
Vaughan, Grady, 208
Virginia Military College (VMI), 19
Virginia Places & Features: Aiken's Landing, 47; Appomattox, 168-169, 176-177; Ashby's Gap, 84, 101; Atlee's Station, 143; Baltimore Crossroads, 29; Banks Ford, 72; Berryville, 84; Bethesda Church, 143; Bloody Angle, 138, 140-141; Bowling Green Road, 53; Brock Road, 131, 134; Burkeville, 177; Burnt Chimney, 31; Camp Bryan, 23; Camp Lamar, 23; Camp Lee, 36; Camp Sally Twiggs, 28; Camp Tom, 47-48; Cedarville, 151; Chaffin's Bluff, 147; Chancellorsville, 67; Charlottesville, 129; Chester's Gap, 150; Chester's Station, 148; City Point, 159; Clarke County, 166; Cold Harbor, 143; Crafton Church, 23; Crooked Run, 152-154, 157; Culpeper Court House, 78, 84, 102, 148, 150; Dam No. 2, 28-29; Darbytown Road, 32; Deep Run, 53; Fairfield Racetrack Camp, 29; Farmville, 177; Federal Hill, 50; Flint Hill, 150; Fort Monroe, 26; Fredericksburg, 50-54, 67, 71, 131; Front Royal, 101, 150-151, 165; Germana Plank Road, 131; Gordonsville Camps, 129-131; Guard Hill, 151-153; Hampton, 161; Hampton Roads, 25-26; Hanover

291

Junction, 102-103, 142; Harrison's Landing, 35; Hazel Run, 53-54; High Bridge, 177; Howison's Mill, 53-54; James River, 21, 26, 32, 37, 146-147, 166; Lee's Hill, 56; Lee's Mill (Dam No. 1), 27; Leesburg, 37; Loudon County, 158; Mechanicsville, 131; Malvern Hill, 32; Marye's Heights (Hill), 50, 53, 55-57, 59-60; Massanutten Mountain, 150; Millwood, 101; Mine Road, 71; Mitchell's Station, 148, 150; Mule Shoe, 138-141; Nansemond River, 166; New Market Road, 32; Nine Mile Road, 31; Newport News Road, 23; North Anna River, 142; Orange Courthouse, 102, 131; Orange Plank Road, 131-132, 134; Orange Turnpike, 131; Parker's Store, 131; Paumunkey River, 29; Petersburg, 16, 25, 146, 168; Plank Road, 67, 71; Rapidan River, 101, 103, 130-131; Rappahannock River, 50-51, 53-54, 59-60, 64, 67, 72-73, 78, 84; Richmond, 15-17, 19-21, 24, 28-29, 31, 36, 61, 103, 168, 175-177; Richmond & York River Railroad, 29, 31; River Road, 72; Salem Church, 71; Shenandoah River, 84, 101, 150-151, 153-154; Shenandoah Valley, 84, 142, 150, 158, 165, 175; Smith's Hill, 67; Snicker's Gap, 84; Spotsylvania Court House, 131, 136-138, 141; Stafford Heights, 51; Suffolk, 25; Telegraph Road (Sunken Road), 53-55, 58-59, 76; Timberlake's Store, 32; United States Ford, 67; Upperville, 84; Waller's Tavern, 102; Warwick River, 26-28, 75; West Point, 23; Williamsburg, 28-29, 75; Williamsburg Stage Road, 32; Winchester, 47, 151; Winchester Pike, 151, 153, 156; York River, 21, 23; Yorktown, 23, 75, 207; Yorktown-Williamsburg Road, 23

Walker, Gen. W. H. T., 82
Walton, George, 2
Walton Volunteers, 17-18
Washington Artillery, 54, 57
Washington, D C, 158, 161
Washington, Pres. George, 188
Watie, Gen. Stand, 172
Watkins, Pvt. Sam, 110

Watson, "Cotton" Tom, 191
Wayne, Gen. Henry C., 13
West Virginia Places & Features: Bunker Hill, 101; Camp Lizzie, 47; Harper's Ferry, 38, 42-44, 158; Martinsburg, 47, 84; Mill Creek, 101
Western & Atlantic Railroad, 104, 184
Wheeler, Gen. Joseph, 112
Whelchel, Davis, 10
Whitworth Rifles, 81
Whitworth Sharpshooters, 81
Wickham, Gen. Williams Carter, 151-152
Wigfall, Gen. Louis T., 62
Wilderness, Battle of, 131-136, 176, 207
Williams, James T., 208
Wing, Henry, 135
Winn, Courtland S., 208
Winn, Richard D., 10
Witham, W. S., 208
Wofford, Gen. William Tatum, 51, 61-62, 65-73, 75-79, 81, 85, 90-96, 99, 101, 103, 105-110, 112-113, 118, 121, 125-126, 128, 131-135, 137-138, 141, 144, 148, 150-151, 153-155, 175-176
Wood, Pvt. James R., 73
Woods, Pvt. Joseph White, 24
Wright, Gen. Ambrose, 32
Wright, Gen. Horatio G., 139
Yellow Tavern, Battle of, 142
Young Harris College, 187-188
Zook, Gen. Samuel K., 56